Acclaim for Brian Orend's
Introduction to International Studies

"There are several reasons why this book is badly needed and so well conceived. First, it is clearly written, and its arguments, while based upon a solid understanding of the most sophisticated of recent scholarship, will be well understood by undergraduates. Second, the approach is genuinely interdisciplinary. Dr Orend has an impressive command of the central debates not only in philosophy, his own discipline, but also in economics, international relations, political science, and history. Third, *Introduction to International Studies* incorporates Canada within the discussion of international policy. The inclusion of Canada reflects not nationalism but rather a recognition that a focus on great powers alone can distort a broader understanding of relations between states.

"I am sure that undergraduates and others within and beyond the university will enjoy and greatly profit from Brian Orend's extraordinary *Introduction to International Studies*."

— John English, Distinguished Professor Emeritus, Department of History,
University of Waterloo

"Brian Orend's book does justice to the daunting scope and complexity of international studies without compromising substance and critical reflection. Though billed as an introduction, his work presents the fascinating features and amazing transformations of our globalized world with mastery and clarity so as to inspire genuine interest and active engagement. Adeptly weaving historical and conceptual backgrounds with contemporary debates and current events, Orend offers novices and experts alike a treasure trove of refreshing insights."

—Thomas Pogge, Leitner Professor of Philosophy and International Affairs,
Yale University

"No other book on the market addresses international studies this way. . . . It has a very clear format and brings the interdisciplinary element of international studies to the forefront."

—Logan Masilamani, Department of Political Science,
Simon Fraser University

Introduction to
International Studies

For Jenny,
with love and joy!

Introduction to

International Studies

Brian Orend

OXFORD

UNIVERSITY PRESS

OXFORD
UNIVERSITY PRESS

Oxford University Press is a department of the University of Oxford.
It furthers the University's objective of excellence in research, scholarship,
and education by publishing worldwide. Oxford is a registered trade mark of
Oxford University Press in the UK and in certain other countries.

Published in Canada by
Oxford University Press
8 Sampson Mews, Suite 204,
Don Mills, Ontario M3C 0H5 Canada

www.oupcanada.com

Library and Archives Canada Cataloguing in Publication

Orend, Brian, 1971–
Introduction to international studies / Brian Orend.

Includes bibliographical references and index.
ISBN 978–0–19–543938–0

1. World politics.   2. World history.   3. Civilization.
4. War.   5. Globalization.   6. Competition, International.
7. World health.   I. Title.

JZ1242.O74 2012   327   C2012-902694-8

Cover image: Shigemitsu Takahashi / Alamy

Oxford University Press is committed to our environment.
This book is printed on Forest Stewardship Council® certified paper
and comes from responsible sources.

Printed and bound in Canada

1 2 3 4 — 16 15 14 13

Contents

PART II   CORE DYNAMICS: NATION VERSUS WORLD

PART III   TRADITIONAL ISSUES OF HARD POWER: BUCKS AND BULLETS

PART IV   NEWER ISSUES OF SOFT POWER: IMPROVING WELL-BEING

Acknowledgements

I'd like to thank Oxford University Press for its commitment to this book. The idea for such a volume came to me long ago. Oxford, happily, saw its promise immediately, and proceeded to sign me up. Then they waited for me to deliver. They waited too long, and I thank them, with great appreciation, for their patience.

Special thanks are due to Patti Sayle and Eric Sinkins, my talented and gracious editors. Thanks, too, to all the great production and design team, the permissions department, and the anonymous reviewers who saw a really rough draft, and whose constructive criticism improved the whole work substantially.

Above all, I am deeply grateful to my acquisitions editor, Katherine Skene, whose original enthusiasm for the book never faltered, and without whom, there would simply be no book at all. Thanks so much, Kate!

I wrote this book on a big black desk, bought for me as a gift by my grandmother, Alvena Schuett. She died recently, and I'm grateful for her memory, and for her love and support, together with that of my grandfather, Dr Leo Schuett.

Thanks, as always, to my family, for all their love and support: my mom, Mary Lou Orend; my father-in-law, Barry Turk; and my sister, Krista Vines. Particular thanks must go to my super-special son, Sam. It has been a total blast watching you grow into such an incredible young man. Our shared times—and Superbowls—are a ton of fun (especially when the G-men keep beating Brady!) Being your dad is the best.

More than anyone, Jennifer McWhirter deserves my deepest thanks and gratitude. She's my talented co-author on the global public health chapter—one of the book's most important—and has aided the whole book's development in countless wonderful ways. I can hardly express how amazing our journey together has been. Jenny, this book is dedicated to you with abundant joy and abiding love.

Brian Orend
April 2012

Introduction

"Life is the continuous adjustment of internal relations to external relations." —*Herbert Spencer (1820–1903), British biologist and political essayist*

It is a joy to teach international studies. And I mean international *studies*, and not international *relations*. The latter is the standard way of approaching the subject, emphasizing the foreign policies of nation-states, and how they each strive—on the global stage—to get what they want. While that is very important, and while it certainly is *a part of* international studies, the plural term "studies" implies something larger than a focused analysis of foreign affairs.

INTERDISCIPLINARITY

It is often said that international studies, or global studies, is "interdisciplinary." What does this much-used—even trendy—term mean? The pursuit of knowledge, historically, has involved the creation of different disciplines. A **discipline** is a unique way of approaching, and achieving, the advance of human knowledge, and it comes with its own particular set of theories and methods. Mathematicians, for example, use number theory; psychologists use various experiments to study human behaviour; and lawyers read legal rules and past cases—and learn how to follow court procedure—in an effort to construct the strongest case for their client. Until recently, colleges and universities have been organized along disciplinary lines: there are various "faculties"—of arts, science, engineering, law, medicine, and so on. And within each of these faculties there are various "departments": biology versus chemistry versus physics in any faculty of science; history versus English versus philosophy in arts; psychology versus economics in social science; and civil versus electrical engineering.

There is much to be said in favour of the discipline of a discipline. The focused and rigorous training that a discipline provides is good exercise for the mind, and offers many valuable skills and tools. Potential problems arise, though, when—as is quite common—people come over time to see *every* issue solely through the *one* lens of their own pet discipline. Further problems arise when the subject matter itself proves so complex and multifaceted that it cannot be fully captured or understood through the perspective of one discipline. To counteract these problems, the idea of interdisciplinarity was devised.

Being **interdisciplinary** means using the tools and insights of *various* disciplines, both (a) to eliminate narrow-mindedness, and (b) to arrive at a more thorough appreciation of the subject matter. For instance, in recent years, economists who study the spending behaviour of consumers—like you and me—have benefitted from using the insights and experiments of psychologists regarding why people make the choices they do; and moral philosophers, wrestling with abstract questions of right and wrong, have benefitted from studying detailed legal decisions about such tricky ethical dilemmas as abortion, online privacy, and the rights of minority groups.

Since the subject matter of international, or global, studies is the world as a whole, the complexity of it *demands* that we use the tools of various disciplines. The whole world simply cannot be reduced to the methods or conclusions of any one discipline. To borrow (with reluctance) a much-used analogy, knowing the world is somewhat like trying to know an elephant. And to know an elephant, you cannot merely examine its trunk, or just the huge legs and floppy ears, or only the tiny tail, or simply the sharp tusks. You must, to the contrary, try to examine *all* the parts, *and* how they come together to form a unique whole.

I cannot pretend—in this one, introductory-level, book—to have delivered the whole world on a platter. But I can say that many different disciplines are here represented, and strongly so, in a quest to arrive at a fuller and better basic understanding of our increasingly complicated, multi-layered, fast-changing, and interconnected world. And the goal here is *not* complete knowledge or mastery but merely a useful and clear introductory understanding of major features of our world, from various valuable viewpoints. So, for example:

- in the chapter on population and resources, we shall use facts and theories from demography and "environment and resource studies;"
- in the chapter on comparative culture, we will look at education, political theory, new media, and religion;
- in the foreign policy chapter, we shall apply the tools of political science and international relations theory;
- in the chapter on international law, we will discern both the law itself and how international lawyers think through various global problems;
- in the international trade and business chapter, we will use the tools of economics;
- in the chapters on armed conflict, we will witness what military science, just war theory, international law, and "peace and conflict studies" have to offer;
- in the human rights chapter, we will rely not only on international law once more but also on the emerging fields of human rights studies and women's studies;
- in the global public health chapter, we will explore the tools of health science and public health policy;
- in the chapter on foreign aid and international development, we shall become acquainted with development economics;
- throughout, maps and photos will supplement our account, thus drawing on geography and, I suppose, a bit of psychology as well. Finally, some tables and conceptual figures will be presented, as visual aids to understanding.

I ought to confess that my own academic training is in history, philosophy, economics, and the law; and so I suppose these ways of understanding may—perhaps inescapably—be more prominently featured here than others. Happily, though, history is hugely relevant for each of these subjects, and international law and economics are not too far behind. Philosophy, presumably, helps with clarifying the concepts and theories, and for explaining how they all might hang together.

Chapter Structure

All of the chapters, in spite of their different content and the different disciplines they draw on, sport the same structure. That structure comprises the following parts, in order:

- an opening, pithy *quote* that captures a crucial aspect of the chapter's subject matter

- a bullet-form set of *learning objectives* outlining goals that the reader should attain by the end of the chapter

- a brief *introduction*, setting out what will be covered in the chapter

- the *body* of the chapter

- a succinct *conclusion*

- a list of prominent *websites* that are useful for further research

- ten *questions* for both summary and review (and potential testing purposes)

- numbered *endnotes*, showing my own (and further recommended) sources of research. (I should mention how my citation style is to keep noting to an uncluttered minimum: at the end of each section or paragraph, as merited, unless a direct quote is involved.)

Nested in the body of each chapter—set apart from the main content—are two highlighted feature boxes. One deals with new technology and how it relates to the subject matter of the chapter. For example, in the foreign policy chapter, this section examines the recent, high-profile Wikileaks scandal. In the chapters on armed conflict, the technology boxes deal with cyberwarfare. The box in Chapter 9, on human rights, deals with new proposals to make access to the Internet a worldwide human right. And so on.

The other feature box examines Canada and how it relates to the rest of the world. This is fitting not only to serve the interests of Canadian students but also to ensure that the contribution of an active, productive, smaller country like Canada doesn't get lost in the huge, swirling tides of global affairs—tides that are often substantially determined by such great powers as the United States, China, the European Union (EU), India, Japan, and Russia.

LITERACY IN INTERNATIONAL STUDIES

One of the more particular pleasures of teaching international studies comes from the feedback I get from my students. A common one runs something like this: "I am so glad I took this course. There's a ton of content, but it truly opened my eyes to a whole range of international issues about which I knew nothing. The world is a crazy place!"

Crazy, yes. Complex and fascinating, too. Plus, it's our home. I think everyone needs to know the basic contours of our world, and this book tries to contribute to that task. I love the concept of *literacy*, and the goal of my own course, and this book, is precisely to provide for students a core literacy in international studies. I want students to come away from this knowing (a) the basic terms for and facts about these different subjects, (b) the historical and contemporary context surrounding them, and (c) the leading theories about such, which shed light on the concepts and contexts. I err slightly on the side of the concepts and theories, as they endure longer while facts can change much more readily. Yet the book remains chock-a-block with facts and figures, and—as mentioned—maps and tables and photos.

> *I love the concept of* literacy, *and the goal of my own course, and this book, is precisely to provide for students a core literacy in international studies.*

Above all, I want students to feel empowered about their knowledge of our complicated world, and to feel comfortable moving on to more advanced studies in each of these fields, should they wish to do so. I am also especially concerned, in each chapter, to stress and explain *how all of these subjects interconnect and impact each other*. I often find this last point is something students find interesting, unexpected, and useful: knowing, for instance, how culture affects the economy, how population relates to health, how war impacts the environment, how trade is related to aid, and how international law bears on human rights.

All together, it adds up—I hope—to a substantial, empowering tool for achieving basic literacy in international studies. Students can then, if they wish, embark on more intensive, advanced studies to further add to their fluency and expertise.

CHAPTER ORDERING AND RATIONALE

Of course, professors are free—and encouraged—to assign whichever chapters in whatever order best suits their plans. That said, it seems appropriate to offer a word or two to explain my own ordering of the chapters here.

First, the (world) stage needs to be set—in a sweeping way—before we can move on to examine particular subjects. We need to know, straightaway, some *core concepts* that will be present throughout the book. And we need to appreciate some *historical context*: how have we come to be where we are? How has the so-called **interstate system** (i.e. today's prevailing international order) come into being, and why? Whose interests does the system serve, and whose does it thwart? Such is the subject matter of Chapter 1, which concludes with a case study examination of whether we live in an Age of American Empire. Widely seen as the world's most influential society—militarily, politically, culturally, and economically—to what extent does (and should) the United States set the tone for the rest of the world?

We move from there to consider basic facts, theories, and projections that affect us all as human beings, regardless of which country we happen to live in. So, we delve into population growth and the pressure this puts on natural resources, and we examine relentless **urbanization**—the growth of cities at the expense of the countryside—and its pros and cons. We consider, in detail, the clash between optimist and pessimist regarding the environment, and whether a growing human population can restrain itself—and "grow green" in a sustainable way moving forward—or whether we shall poison ourselves with our own pollution.

Population and the interaction between humanity and Earth set the world stage. So, too, does **comparative culture**: how different people (and groups of people) believe different things, adopt different values, and behave in various ways, according to local custom. *Culture mediates all our international interactions*—causing both conflict and creativity—and so we need to understand in detail such sources of culture as social institutions, political values, religion, education, and, increasingly, new media and technology.

Act Two of this book concerns a core dynamic—or fundamental tension—between nation and world (and, relatedly, between realism and idealism). Our world is composed of nations, many of which have their own state. A **nation** is a group of people that sees itself as being a people, in other words, as belonging together in some meaningful sense as a unit, and as having its own identity, and as being separate and distinct from other comparable groups. The basis of this national uniqueness is thought to include some, or all, of the following shared characteristics:

- racial or ethnic background

- common language

- shared historical experiences

- religious beliefs and cultural practices

- diet/cuisine and fashion choices

- common ways of believing about, and behaving in, the world.

The idea of the nation has been historically very potent, and nationalism has been one of modern history's biggest driving forces. **Nationalism**, generally, means recognition of, and attachment to, one's nation. In its narrowest sense, however, nationalism implies an impulse of a nation, or a people, to get and form its own separate country, governed by a state of its own choosing. A **state** refers to the government of a country. This is the group of people responsible for making, and enforcing, the rules that regulate the collective life of a people and thereby make an orderly social life possible within a given territory. Every country has a government, and often it is the single most powerful association, or institution, in that society.

Realism is the doctrine that says, first and foremost, that one's nation or country must look out for its own interests and advantages on the world stage. "Looking out for number one" is a way of life for realists, and it expresses *an ethos of national egoism*. A very influential doctrine—especially among policy-makers—realism is opposed by idealism. **Idealists** believe that the most important thing for nations and countries to do is *not* to tend to their own self-interest but, rather, to contribute what they can towards the creation of a better world for all. Idealists believe in *an ethos of universal improvements*—of thinking globally, and acting globally, too, we might say—whereas, for the realist, it is all about one's nation-state.

This clash between nation and world permeates every major international issue: global pollution, international trade, population growth, the generation and distribution of food and water, war and peace, the distribution of both wealth and health, and how to structure the world and whether to create new institutions. In chapters 4 and 5 we will examine this clash in detail, first from the realist side, emphasizing power and self-serving foreign policy strategies, and then from the idealist side, stressing co-operation, the rule of international law, and the formation of global governance institutions.

The clash between nation and world permeates every major international issue, from pollution and trade to war and peace and how to structure the world.

Indeed, nations and states are very much concerned with **power**, which can be generally defined as the ability to get what you want. Recently thinkers such as Joseph Nye have carved a deep distinction between hard power and soft power.[1] **Hard power** is thought to be the most reliable and effective—at least in the short term—and it boils down to *wealth* and *strength*. The richer you are, and the stronger you are, the more likely it is that you can use these tools to get what you want: either you just buy it, or you bribe others to get it, or you take it by force from others. In terms of international politics, hard power is "**bullets and bucks**," economic wealth and military strength. So, in Act Three, we discuss in detail these topics, which are the traditional, classical subjects of global affairs: international trade and business, armed conflict, and the pursuit of national security by state governments.

Recently, the "hard power" paradigm has been challenged, both by experts and by ordinary people. Even Nye has said that—while, in the short term, "bullets and bucks" may be the most potent—over the long term it is culture (beliefs and values especially) that comes to determine things. After all, there is no more thorough way to influence others than to have them agree with you, in other words, to think the way you do, share the same set of values as you, behave the way you do. And the various aspects of culture are known as **soft power**. (Some have said that while hard power is the use of "coercion and/or payment" to get what one wants, soft power is the use of "attraction and/or co-option" to do the same.) A nice historical illustration of soft power would be the way the British have spread their language, literature, pop music, culture, and values throughout the world: first directly, through the iron fist of their Empire, and now indirectly, through the amazing spread of the English language and such typically British values as the rule of law, free trade, individual liberty, intellectual invention and creativity, and democratic governance.[2]

There's another, emerging sense of "soft power," and this has to do with the well-being of one's people. Increasingly, ordinary people, social activists, and political thinkers (such as Mary Kaldor) have stressed—instead of the national security of a country—the human security of individual persons.[3] Human security stresses that, above and beyond money and protection from violence, ordinary people also require education, healthcare, and basic regard from social institutions for their continued growth and development. This rising concern for human security goes hand in hand with another, clear, post–World War II trend in world affairs: the growth in human rights awareness and the insistence on minimally decent standards of conduct that governments must observe, both regarding their own people and internationally.[4]

Putting these trends all together, one discovers the final set of subjects in this book: the "soft power" focus on improving not just the wealth and strength of countries but, moreover, the well-being of individual persons worldwide. We shall thus close out this book with chapters on human rights, global public health, and poverty alleviation via foreign aid and international development programs.

CONCLUSION

And now, to end the beginning: Pierre Trudeau was a brilliant student, and a dashing figure, who went on to become one of Canada's longest-serving and most successful prime ministers. When he was a Master's student at Harvard University, he taped the following sign to the door of his dorm room: "Pierre Trudeau, Citizen of the World."[5] That was, perhaps, a bit ambitious for his time and place. But, nowadays, we are all—truly—world citizens. I wish you good reading, and good luck, on your journey across the globe.

NOTES

1.   J. Nye, *Bound to Lead* (New York: Basic Books, 1991).
2.   J. Nye, *Soft Power* (New York: Public Affairs, 2004).
3.   M. Kaldor, *Human Security* (London: Polity, 2007).
4.   B. Orend, *Human Rights: Concept and Context* (Peterborough, ON: Broadview, 2002).
5.   J. English, *Citizen of the World: The Life of Pierre Trudeau, 1919–1967* (Toronto: Knopf, 2008).

I

Setting the World Stage

1 Core Concepts and Historical Contexts

"We find ourselves thrown into the world." —*Martin Heidegger (1889–1976), German philosopher*

LEARNING OBJECTIVES

After studying this chapter, you will be able to:

▸ define all the bolded key terms and concepts

▸ understand and define the core components of any country

▸ grasp how the modern nation-state constitutes a midpoint between the tiny city-state and the giant cosmopolitan empire

▸ discuss the essence of empire—the complex relationship between a metro-pole and its colonies—and explain how important European imperialism and colonization have been in shaping today's world

▸ define *North versus South* and *the West versus the Rest*, and be able to explain the significance of these distinctions

▸ consider whether the United States is a present-day empire and, if so, whether this is good or bad for the world

▸ understand and explain, generally, how Canada fits into this historical context, regarding state-formation, European imperialism, and American hegemony.

INTRODUCTION

I love the opening, dramatic quote from Heidegger: of all of us being "thrown into the world."[1] And it's true: no one asked whether we wanted to be born, or to which parents, or into which race, ethnicity, gender, epoch, or society. We just find ourselves here—thrown, as it were, or catapulted into the world at this time and place—and eventually we wind up asking questions about what kind of world this is, and what we should do with our lives. Hence, we need some basic historical and conceptual orientation, in this subject and others.

COUNTRIES

International studies, by definition, involves studying things *between nations*, specifically by looking at how different countries relate to, and deal with, each other, in all kinds of important ways: economically, politically, culturally, militarily, and so on. This raises an obvious, yet fundamental, question: *what is a country?* There are over 200 countries in the world today, and every single part of planet Earth has been claimed by some country, or group of countries. There are *three general exceptions* to this observation: (1) Antarctica;

(2) **atmospheric near-space**, on the edge between the atmosphere and outer space; and (3) **the high seas**, in the middle of the oceans. These have been deemed **international public spaces**, like parks (as it were, unowned by any one person or nation), thereby allowing for any country to use them, theoretically for the general benefit of humanity.

Territory and Resources

Countries have *four basic elements*, as diagrammed in Figure 1.1. First, there's *a physical environment, defined by borders* (whether politically human-made or else naturally present, like a coast or river). This physical environment most importantly features **territory** (we all have to live somewhere) and all the natural resources on top of, or below, or surrounded by it. The most vital **natural resources** include:

> *Countries are considered to be the owners of their territories, and all the natural resources therein.*

- water
- food crops
- other plants
- animals
- timber
- useful rocks and minerals, such as silver and gold, coal and oil.

Countries are considered to be the owners of their territories, and all the natural resources therein. The top 10 countries, by territorial size, are (in order from top to bottom, as of 2010):

1. Russia
2. Canada
3. United States

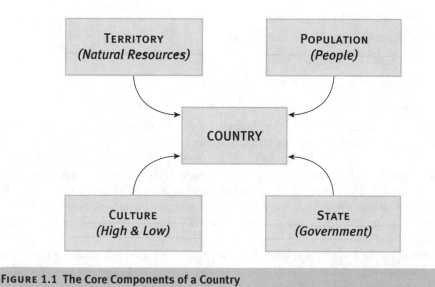

FIGURE 1.1 The Core Components of a Country

4. China

5. Brazil

6. Australia

7. India

8. Argentina

9. Kazakhstan

10. Sudan (before the partition, in 2011, into North and South Sudan).[2]

Population: People and Nations

On the territory, a country has a **population**, its people. A country's population can be highly unified and quite similar, in terms of its racial and ethnic background, cultural practices, languages spoken, beliefs and behaviours, and so on. Iceland and Japan are frequently mentioned in this regard. Or, a country's population might be a collection of highly diverse groups and individuals. This is especially true of the so-called **immigrant societies**, those countries populated—over the years—by waves of immigrants from many different parts of the world. These countries would include especially, Australia, Britain, Canada, Israel, and the US.

An important term here, stressed in the book's introduction, is "nation." This is often used interchangeably with "country" or "state," but technically it's different—and importantly so. A **nation** is a group of people that sees itself as *being a people*, that is, as belonging together in some meaningful sense as a unit, and as having its own identity, and as being separate and distinct from other comparable groups. The basis of this national uniqueness is thought to include some, or all, of the following shared characteristics:

- racial or ethnic background
- common language
- shared historical experiences and memories
- religious beliefs and cultural practices
- diet/cuisine and fashion choices
- common ways of believing about, and behaving in, the world.

The nation, and also the state (see below), of which we are members, has come to shape us in many profound ways, and it's safe to say that, among the many identities that each of us sports as individuals, our national membership would rank highly in the list of most consequential (alongside such other crucial aspects as, say, gender, age, career, and sexual orientation). The languages we speak, the food and drink of which we partake, the institutions we interact with, and the immediate social context of our daily lives have all been deeply contoured by the history of our country, by how it is governed, and by the kind of people who live there.

As noted in the book's introduction, many historians assert that **nationalism**—the drive of a nation to get its own state—has been one of the most potent forces of modern history, emphatically since the American (1776–83) and French (1789–1800) revolutions.

Nationalism has inspired people, created deep senses of belonging and identity, but also caused numerous wars and armed conflicts, and has completely overhauled the political map of the world through time.[3]

Populations don't just have ideals and identities: they also have practical needs and attributes. For example, a population is highly valuable to its country as a source of labour and talent; yet it also requires a vast infrastructure to feed it, water it, house it, transport it, clothe it, educate it, tend to its health, and so on. And so every country must concern itself with such **core infrastructure** needs, and some are better at this than others, and some face steeper obstacles to this than others. We shall see this in future chapters, such as those on aid and development and on global public health. For now, we note that the top 10 largest countries, by population, are (in order from top to bottom as of 2010):

1. China
2. India
3. United States
4. Indonesia
5. Brazil
6. Pakistan
7. Bangladesh
8. Nigeria
9. Russia
10. Japan.

Culture: High and Low

Peoples have cultures, or ways of life. They also form many groupings, even within their own nation. **Culture** refers to how people live, think, and behave; it's often split into "high" and "low" forms. **High culture** is thought to be of especially good quality, or enduring merit, and is thought to represent, in some sense, the very best and most meaningful pieces of culture. High culture would include such things as groundbreaking works of art, housed in prestigious museums; Picasso's paintings could be said to represent an important part of Spanish high culture. It would also include music of great beauty and sophistication, such as Tchaikovsky's for Russian culture. Brilliant and beautiful pieces of architecture would also count, like India's Taj Mahal or France's Eiffel Tower. Landmark works of poetry and literature are also forms of high culture, for instance the works of Shakespeare for the English-speaking countries. The top 10 languages spoken and used in the world today are (in order by number of speakers, from top to bottom as of 2010): Chinese Mandarin, Spanish, English, Hindi-Urdu, Arabic, Bengali, Portuguese, Russian, Japanese, and French.[4]

Low culture refers to more common or widespread forms of belief and behaviour, such as dietary

High culture is often associated with national identity, as it is with this performance by Korean dancers. How is the line between high and low culture drawn? Is it movable or fairly fixed? (© Richard Lindie/iStockphoto)

(i.e. food and drink) practices, popular music and books, sports, TV and radio content, Internet and new media content, popular recreation and leisure activities, common ways of speaking and dressing, and so on. Religious practices would probably count here, on grounds of their widespread nature. The world's top 10 religions, by number of believers, are (in order from top to bottom, as of 2010):

1. Christianity (Catholic, Protestant, and Orthodox counted together)

2. Islam

3. Hinduism

4. Chinese folk religion (or Confucianism)

5. Buddhism

6. Indigenous folk religions (such as Shintoism)

7. Judaism

8. Sikhism

9. Baha'i

10. Jainism.

The number of non-religious, or **secular**, belief-systems (like secular humanism) is estimated to be enough to be third on this list.

We will explore culture in much greater detail in Chapter 3, on comparative culture. For now, we note how a culture defines what a country thinks and feels, and what it does and how it behaves. We recall from the book's introduction the distinction between hard and soft power, and how the cultural influence of a country is defined as its soft power. We shall also see, further on in this chapter, how culture can come to define a civilization and how it differs from other world civilizations. This means that culture can serve to unite like-minded countries (creating a civilization), but then it can also—depending on the differences—serve to divide countries, even causing wars and clashes of civilization.

Religious groups are only one kind of important grouping, or association, within a country. It is now common to distinguish between states (or governments), on the one hand, and, on the other, so-called "non-state actors." **Non-state actors** are non-governmental groupings or institutions. Some of the most important and influential include businesses or corporations, churches or religious groups, charities, sports leagues, fan clubs, social movements, and interest groups. (Most of the *charitable* non-state actors get referred to collectively as **non-governmental organizations**, or NGOs.) **Social movements** are broad-based and widely dispersed groups of people devoted to a certain cause, like the environment. **Interest groups** share a similar shape, yet tend to be more highly organized and more politically involved, determined to get their particular interest onto the agenda of government and society, for the sake of change and securing some kind of benefit. Interest groups include such bodies as the National Rifle Association (NRA) in the United States and the Dairy Farmers of Ontario (DFO) in Canada. In terms of international studies, the most influential and important of the non-state actors would be:

- **multinational corporations** (or MNCs—big businesses with multiple units in multiple countries)

- aid and development charities, or NGOs (sometimes religious in nature)

- social movements or international interest groups (especially ones connected with peace, health, human rights, and environmental issues)

- terrorist groups, insurgent forces, and private militias.

A **terrorist group** is an armed group that deliberately uses violence against civilian populations—as opposed to military targets—in hopes that the resulting spread of fear (or terror) amongst the people will further a narrow political agenda that the group has. **Insurgent forces** are revolutionary armed groups, committed to the violent overthrow of the government of their society. And **private militias** are armed groups that are *not* part of any country's official military. They may be either political or mercenary in nature; in other words, either they have a private political agenda of some kind, or they simply sell their military services to the highest bidder. The latter kind, the mercenary kind, get referred to today as **PMCs**, or **private military companies**.)[5]

The State: Government and Its Powers

Finally, a **state** refers to the government of a country. This is the group of people responsible for making and enforcing the rules that regulate the collective life of a people and thereby make an orderly social life possible on a given territory. Every country has a government, and often it is the single most powerful association or institution in that society. Governments make the rules and enforce them with police; they also arm and train national military forces, both to protect that society from external attack and to help keep the peace internally. Governments decide which kind of activity is legal or not, and with their powers of taxation, usually have massive financial resources to realize their will. Governments patrol borders, and decide who gets in and who doesn't by setting standards for immigration and membership. Governments negotiate trade deals with other countries, and decide such momentous issues as war and peace, and how to respond to public emergencies, such as an outbreak of disease, a storm, an earthquake/tsunami, or an environmental catastrophe. Though non-state actors are of increasing importance in international life, it seems fair to say that states remain the most influential agents. In many ways, and both for better and for worse, the world we have today is the world created by nation-states.

Though non-state actors are of increasing importance, it is safe to say that states remain the most influential agents in international life today.

State Formation

But how did states come into being? How did Earth come to be divided up between 200 or more countries, each having these four different parts as described above? After all, in the beginning—as they say—there were no states and countries: only human beings and the planet itself. So, how from that original point did the current state of international affairs—which some experts label **the interstate system**—come into existence? And who are the winners and losers in such a system?

Studies in Technology

The Birth of the Internet

The Internet is, of course, closely tied with today's culture. Most all of this book's technology boxes will deal with new computer-based, and Internet-based, technologies, and so it seems appropriate to have this first one offer a quick history of this amazing piece of technology.

As soon as computers were invented, in the 1940s and 1950s, engineers and computer scientists began working on how, and whether, point-to-point communication between different computers might happen. All the funding for all this original research was given by the US federal government, and much of the initial concern was with potential military applications. The government was particularly interested in creating a system of basic communication between key institutions across the country, a system that might be able to withstand even a nuclear war and keep working. Hence, it funded DARPA, the Defense Advanced Research Projects Agency. DARPA created ARPANET, the world's first system of interconnected computer networks, featuring the world's first-ever e-mail. This was in the very late 1960s and early 1970s.

In 1982, the term "Internet" was coined to describe the dream of not just a nationwide, but a worldwide, network of fully interconnected "protocol suites"—sets of rules governing the exchange or transmission of data electronically between computers. The Internet moved out of the purely military world into universities and research institutes, with help from the US National Science Foundation (NSF) and its own network, NSFNET. The Internet also moved overseas, when Tim Berners-Lee of Europe's CERN agency (the European Organization for Nuclear Research) both coined the term "World Wide Web" and developed the most basic Internet language, HTML, in the late 1980s.

The Internet became commercialized and widely distributed when NSFNET was **privatized** (i.e. sold to for-profit companies), and commercial Internet service providers (ISPs) came into being, in the mid-1990s. Since then, the Internet has exploded in growth, with wide-ranging impacts on human culture. For example, in 1992, an estimated 1 million people worldwide had access to the Internet. In 2011, that number is now 2 billion.

The Internet's impact on culture and on how we live our lives has been enormous, allowing for: near-instant communication between remote correspondents, worldwide; global information-sharing; social- and business networking; and online shopping, research, and entertainment. More on the fuller consequences of the Internet will be shared throughout this book. For now, consider the world's top five most-visited websites on the Internet, as of 2011:

1. Google
2. Facebook
3. YouTube
4. Yahoo
5. Wikipedia.

How many of these have you visited today?[6]

The contemporary interstate system has its origins in European history, and through European colonialism and imperialism, it spread to cover the whole world. So, we need first to set the stage *within* Europe, and then to describe the ugly and problematic, yet historically crucial, phenomenon of European imperialism.

State Formation in Europe

Details on the ultimate origins of government are lost in the sands of time, but many argue that as soon as the very earliest humans stopped being nomadic hunter–gatherers and became settled agricultural people, the need for governments to organize communities and to protect the farms (and their produce and livestock) from foreign invaders, not to mention local thieves, was born. Hence, so was the need for government.[7]

It is thought that the earliest humans evolved over millennia from the ape family of mammals, with the first known human—or *Homo sapiens*—appearing approximately 200,000 years ago. It is widely agreed that humanity first evolved in Africa, in the temperate middle region comprising present-day Kenya and Ethiopia. From there, humans spread out in a vast migration across the world, to the east into the Near/Middle East and Asia, and then to the north and west into Europe. It is thought that our earliest ancestors lived as **nomadic hunter–gatherers**, never having one home base but, rather, moving from site to site in the pursuit of animals for food and the flight from predators and each other. This is what drove early humans—eventually—across the whole planet. But, around 10,000 years ago, the **first agricultural settlements** were created, as people came to realize that they could effectively raise their own food instead of chasing it, and that coherent, permanent settlements offered a range of social, cultural, and economic benefits besides. The oldest such settlements thus far found have been in the Middle East, in the Mesopotamia area between the Tigris and Euphrates rivers, in what is now Iraq.[8]

Even in Europe's beginnings, there weren't any countries or nation-states. There were cities, and then there were empires. It's commonly said that the origins of modern Europe are to be found in ancient Greece (starting around the eighth century BCE). But ancient Greece was a collection of so-called **city-states**: not big national communities governed by state structures but, rather, tiny cities—usually on coasts or waterways—ruled by local or municipal governments.

The most prominent of the ancient Greek city-states included Athens, Delphi, Knossos, Marathon, Olympia, Sparta, and Thebes. Greek civilization is thought to have enjoyed its height of achievement between 600 and 400 BCE. It was often lamented—at that time and since—that in spite of their massive accomplishments, and all they did to advance human civilization, the ancient Greeks never were able to overcome their local loyalties and to create a national government uniting all the Greek-speaking people, with their common culture, religion, literature, and ways of living. This failure of unity left them wide open to military conquest, first by the Macedonians under Alexander the Great, and then at the hands of another city—an ultra-ambitious and aggressive city—based not in Greece but in Italy: Rome. Rome's conquest of Greece is usually dated around 146 BCE.[9]

With Rome we see the first great European empire, succeeding that of Alexander's (which broke apart almost as quickly as he had put it together, following his sudden death). Empire is as old as the hills, and can be seen throughout world history, in such far-flung places as ancient Egypt, the Middle East (especially Persia, centred around present-day

Iran), the Aztec, Incan, and Mayan civilizations of Latin America, the Mongolian empire of the Khans, and, of course, in ancient China and India. What do we mean by empire?[10]

Empire

Empire is a system of governance forged in military conquest (as opposed to, say, the freely given consent of people). In an empire, there is an imperial core, sometimes known as a "hub of empire" or **metropole** (i.e. "mother city" or "mother country"—literally the pole around which the rest of the empire revolves). And then there are the **colonies**, which are the conquered and subjected lands, "the dependencies" on the periphery of the empire. Substantial inequality between metropole and colony, and the domination and subjugation of the latter by the former, are of the essence of empire. Consider the conceptual Figure 1.2, illustrating the basic relationship in this regard.

The metropole conquers the colony by force. It subjects the colony to its rule and sends leaders from the core to govern the periphery in a way that pleases the metropole (and often is, in fact, a pale imitation of the method of governance within the metropole itself). The metropole also offers military protection, of a kind, to the colony, at least from conquest by other, would-be imperial powers. Often, the metropole must invest to some extent in the colony, particularly in terms of such physical infrastructure as roads. However, this investment tends to be highly selective and mainly designed to maximize the extractive agenda of

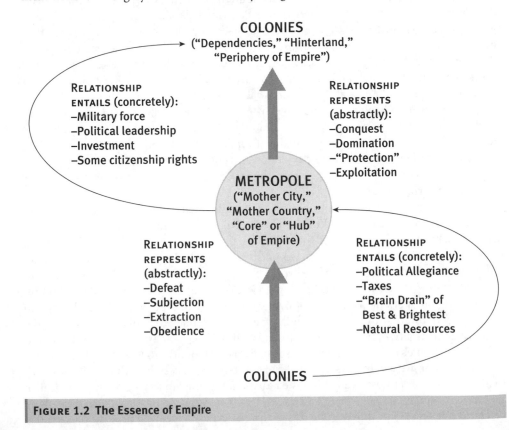

COLONIES
("Dependencies," "Hinterland," "Periphery of Empire")

Relationship entails (concretely):
–Military force
–Political leadership
–Investment
–Some citizenship rights

Relationship represents (abstractly):
–Conquest
–Domination
–"Protection"
–Exploitation

METROPOLE
("Mother City," "Mother Country," "Core" or "Hub" of Empire)

Relationship represents (abstractly):
–Defeat
–Subjection
–Extraction
–Obedience

Relationship entails (concretely):
–Political Allegiance
–Taxes
–"Brain Drain" of Best & Brightest
–Natural Resources

COLONIES

Figure 1.2 The Essence of Empire

the metropole. At times, metropoles (such as Rome) have offered citizenship rights, of various degrees, to the people within their colonies as an effective way of cementing obedience and as of attracting some of the "best and brightest" from the colonies to the metropole.

At the heart of the logic of empire is the growth and success of the metropole. Thus, in exchange for the benefits of military protection and being part of the empire (with potential citizenship rights), the conquered people within the colonies commonly must offer the following back to the metropole: political allegiance (especially vis-à-vis any rival empires); taxes and other financial tributes; local troops to help out with the protection and defence of the colony; and, perhaps above all, a steady and large flow of natural resources that meets the metropole's extractive agenda. Indirectly, as mentioned above, the colony usually also winds up suffering a **brain drain**, as its best and brightest people seek better opportunities for themselves within the heart of the metropole.[11]

The Roman Empire was one of, if not the, most successful in the history of the world. At its peak, it stretched from Britain in the north to Egypt in the south, and from Spain in the west to Syria in the east, controlling for over 1,000 years the fates of hundreds of millions of people. It brought peace and stability, legal coherence, cultural advance, and technological innovation to the entire Mediterranean world. Rome began as an imperial power around the year 500 BCE and ended, in western Europe, in 476 CE. But, in eastern Europe and the Near East, it went on to last 1,000 *more* years as the remodelled Byzantine Empire (which fell in 1453 CE).

Both the rise of the Roman Empire and its collapse contributed substantially to state formation in Europe. On the one hand, the Romans showed how it could be done, governing vast stretches of territory in an effective, prosperous, and stable way. Their ruthless skill at military conquest, their genius for engineering public infrastructure, their enthusiasm for trade both by land and by sea, and their legal capacities for organizing and controlling populations would all prove very instructive to later powers. On the other hand, we might term the governance of the Roman Empire a form of **cosmopolitan governance**, at odds with that of the modern nation-state. For the Roman Empire featured one city governing an enormous, far-flung, non-contiguous territory containing a vast multitude of different cultures and peoples. We might say then that, between the Greek way (of the tiny city-state) and the Roman way (of the vast cosmopolitan empire) lies the middle way of the European nation-state. And it is with the collapse of Rome in the West that we begin to see how this form of governance comes into being.[12]

After Rome

The Roman Empire collapsed in western Europe in the late 400s CE, fragmenting in the face of repeated barbarian invasions, especially from what is now Germany. The Roman Empire had grown too large to govern efficiently, and too often its governors were corrupt and incompetent. It managed to endure in the Near East, as mentioned, for over a thousand years more (in remodelled form), but in the West the only institution to survive the collapse of Roman civilization was the Roman Catholic Church (Christianity having been made the state religion by the emperors Constantine and Theodosius). The Western empire otherwise dissolved into a series of small ethnic groups and tribe-like families, and many wars between them ensued. Not much information survives from this period, and so we call it the Dark Ages. What little does survive tells us, sporadically, of an anarchical and bloody existence, a dirty and decrepit life. Europe took major steps backward during the Dark Ages, which lasted anywhere from 500 to 1000 CE. At the same time, Islamic civilization in Persia and North Africa, and Far Eastern civilizations in China and India, flourished.[13]

During the Dark Ages' later years, starting around the year 800, ambitious local warlords made bold attempts to consolidate their control over larger pieces of territory. Alfred "the Great" (849–899) did this in Britain, and Charlemagne (742–814) on the Continent. While not immediately successful, these efforts pointed the way towards the future: local tribal heads gradually winning control over larger and larger pieces of territory, declaring themselves "champions of the people" in the process. They re-established law and order, by force of arms, farm-by-farm and forest-by-forest. A handful of these warlords eventually became self-styled kings, monarchs of their realms. Latin, the official language of the Roman Empire, fell into disuse and there arose in its place numerous national languages, some of which (such as French, Italian, and Spanish) were clear derivatives from the original Latin. In short, we see over centuries (during the Middle Ages, circa 1000–1500 CE) the rise of the European nation-state, with:

- its own territory, mid-size between city-state and empire;

- its own national language and literature;

- its own kings, queens, and system of governance;

- its own customs and cuisines; and

- its own religion, as we will see.[14]

For a thousand years, the Roman Catholic Church had been the *only* religious organization in Europe. It was immensely powerful, surviving the collapse of the Roman Empire and entrenching its influence—economically, politically, culturally—for centuries. But in 1517, German priest Martin Luther (and others) demanded changes in the structure, teachings, and practices of the Church; they "protested," hence came to be called Protestants, and the Protestant Reformation began. When the Church refused their demands, the reformers broke away and formed rival Christian churches (e.g. Lutheran, Anglican). Needless to say, bad feelings were created, and violence eventually erupted. National political leaders—kings and queens, barons and earls—chose sides, and soon full-scale battles and even wars broke out, as Europe split religiously into a mainly Protestant north and a mainly Catholic south. The worst of these religious wars was the Thirty Years War (1618–48), which, for instance, resulted in the death of *one-third* of the population of Germany.[15]

Westphalia

After three decades of such savagery, the national leaders of Europe got together to make a deal for peace. This deal has come to be known as the **Treaty of Westphalia** (1648), and many credit Westphalia as forming the real and true birth of the modern interstate system we know, and must live with, today.[16] The essence of the deal struck at Westphalia was this: "Let's stop trying to kill each other over our religious differences. We—Catholics and Protestants—both admit that we cannot fully kill off the other side; each is here to stay. So, *you* decide which religion will prevail in *your* country, and *we'll* decide which will prevail in *ours*. We won't try to convert each other by force of arms." It was an agreement to lay down arms, to live and let live, and it represents a kind of deal known as a ***modus vivendi*** (i.e. a way to live), meaning something we can all live with, even if it's not our preference.

The Treaty of Westphalia is one of the earliest expressions of some kind of tolerance for difference found in any legal system. The major importance for modern international affairs, though, has to do with the fact that Westphalia affirms the core "state-centric" values of political sovereignty and territorial integrity. These values are **state-centric** in that they place countries, or the nation-state, at the very heart of international affairs and at the centre of the global system of power and order. These values thus privilege the nation-state over such other entities as NGOs, MNCs, international institutions like the United Nations (UN), and perhaps—some fear—even individual human persons.[17]

Sovereignty and Territory

Political sovereignty refers to the right of a group of people to rule themselves. "Political" refers to power, or *polis*, an ancient Greek term for a group of people living together as an ongoing community, whereas "sovereignty" means the entitlement to rule (literally the power of a sovereign, or king). To be sovereign is to be self-ruling, acknowledging no higher authority over oneself. More fully, then, political sovereignty is the most basic right of a country in modern international law and global affairs: the right of a country to make its own laws and to govern itself, *provided*—crucially—that it respects the right of all other countries to do the same. Every country on Earth thus jealously guards, and is proud of, its national or state sovereignty.

But this sovereignty must be exercised *somewhere*. To be real, the abstract right of political sovereignty must imply some secure space on which to live, and in which to enjoy self-rule. Hence, the right to **territorial integrity**: a community or country has a right to some livable territory and is considered—as mentioned above—to be the general owner of all the natural resources on, under, or above its land. That's the "territorial" part; the "integrity" part refers to that group's right not to have other countries invade its territory or attempt to seize its resources. A community needs not only, or merely, *to have* territory and resources; it needs to be able to count on having such resources moving forward, if it is to remain—as Aristotle said—an ongoing partnership formed for the general good of its members.[18]

Spread of State Formation from Europe throughout the World

Thus, with Westphalia, the European interstate system was formed: nation-states had finally gelled, and they agreed (at least in theory) to deal with each other in terms of the values of political sovereignty and territorial integrity. How did the rest of the world come to share the same structure and (eventually) to be brought into the same system (the so-called **Westphalian system**) that remains in force today? The answer, as noted, is through the experience of European colonialism and imperialism, one of the major drivers of modern world history, lasting from about 1500 until 1975.

While empire, as we've mentioned, is as old as the hills, European imperialism became reborn once Columbus "discovered" (more accurately "made contact with") the New World in 1492. While there were, of course, Native or Aboriginal peoples who had been in the Americas for centuries, these territories were brand-new to the Europeans, and their discovery sparked off a massive "land rush" to gain control of as much of the New World as possible. The kings and queens of Europe urged their citizens to settle abroad, seeing an opportunity to grow the power, wealth, and prestige of their relatively young and still growing nation-states. The result was the rapid spread of empire—along the lines of the system described, and diagrammed, above—throughout the Caribbean and North, Central, and South America. Later, as technology for longer travel and effective conquest improved, the Europeans were able to look farther afield into Southeast Asia, the South Pacific, Australia/New Zealand, and the heart of Africa. The original imperial powers were Portugal and Spain, but they were quickly followed by the Netherlands. Next came France, England, and Russia, and by the early 1900s, even Belgium, Italy, and Germany were trying to found colonies in Africa.[19]

Table 1.1 shows the most prominent colonial holdings of the European imperial powers during this period. We can see that the table covers almost all the world, reflecting the extent to which Europeans came to spread, by force, their own mode of governance across the planet. In so doing they established the interstate system we know today, according to which (a) countries are the major players in international affairs, and (b) they must (at least try to) deal with each other on the basis of political sovereignty and territorial integrity.

European imperialism had a profound effect on world history. Not only was the interstate system created, but much of the world was used as a vast resource base for Europe, with people, money, and natural commodities flowing from around the world into the heart of such European capitals as Madrid, Amsterdam, London, Paris, Berlin, and Moscow. This was all for the good in Europe, of course, but much to the disadvantage of the rest of the world. The American colonists were among those who recognized this injustice and took steps to end it, overthrowing British rule and establishing their own republic during the American Revolution (1776–83). Most other countries weren't so lucky, and they endured centuries of exploitation and resource extraction at the hands of the European empires. And it wasn't just political and economic exploitation that occurred. In many instances European imperialism was founded on ferocious military violence, and it came to express deep cruelty and social dominance, and racial and other forms of bigotry and prejudice, which left massive scars on colonial societies.[20]

END OF EUROPEAN IMPERIALISM

How, then, did such a powerfully entrenched, worldwide, imperial system come to an end? The answer is that it was destroyed by the Europeans themselves . . . but, not intentionally. During the entire period of colonization and imperialism, there were of course huge rivalries between the European empires. Even though, *in theory* after Westphalia, they were committed to dealing with each other as equals—each with sovereignty and territory—*in practice* they engaged in fierce competition with each other, to see who could have the biggest, richest, and most powerful empire. This process sparked many wars over the centuries, but none bigger than the two world wars. World War I (1914–18) really marks the high-water point for European imperialism around the world. The war—begun as a struggle of imperial rivalries between Germany, Austria–Hungary, and Turkey on the one side and Britain, France, and Russia on the other—degenerated into a long and tragic slaughterhouse of destruction. The war only halted when the United States intervened in 1917, on the side of Britain and France.[21]

But, in many ways, the First World War left things unsettled, and in rapid fashion war returned. The **Treaty of Versailles** (1919), which ended the Great War, broke up the German and Austro-Hungarian empires, as well as the Turkish (or Ottoman) empire. The

TABLE 1.1 European Nations and their Colonies, *c.* 1500–1950

European Nation-State	Prominent Colonial Holdings
Portugal	• Brazil • some cities in India (e.g. Goa)
Spain	• Mexico • Central America • most of South America (excluding Brazil) • parts of the southwestern US (e.g. California, Texas) • the Philippines
the Netherlands	• South Africa • some Caribbean islands (e.g. Aruba) • parts of Indonesia • early settlements in eastern North America (e.g. New York)
France	• North America (Quebec & Middle America, from Detroit south to Louisiana) • some Caribbean islands (e.g. Martinique) • cities on the coast of India • some South Pacific islands (e.g. French Polynesia) • West and North Africa (e.g. Ivory Coast, Algeria) • parts of the Middle East (e.g. Syria, Lebanon) • Vietnam
England	• the United States (originally the "Thirteen Colonies") • Canada • many Caribbean islands (e.g. Bahamas, Bermuda) • India • Burma • Hong Kong • Singapore • Australia/New Zealand • some South Pacific islands (e.g. Fiji) • parts of the Middle East (Egypt, Iraq, Palestine) • central and East Africa (e.g. Sudan, Kenya, South Africa, Nigeria)
Russia	• Alaska • large parts of Poland and Finland • Ukraine • some Baltic states (e.g. Latvia) • most of central Asia (e.g. Armenia, Georgia, Kazakhstan, Uzbekistan)
Italy	• Ethiopia • Libya • Somalia
Germany	• Cameroon • Namibia • Tanzania

British and French hungrily helped themselves to portions of their defeated rivals' colonial holdings. Further, steep terms of punishment and reparations payments, were placed upon Germany, and this caused deep resentment and ultimately severe social dislocation. So desperate did the situation become in Germany that by the 1920s, German people were looking towards radical, extremist "solutions" to their many political and economic problems. This provided oxygen, so to speak, for Adolf Hitler's Nazi Party. Hitler promised to tear up the Treaty of Versailles, re-conquer the lost lands of the German Empire, and grow the German economy through military buildup, modernization, and a renewed round of conquest within Europe. After the Nazis won power in the 1930s, Hitler kept his word, and the world marched directly towards another massive war.[22]

World War II (1939–45) was the biggest war the world has ever seen. Over 50 million people died in fighting that raged all around the globe, pitting the Axis powers of Germany, Italy, and Japan against the Allies of Britain (including its huge list of colonies, like Canada), China, France, Russia, and (as of 1941) the United States; in fact, by 1945, 50 different countries were part of the Allied cause. The two world wars had a tremendous significance for European imperialism. For even though the Allies ultimately won World War II, the two wars had exacted such enormous damage and costs upon Europe that none of the European powers could afford to maintain their empires. Even Britain and France, though victorious, had to shed their colonies. Thus began the process of **decolonization**, which lasted from about 1945 until 1975. Old European colonies became newly liberated and independent nation-states, left to fend for themselves in the interstate system. Sometimes, this process occurred smoothly. More often than not, it was very difficult, complicated not merely by political conflict but by all-out war (such as involved the French in Algeria and Vietnam, and the British in the Middle East).[23]

NORTH VERSUS SOUTH

Thus far, we have defined and explored countries, nations, states, and their various parts; these are truly the most basic units of global relations. Then we enjoyed a sweeping, yet informative, history as to how such entities and forces have come into being: how they have set the stage for international studies today. There remain, in this opening chapter, two large and truly vital concepts that need to be defined and explained. These concepts relate to the distinctions between, first, North and South, and second, Western civilization and non-Western civilizations.

In many ways, the distinction between North and South (see Figure 1.3) has replaced the older frameworks of "developed versus developing" and, certainly, "First World versus Third World." **The North** refers generally to countries in the Northern hemisphere, above Earth's equator, with the important exception of Australia and New Zealand. **The South**, then, refers generally to countries south of the equator. But here, too, the strict geography is misleading, as for example Afghanistan, North Korea, and Haiti are all north of the equator yet have many more of the characteristics of nation-states of the South. The North–South distinction is thus crude and sweeping, and in many ways "developed versus developing" is more accurate. The controversy with this latter distinction, though, is that it may seem to imply that some countries have "made it," achieved full development (or some kind of social nirvana), whereas others race desperately to catch up. Yet it seems more correct to

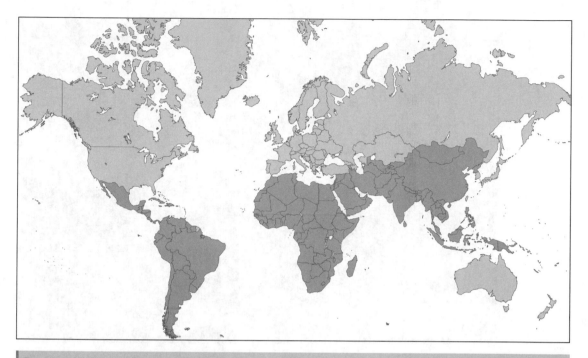

FIGURE 1.3 The North and the South

It is generally accepted that 25 per cent of the world's population lives in the developed Global North, whereas 75 per cent resides in the developing Global South.

say that *all* countries are, in an important sense, always developing further, always with room to improve. Thus, "more developed" versus "less developed" is probably best. In any event, **Northern**, or **developed**, or **more developed countries** tend to be wealthier, better educated, healthier, less populated, more technologically advanced, more urbanized, more influential internationally, and more attractive to immigrants. They have lower rates of crime, poverty, and unemployment; they have more stable governance and social peace; and they have longer life expectancies and even higher average rates of personal happiness and life satisfaction. By contrast, **Southern**, or **developing**, or **less-developed countries** are more populated, yet less wealthy, less educated, less technologically advanced, more rural, and with higher rates of **emigration** (i.e. people leaving) than **immigration** (i.e. people coming in). Southern countries have less power internationally and higher rates of crime, disease, poverty, and unemployment. They have more political instability, greater instances of violence and warfare, and shorter life expectancies and lower rates of average personal happiness and life satisfaction.[24]

Why the world has become divided in this way is an interesting, important, and complex question. One big piece of the puzzle, though, is the recent 500-year history of European imperialism and colonialism. As we have seen, the process involved, among other things, draining very valuable resources—both material and human—from the South and into the North. We could say that the South today is playing catch-up in a rather grim

Nycole Turmel steps out of a shelter being used as temporary lodging for Aboriginals in Attawapiskat, Ontario, during her time as interim leader of the federal New Democratic Party in November 2011. (© THE CANADIAN PRESS/Adrian Wyld)

game in which Northerners have (a) had a 500-year head start, and (b) given themselves that head start, while putting the Southerners far behind. Now, it's not quite so simple—as we'll find in the chapter on international aid and development—but it's clear that imperialism and colonialism are major reasons why the North is so advantaged and, especially, why the South stands so disadvantaged. An important question, which we'll put off for now but return to in that future chapter, is this: *given the history of colonialism, what does the North owe to the South, by way of assisting their development?*[25]

As noted earlier, generally, *any* country can be placed in *either* the Northern/developed/more developed category *or else* the Southern/developing/less developed category. Yet notice that even this is not quite so straightforward, as there are regions within even very advanced countries where life seems to share more in common with the Global South. One thinks of the lives of some Aboriginal people in Canada (see the photo above) or Australia, or of some of the homeless people living in some of the biggest, richest cities of North America or Europe. And vice versa: there are pockets of amazingly advanced comfort and privilege in otherwise developing societies. Consider the rich suburbs of Rio or Buenos Aires, or those of Mumbai, Cairo, or Jakarta. Or, perhaps most graphically, note the glittering, air-conditioned, ultra-modern, "oil-money" skyscrapers of Dubai, set amidst the emptiness of the scorching Middle Eastern desert.[26]

THE WEST VERSUS "THE REST"

The Global South is, by now, a much-used term of art. It is much more common than "the North." When speaking of northern, developed societies, the preferred phrase is generally "the West." So, we have a rather funny situation (one that would no doubt cause a compass confusion!) wherein in international politics, the terms "North" and "West" refer, basically, to the same thing. And we need to focus on the West, at least for now, owing to its leading role in the development of the international system: through the experience of European imperialism, and later through the influence of powerful countries like the United States, Western civilization has had disproportionate impact on the current state of international society.

We need to consider civilization in general before we can talk about Western civilization and how it differs from others. "Civilization" can be a controversial term, as its deepest roots lie in a distinction between "civilized" and "uncivilized," wherein the former refers generally to someone who is urban, wealthy, educated, law-abiding, sophisticated, polished and well-mannered (there is, after all, an obvious connection between "civilization" and "civility"). "Uncivilized," by contrast, would refer to someone who is rural, poorer, uneducated, crude, and unpolished. Scholars stress that the deepest connections between "civilization" and its root word, "civil," relate to (a) the city (think citizen, civilian) and (b) the law (as in civic order, civil law).

Today, however, references to civilization have outgrown these older, sweeping associations, and experts like David Wengrow generally use the term "civilization" as an equivalent to "culture" in its broadest sense, that is, as a way of life. So, there are no "civilized" versus "uncivilized" cultures (much less the older distinction between "civilized" and "barbarian"); rather, there are only *different kinds of civilization*. It is this broader, non-judgmental sense of civilization that we are here interested in. In many ways, **civilization** means a pervasive culture (or way of life), shared by many countries, impacting a large region of the world over time. A civilization tends to have the same, or at least similar, systems of law and governance, economic organization, patterns of living and settlement, types of food and subsistence, and kinds of culture, both high and low (especially in terms of worldview, religion, and shared values). Figure 1.4 shows Samuel Huntingdon's influential map of world civilizations.[27]

Loosely speaking, "Western civilization" has two meanings: (1) the simple *geographical* reference to western Europe and the colonies it created, especially throughout the Americas and Australia/New Zealand; and (2) the much more important reference to *shared values*, especially regarding how, ideally, to run a society. The West, so to speak, is a state of mind. The core ideals—which, of course, don't always get realized perfectly—of the West are commonly thought to include the following:

1. *Individualism.* There is a commitment to every individual person's human rights to life, liberty, and the pursuit of happiness. This would be in contrast to civilizations in which the primary unit of concern might be the family, or the nation, and the job of the individual is to find a way to fit in and contribute.

2. *Limited, democratic government.* Government is seen as the servant of the people, kept under control by written constitutions, the rule of law, checks and balances, and **democracy**: free and fair regular public elections wherein there is one person, one vote, and the majority rules. This would be in contrast to civilizations in which

FIGURE 1.4 Huntingdon's Map of World Civilizations

Huntingdon hypothesized that there was a greater chance of war between civilizations whose core values were most dissimilar, as they would lack mutual respect for and understanding of each other.

government might be seen as leading or controlling the people, and as having its authority coming *not* from elections but from, say, military power.

3. *Free-market capitalism.* Most generally, **capitalism** is a kind of economic system that:
   a) allows for the **private-property ownership** (i.e. the non-governmental owner-ship) of the means of economic production (such as natural resources and one's own labour power);
   b) allows businesspeople the freedom to set up their own businesses and to keep some of the profits they earn for themselves and for their own private enjoyment;
   c) encourages *trading* between buyer and seller as the means of distributing goods and services in the economy (this is the "free market" part, as opposed to, say, the government dictating who gets what);
   d) uses money as the means of exchange, to facilitate the trading of goods and services (i.e. the buyer and seller in a transaction agree upon a price that is mutually acceptable); and
   e) features a court system of public laws for the peaceful handling, and non-violent resolution, of economic disputes.

Free-market capitalism operates in contrast to economic systems such as **commu-nism**, wherein the state owns and controls everything, and/or where the private profit motive is not so central, usually because the state taxes back all the gains for its own public purposes. Capitalism is also in contrast to earlier, more primitive economic systems of **barter exchange** (i.e. good-for-good or favour-for-favour, *non-money* exchanges) or **forced exchange** (the use of *violent coercion* to conquer and control the means of economic production, notably including territory and resources).

4. *A history of Christianity being the dominant religion.* Note, however, that in Western civilization today there is a **separation of church and state**, wherein the government does *not* try to enforce any particular religious vision. This model would be in contrast to civilizations where the state may very well use its power to try to realize a religious vision, and force people's beliefs and practices in this regard.

5. *Commitment to science and technology to improve people's lives.* Though most civilizations value technological improvements, this is not always so: some civilizations have rejected scientific breakthroughs—the birth control pill, for example—for reasons of religion or their views on gender roles.

6. *Urbanization.* Western civilization favours the growth and health of cities as the economic, cultural, and social engines of modern society.

7. *Robust civil society activity.* "**Civil society**" refers to all associations of people that are not official government groupings or institutions; it includes everything from businesses to churches, and from sports teams and volunteer organizations to NGOs. Often, in non-democratic, un-elected **authoritarian regimes**, the state does not allow other institutions to rival its influence and prestige, and so it outlaws them, or keeps their resources very low, as a result shrinking the size of civil society.

Again, these are only general, idealized characteristics, and the West does *not* fulfill them perfectly. Nor are these seven things immune to criticism, even as ideals. There are drawbacks to free-market capitalism, as we shall see later on in this book, and some societies disapprove of the West's separation of church and state, and its growing **secularization** (i.e. lack of religious belief). Perhaps above all, many other world civilizations find the individualism of the West to be harmfully at odds with family attachment, social togetherness, and even the success of the nation. All that is being claimed here is that there are, *as a matter of fact*, these seven major tendencies in Western countries, and they shape the sorts of societies they are, in addition to the previous characteristics mentioned above regarding the developed North. Put them together, and you have quite a full picture of how Northern/Western developed countries differ substantially from the other civilizations and countries of the still-developing Global South. (Much more will be said about the content of non-Western civilizations, in their own right, in the chapter on comparative culture.)[28]

Relevance of Civilizational Differences: Huntingdon's "Clash of Civilizations"

It should be obvious that the differences between world civilizations are extremely relevant: after all, they concern the ways vast regions of the planet differ from each other in terms of their core beliefs, their structures of governance, and how people lead their daily lives. A further—more recent and graphic—illustration of how important it is to pay attention to these differences comes from Huntingdon, who, in the early 1990s, wrote about a coming "clash of civilizations."

The timing of Huntingdon's work is important. For in the early 1990s, the major event of world historical importance was the end of the Cold War and the collapse of communism around the world. The **Cold War** (1945–91) refers to the multi-generational global showdown between the United States and the USSR (i.e. the Soviet Union, which included Russia and several other republics, especially in central Asia, that are now independent). The US and Russia were the two biggest winners of the Second World War, yet they did not trust each other and championed completely different social systems: the US, that of free-market, or capitalist, democracy, and Russia, that of police-state, planned- or command-economy communism. The Cold War *was* a war, in that it was very much a struggle between these nations as to whose social system would triumph and survive, and whose would fail and collapse. But the war was *cold*, in that there never was a **hot war** exchange of live-fire hostilities directly between the US and USSR. They did clash indirectly, though, in so-called **proxy wars**, mainly in the developing world. These wars involved "proxies," or pawns, in the sense that the US would support one side and Russia would support the other, and those sides would themselves fight directly in a live-fire exchange of hostilities. Vietnam (1954–74) and Afghanistan (1979–89) were Cold War proxy wars, and others were fought throughout Latin America and Southeast Asia. The US and Russia never fought directly because they were both nuclear powers, and each feared total destruction at the hands of the other's nuclear arsenal. This was known, notoriously and widely, as MAD, the doctrine of **mutually assured destruction**. Nuclear terror deterred, or prevented, any kind of direct armed clash between them, lest things escalate and spiral out of control towards an apocalyptic exchange of nuclear weapons.[29]

The US eventually won the Cold War, for a variety of reasons. Many agree that a very important one was the fact that Russia's not-for-profit, command-and-control, state-owns-everything economy could not out-produce the American capitalist economy over the long term, and Russia fell broke trying to keep up with the US's military spending. (It is sometimes amusingly said that the Americans "drank the Russians under the table.") Also, the non-democratic nature of communist countries could only alienate their citizens and make them feel detached from, and uncaring about, supporting such regimes; it really seems as if most people want the right to participate in their own governance. As a result, in the 1990s, the Soviet Union broke apart, and Russia's political, economic, and social systems collapsed and had to be reconstructed completely along more Western, free-market, democratic lines, as described above.[30]

When Huntingdon saw that the US—as the latest champion of Western values—was going to win the Cold War, he asked himself, as a political scientist concerned with the future: *who would be the next great enemy of Western civilization?* Where would the next huge wars be fought, and over what? His answer: the Arab world and Islamic civilization.[31] He wrote this thesis around the time of the outbreak of the first war in Iraq, the Persian Gulf War of 1991, triggered when Iraq invaded Kuwait to take over the latter's territory and gain control of its oil and gas resources. At the time, many people argued that the war was all about oil and who would control this valuable commodity moving forward.[32] Huntingdon argued, by contrast, that economic resources (like oil) are merely flashpoints or sparks, and that *what really sustains wars*—and what would sustain this future clash between the West and the Arab world—*is a clash over different civilizational values*. At the time, he was criticized as being an ignorant, provocative, pro-Western warmonger (and worse),[33] but many people have come to admit that his thesis really did seem to predict the next set of wars, and to be worthy of serious consideration in its own right.

Here's Huntingdon's view. There are different global civilizations, as noted above in his map. Each one has its own civilizational values and practices. Some civilizations have values and practices that overlap with those of other civilizations, but many are unique. Huntingdon conjectured that the farther apart two civilizations are in terms of their values, the more likely it is there will be wars between them, as they lack respect for each other and mutual understanding. And the closer two different civilizations are geographically, the greater the odds of armed conflict between them, as they share grinding flashpoints of contact, or fault lines of rupture.

For the Islamic world and the West, such flashpoints of contact include oil—the Arab world's huge supply of it and the West's enormous consumer and industrial demand for it. But the flashpoints extend beyond that to include the considerable numbers of events and territories in which the Islamic world and the Western world have previously come into contact, and conflict, starting with the **Crusades** (of Christianity versus Islam, from 1000–1300 CE) and moving through the Ottoman Empire (present-day Turkey, which touches both Europe and the Middle East), North Africa, southern Spain, and even central and eastern Europe (the former Yugoslavia especially). Add to that England's and France's recent imperial control over Algeria, Egypt, Lebanon, Iraq, Palestine, and Syria, and one begins to see the depth of flashpoint contact between these two massive world civilizations. To ice it off, consider that when Huntingdon looked around in the early 1990s and compared the above-listed Western values and practices to the ones prevailing in the Middle East, he saw minimal, if any, agreement. (The Islamic world at the time did not favour individualistic free-market capitalism, or democracy, or the equality of women, or the separation of church and state, or the full application of science and technology, or the prospect of having a robust civil society, and so on.) Thus, Huntingdon's theory predicted that with lots of historical and geographical flashpoint contact but with maximal distance on values and practices, the next huge set of wars involving the Western powers would be in the Middle East, and against countries where the majorities are both Arab and Islamic. Once more, he wrote this in the early 1990s, *before* the September 11 ("9/11") terrorist strikes in the US, the July 7 ("7/7") terrorist strikes in Europe, the American invasions of Afghanistan and Iraq, the sharply rising tensions in Europe between native Europeans and Muslim immigrants, and the 2010 Arab Spring, with the related NATO invasion of Libya in 2011.[34]

Case Study: The American Empire?

Let's try to draw some threads together in this final section of the chapter. We have looked at countries and their components, the development of cities and empires, the growth of the nation-state and how it has come to dominate the contemporary international system, the history of European imperialism, and the resulting split of the world into *North versus South*, and *the West versus the Rest*. In order to help these themes gel, and then apply them to today, we will focus on one country: the United States. The US is a natural choice for this exercise because (a) it is a country, (b) it is currently the world's most influential country, (c) it is both a Northern and Western country, and in many ways is the flag-bearer of Western civilization in our time, and (d) sharp questions actually arise about whether it is an empire. Do we live in an Age of American Empire?

Many Americans, if you ask them, will deny quite strongly that they are, or have, an empire. They will say that empire is a cynical, old-world game played by other peoples, especially Europeans, and it is all about power and status. But the US was formed on a non-cynical—indeed, optimistic—moral vision about what a political community could be like. It could be, and ought to be, about things more sublime than power, and who's on top and who's on bottom. Political society should be about securing individual rights to life, liberty, and the pursuit of happiness. America, to that extent, was created in 1776 to be a new kind of society, and thus to tar it with the same old brush of European imperialism and colonialism just isn't right. In other words, the accusation that America has an empire goes against everything that Americans have learned about their country in school, and so it meets with very strong resistance.

But these deniers—such as Patrick Buchanan—aren't just in denial: they do have a point. These American patriots argue that empire—as defined above—is about a formal relationship of dependency and exploitation between the metropole (the mother country, the locus of empire) and the periphery (the colonies, the dependencies, the hinterland). The peripheries were run by, and used for the benefit of, the cores. Resources were sucked from the colonies into the capitals. People were sent out from the cores to claim the hinterland and to colonize it on behalf of the mother country, replicating and reproducing its way of life elsewhere. The peripheries were governed by state structures set up by the core and run by officials who came from the core. Such was European imperialism, from the dawn of time until about 1975 or so. But the US, these empire-deniers say, has no such formal relationship with countries outside its own borders (with a few, very small exceptions, like some islands in the Pacific taken over during the Pacific phase of World War II). The US might be incredibly powerful—the global **hegemon**, as they say (i.e. the world's most powerful country)—but, technically, it's *not at all* an empire. People who talk of "empire" in the American context do so because of the word's negative connotations—they want to criticize the US because they are jealous of its power and wealth.[35]

For those who retain the idea that the United States *has* an empire, what reply can they make to this line of argument? Their reply focuses on making a distinction between formal and informal empire. **Formal empire**, as defined and illustrated above, is an old-style, European model of empire. The US may not exactly fit that mould, admittedly. But there can be *other* modes of power and dependency that are just as relevant, the pro-empire people say. In an **informal empire**, there are no formal, legally declared links between core and periphery, nor formal, publicly declared relations of dependency. But the US today is, nevertheless, able to set up the basic ground rules of the world system in its favour. It chooses not to declare an empire formally, in other words, but that doesn't mean that it's not there. These people, like Ivan Eland,[36] say that America fulfills all the traditional criteria of **an imperial core**: it has the biggest economy (or very nearly so) and the biggest military (by far); it is politically the most influential; it has the biggest consumer base (in terms of per capita spending), and is a magnet for both foreign investment and immigration. Also, the US *does* have some of the more formal aspects of empire. Did you know, for instance, that the United States currently operates 700 military bases *outside* its own borders?[37]

There are even **revisionist historians**, such as Sidney Lens and Don Meinig,[38] who dispute the happy tale about America's founding values, suggesting that that vision is pure myth-making, telling people what they want to believe. They argue that we should re-examine the prevailing, conventional narrative of American history and see the US, instead, as an imperial project *right from the start*. From the very first moment of its founding in 1620, by the Pilgrims at Plymouth Rock, the US has witnessed one steady outwards expansion, as its core communities sought to gain territory, subject peoples who stood in their way, and claim land and power for themselves, from east to west and down to Texas and Florida. Looking at a historical map of the growth of the United States (see Figure 1.5), one is struck by this clear, relentless, westward and

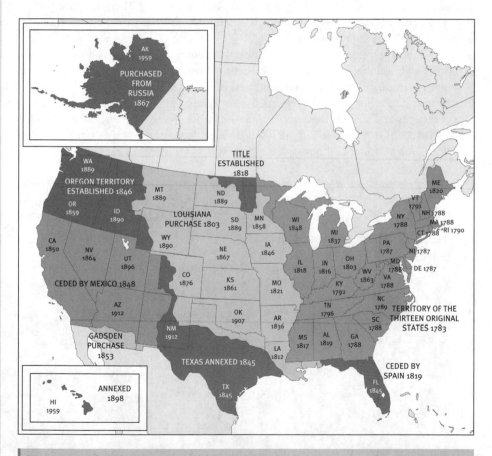

Figure 1.5 Historical Growth of the United States

From the very first moment of its founding in 1620, by the Pilgrims at Plymouth Rock, the US has undertaken a steady outwards expansion—but does that mean that America has imperialism running in its veins?

Source: Adapted from "Admission of States and Territorial Acquisition", US Bureau of the Census, Perry-Castañeda Library Map Collection. Courtesy of the University of Texas Libraries, The University of Texas at Austin.

southward and northward expansion of territorial control; then, as the continent filled up, one starts to see American growth spreading over into Alaska and Hawaii and then, after World War II, into Germany and Japan. Now, today, the US has extensive entanglements *all over the globe*, especially in the Middle East (to secure the oil supply there, and provide protection for its ally Israel). America has imperialism running in its veins, the revisionists say—you better believe it's an empire.[39]

Let's leave, for now, the *factual* question of whether America has an empire and turn to the following, *normative*, issue: entertaining the notion that the US *may* have some kind of empire, *is this good or bad?* "Empire" is a bad word, generally, because we associate with it the infliction of power, the assertion of dominance, and the absence of democracy and the self-rule of a people. But, need it be? There is a group of people who actually say that, yes, America *is* an empire, but that this is a *good* thing for the world. What is their argument?

Their argument is that the US is the only country on Earth capable of bringing some order to the globe, and capable of preventing it from sliding back down into **anarchy**— that is, an ungoverned, chaotic condition of all-out fighting and conflict between the various national groups and regions. So, American empire is good because it's a source of security and stability that everyone benefits from. These thinkers, like Paul Wolfowitz, also argue that American empire has been great for raising people's standards of living. If we look at world GDP (gross domestic product, a measure of economic activity) since

Protesters in the Philippines hold a star-spangled banner that reads "IMPERIALISM— A PLAGUE TO THE WORLD." Why do you think the US is such a flashpoint for protests around the world? (© CP/AP Photo/ Pat Roque)

the US established itself as the clearly dominant *Western* power (in 1945, after the end of the Second World War and the collapse of the British and French empires), and then since the US became the dominant *world* power (in 1991 or so, following the collapse of the Soviet empire), we see very steady and quite remarkable increase (even in spite of the latest recession). This, the fans of empire say, is a product of the values of capitalism and free trade, for which the United States stands so proudly. Americans know how to run profitable businesses and how to run a productive free-market economy, which increases everyone's standard of living. So, American empire has generated more money, and a higher standard of living, for its subjects and beyond. Finally, the American empire proponents say that the American empire stands for great values: human rights, individual freedom, free markets, democracy, free and fair elections, separation of church and state, and the growth of science and technology. To the extent that the US spreads these values, it does the world a favour. American empire is nothing to apologize for, these supporters say: it has generated very good consequences and has made the world a better place. We should all be happy with the dominance of the United States in the world today. What's that famous phrase again? Oh yeah: *God Bless America!*[40]

Noam Chomsky—American himself, and a distinguished professor at MIT in Boston—has been one of the foremost critics of the American empire. He wants the USA, as the bumper sticker says, "Out of everywhere!" He believes that even if the United States started out nicely, it has since turned into a fat, corrupt society run mainly for the benefit of the ultra-rich and powerful elites, "the masters of the universe," focused only on their own narrow self-interest. These elites are essentially the East Coast power, finance, industry, and money barons of Washington, DC, and Wall Street in New York City. The US, in this sense, is an empire *just like every other historical one*: the ultra-elite use their money and power to run the entire empire for their own benefit, using the common people (whether in the US or elsewhere) to secure these benefits, and only doling out those rewards they must to keep the social peace and to let them keep their hold on society. These money and power elites use the US military, based around the Pentagon, to protect themselves and their interests, and they offer lots of great entertainment out of Los Angeles to keep the powerless people happy, distracted, and stupefied. Chomsky's is, in many ways, the ultimate **conspiracy theory**. But the direct historical analogy here, Chomsky says, is to the Roman Empire: what may have started out nicely and with real benefits for its subjects grew increasingly corrupt and degenerated into a struggle for power and money between the ultra-elites, on the one hand, and a pointless existence—of rounds of work, food, booze, and cheap entertainment—for the masses, on the other. Chomsky views *any* form of empire as a violation of democracy and the rights of peoples around the world to choose their own forms of governance. But he also thinks that American empire is especially bad because Americans know so little, and care so little, about the world outside their borders. As a result of this ignorance, they are not likely to be good imperial masters; they will be apt to screw things up, like (Chomsky would say) they did in Vietnam or the Middle East: areas the US was very willing to intervene in, yet—incredibly!—with next to no knowledge of, or historical involvement with.[41]

Niall Ferguson, in his acclaimed books *Empire* and *Colossus*, argues that while the US *could* be a force for good in the world, presently it is *not*. He argues that, contrary to popular belief, empires *can* be good. The ancient Roman Empire, for example, brought peace, prosperity, civilization, and technological advances to the entire Mediterranean world for hundreds of years. And the British Empire—Ferguson's favourite example—likewise generated remarkable prosperity, political stability, and cultural advance for its subjects. Indeed, some of the most developed and successful societies on Earth are former members: the US, Australia, Canada, and the UK itself. And the benefits of the British Empire weren't measured simply in terms of wealth and security but also, Ferguson says, in terms of important moral and legal values, such as individual liberty, free trade, the impersonal rule of law, and parliamentary democracy. By population, the world's two largest democracies are ex-Empire members: India and America. The record is marred by flaws, of course: the British Empire, early on, was involved in African slavery; it lost the States to revolution; and there were sore spots of protracted violence, including Ireland and parts of the Middle East. And the handling of both Indian and Israeli independence was a mess. Ferguson doesn't deny such realities; he merely wishes to point out the other, positive side of the ledger. The words sound strange but, historically, empire has had some advantages.[42]

> *Every aspect of international studies—war, trade, development, pollution—is hugely influenced by American policy.*

But Britain was a good imperial overlord because it *cared* about the societies it governed, and because it wasn't afraid to admit that it had an empire. Indeed, it took great pride in that fact, with officials famously bragging that, owing to its far-flung, worldwide nature, "the sun never set on the British Empire." But the United States, Ferguson asserts, is an *empire-in-denial*. It refuses to admit that it has an empire, much less does it fully live up to its potential for developing its dependencies into decent societies. Ferguson says that the US must stop "the half-assed job" it is currently doing as the global hegemon. It ought to be like Britain and train future leaders in its dependent societies, it ought to know more about those societies, it ought to invest in those societies, and it ought to develop the good institutions necessary for those societies to succeed over time. Then, it will preside over a "*Pax Americana*," modelled after the legendary *Pax Romana*, the peace established by the dominance of Rome for centuries.

Ferguson notes that, during the heyday of the British Empire, the young British elites would compete amongst each other for the plum imperial positions, and take pride in helping their colonies develop in a good, peaceful, prosperous way. But today's young American elites, he notes, have no interest at all in living outside the United States, much less in being, say, president of Iraq. Young American elites want to make it in one of three cities, depending on their main career interest: New York (money), Washington (power), or Los Angeles (fame). Unless and until that changes, Ferguson concludes, the American empire will not be a successful venture for the world as a whole.

Whether the United States is in command of an empire or is merely a hegemon or great power, it clearly is the world's most influential society. As such, every aspect of international studies—war, trade, development, pollution—is hugely influenced by American policy. The debate on American empire allows us to think through the pros and cons of this hegemony, as well as to see more clearly both the strengths and weaknesses of American society and the nature of its impact on the rest of the world.

Canadian Insights

Canada: Standing at the Crossroads of European Empire and American Hegemony

Where does Canada fit into the themes of this chapter—state formation, European empires, American hegemony? Well, Canada's founding was largely shaped by the imperial rivalry between Britain and France. Although there were Aboriginal people here first, and though the Vikings (from Scandinavia) landed briefly in Newfoundland around 1000 CE, the "discovery" of Canada is commonly credited to French explorer Jacques Cartier in 1534. Founding the colony of New France (now Quebec), Cartier and other hardy, enterprising immigrants from France were truly the first *canadiens*. The basis of the first colony was overwhelmingly agricultural, with the French colonists seeking arable land they could not attain in their native country. The early settlers forged surprisingly warm and co-operative relationships with the Aboriginal people, who helped them hunt animals for both food and fur.

As the English rose in global power, they came to challenge France's claims to Canada repeatedly. This culminated in the Seven Years War (1754–63), which some historians label the first true world war. Britain won, claiming Canada amongst its many prizes; however, as the Quebec province was already so firmly settled and established, the British promised *accommodation* (and not assimilation) of Quebec's special French culture. Otherwise, English colonization spread out across the rest of the country, marked generally by more hostile interactions with the country's First Nations than the French had experienced. Economically, Canada started out—and remained until very recently—a gigantic natural resource base for export into the imperial hubs of Paris, London, and, even now, the US. What started out as the export of beaver pelts into fashion-conscious France grew into the enormous extraction of Canada's rich natural bounty of timber, food, oil, gas, and countless minerals for export to the growing industrial empires of England and the US.

Canada was governed firmly as a colony, first by France and then by England, in complete accord with the model illustrated in Figure 1.2 above. This was, in the first instance, to protect the Europeans' economic interests in Canada. But the model did have some beneficial effects on the colony, as England brought over quite capable governors and, in fact, jealously protected the independence of Canada from the rising superstar to the south. (In the War of 1812, Britain and the Canadian colonists fought off an American invasion, and Britain sided repeatedly with Canada, against the US, as the border between the latter two was negotiated and drawn, bit by bit, across the continent.) Political developments in England rippled over into Canada, including such virtues as the rule of law, the doctrine of "peace, order, and good government," and, in time, democracy. Meanwhile, Canada stood as one of the firmest, and most useful, allies of both England and France throughout the many devastating wars fought in Europe from 1789 to 1945. Though Canada remains today, technically, a constitutional monarchy—with Britain's monarch as its head of state—everyone knows this is both a formality and a deliberate Canadian choice; and that, certainly since the end of the Second World War, Canada has become a completely independent and developed democracy. (Three legal events tend to highlight Canada's growing independence from England: the **British North America Act of 1867**, whose passage brought about Confederation, which we celebrate every year on the first day of July; the **Statute of Westminster of 1931**, wherein Britain allowed its colonies to have independent foreign policies; and the **Canada Act of 1982**, when Canada patriated the Constitution, gaining the right to amend it without British consent—the first of these amendments came with the passage of the **Constitution Act of 1982**, which added the **Charter of Rights and Freedoms**.)

So, Canada was a colony for most of its existence. And, depending on your views regarding American empire, you might even be tempted to opine that Canada remains a colony today: a chilly yet peaceful outpost on the northern fringe of the enormous American empire, eager to sell its wares into the United States in exchange for the lucrative benefits of doing so. Never content to simply remain a bed of resources for others to exploit, Canada struggled over time to develop homegrown advanced industries, first through the railroads, then the factories, and today with such high-tech products as automobiles, high-speed trains, and the famous BlackBerry smartphone and related products. But Canada is massively influenced by American pop culture, and its economic links with the US account for about 30 per cent of its national wealth. Moreover, Canada generally supports the US in most of its foreign policy decisions. Yet, Canada retains its European heritage and its robust links with both Britain and France. It is a bilingual country, and one with a much stronger **welfare state** than exists in the US, with particular strengths in quality public education and universal healthcare coverage. Canada (population now 33 million) is one of the world's biggest immigrant societies, receiving people from all over the world, and is much more conscious than the US of the founding role of its Aboriginal peoples, a point exemplified by the fact that Inuit leaders democratically control the two legislatures of Northwest Territories and Nunavut. So, for all the cynical talk of Canada's still being a colony, the country boasts many salient and admirable qualities that set it apart from the US.[43]

(For more on Canada–US relations and how the two countries differ and yet co-operate substantially in foreign affairs, see the extended case study in Chapter 4, on foreign policy.)

CONCLUSION

Countries are the basic units of international studies. So we began this chapter, and this textbook, by looking at countries and their parts: population, territory, culture, and government. We came to understand the growth of nations and states, and how they constitute a middle way between the tiny city-state and the massive, far-flung, cosmopolitan empire. To chart the growth of the nation-state, we needed to consider the history of state formation, first in Europe and then—through European imperialism and colonialism—across the globe. In so doing, we took note of how deeply European imperialism has shaped our world, in terms of both *North versus South* and the spread of the interstate system. We also witnessed how civilizations differ from each other, and how these differences can result not just in friction but in sustained, and world-changing, armed conflict. We spent some time looking at the essential elements of Western civilization, and how it differs from others, on grounds that it has, through European colonialism and the strength of the US, come to be the leading civilization of our times. Strengths and weaknesses of the West were noted, and then extended case study consideration was given to whether the United States, as the leading Western nation, is in fact an empire, a revival of old-style imperialism and colonialism. Given the pervasive impact of the US on international society and international studies, this focus was a helpful first case study, as we start to think through more deeply the scope and limits of our world.

REVIEW QUESTIONS

1. How has your national membership shaped your personal identity? How meaningful is it to you, and how has it affected your view of the rest of the world?

2. In what ways are non-state actors (MNCs, NGOs) becoming more important in international life? In what ways might the roles of national governments be decreasing? Some experts have even written of "the death of the state" in this regard: do you agree?

3. Reading the various "top 10" lists (i.e. of territory, population, languages, economies, etc.) did anything surprise you, and/or concern you? How do you think these lists might change over the course of your lifetime?

4. Even though everyone agrees that Europe begins in ancient Greece, revisionist historians have recently argued that ancient Greece was, in turn, heavily influenced by ancient Egypt and Mesopotamia/Persia. Research and comment on the debate raging around M. Bernal's provocative work *Black Athena: The Afro-Asiatic Roots of Classical Civilization*, vols 1–3 (New Brunswick, NJ: Rutgers University Press, 1991).

5. Explain how state formation happened in Europe, and how the state-centric model of international relations spread from there throughout the whole world.

6. What's the significance of both the Treaty of Westphalia and the Treaty of Versailles to our world today?

7. How was decolonization triggered? Pick a former European colony and research (a) how it was impacted by imperialism, and (b) how it handled decolonization.

8. What do you think are the pros and cons of Western civilization?

9. Do you agree with Huntingdon's thesis about "The Clash of Civilizations"? Why or why not? In general, what's the value of comparing different world civilizations for international studies?

10. In your view, does America have an empire? If not, why not? If so, *what kind*, and *is this good or bad* for the world?

WEBSITES FOR FURTHER RESEARCH

The American Empire Project www.americanempireproject.com
– critical of US foreign policy

Project for the New American Century www.newamericancentury.org
– supportive of US foreign policy

The Nationalism Project www.nationalismproject.org
– advanced research about nationalism's historical impact

The North–South Institute www.nsi-ins.ca
– advanced research about the differences, and relations, between North and South

The Dominion Institute www.dominion.ca
– information on Canadian history and heritage

NOTES

1. M. Heidegger, *Being and Time*, trans. J. Macquarrie & E. Robinson (New York: Harper, 2009).
2. Material for this and all subsequent "top 10" factual lists in this chapter comes from (a) the United Nations Statistics Division, www.unstats.un.org/unsd, and (b) the CIA World Factbook, www.cia.gov/library/publications/the-world-factbook
3. E. Gellner, *Nations and Nationalisms* (Ithaca, NY: Cornell University Press, 2nd edn, 2009).
4. Some experts consider English to be the world's most prevalent language, as it's thought to be, by far, the most common *second* language learned around the world. Thus, combining mother-tongue with second-language would result in a different ordering, with English on top.
5. W. Wallace & D. Josselin, *Non-State Actors in World Politics* (London: Palgrave Macmillan, 2002).
6. M. Campbell & W. Aspray, *Computer: A History of the Information Machine* (New York: Basic Books, 1996); J. Abbate, *Inventing the Internet* (Cambridge, MA: MIT Press, 1999); R. Stross, *Planet Google* (New York: Free Press, 2008).
7. F. Fukuyama, *The Origins of Political Order* (New York: Farrar, Strauss & Giroux, 2011).
8. A. Gibbons, *The First Human* (New York: Anchor, 2007); R. Chadwock, *First Civilizations: Ancient Mesopotamia and Egypt* (London: Equinox, 2006).
9. C. Freeman, *Egypt, Greece and Rome: Civilizations of the Ancient Mediterranean* (Oxford: Oxford University Press, 2004).
10. T. Harrison, *The Great Empires of the Ancient World* (Los Angeles: Getty Museum Publications, 2010).
11. M. Hardt & A. Negri, *Empire* (Cambridge, MA: Harvard University Press, 2001).
12. J. Burbank & F. Cooper, *Empires in World History* (Princeton, NJ: Princeton University Press, 2011).

13. C. Wickham, *The Inheritance of Rome: Illuminating the Dark Ages, 400–1000* (New York: Viking, 2009).
14. W. Duiker & J. Spielvogel, *The Essential World History: To 1500* (London: Wadsworth, 3rd edn, 2006).
15. D. MacCulloch, *The Reformation: A History* (New York: Penguin, 2005); P. Wilson, *The Thirty Years' War: Europe's Tragedy* (Cambridge, MA: Harvard University Press, 2008).
16. I. Wallerstein, *The Modern World-System, Vol. 1* (Berkeley, CA: University of California Press, 2011).
17. C.V. Wedgewood, *The Thirty Years' War* (New York: NYRB Classics, 2005); J.L. Brierly, *The Law of Nations* (New York: Waldock, 6th edn, 1963).
18. H. Kelsen, *Principles of International Law* (New York: Holt, Rinehart and Winston, 1966); Aristotle, *The Politics*, trans. C. Lord (Chicago: University of Chicago Press, 1985).
19. D. Abernathy, *The Dynamics of Global Dominance: European Overseas Empires, 1415–1980* (New Haven, CT: Yale University Press, 2001).
20. J. Hart, *Comparing Empires* (London: Palgrave Macmillan, 2008); P. Curtin, *The World and The West* (Cambridge: Cambridge University Press, 2002).
21. J. Keegan, *The First World War* (New York: Vintage, 2000).
22. M. MacMillan, *Paris 1919* (Toronto: Random House, 2003); H. Arendt, *The Origins of Totalitarianism* (New York: Schocken, 1951).
23. J. Keegan, *The Second World War* (New York: Vintage, 1990); M. Chamberlain, *Decolonization: The Fall of the European Empires* (London: Wiley-Blackwell, 2nd edn, 1999); D. Rothermund, *The Routledge Companion to Decolonization* (London: Routledge, 2000).
24. A World Bank Report, *Atlas of Global Development* (Washington, DC: World Bank Publications, 2nd edn, 2009).
25. S.A. Marston, et al., *World Regions in Global Context* (New York: Prentice Hall, 4th edn, 2010).
26. J. Rigg, *An Everyday Geography of The Global South* (London: Routledge, 2007).
27. D. Wengrow, *What Makes Civilization?* (Oxford: Oxford University Press, 2010).
28. J. Spielvogel, *Western Civilization* (London: Wadsworth, 2003); S. Huntingdon, *The Clash of Civilizations* (Cambridge, MA: Harvard University Press, 1991).
29. M. Walker, *The Cold War: A History* (New York: Henry Holt, 1995).
30. S.R. Dockrill, *The End of The Cold War Era* (London: Bloomsbury Academic, 2005).
31. S. Huntingdon, *The Clash of Civilizations and The Remaking of World Order* (New York: Simon and Schuster, 1996).
32. I. Eland, *No War For Oil: U.S. Dependency and The Middle East* (San Francisco: The Independent Institute, 2011).
33. G.E. Perry, "Huntingdon and His Critics," *Arab Studies Quarterly* (2002), pp. 1–12.
34. J. Sacks, *The Dignity of Difference: How to Avoid the Clash of Civilizations* (London: Continuum, 2002).
35. P. Buchanan, *A Republic, Not an Empire* (New York: Regnery, 2002).
36. I. Eland, *The Empire Has No Clothes: US Foreign Policy Exposed* (Stanford, CA: The Independent Institute, 2008).
37. A.J. Bacevich, *American Empire: The Realities and Consequences of US Foreign Policy* (Cambridge, MA: Harvard University Press, 2002).
38. S. Lens, *The Forging of The American Empire* (London: Haymarket, 2003); D.W. Meinig, *The Shaping of America* (New Haven, CT: Yale University Press, 2004).
39. E. Foner, *Give Me Liberty! An American History* (New York: W.W. Norton, 2008).
40. See the "Project for the New American Century" at www.newamericancentury.org
41. N. Chomsky, *Making the Future: The Unipolar Imperial Moment* (San Francisco: City Lights, 2010).
42. N. Ferguson, *Empire* (New York; Basic, 2004); N. Ferguson, *Colossus: The Rise and Fall of American Empire* (New York: Penguin, 2005).
43. R. Bothwell, *The Penguin History of Canada* (Toronto: Penguin Global, 2008); Statistics Canada, www.statcan.gc.ca

2   Population and Environment

"Those who contemplate the beauty of Earth find reserves of strength that will endure as long as life lasts." —*Rachel Carson (1907–1964), author of* Silent Spring

LEARNING OBJECTIVES

After studying this chapter, you will be able to:

▸ define all the bolded key terms and concepts

▸ understand and explain population-related contrasts, such as (a) big versus small, (b) fast-growing versus slow-growing, (c) immigrant versus native-born, (d) migrant worker versus refugee, and (e) urban versus rural populations

▸ grasp the pros and cons of urbanization, and how industrialization—as begun during the Industrial Revolution—has played a crucial role not only in urbanization but regarding pollution, too

▸ apprehend the arguments of both environmental optimists and neo-Malthusian environmental pessimists, and be able to speak intelligently on the pros and cons of both

▸ define "the tragedy of the commons," and evaluate the two most common solutions to this tragedy: national enclosure and international public park protection

▸ reflect on whether resource management is enough, or whether sustainable development demands deeper changes to contemporary capitalism

▸ enjoy expanded literacy about key environmental problems like deforestation and climate change, as well as crucial resource issues like energy and oil, and having enough food and water for the world's population.

INTRODUCTION

The chapter-opening epigraph comes from American conservationist Rachel Carson. Her 1962 book, *Silent Spring*, is often credited with sparking the modern environmental movement. In it, she drew on her training as a biologist to explore why, in some parts of the US, the migrating songbirds of spring had gone missing (hence, silent). Her finding: uncontrolled pollution, especially of pesticides, was to blame. In particular, the chemical DDT was destroying the eggs of the songbirds before they could hatch. The reaction of the American people to this discovery helped spur the banning of DDT, and the social movement that grew out of her book helped develop political support for creating the **Environmental Protection Agency** (EPA), the main government department in charge of natural resource stewardship in the US. After death, Carson was awarded the President's Medal of Freedom, the highest civilian honour in America.[1]

In this chapter, we will explore the issue of environment and resources. Related to this, of course, is the topic of human population. How many people there are and how they live impact the planet enormously; *Silent Spring* details just one tiny example. Few things could be more foundational to global studies than the issue of how humans interact with the planet. First up: population.

POPULATION

On the last day of October 2011, Earth reached a milestone, welcoming its 7 billionth human to the planet. This is up, very sharply, from 1 billion in the early 1800s. (It took humanity nearly 10,000 years to hit the first billion, and then *not even 200 years to add six billion more!*) Most experts say that population growth will continue until it approaches the 10 billion mark, perhaps around 2100, at which point it is expected to level off. Still, note the dramatic degree of increase, as illustrated in Figure 2.1.[2]

According to demographers, like Massimo Livi-Bacci, almost all future population growth is expected to occur in the Global South, and the number is supposed to level off as the developing world becomes richer and more developed. For, one of the clearest statistical associations is this: the wealthier people become, the fewer children they have. Kids, after all, cost money, and gone are the days when the family farm dominated the economy and you needed as many young helpers as you could get. Advances in healthcare have substantially increased the survival rate for children in the West; so gone, too, are the days

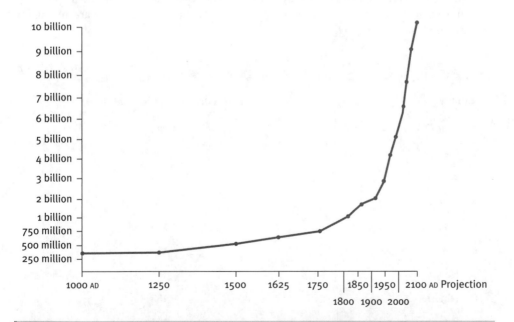

FIGURE 2.1 The Growth of the World Population: Real and Estimated Future Growth

Source: Data from J.R. Weeks, *Population: Concepts and Issues* (London: Wadsworth, 11th ed., 2011); and the United Nations, www.un.org/esa/population.

when it was thought you needed to have many kids in order to ensure that enough survived to take care of you, as you became elderly and infirm. Finally, increased career opportunities, access to birth control, legal rights, and socioeconomic resources for women have translated, on average, into their having fewer children than previous generations did.[3]

Almost all future population growth is expected to occur in the Global South.

Table 2.1 lists the world's 10 largest countries by population; Table 2.2 lists the countries with the fastest and slowest rates of population growth, as of 2010. Note, in Table 2.2, that nearly all of the fastest-growing populations are *in the developing world*—almost all in Africa—and that they have had consistent annual population growth of at least 3 per cent over the past few years. By contrast, the 10 countries with **the slowest-growing** populations have actually had **negative population growth** in recent years (i.e. their population is shrinking, not growing), and they tend to be either tiny islands—with people leaving for better work opportunities elsewhere—or else situated, disproportionately, in central and eastern Europe.[4]

The Problem with People

Fast-growing populations have a greater number of younger, than older, people; as a result, they have big demand for the services young families with children require, such as schools and physical infrastructure, like roads and the kind of affordable housing that is often found in suburban subdivisions, outside the city core. There is also a need to create jobs to keep those children occupied once they reach working age. These requirements put large pressures on governments, and the poorer governments of the Global South are among the least capable of delivering in this regard.

TABLE 2.1 The 10 Biggest Countries, by Estimated Population (2010)

Country	Estimated Population (millions)
1. China	1,300
2. India	1,200
3. America	311
4. Indonesia	238
5. Brazil	195
6. Pakistan	175
7. Bangladesh	164
8. Nigeria	158
9. Russia	141
10. Japan	127

Source: Data from *The CIA World Factbook*, 2010 edition.

TABLE 2.2 Countries with the Fastest-Growing and Slowest-Growing Populations (2010)

Fastest-Growing Populations	Slowest-Growing Populations
1. Zimbabwe	1. Mariana Islands
2. Niger	2. Cook Islands
3. Uganda	3. Bulgaria
4. Turks and Caicos Islands	4. Montenegro
5. Burundi	5. Estonia
6. United Arab Emirates (UAE)	6. Ukraine
7. Ethiopia	7. Latvia
8. Burkina Faso	8. Russia
9. Yemen	9. Serbia
10. Zambia	10. Guyana

Source: United Nations, Population Division of the Department of Economic and Social Affairs: www.un.org/esa/population.

Slow-growing, or negative-growth, populations have—by contrast—a greater number of older, than younger, people, and so they have big demand for the services that older people require, such as healthcare and old age or retirement pension payments. This puts its own considerable pressures on governments, which often must tax a smaller base of younger workers to afford these kinds of social programs. But often in these countries, younger workers are leaving to secure better opportunities in larger, faster-growing economies.[5]

So, regardless of growth status, population brings challenges to *any* kind of country and to *any* kind of government. Different governments deal with these challenges differently. For instance, faced with its enormous population pressures, the government of China in 1979 instituted its **one child policy**, a set of regulations governing family size and the spacing of children in cases where a second child is permitted. To the upside, this *does* seem to have had a positive effect on containing that nation's enormous population growth (much of it occurring along the coast—China's population is *not* evenly distributed, geographically); the country's rate of natural increase—its growth rate based on births and deaths—fell from 1.7 per cent in 1975 to 0.6 per cent in 2006.[6] To the downside, though, there is evidence that this policy has increased abortions and the abandonment of baby girls, as some parents seem to value a boy more highly. Over the long term, there are fears such actions will skew China's **demographics** (i.e. the composition of population), resulting in an unhealthy disproportion of boys to girls. There are, moreover, indications of unfairness to this policy, as some wealthier couples can bribe officials to look the other way, and of course, there's the fundamental issue of the huge restriction on personal freedom to begin with. On the one hand, we can appreciate the enormous practical problems such a giant population would put on everyone, government planners especially; we can see why they'd want some population control. On the other hand, I doubt many of us want to be told by our governments how many children we can have: it's one of life's biggest, and most personal, decisions. The government of India has gone another way in its pursuit of population control: aggressively distributing birth control pills and aggressively disseminating information on sexual health and reproductive technologies, among the young female population in particular.[7]

There are a handful of **pronatalist** governments around the world. ("Pronatalist" describes governments that want to *promote* birth and population growth, as opposed to *restricting* birth and curbing population growth, as in the case of China and India.) Pronatalist governments—such as those in the slow-growth countries of eastern Europe, and even here in Canada, in Quebec—take measures to increase population, such as offering tax breaks, or baby-bonus cash payments, to new parents. More extreme pronatalist policies can be found in cultures where religious law proscribes the use of birth control. This accounts, in part, for the high population growth rates in some Muslim countries in the Middle East.

The Distribution of Population

The world's population is not distributed equally, of course. We saw, last chapter, how humans first evolved in Africa and migrated from there to the east and south through the Middle East and into Asia, and also to the north and west into Europe. Historically, the world's largest *voluntary* migration was the movement of Europeans into the Americas, from about 1500 to 1975; the world's largest *involuntary* migration was the coercive movement of Africans—as slaves—into the Americas (especially the Caribbean and the United States), from about 1500 to 1865.

Asia, with more than 4 billion people, contains fully 60 per cent of the entire world's population. (Indeed, the two giant neighbours, China and India, contain over one-third of all humanity within their borders!) Africa has about 15 per cent of the world's population, with roughly 1 billion people calling that continent home. Next comes Europe, with just over 10 per cent of the world's population, or about 725 million inhabitants. Then follows North America, with approximately 8 per cent (525 million people) and South and Central America, at 5 per cent (385 million). Rounding things off is Oceania (Australia, New Zealand, and other islands of the South Pacific), with under 1 per cent of the world's population (38 million).[8]

Another important measure is **population density**, which tracks how many people there are in a given mile or kilometre. Asia is the most densely populated continent by far, followed by Europe. Trailing those two rather distantly are, in order, Africa, North America, South and Central America, and Oceania.

Immigrants

Typical in the developed world—especially Canada and Europe—is a phenomenon whereby, without immigration, the population would actually decrease. This is to say that, among the native-born population, the growth rate is slow or negative. To keep population—and the size of the economy and tax-base—up, governments in this position can aggressively encourage immigration from around the world, inviting foreigners to leave their home countries to establish a new life and a new membership status in the receiving country. The top 10 **immigrant-receiving societies** are, in order:

1. United States

2. Russia

3. Germany

4. Ukraine

5. France

6. Saudi Arabia

7. Canada

8. India

9. Britain

10. Spain (with Australia nearly tied with Spain).[9]

The three biggest immigration corridors in the world today are from Mexico into America, from Ukraine into Russia, and from Bangladesh into India.[10] (An **immigration corridor** is a heavily travelled route taken by people immigrating to one country from another.)

Immigrants bring many benefits to the receiving country, including diversity, new ways of life, new skills, and reinforcements for the workforce. Immigrants, typically, are younger, too, and so they bring youthful energy and may choose to start a family in the new country, further bolstering the host country's population. But immigrant-receiving societies also face challenges helping new members adjust to, and integrate in, their new home countries. This is a challenge for every society, but recently the issue has received high-profile attention throughout Europe, where some minorities—especially those of Arab ethnic descent and Muslim religious belief—are growing much more quickly than the native populations. (For more on precise meanings of "Arab" and "Muslim," please see the next chapter, on culture.) These minorities are sometimes much more religious than the native population, and some are requesting that aspects of their traditional social and legal understandings, such as those pertaining to the division of assets upon divorce, be incorporated into European laws. Moreover, these immigrant communities often live together in closely connected and densely populated pockets within the receiving population, arguably forming societies within societies, or nations within nations. These realities are strongly challenging the identities of some European countries, and raising issues about the coherence and integrity of a national culture, on the one hand, versus the need, on the other, to be **multicultural** (i.e. to respect cultural diversity while still maintaining social peace and political unity).[11]

Case Study: The French Ban on Muslim Head Scarves

A recent example of the clash between immigrant and receiving cultures occurred in France. After many years of tension, the French National Assembly passed a law in 2004. This law prohibits the wearing of any conspicuous (i.e. prominent and visible) religious symbols while attending publicly funded elementary and secondary schools. Though the ban applies to the symbols of *all* religions, many consider the law to be targeting the Muslim minority, specifically the practice of its young girls wearing headscarves (*khimar*) as part of traditional female modesty (*hijab*). The law is commonly referred to as the "French head scarf ban."

In practice, this *is* how this law has been applied. Though the legislation was initially greeted by substantial protests by the Muslim community throughout France, the law today remains on the books, and is enforced by the government of France as a commitment to equality and **secularity** (i.e. non-religiousness) in its public schools.

Migrant Workers

In a number of countries, there is a large population of **migrant workers**. These are people who have citizenship and a permanent home in one country but live temporarily, for work purposes, in another. They tend to work in industries that pay very little and that are very **labour-intensive** (i.e. they are not heavily mechanized and require a lot of "people power," such as picking delicate fruit when ripe, or washing dishes in a restaurant, or cleaning people's houses, or gardening). Agriculture is perhaps the largest example. In Canada, for example, there are large numbers of **seasonal migrant workers** who enter the country, especially from the Caribbean and Mexico, during harvest time. It is hard to tally precisely the population of migrant workers in any given country, as many of them are **illegal immigrants** who have entered the "work country" without any passport, visa, or permission.

The issue of illegal migrant workers has been a contentious one in the United States, where the government has sometimes extended **amnesties for illegal migrant workers**. According to this policy, illegal immigrants who could prove they've worked for at least one full season in America's migrant worker industry could sometimes qualify for legal immigrant status in the US. Recently, though, a number of states—Arizona leading among them—have resisted such measures, and have favoured cracking down on, and even deporting, people working in the US illegally. While no one wants to condone law-breaking, the other side of the equation is that the vast majority of the jobs "taken away" by migrant workers seem to be jobs that native-born Americans show absolutely no interest in performing, given their demanding physical nature and the substandard wages and benefits. Some scholars, such as Daniel Rothenberg, have even argued that cracking down on illegal migrant workers could actually do much damage to the economies of states such as California, where the cheap labour performed by illegal workers helps to keep agricultural prices low. The figure of the migrant worker thus seems something of a murky shadow, given how much associated with it exists across national borders, under the radar of the legal system, and below the poverty line.[12]

Refugees

There is an important difference between being an immigrant and being a refugee. **Immigrants** leave their home country voluntarily, seeking to make a new and better life for themselves and their children. This is to say that the motives of an immigrant, or a migrant worker, are usually economic. A **refugee**, by contrast, is a person who has *been forced to leave* his or her home country involuntarily, usually for reasons of war or persecution. The

United Nations High Commission on Refugees (UNHCR), headquartered in Geneva, Switzerland, lobbies United Nations member countries on behalf of refugees to ensure that refugees receive decent treatment from receiving countries until they manage to find a new home. (For more on the UN in general, see Chapter 5.) A refugee being offered admission into a new home country is said to be granted **asylum**. The UNHCR estimates that as of 2009 there were between 8 million and 10 million refugees worldwide; however, there were about 36 million people forming the worldwide **population of concern**, which includes both refugees and **internally displaced persons** (IDPs), who are like refugees *but in their own country*: they have been forced out of their home region into a different region of the same country. Sudan is home to a number of IDPs.

Case Study: The Darfur Region of Sudan

Sudan contains a northern, mainly Arab and Muslim, population, and a southern, mainly black and Christian, population. The central government is controlled by the Arabs, and it has been—for at least the last 10 years—permitting radical Arab groups, or militias, to push the black Christians out of the Darfur province. This practice of trying to drive out a whole, distinct people from a certain territory where they've been clearly established and living as a community is known as **ethnic cleansing**. Fighting has erupted between the groups, with casualties pegged at 300,000 and climbing. Following a referendum in January 2011, the southern region seceded and, in July of the same year, established a separate independent state, called South Sudan. (The northern region has since adopted the name North Sudan.) However, if history is any guide, there will likely continue to be disputes over such matters as control of the lucrative oil fields and details concerning where the border between the two new countries ought to go.[13]

A mother and her children at the UN's Zam Zam Camp for internally displaced persons in Darfur, Sudan. Such camps are very much needed on a temporary basis, but what's a more promising, more permanent solution to refugee flows? (UN Photo/Eskinder Debebe)

Refugees and IDPs are very vulnerable populations, since they lack a home and the protection of a national government. Their human rights and quality of life are tenuous and uncertain. Organizations like the UNHCR try to urge national governments to grant them asylum and to put them on track for immigration and new citizenship. But the process is a difficult one, for a couple of reasons. First, the process of being awarded citizenship takes a long time, and the population of concern needs resources and protection in the interim.

Second, the countries into which the refugees have fled are often themselves impoverished and lacking resources. For example, wars, dire poverty, ethnic cleansing, and disease in sub-Saharan Africa have recently generated millions of refugees, who are often forced to rotate between countries, as governments agree to take them in for short periods only—and then they must move on. Wealthy countries, for their part, fear being swamped by the world's refugees if they were simply to open their borders and welcome anyone: 36 million, after all, is *not* a small number.[14]

Urbanization

A final, vital population difference—alongside big versus small, fast- versus slow-growing, immigrant versus native-born, and migrant worker versus refugee—is the difference between urban and rural populations. **Urbanization**—the growth of the population of cities at the expense of rural or countryside areas—has been a relentless population trend in recent world history, in both the developed and the developing worlds. Consider Table 2.3 and note how the 10 largest cities are split between the North and the South.

To make sense of urbanization, we need to consider the **Industrial Revolution**. In the early 1700s, enormous changes began to be made regarding the production of goods. Sparked by new inventions, such as the steam engine and the cotton gin, machine-driven production of goods became possible, replacing the piece-by-piece, handcrafted production of goods. In England notably, the first factories were built to take advantage of this and to mass-produce as many goods as possible, eventually leading to such innovations as the assembly line. The Industrial Revolution had enormous impact on society: people became much wealthier, goods were being created much more quickly and cheaply, and the nature

TABLE 2.3 The 10 Biggest Urban Areas, by Estimated Population (2011)

City	Population (millions)
1. Tokyo, Japan	32.5
2. Seoul, South Korea	20.5
3. Mexico City, Mexico	20.4
4. New York City, USA	19.8
5. Mumbai, India	19.2
6. Jakarta, Indonesia	18.9
7. Sao Paulo, Brazil	18.8
8. Delhi, India	18.6
9. Osaka/Kobe, Japan	17.3
10. Shanghai, China	16.7

Source: Data from *The CIA World Factbook*, 2010 edition.

of work and the economy was utterly transformed. More about the consequences of the Industrial Revolution will be discussed later this chapter. For our purposes here, we need to note how the Industrial Revolution spurred urbanization: farm workers flooded the cities, leaving agriculture behind to participate in the newly developing industrial economy, headquartered in the factories.[15]

When the Industrial Revolution began, only 3 per cent of the world's population lived in cities. Recently the world reached the landmark threshold of 51 per cent: in other words, for the first time in all of human history, the majority of the world's population is now urban.[16] (There remain, however, stark and significant regional differences: in the US, for instance, 80 per cent of the population is urban, whereas throughout the Global South, 70 per cent of the population is still rural.) A striking illustration of the growth of urbanization: in 1850, London and Paris were the only cities in the world with populations over 1 million; today over 600 cities around the world have hit that milestone mark.[17]

Urbanization has its pros and cons. In terms of cons, the growth of cities has, historically and currently, come at the expense of rural areas. This is known as **rural flight**: people leave the country in the hope of finding better opportunities in the city. Those who view the rural way of life positively, as being more traditional, will regret what they might perceive to be an *erosion of traditional values*. (For example, it's often said that the family farm is now dead, having been replaced with a handful of giant agricultural companies that mass-produce food products for hungry urban centres.) As cities grow and sprawl, they also take over farmland and formerly wild spaces, threatening several animal and plant species by eliminating their habitat. Cities concentrate people, and so they also produce a concentration of the bad things people cause—crime, traffic, lack of civility, gridlock, overcrowding and sprawl, pollution (water, air, noise, smell), and so on. Cities bring with them enormous problems of management—in terms of housing, transportation, garbage collection, infrastructure renewal—on a scale and complexity much

For the first time in all of human history, the majority of the world's population is now urban.

greater than rural areas. This is one reason why, for example, the mayors of big cities are often major political figures in their own right, and why the municipal budgets of some city-centres can dwarf those of full-blown nation-states. (Indeed, note that the population of the world's biggest city, Tokyo, is equal to the entire national population of Canada.)

But urbanization does have its benefits. Historically urbanization has been deeply intertwined with both *modernization* and *industrialization*. It will be considered good insofar as one favours wealth creation over pollution and modern values over traditional ones. For instance, city-centres have often been sources of secularization, diversification, and female liberation. Polls and studies confirm that rural populations are much more religious than urban centres, and are much less racially, ethnically, and religiously diverse than cities. Cities have thus been seen as centres of liberation for those who, historically, have felt stultified by more traditional ways of life, such as racial and ethnic minorities, sexual minorities, and women. Cities also tend to offer much better quality of social services, in terms of education, entertainment, healthcare, and poverty management in particular. (People often wonder why there are so many more poor and homeless people in cities; the answer is that there are so many more services that cater to their needs and problems.) Cities also, with their concentration of wealth and population, tend to offer much greater socioeconomic opportunities—and more upward, merit-based mobility—than the rural

Canadian Insights

CSRs and the GTA

Urbanization has led some experts, such as Canadian economist Tom Courchene, to consider some cities as **city-state regions** (or CSRs). We saw last chapter that, before the Treaty of Westphalia and the formation of the great nation-states, urban centres dominated, and "countries" counted for little. For example, there was no Italy, but there *were* the great cities of Florence, Milan, Venice, and Rome itself—the "Eternal City." Some **futurists** (experts at predicting the future) are suggesting that, with increasing globalization, we may well see that same trend occur again, that nations will become less important, and cities much more so. Some experts have even predicted the death of the nation-state, at least economically.[18] These experts say that, if you look around, everywhere you see the formation of CSRs: areas that are almost self-contained, with all of life in the region centred around that municipality. For example, in southern Ontario, the CSR would of course be Toronto. Toronto proper, and the Greater Toronto Area (GTA), together account for *fully half* of Ontario's population *as well as* half its total economic activity. (Indeed, the GTA accounts for almost 25 per cent of Canada's *national* economy.) The area around the GTA grows food to feed the GTA, manufactures goods used in the GTA, cheers for Toronto sports teams, flies into and out of Pearson International Airport, sends local politicians to Toronto to represent them, sends tons of commuters to work every day in the GTA, and, ultimately, raises its kids to grow up and begin their careers in the GTA, so that the cycle can repeat. So dominant is Toronto, in the context of Ontario, that it's almost tempting to note recurrent themes of "metropole and periphery," as learned last chapter.[19]

regions can. Some experts even argue that cities—or, certain kinds of cities—don't necessarily have to be bad for the environment, for the greater concentration of humanity in cities leaves more of nature to Mother Nature (as long as the cities are built more *up* than *out*). Moreover, urban dwellers have, on average, fewer children than rural people do, and so urbanization decreases the population pressure on natural resources.[20]

Referring to the above "Insights box", one can certainly appreciate the formation, and growing influence, of these "CSRs." In Canada, one thinks not only of Toronto but also of Montreal, Ottawa, Halifax, Vancouver, Calgary, and Edmonton. In the US the list expands to include New York, Chicago, and Los Angeles especially, but also Boston, Dallas, Denver, Houston, Miami, Seattle, and Washington, DC. Every country in the world has at least one CSR, and possibly several, and they tend to set the tone and pace regarding both culture and standard of living. Paris may well be the boldest international example of this, as without question it dominates the tone of life in France. Increasingly, to borrow and revise a famous Latin phrase, *urbi est orbi*: the city *is* the world.

Studies in Technology

Creative Cities

We do not, of course, mean to imply that all cities are equal. Each has its own unique composition, its own particular strengths and weaknesses. Some cities—think of Detroit—seem to be struggling, whereas others, such as Shanghai, are booming. More commonly, cities endure through good times and bad. Of recent interest, though, is the new theory of "the creative city." This is thought to be of special relevance to the developed world. For as the manufacture of goods increasingly moves offshore to low-cost labour countries like China, it becomes important for developed societies to provide highly value-added services if they are to remain competitive in the global economy. (**Value-added** here means that people take rather routine inputs and, through invention and ingenuity, transform them into outputs, or goods and services, that are much more useful, valuable, and expensive.)

So what is **a creative city**? Urban experts like John Howkins and Richard Florida define it as a dynamic, growing city wherein there is (1) a substantial creative class, (2) a creative economy, and (3) creative, pleasing city conditions. The **creative class** is that segment of the workforce that gets paid to think. This would include not only people in such obviously "creative" industries as entertainment, fine arts, culture, publishing, and fashion, but also engineers, scientists, professors, lawyers, doctors, accountants, software designers, high-tech people in general, and so on. A creative city has at least 30 per cent of its workforce labouring in such activities that together constitute **the creative economy**: inventive "white-collar" work that provides services that improve quality of life (like education or medical advice) and/or difficult-to-design, value-added goods (such as software, TV programs, and Internet applications).

Pleasing city conditions might be more vague, but the general idea is that the city is not primarily industrial, nor is its layout routine, nor is its physical infrastructure drab and/or decrepit. The layout, rather, is interesting and inventive, with lots of green space and an intriguing blend of human spaces (like houses and buildings) with natural spaces (like parks and waterfront). There is some effort to make the city-space pleasing, people-friendly, and imbued with the promise of a high quality of life: it's not endless, "cookie-cutter" suburbia, nor is it a rusting old town whose manufacturing heyday is done and gone. And the "pleasing conditions" aren't just physical; they are social, too, with a stress above all on tolerance and a lack of tension and bitterness between the city's various groups. Florida has popularized this slogan, summarizing the essence of a creative city: "Talent, Technology, and Tolerance." Cities scoring highly on the various "creative city indexes" include Toronto, Vancouver, San Francisco, Seattle, Boston, Austin, Washington, DC, and New York. Internationally, cities like London, Paris, Hong Kong, and Sydney do well.[21]

TRANSITION FROM HUMAN POPULATION TO NATURAL ENVIRONMENT

It's easy to make the transition from issues concerning human population to issues concerning the natural environment. Perhaps the most evocative way to do this is to cite English economist Thomas Malthus and the social demographers influenced by his work, the so-called neo-Malthusians. Malthus back in 1798 wrote a famous essay in which he warned that the explosive growth in human population would soon exceed the ability of Earth to sustain such numbers, resulting in gruesome eventualities like mass starvation. This theme, or concern, comes up again and again in more recent writings, such as Paul Ehrlich's alarmingly titled book *The Population Bomb* (1970) and the Club of Rome's influential report *The Limits to Growth* (1972). **Neo-Malthusians** believe that the incredible growth of the human population—illustrated above in Figure 2.1—simply cannot be sustained, and that soon enough (though the neo-Malthusians never seem to agree on when exactly) humans will be too many in number for the planet to feed, water, clothe, and house us all.[22]

ENVIRONMENT AND RESOURCES

The environment refers, very broadly, to the natural setting in which human beings exist. Humans live in a complex environment composed of both artificial (i.e. human-made) and natural (i.e. non–human-made) settings and systems. When we talk of the environment we mean chiefly the latter—the natural context—and how both natural and human-made elements interact, and how this interaction impacts the future well-being of both. Thus, **the environment**, for our purposes, refers to Earth's various, and most vital, natural cycles and systems, which we depend upon for life and well-being: the atmosphere, the land, resources under the land, the water, sea life, the plant world, and the animal kingdom. To humans, all of these things are **resources**—inputs used to produce something, such as food, whether it is for one person or for the population of a **metropolis** that is home to tens of millions of people.

But humanity also deposits the waste, or by-products, of its activities into Earth's various natural systems, and this is called **pollution**. Every single human activity creates some waste—just drinking water will, eventually, produce urine, and even the simple, automatic act of breathing produces carbon dioxide (CO_2) as a by-product. There is thus no possibility of humans creating zero pollution, much as that might sound appealing as an ideal. The inescapable fact is this: we *need* the natural environment, yet we *pollute* it, too.

Pessimists Open the Argument

This complex fact of our existence has led many to speak of a massive, ever-worsening environmental crisis. Let's call these people **environmental pessimists**, or just "pessimists" for short. (Some are neo-Malthusians, but they don't all have to be.) They tend to focus on two facts above all:

1. the enormous and very rapid growth in human population (as discussed above)

2. the rise of **industrialization**—mechanized mass-production using large-scale advanced machinery and artificial measures—since the Industrial Revolution first began around 250 years ago.

Pessimists such as James Lovelock fear our enormous, and omnivorous, population will soon exceed what they call Earth's **carrying capacity**.[23] This refers to the idea that Earth and its resources are *finite*, not infinite, and that there is a limit of population growth, and resource use, that the Earth can sustain, which we must eventually reach. Simply put, there are only so many people the Earth can carry without becoming completely used up, exhausted, lifeless, and useless—like a giant garbage dump. In terms of the second item— industrialization—the pessimists fear not only that our population is sucking too much out of the Earth, but that—with mechanized mass production for a global marketplace—we are putting far too much pollution back into Earth's various systems, those of air, land, sea, and water. We are thus poisoning the plant and animal kingdoms, hence undermining our own ability to survive and thrive as a species moving forward. Lovelock goes so far as to liken Earth to a living organism ("Gaia," he calls it), and to liken the human population to a deadly, cancerous tumour within it.[24]

The Example of Easter Island

The future most feared by environmental pessimists is something very much like what happened on **Easter Island**. Easter Island (a.k.a. *Rapa Nui*) is a remote South Pacific island. In ancient times, there grew a venomous rivalry between the different tribal groups who lived there. This spilled over into a vicious, multi-generational war. So possessed did they become by the war and by the goal of victory for their tribe that the island's inhabitants relentlessly, irrationally made as rapid use as they could of every natural resource they could get their hands on: crops, livestock, drinkable water, nearby fish, trees and timber, and so on. They couldn't stop themselves, and they ended up exceeding the carrying capacity of the island, and everyone died either from violence or starvation.[25]

The fate of humanity? (© Ralf Hettler/iStockphoto)

For all practical purposes, no one lives anymore on Easter Island, and nothing grows there except some wild grass. All that remains are the enormous, eerie stone heads that were erected as monuments to the ancestors of the various groups. Environmental pessimists fear that if we are not careful—if we fail to curb irrational human impulses like rage or, in this case, greed and gluttony—the fate of our civilization might wind up like that of Easter Island. *If it happened before, it can happen again.* But this time the stakes involve the whole world and not merely one island. Perhaps one day the giant skyscrapers of our great cities—New York and Dubai, Paris and Shanghai—will one day be empty towering husks, just like the giant stone heads of Easter Island.[26]

Challenges

Now, there are environmental optimists—like Julian Simon—who doubt these grim fears will come true. They give a number of compelling reasons why the Earth is *not* Easter Island. What I would like to do, however, is to come back to this all-important clash between pessimist and optimist *at the conclusion* of our discussion of the environment. For it seems fair to say that much of the discourse and research surrounding the modern environmental movement leans towards the pessimist side. This side has **set the agenda**, as they say. So let us follow that agenda, for now, and consider the many challenges that the environment poses to us (or vice versa) in the contemporary world. Once we discern the full range and scope of environmental problems, we can more plausibly judge whether these challenges can finally be overcome.[27]

Environmental Management and Sustainable Development

With regards to managing the environment, the modern nation-state is like a person on a diet, who is trying to exercise the will-power to eat less, and better. On the one hand, countries and the people who live in them want to take advantage of their natural resources in order to become wealthy; on the other, they don't want to deplete natural resources so completely that they can no longer use them. And yet that happens *all the time.* The world's fisheries, for example, are nowhere near the levels they used to be, as consumers' huge demand for seafood outpaces the ability of the fish to replenish their numbers sufficiently. During the 1990s, Canada had to shut down its East Coast cod fishery almost completely lest the resource become completely captured and destroyed. The key, then, is **environmental management**: finding a smart balance between using enough resources to satisfy *present* demands and yet not using all the resources, so that there will be—as John Locke famously said—"enough and as good" for *future* generations. This idea has been captured in the concept of **sustainability**: not using resources to exhaustion, not polluting the environment to the point of its being poisoned, but rather managing growth and consumption so that future generations will continue to enjoy the resources we benefit from today. Devising a long-term plan to replenish, on an ongoing basis, the resources we consume—as opposed to exhausting and destroying key resources with short-term "**gold rushes**"—is of the very essence of sustainability.[28]

Some environmental critics, like Lovelock, argue that environmental "management" is not enough. They feel that the problem is deeper, and may well lie in the very makeup of industrial capitalism (whose components were described last chapter). Committed to relentless growth, and to plying consumers with every imaginable product or service, capitalism is practically designed to be the sort of economic system that could cause people to exceed Earth's carrying capacity.[29]

Moreover, with its focus on *private* profits and rewarding *individual* greed, capitalism, in the eyes of some, is seen to be at odds with the kind of social, *public* co-operation and solidarity that is going to be needed to (a) curb pollution, (b) clean our air, land, and water, and (c) transform our economy into one that operates on a smaller scale and is more local, more clean, and above all, more green. In fact, environmentalists, economists, and policy-makers—most famously in the so-called *Brundtland Commission Report* of 1987—have created the concept of **sustainable development**. This refers to economic progress that is based not on growth for its own sake but rather on growth that is measured, paced, reasonable, and consistent with Earth's carrying capacity. It is growing an economy—i.e. making people richer and better off—in a way that can be continued or sustained in the future. Many in the modern environmental movement would like to see the paradigm of sustainable development replace that of industrial capitalism. Some even see this paradigm as part of what they call a **post-industrial green economy**.[30]

> *Many in the modern environmental movement would like to see the paradigm of sustainable development replace the old model based on industrial capitalism.*

The Tragedy of the Commons

Countries not only face environmental problems *within* their own borders; they also face challenges with pollution and resources that *cross* borders or that exist in common, unowned areas between them. We noted, last chapter, three examples of unowned areas: the high seas, near-space, and Antarctica. The problem with these common spaces, captured by economists in the phrase "**the tragedy of the commons**," has been well documented in hundreds of historical cases. The tragedy is this: when things are owned in common, or are unowned, the result tends to be a decline in both the quality and quantity of the thing. When there is no one specifically to care for, and to pay the price for the decline of, an asset, that asset tends to fall apart or get completely used up. A famous case of this occurred in England, where during medieval times, grazing areas for herds were public and common. The result was that these areas were completely chewed up and left useless: eventually, everyone lost. The **enclosure movement** was a response to, and attempt to remedy, this situation: the common areas were divided up and sold to individual farmers, who then "enclosed" their areas with fences and shrubs to prevent nomadic grazing herds. These owner–farmers then planted grass and crops, and the lands sprung back into fertile life.[31]

To an extent, we can see that this way of thinking was behind the United Nations' Convention on the Law of the Sea (UNCLOS). UNCLOS, an international treaty drafted in 1982, took 10 years just to negotiate. It deals with the regulation of the oceans, which exist as public, unowned, common space. The **high seas** are thus vulnerable to a range of environmentally destructive practices, as states and non-state actors (especially corporations) exploit the unregulated domain. Garbage gets dumped there (including toxic, and even nuclear, waste); oil gets spilled there; and unrestricted fishing and piracy occurs there. (For example, did you know that, in the Pacific Ocean, there is a floating island of human-made garbage that is twice the size of France?[32] Google this: "Great Pacific Garbage Patch.") To try to contain such problems, UNCLOS sets out clear rules as to who is responsible for what on the high seas. It establishes that states may consider water adjacent to their territory to be their own sovereign territory, out to a distance of 12 miles (22.2 km) from shore. This is for purposes mainly of shipping and of sovereign entitlement and responsibility. But for economic activities like fishing, deep-sea mining, and oil/gas/mineral rights, UNCLOS gives states rights out to 200 miles (322 km) from their shores. Beyond the limits of these **exclusive economic zones (EEZs)**, the high seas remain common, public, and unregulated.[33]

Some people don't like national enclosure as a solution to the tragedy of the commons, and their preferred international treaty deals with Antarctica. They point to it as an entirely different (i.e. public and co-operative) model of how to achieve global environmental care. The **Antarctica Treaty** (1959) essentially turned that entire continent into a kind of international ecological "park": it was agreed that no country owned any part of Antarctica, that no military activity would occur there, that neither nuclear weapons nor nuclear waste would be stored or dumped there, and that the main purpose of human activity in

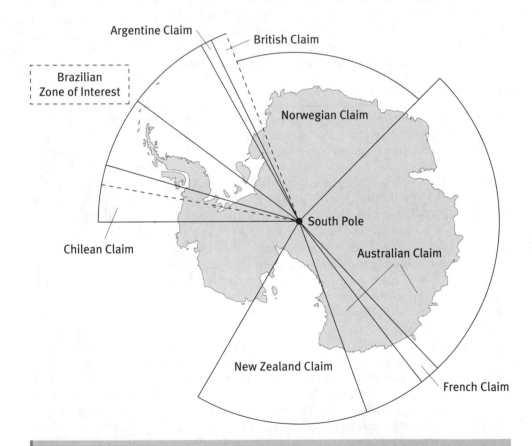

FIGURE 2.2 Antarctica, an International Public Park

As the map shows, several countries have established claims to parts of Antarctica for the purpose of scientific research. Compare this with the Arctic (Figure 2.3), where the competing national claims surround the lucrative untapped oil and gas reserves.

Antarctica would be scientific research. Almost all countries with the capability of establishing a presence in Antarctica have signed, ratified, and—moreover—largely observed the terms of this treaty.[34]

Supporters of national enclosure find these "public people" too idealistic, and they suggest (with realist savvy) that the only reason the Antarctica Treaty works is that the

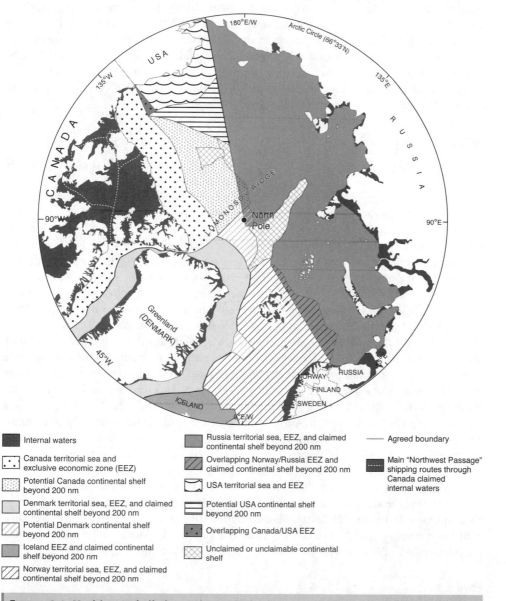

FIGURE 2.3 Maritime Jurisdiction and Boundaries in the Arctic: Competing National Claims

Source: International Boundaries Research Unit, Durham University at www.dur.ac.uk/ibru/resources/arctic.

continent is simply too remote, too hostile for human habitation, and too lacking in any valuable resource. These realists note that the other pole—the Arctic—has *not* been set up as a public commons but, rather, is carved up into competing territorial claims by the **circumpolar powers**—Canada, the US, Denmark, England, Norway, and Russia. That's because the Arctic is much closer and more hospitable, and has resources (some speculate there may be huge oil and gas reserves under the Arctic ice). And so, realists suggest, *either* the Antarctica agreement will stay the way it is—because the facts about its forbidding nature will stay the same—*or*, as soon as a valuable resource is discovered down there, then all bets will be off, and the treaty will fall apart in a "gold rush." In short, idealists tend to favour the international public park solution—the Antarctica answer, as it were—to the tragedy of the commons, whereas realists favour national enclosure.[35] (We shall return, in detail, to the clash between realist and idealist in Chapter 4.)

Deforestation

A similar problem concerns areas that are of truly *global* environmental concern yet are entirely *within the borders* of a handful of nations. The Amazon rainforest, situated primarily in Brazil, is an example. Forests are crucial as cleansers of air—**carbon sinks**, some say—as they soak up carbon dioxide and release oxygen. And some forests are especially good at this, like the Amazon rainforest, which is also a cornucopia of plant and animal life (i.e. **biodiversity**), and which has been proven instrumental in the creation of many beneficial medicines and pharmaceutical treatments. The problem, in the case of Brazil, is that until recently the government of that country saw the rainforest purely as an economic resource to be logged, cleared away, and sold. This grew the Brazilian economy, and the Brazilian government viewed with suspicion any suggestion from outside—from the developed world especially— that it shouldn't develop its society at the expense of this resource. Abstract claims about "a global carbon sink" just couldn't compare with cash in hand gained by selling all that lumber. Over time, though, Brazil came to see that non-stop cutting and clearing would only generate short-term sales and could not be sustained forever. Recognizing that preserving the rainforest had become a global priority, the Brazilian government put a proposal to the international community, challenging its trading partners to put their money where their environmental mouth is by paying Brazil *not* to overuse this resource. And so, the international community—through complex agreements with lumber and pharmaceutical companies—has done exactly this: it has paid Brazil to preserve a globally valuable environmental asset. Logging still happens, of course, but with careful planning and aggressive re-planting.[36]

Creative deals like this give heart to environmental optimists. Similar deals have been done between the rich, developed nations and such forest-rich yet economically struggling states as Indonesia, Malaysia, Madagascar, and Russia. A variation of this idea is a **debt-for-nature swap**, where a country's international trade partners offer national debt forgiveness, in lieu of direct payment, in exchange for environmental preservation.

Food

Experts agree that around 1 billion people in the world today lack the minimum calorie intake needed for their stage of growth.[37] Moreover, there is a gross distortion in the distribution of food globally, with so much *excess* in the Global North and shockingly *insufficient* food quantities in the South. Evidence of the North's excess: the UN's **Food and Agriculture Organization** (FAO) says that the average person in North America *throws away* 253 pounds of food a year! Obviously, with the greater part of projected population growth expected to occur in the starving South, this maldistribution of food resources needs to be rectified.

Things would be even worse today without the **Green Revolution**. Between 1940 and 1980, the movement helped to export the North's latest know-how in agricultural production to the Global South. (Increasingly, international aid and development involve this kind of **technology transfer**, designed to give not just goods or cash but also—indeed, *preferably*—technology and expertise to help the South develop more rapidly.) Specifically, the Green Revolution brought to the South new methods of planting and **irrigation** (i.e. watering crops), better fertilizers and harvesting techniques, and **genetically modified** (GM) **crops** and foods, whose genes have been artificially manipulated so that they are more resistant to disease, giving them superior durability and freshness. As a result of the Green Revolution, world grain production has *tripled* over the last 50 years, yielding enough basic foodstuffs—including the world's top three crops: wheat, rice, and corn—to feed all of humankind, if only distribution were better. This sort of technological innovation, in the face of serious challenge and apparent scarcity, also gives huge hope to environmental optimists. Some pessimists—while of course applauding the increase in food for needy humans—point out that the Green Revolution nevertheless has had some negative environmental consequences, such as pollution into groundwater from the new chemical fertilizers.[38]

Another thing that pessimists emphasize, and rightly so, is *food prices*. Applying the kinds of advanced new methods just described costs money, and so in order to make a profit, farmers must increase prices they charge for the crops they produce. Bad weather—on its own, and as predicted to increase owing to global warming—can destroy crops, cutting supply and thus raising prices. Finally, it requires a lot of energy, especially in the form of oil and gas, to power agricultural machinery and to transport food from rural farms to urban kitchens. When energy prices go up—as they have recently—food prices follow. This affects us all, but it hurts the global poor most. It is estimated that some people living in the developing world already spend about two-thirds of their income on food;[39] any substantial increase in food prices means even less money for other essentials, like shelter, or else more hunger. Either seems unacceptable. And increases in food prices don't merely have these *moral* or *health* consequences to them. History shows that few things are more *politically* destabilizing than food shortages or big increases in the price of food staples like bread, rice, and corn.[40] Many a major revolution has been sparked by food shortages as much as by radical ideas: this is true of revolutions ranging from the French Revolution of 1789 all the way to the Arab Spring of 2011 (which we'll examine in detail in Chapter 9). Environmental pessimists believe that, owing to all these pressures—population crush, maldistribution, climate change, rising energy prices—there will not be enough food in the future, causing serious political disruption and human suffering worldwide.[41]

Water

Water is a vital human need. We need it not only to drink and to clean with, but also to water our crops and to give to animals. Water is also used in many industrial processes. It is absolutely essential to modern civilization, in hundreds of ways. The problem is that, even

Human development can have adverse effects on water sources. Can you think of some? Consider everything from delicate ecosystems to municipal water supplies.
(© Bart Coenders/iStockphoto)

though 70 per cent of Earth's surface is water, the vast majority of that is saltwater. While it is possible to remove the salt from water so that it is fresh, usable, and drinkable, **desalination** is expensive and time-consuming on a mass scale. As a result, nearly all the water we use comes from freshwater rivers, lakes, and streams, and from groundwater and rainwater. These freshwater sources represent only a tiny portion of Earth's seemingly huge supply of H_2O.

Experts worry whether there will be enough water in the future. Indeed, they point out that there's not enough water now: between 1.1 and 1.2 billion people—almost all in the Global South—lack reliable daily access to **potable** (i.e. **drinkable**) **water**. Growth in population will only make this worse. Water also gets polluted and wasted. It gets polluted with garbage, sewage, oil spills, fertilizer runoff from farmers' fields, salt runoff from streets and sidewalks in the winter, and industrial pollution from factories. It gets wasted especially in developed countries of the North, where people are used to bounteous, seemingly endless quantities of fresh water spilling out of their taps and faucets. The two biggest water-consuming nations—by far—are Canada and the US. Per capita, Americans use about 350 litres—and Canadians, 335 litres—of fresh water *every single day*! These amounts are double even the western European average. Consider, for a moment, how these amounts compare to the water use of those 1.1 to 1.2 billion people who, some days, consume zero litres, and once more the depth of the difference between the top and the bottom in world consumption reveals its enormous magnitude. The **water-poor** are defined as those who live on five litres (or less) of potable water a day: the very amount used by most North Americans in a single flush of one solitary toilet.[42]

Oil

Energy is one of the most important environmental issues. Along with food and water, we require energy for everything we do, whether in the form of the calories and muscle energy we need to walk and talk, or the gasoline to power our vehicles, or the enormous amount of electricity required to light up a city. The top five sources of energy in the *developed* world are, in order:

1. oil
2. coal
3. natural gas
4. nuclear energy
5. hydroelectricity.

Compare these with the top three sources in the *developing* world:

1. coal

2. oil

3. **biomass** (i.e. wood, charcoal, and animal waste, all burned to make heat).

Total world energy consumption per year is the equivalent of burning 10 to 12 *billion tons* of oil. This has increased *twenty-fold* since 1850, owing to the rise in both population and industrialization over that period. We are only going to need more energy in the future, as both these trends continue worldwide.[43]

The problem is that each major source of energy listed above generates significant pollution and other problems. With oil—source of 40 per cent of the world's current energy supply—there are oil spills, particulate air pollution and greenhouse gases from burning it, and political difficulties, as we will see below. Natural gas also creates greenhouse emissions and local air pollution, and it brings some safety concerns with the possibility of pipeline explosions. Coal causes substantial smog-creating particulate air pollution that contributes to **acid rain**, which, when it falls, can burn the leaves and even the bark off trees and can actually kill fish species living in rivers and lakes. The drawbacks of nuclear energy include the cost (it is very expensive to build nuclear reactors), concerns about radioactivity, and fears about potential disasters (heightened since Japan's 2011 nuclear crisis). Hydroelectric power can cause flooding in vast areas—as with China's Three Gorges Dam—and is, besides, heavily dependent on finding the right location. Each of these forms of power production requires massive outlays of money, manufacturing, and elaborate and enormous distribution networks, be they pipelines or electricity cables. (Even smaller-scale biomass requires whole forests of trees, produces a lot of acrid smoke, and is responsible for many property-destroying fires.)[44]

Oil is worth added focus, as it is the world's leading energy source (and, not coincidentally, its most valuable commodity by price). Mechanized, industrial economies are driven by oil: factories require oil to power and lubricate machinery; consumers need fuel for their cars and trucks; and many homes are heated by oil and natural gas. Such is the enormous demand that the developed world is a net *importer* of oil and gas, while the developing world is a net *exporter* of oil and gas. (Crudely and cynically—and echoing last chapter's discussion of colonialism—one might say that the North uses the energy resources of the South to power its advanced industrial society.) Consider the North–South distribution of the countries boasting the world's top 10 oil reserves:

1. Saudi Arabia
2. Canada
3. Iraq
4. United Arab Emirates
5. Kuwait
6. Iran
7. Venezuela
8. Russia
9. Libya
10. Nigeria.[45]

Two comments related to this list of countries are crucial. The first has to do with **OPEC**, the **Organization of Petroleum Exporting Countries**. OPEC was founded in 1973, and is one of the most important cartels in the world. (A **cartel** is a small group of suppliers that controls the majority of the supply of a good.) When its members co-operate, a cartel can influence heavily the price of the good in question. By cutting back supply, for instance, it can increase the good's price. OPEC, whose leading members include Saudi Arabia, Iran, Iraq, Kuwait, UAE, Libya, Algeria, and Qatar, was founded by Arab states of the Persian Gulf region mainly for two reasons: first, to increase the price of oil, thus generating more money for themselves; and second, to punish the West—especially the US—for its ongoing support of Israel. (For more on the Arab–Israeli conflict, see the next chapter.)

When it was first formed, OPEC immediately cut the supply of oil, substantially driving up its price (as demand only continued to increase). This caused the first big **oil crisis** in Western society, which brought gas shortages, huge lineups at gas stations, and, as the price of oil affects the price of everything else (via transportation costs), sustained price increases (i.e. **inflation**) throughout all of Western society. A second, much smaller oil crisis followed in 1979. These "**oil shocks**" created **stagflation**—inflation and stagnant (or slow) economic growth *together*—as the higher cost of oil and gas cut into the budgets of businesses and consumers alike, leading to decreases in spending and investment. Decreased consumer spending and business investment generated fewer tax revenues, and so even big Western governments had less to spend. It took over a decade for the stagflation and "malaise" of the 1970s to wear off and give way to a period of low-inflation growth and optimism. On the other side of the coin, the formation of the oil cartel generated almost unheard-of wealth for OPEC's member states, who learned just how much political and economic power they could wield.[46]

The oil crises ended for several reasons. First, the West increased other sources of energy, notably nuclear. The crises also pushed Western countries to devise and introduce measures to conserve oil, such as new mileage requirements on gasoline tanks in vehicles. But perhaps the greatest factor in ending the oil crises was the fact that OPEC (especially Saudi Arabia) decided—of its own accord—to relax the price of oil, realizing that it was in its own long-term self-interest not to turn the West off oil completely, but, rather, to keep it coming back for more. OPEC survives today, and counts among its member several non-Arab members countries, including Nigeria, Venezuela, and Indonesia. There are also major oil- and gas-producing nations that are *not* OPEC members, notably Canada, Britain, China, Kazakhstan, Mexico, Norway, and Russia.

The second important thing to note about the top 10 oil-producing countries is that *not all oil is created the same*. Simply speaking, there's easy oil and difficult oil. **Easy oil** is oil that is readily available, cheap to extract and purify, and ready to go. To put it crudely, you just have to stick a straw in the oil field and suck it out. The oil of the Arabian peninsula and Persian Gulf region is easy oil. **Difficult oil** is oil that is remotely located (e.g. offshore), expensive to bring out, laborious to purify, and not at all ready to go. It needs to be processed. An example of this is Alberta's enormous stock of **oil sands**. These reserves are huge—almost rivalling those of Saudi Arabia—but, as the name indicates, they are made up of oil mixed together with sand. It takes a lot of time and treasure to extract the oil from the sand, and then to purify it enough to substitute for easy oil. (You can't have sand in your gas tank, after all.)[47]

Environmental pessimists have enormous problems with our addiction to oil. First, oil (and all fossil fuels) create pollution when burned for energy. (**Fossil fuels** include coal, oil, and natural gas, which together account for nearly 90 per cent of current world energy consumption.) This fossil fuel pollution is of three main kinds: spills; smog and particulate in the present; and contribution to greenhouse gases and climate change in the future. Second, because oil is so central to the energy requirements of the world economy, oil-rich areas are prone to conflict and even war, as major powers seek to secure sufficient oil supplies for their massive requirements. The history of the Persian Gulf region since oil was first discovered there in the late 1800s bears witness to this. Third, oil is a finite resource. Mother Nature isn't making new oil, and so all we can do is extract and use it. Fossil fuels in general are thus **non-renewable resources**, unlike solar, wind, and water power, all **renewable resources**. In spite of enormous oil reserves, we will one day run out (in, perhaps, a century or so).[48]

> *In spite of enormous oil reserves, we will one day run out.*

Peak oil theory is based on speculation about when oil production will reach its peak (or maximum output), beyond which there will be less and less oil to extract, yet more and more demand for it (owing to population growth and industrialization). Most peak oil theorists, such as Kenneth Deffeyes,[49] suggest that we are, worldwide, at that peak point right now. Interestingly, when peak oil experts—like M.K. Hubbard—have applied their global theories to national cases, they have had a very strong track record of predictive success. For example, the United States used to be a net *exporter* of oil, with big reserves in Pennsylvania, Texas, and Alaska. Today, however, the US is *by far* the world's biggest importer of oil, a fact that many people believe has been crucial in drawing the US into various Middle Eastern wars.[50] So, peak production of oil in America was correctly predicted to have been around 1970, and indeed since then, the US has had to chase oil reserves elsewhere, with unhappy consequences both politically and environmentally. Worldwide, according to the peak oil people, what will happen once the easy oil is tapped out and we increasingly turn to difficult oil is that oil's price will skyrocket, hurting everyone and turning the entire world economy into one suffering from 1970s-style stagflation: low growth, low employment, reduced incomes, yet higher prices for everything.

Global Warming and Climate Change

The authoritative source on climate change and global warming is the **Intergovernmental Panel on Climate Change** (IPCC). Its 2007 report, reviewed by 2,500 expert scientists, concluded that global warming *is* happening, and that it is being caused by *human activity*, especially ongoing industrialization and the burning of fossil fuels used in the process.[51] The causal linkages, described effectively by Al Gore in his 2005 documentary *An Inconvenient Truth*, are supposed to work like this:

1. The burning of fossil fuels releases enormous amounts of carbon dioxide (CO_2) into the atmosphere.

2. Carbon dioxide acts as a **greenhouse gas**, trapping sunlight in and below the atmosphere, causing Earth's temperature to rise.

3. The result, since industrialization began, has been a steady increase in average global temperatures.

The consequences of global warming will be severe:

- Polar ice will melt into the oceans, reducing freshwater stores and creating **rising sea levels**, flooding low-lying countries like the Netherlands and the South Pacific islands, as well as coastal cities like New York and Shanghai.

- Inland **desertification** (i.e. the spread of deserts) and water scarcity will intensify.

- Extremes of weather—especially wind- and rainstorms—will grow.

- Diseases will increase as tropical diseases like malaria spread north.

- Plagues of insects and mould will occur, as warmer temperatures allow these organisms to thrive more readily.

- Some animals, such as polar bears, will become extinct with the flooding of their habitat.

- Ditto for some ecosystems, such as coral reefs, that cannot support higher temperatures.

And there will be further consequences not yet known, as climate change kicks off a cascade of **feedback loops** throughout the world's ecosystems, with each change producing another that, in turn, reinforces the first.

There is strong evidence that the average global temperature *has* increased since 1700, and that the level of carbon dioxide in the atmosphere has risen from historical norms of 280 parts per million (ppm) to 380 ppm today. Roughly 12 of the past 15 years have seen the highest global surface temperatures since 1850, a statistic that is illustrated in the famous "hockey stick" chart of rising average temperatures (see Figure 2.4). Note how similar this diagram is to the one in Figure 2.1, on population growth. For the environmental pessimist, this striking sameness is, of course, no mere coincidence: *more people must equal more pollution.*[52]

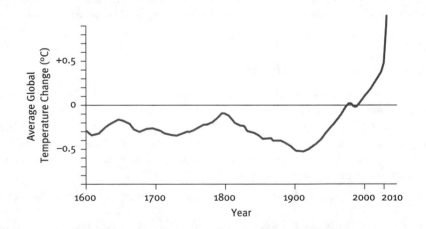

FIGURE 2.4 The "Hockey Stick" Chart of Rising Global Temperature

Note the similar shape of the previous chart showing the growth of the human population (Figure 2.1) and this chart showing the rise in global temperature.

As a result of concern regarding global warming, there have been various attempts at regulating and cutting greenhouse gas emissions. Most famous is the **Kyoto Protocol** of 1997. This international treaty stands as a failure, much to the lament of environmentalists. Why has it failed? There is a very sharp North–South split on the issue. Developing nations of the Global South—especially India, China, and numerous African countries—want to use cheap fossil fuels to industrialize and grow their economies. And OPEC countries—obviously—want to keep selling oil. Only societies that have already become industrialized—especially in Europe—seem committed to cutting greenhouse gas emissions and reducing their dependency on oil and coal. Developing societies like China, India, and Brazil were thus excluded from the strictest terms of Kyoto, as an incentive to get their general support; these countries have agreed to take voluntary, non-binding steps to curb emissions. But countries such as the US have asked, why should we commit to cutting *our* oil and coal use, if China—the world's largest emitter of greenhouse gases today—is *not* obliged to meet similar targets? Since the US recognizes that China might become a global rival—economically, politically—it has decided to say no to Kyoto, too.[53]

There have been a number of attempts to revive negotiations surrounding climate change, including the 2007 "Bali Roadmap" and the 2011 UN conference on climate change in Durban, South Africa, where the Kyoto Protocol was extended. But these attempts have, by and large, achieved small, if any, success. In fact, immediately following the Durban conference, Canada officially withdrew from Kyoto, claiming the protocol's targets are impossible to achieve (especially for a country that plans to continue extracting oil from Alberta's tar sands). The point remains that if the world's most powerful and most polluting economies—notably the US and China, not to mention Canada—refuse to sign on to Kyoto's legally binding measures, then any deal is going to be very limited, in terms of the progressive environmental impact it can make.

A quick word about scientific controversy is in order. Most everyone agrees on the temperature record, and thus that global warming *is occurring* to some degree. The debate is over whether industrialization is chiefly to blame.

Doubters say that carbon dioxide is much too small a component of atmospheric gases to have the effect imagined by "global warmers." The same skeptics point out that the main drivers of Earth's climate have always been the sun and its effect on Earth's oceans. A longer look at historical temperature records will show that temperatures move up and down in long waves. In fact, they argue, the "hockey stick" graph is a misleading, sensationalist snapshot of just a small part of the historical record; take a longer view, and the upward-curving stick becomes but a hill or a wave in a long series of such. Moreover, these long waves of temperature movement are most closely associated with changes in solar activity. When the sun heats up and produces solar flares, there's global warming; when the reverse happens, we experience cooler temperatures, even an ice age. In conclusion, these doubters assert that if there's global warming, then it's because of the sun and its impact on ocean temperature and current; it is *not* a result of human-made CO_2 emissions. And so, to call for restrictions on economic activity or a cutting back on industrialization is completely unfounded, and with severe consequences to the world's economy and especially to the development aspirations of the Global South.

> *Most everyone agrees that global warming is occurring to some degree. The debate is over whether industrialization is chiefly to blame.*

This latter argument is the climate change doubter's standard reply to the supporters' use of the so-called precautionary principle. A much-cited tenet of environmentalism, **the precautionary principle** stipulates that if you're unsure of whether a practice is safe—or, if you think it *might* be dangerous or polluting—then, as a matter of prudence, you ought *not* to continue it. Thus, even if we are unsure about the effects of carbon emissions on Earth's temperature, we should cut back on burning fossil fuels *in case* this is contributing significantly to global warming. The skeptic replies by urging us to consider the clearly negative consequences of requiring big cut-backs in greenhouse gas emissions: economic damage for the North and dashed development hopes for the South. It is thus, for them, not prudent at all to adopt the precautionary principle in this case.[54]

OPTIMISM VERSUS PESSIMISM

We return, then, after our survey of pressing environmental problems, to the clash between optimists and pessimists. Let's summarize the case of the optimists before letting the pessimists have the final say.

The Case for Environmental Optimism

We can summarize the optimist's arguments thus:

- For many environmental problems, solutions *are* known, and in a number of respects, things are getting better. Acid rain and smog, for example, used to be much worse in the developed world, before effective treaties and air quality laws came into being. Even with trickier global issues, the Montreal Protocol on ozone shows that strengthening environmental laws, and improving our actions, *can* make a difference. The Montreal Protocol was drafted, signed, and ratified in response to concerns about the **ozone layer**, that part of Earth's atmosphere responsible for filtering out some of the most harmful (i.e. skin cancer–causing) ultraviolet rays from the sun. By the mid-1980s, there was expert consensus that (a) the ozone layer was thinning, and even had holes at both of Earth's poles; and (b) industrial chemicals used in refrigeration, known as **chlorofluorocarbons** (or CFCs), were largely responsible. **The Montreal Protocol** set guidelines for restricting and then eliminating the use of CFCs. In the developed world, CFCs stopped being made in 1996, and this is almost true today for the developing world, too. Happily, there is evidence that the ozone layer is now recovering as a result, with global public health gains for all, especially for those in the southern hemisphere, where ozone thinning was at its worst.[55]

- For optimists such as Bjorn Lomborg, the pessimists grossly underestimate (a) our ability to adapt, (b) nature's enormity and resiliency, and (c) our talents at technological innovation.[56] In the face of many resource pressures before, humans have been able to apply their brilliance and determination to come up with new, more productive ways of doing things, such as refrigeration without CFCs. But the best example here, by far, is the Green Revolution. So much of the pessimist's case is built around the growth of human population and the pressure this puts on finite natural resources. But if we can—through technology—find ways to make those resources go farther (like tripling staple grain yield in the last 50 years), then this pressure becomes substantially reduced. We see this also in the energy field, and in the development of alternative, renewable energy technologies such as solar and wind power, geothermal and tidal energy, nuclear power, and alternative fuels like ethanol, and in alternative modes of transport, like electric cars and better-quality public transportation.

- There are so many reasons for so many different **stakeholders** to care about the environment, and to move towards a more sustainable, less wasteful society. Corporations, for example, want to cultivate a positive public image by developing a green reputation; they also want to avoid polluting fines, reduce the inputs needed to make their goods, and render their profits sustainable moving forward. Governments care about the environment because (in democratic societies anyway) the voters force them to. Governments don't want to pay clean-up costs for pollution, either, and they are increasingly moving towards laws, and urban planning schemes, that aid the environment, such as higher-density development ("building up, not out"), combined with public transportation, instead of car-dependent suburban sprawl. Consumers, for their part, want to live and eat better; they don't want to pay astronomical oil and gas bills; they support local **reduce, reuse, recycle** programs; they celebrate **Earth Day** on 22 April; they love national parks and believe in wildlife and biodiversity preservation; they now vote for various Green parties; and, above all, they don't want to leave to their children a shabbier world than the one they were born into.

- Most countries have domestic government agencies devoted to environmental stewardship: in the US, it's the Environmental Protection Agency (EPA); Canada has a federal (and several provincial) Ministry of the Environment. Internationally, there are scores of agencies, the most influential of them probably the **United Nations' Environmental Program** (UNEP), headquartered in Nairobi, Kenya, and with a variety of regional offices. Also important is the UN **Commission on Sustainable Development** (UNCSD), founded at the 1992 Earth Summit in Brazil to monitor state compliance with environmental promises. There are also many non-governmental organizations with global impact, including Greenpeace, the World Wildlife Fund, the Sea Shepherd Conservation Society, and the Sierra Legal Defence Fund. All of these agencies and organizations exist to help protect the environment.

- And so we are not Chicken Little and the sky is not falling. Earth is not Easter Island—those people were ignorant of the concept of sustainability, and today we know much better. We have the reasons, the laws, the organizations, and the technology to develop a truly sustainable society; it's just a matter of finding the money, ingenuity, and political will to bring it into being. This will be a difficult and ongoing—yet totally achievable—process.[57]

The Case for Environmental Pessimism

The above is a hopeful set of considerations, backed by some solid facts. And yet, while pessimists might *want* the optimists to be correct, on the whole many of them remain unpersuaded:

- Against the handful of successful environmental regulations and treaties, like the Montreal Protocol, pessimists can point out scores or even hundreds of failed resolutions, such as the Kyoto Protocol. Indeed, even when environmental laws *do* get passed, often they are merely **trophy laws**—laws passed for reasons of public display—that remain unenforced. The resources for realizing environmental regulations are, worldwide, very modest. The same may be said for all the agencies listed above as "effective protectors" of the environment. Even in wealthy, developed countries, many pollution inspection systems are years behind, underfunded, and—worse—reliant on data provided by corporate polluters themselves.

- The magnitude of existing limits on resources diminishes the pessimist's enthusiasm for what technology can do. If technology is such a promising way out of these problems of scarcity, then why do about 1 billion people currently lack secure access to both potable water and sufficient food? The breadth and depth of *today's* problems should give serious pause to those believing that, if only we can hit upon the right new inventions, we can readily solve *tomorrow's*.

- While different stakeholders *do* have very good reasons to care about the environment, *this doesn't mean they are always guided by them*. Some companies, for instance, continue to pollute in spite of the reasons listed above, and governments continue to fail to enforce environmental laws, in spite of their good reasons not to. And, while consumers may like to think of themselves as environmentally conscious, the reality (especially in North America) is that they also like cheap gas and huge SUVs, big houses (with well-watered lawns) in the suburbs, and the convenience of living in a "disposable society" that caters to The Consumer as King. We waste food and water in unconscionable quantities, and come election time, we tend not to vote for "green" candidates (witness the poor showing of the Green Party in the 2011 Canadian federal election). Moreover, there is some disturbing evidence that *we only care about the environment when the economy is up and we feel financially secure*. Opinion polls confirm this: interest in, and support for, environmental measures tracks the business cycle—in other words, it goes up when the economy goes up, and it goes down when a recession hits. (For more on the business cycle, see Chapter 6.) This fact seems to suggest that, when push comes to shove, people prefer economic growth over environmental protection. People have to pay the rent and feed themselves, and thus seem unwilling to sacrifice growth in the name of sustainability. And this is, for pessimists, the deeper, remaining truth about Easter Island: people can become obsessed with, indeed consumed by, their short-term drives and needs, and can, in pursuing them, undermine their long-term interests and goals. Are we really so sure we won't wind up like Easter Island?

- The salient fact remains regarding the severe split between North and South. Most pollution comes from the industrial North; most population growth occurs in the poorer South. Interest in environmental protection is much higher in the North, whereas the South fears that any such measures will hamper its ability to develop and grow richer. How to square that circle? How to harmonize such divergent perspectives and interests to forge a unified and effective environmental policy worldwide? Pessimists fear that it simply can't be done, and that in the future, we will be confronted with a long list of ferocious difficulties, including a skyrocketing population, global warming, peak oil, stagflation, pollution, species extinction, resource scarcities (especially food and water), and the dire misery and violent conflict that often go with these.[58]

CONCLUSION

In this chapter, we have surveyed humankind's interaction with the natural environment. First, we examined our fast-growing population and how it is being distributed in interesting, important, and challenging ways across the globe, and within societies. We paid special attention to the rise of urbanization, and its pros and cons, as the majority of people on Earth now live in cities. We then turned our attention to the natural environment, and focused on the clash between optimist and pessimist regarding humans' future relationship with the natural world.

REVIEW QUESTIONS

1. Does Earth have too many people? Who gets to declare such things? Consider how both China and India have adopted quite different methods for controlling their giant populations: which of their policies do you consider better, and why?

2. Nearly every society has issues when it comes to immigration and how to assimilate immigrants into the existing, native-born population. What has immigration added to your country? What challenges has it created?

3. Do you believe Lovelock's idea that Earth, as a whole, is like a huge living organism? And do you believe that humanity exists as a kind of cancer within that organism, or do you find this latter claim dubious and hostile to humanity? How would you characterize our relationship with the environment?

4. Define more fully the concept of sustainable development. How would an economy built on such a principle be different from the current one?

5. What are the top three environmental problems in your country? Your city? (Consult relevant government websites to get a sense of these.) What, if anything, can be done about them?

6. When it comes to solving "the tragedy of the commons," which solution do you prefer and why: national enclosure (as in UNCLOS) or international public park protection (as in Antarctica)?

7. Research the Green Revolution—its causes, consequences, and particular country case studies. Detail the pros and cons of this movement and how it has changed the world. Is it over? Or is this an ongoing thing now, with technology transfer? Can we expect similar progress in the future, or have the big gains already been made?

8. Consider global warming, and the clash between climate scientists. Watch the excellent, rival documentaries *An Inconvenient Truth* and *The Great Global Warming Swindle*. Who has you most persuaded, and why? What, if anything, should we be doing about climate change?

9. Do you really care about the environment? Why, or why not? What do you actually do in your life to prove that you *do* care? What more could, or should, you be doing?

10. All things considered, do you agree more with the optimist or the pessimist regarding humankind's future and the fate of our environment? Explain fully, appealing to your own subjective values as well as to the objective evidence.

WEBSITES FOR FURTHER RESEARCH

Environment Canada www.ec.gc.ca
– Canada's federal ministry for environmental protection

The US Environmental Protection Agency www.epa.gov
– America's federal agency responsible for environmental protection

Greenpeace www.greenpeace.org
– world's first, and perhaps still most aggressive and controversial, environmental NGO

The United Nations Environment Program www.unep.org
– global IGO mandated to advance the cause of environmental protection, interestingly headquartered in Global South

The United Nations Population Program www.un.org/esa/population
– for any of the latest international population statistics

NOTES

1. R. Carson, *Silent Spring* (New York: Houghton Mifflin, 1962); L. Lear, *Rachel Carson* (Seattle: Mariner, 2009).
2. UN News Centre, "As World Passes 7 Billion Milestone, UN Urges Action to Meet Key Challenges," www.un.org/apps/news/story.asp?NewsID=40257&Cr=population&Cr1=; J.R. Weeks, *Population: Concepts and Issues* (London: Wadsworth, 11th edn, 2011).
3. M. Livi-Bacci, *A Concise History of World Population* (London: Wiley-Blackwell, 2006).
4. United Nations, Population Division of the Department of Economic and Social Affairs: www.un.org/esa/population
5. J. Goldstein & S. Whitworth, *International Relations* (Toronto: Pearson Longman, 2005), pp. 515–30.
6. Population Reference Bureau, *World Population Data Sheets* (Washington, DC: Population Reference Bureau, 1975, 2006).
7. Geoffrey York, "Baby Boom a Perk that Only Elite Can Afford," *The Globe and Mail* (8 May 2007); M. Connelly, *Fatal Misconception: The Struggle to Control the World's Population* (Cambridge, MA: Harvard University Press, 2010).
8. Weeks, *Population* (op. cit., note 2).

9. United Nations, Migration Division of the Department of Economic and Social Affairs: www.unmigration.org

10. UN, ibid.

11. R.M. Dancygier, *Immigration and Conflict in Europe* (Cambridge: Cambridge University Press, 2010); C. Taylor, *Multiculturalism and The Politics of Recognition* (Princeton: Princeton University Press, 1994).

12. D. Rothenberg, *With These Hands* (Berkeley, CA: University of California Press, 2000).

13. M. Mamdani, *Saviours and Survivors: Darfur, Politics and The War on Terror* (London: Pantheon, 2009).

14. G. Prunier, *Africa's World War* (Oxford: Oxford University Press, 2009).

15. E.J. Hobsbawm, *Industry and Empire: The Birth of the Industrial Revolution* (London: The New Press, 1999).

16. UN Population Division (op. cit., note 4).

17. Weeks, *Population* (op. cit., note 2).

18. W. Brown, *Walled States, Waning Sovereignty* (London: Zone, 2010).

19. R. Grant, "Drowning in Plastic," *The Telegraph* (2008). Available at: www.telgraph.co.uk/earth/environment/52

20. E. Birch & S. Wachter, eds, *Global Urbanization* (Philadelphia, PA: Penn State University Press, 2010).

21. T. Courchene, *Rearrangements* (Toronto: Mosaic Press, 1992); D. MacFarlane, ed., *Toronto: A City Becoming* (Toronto: Key Porter Books, 2008).

22. J. Howkins, *The Creative Economy* (London: Penguin, 2001); R. Florida, *The Rise of the Creative Class* (New York: Basic Books, 2002).

23. T. Malthus, *An Essay on the Principle of Population* (Oxford: Oxford World Classics, 2008); P. Ehrlich, *The Population Bomb* (Los Angeles, CA: Sierra Club, 1970); The Club of Rome, *The Limits to Growth* (Rome: Club of Rome, 1972).

24. J. Lovelock, *Gaia* (Oxford: Oxford University Press, 1979).

25. Lovelock, ibid.

26. J. Keegan, *A History of Warfare* (London: Viking, 1993).

27. Keegan, ibid.

28. J. Simon, *The State of Humanity* (London: Wiley-Blackwell, 2008).

29. B. Norton, *Sustainability* (Chicago: University of Chicago Press, 2005).

30. Lovelock, *Gaia* (op. cit., note 24).

31. P. Rogers, et al., *An Introduction to Sustainable Development* (London: Routledge, 2008); G.H. Brundtland, et al., *Our Common Future* (Oxford: Oxford University Press, 1987).

32. G. Hardin, *Living within Limits* (Oxford: Oxford University Press, 1995).

33. T. Mensah, ed., *Sustainable Development and The Oceans* (Washington, DC: Law of the Sea Institute, 1995).

34. G. Triggs & A. Riddell, eds, *Antarctica* (London: British Institute of International and Comparative Law, 2007).

35. M. Byers, *Who Owns the Arctic?* (Toronto: Douglas and McIntyre, 2010).

36. M. Williams, *Deforesting the Earth* (Chicago: University of Chicago Press, 2006).

37. R. Parker & M. Sommer, *Routledge Handbook of Global Public Health* (London: Routledge, 2011).

38. J. Perkins, *Geopolitics and The Green Revolution* (Oxford: Oxford University Press, 1997).

39. United Nations Food and Agricultural Organization (FAO): www.fao.org/corp/statistics/en

40. J. Von Braum, *Globalization of Food and Agriculture, and The Poor* (Oxford: Oxford University Press, 2008).

41. J. Clapp & M. Cohen, eds, *The Global Food Crisis* (Waterloo, ON: CIGI, 2008).

42. S. Solomon, *Water* (New York: Harper Perennial, 2011); C. Fishman, *The Big Thirst* (New York: The Free Press, 2011).

43. V. Smil, *Energy: A Beginner's Guide* (London: OneWorld, 2006).

44. D. Yergin, *The Quest: Energy, Security and the Making of the Modern World* (New York: Penguin, 2011).

45. M. Downey, *Oil 101* (London: Wooden Table, 2009).

46. T. Falola & A. Genova, *The Politics of the Global Oil Industry* (New York: Praeger, 2008).

47. D. Yergin, *The Prize: The Epic Quest for Oil, Money and Power* (New York: Free Press, 2008).

48. D. Seifried & W. Witsil, *Renewable Energy: The Facts* (London: Routledge, 2010).

49. K. Deffeyes, *Hubbert's Peak* (Princeton: Princeton University Press, 2008).

50. Yergin, *The Prize* (op. cit., note 47).

51. Intergovernmental Panel on Climate Change (IPCC), *Report on Climate Change* (New York: United Nations, 2007).

52. IPCC, ibid.; M. Mann & L. Kung, *Dire Predictions: Understanding Global Warming* (Berlin: DK Publishing, 2008).

53. D. Archer & S. Rahmstorff, *The Climate Crisis* (Cambridge: Cambridge University Press, 2010).

54. M. Hulme, *Why We Disagree About Climate Change* (Cambridge: Cambridge University Press, 2009); J. Porritt, *Playing Safe* (New York: Thames and Hudson, 2000.

55. IPCC, *Safeguarding the Ozone Layer* (New York: United Nations, 2005).

56. B. Lomborg, *The Skeptical Environmentalist* (Cambridge: Cambridge University Press, 2001).

57. Julian Simon, *The Ultimate Resource 2* (Princeton: Princeton University Press, 1998).

58. T. Easton, *Taking Sides: Clashing Views on Environmental Issues* (New York: McGraw Hill, 12th edn, 2008).

3 Comparative Culture

"Without culture, and the relative freedom it
implies, society, even when perfect, is but a jungle.
This is why any authentic creation is a gift to the
future."[1] —*Albert Camus (1913–1960), French author and Nobel Prize Laureate*

LEARNING OBJECTIVES

After studying this chapter, you will be able to:

▸ define all the bolded key terms and concepts

▸ know the tenets of, and explain the differences among, the three big ideologies of conservatism, liberalism, and socialism

▸ explain the rise of welfare liberalism in the West, and contemplate possible future challenges to it, such as from environmentalism or from immigration

▸ grasp the role religion plays in contemporary culture

▸ appreciate the differences between the major world religions, both Abrahamic/monotheistic and Eastern/polytheistic

▸ reflect on the complex case studies on the Arab–Israeli conflict and the conflict between Tibet and China, and be able to comment on the degree to which they involve political ideology, nationhood, religion, and culture

▸ ponder the role of advanced technology in your own life and culture, and the meaning of the global "digital divide" for international affairs.

INTRODUCTION

We have already discussed many things about culture. In Chapter 1, we defined **culture** as a way of life, as the way that people think, speak, behave, and spend their time, and we noted the distinction between high and low culture. We also spent time defining *civilization*, comparing Western civilization to others around the globe, and discussing Huntingdon's "clash of civilizations" thesis and the role that cultural difference plays therein. In Chapter 2, we considered tensions between immigrants and native-born populations, and the role that policies of multiculturalism can play in easing them. We also examined how urban life differs from rural life, noting the worldwide trend toward urbanization. Finally, we raised deep questions about the developed world's way of life, in terms of food and water consumption, energy use, pollution, and capitalism (versus alternatives such as sustainable development) as the engine driving its economic system. We need not repeat such things here. Instead, this chapter will thus focus on three major drivers of contemporary culture that we've yet to examine: politics, religion, and new media. (A fourth, education, will be discussed in Chapter 11, on international aid and development.)

THE STRUCTURE AND IDEOLOGY OF THE STATE

We saw, in both the introduction and Chapter 1, that national governments have an enormous impact on international affairs and global studies. This is because of the sheer degree of power they have relative to that of other international organizations, such as corporations and NGOs. Though these latter organizations *are* increasingly important, by and large state governments remain the most influential players in both national and international life. How state governments are shaped and run therefore winds up having a huge impact on the culture of the societies they govern. So, let's examine the values and principles that contour these political structures.

> How state governments are shaped and run winds up having a huge impact on the culture of the societies they govern.

Admittedly, not all state governments are run on the basis of values and principles. An **unprincipled state** would be one that is controlled, for instance, by a very small, elite group whose only agenda is to use the power of government to serve itself (in terms of money, influence, and prestige). Another example of an unprincipled state would be a **military dictatorship**, wherein a strongman commands the government, and his power rests on his control of the military; the military's power, in turn, rests on the **coercive** (i.e. violent and unelected) force it exerts over society in general. Recent examples of unprincipled states would include Iraq under Saddam Hussein (1979–2003) and Libya under Mu'ammar Gaddafi (1969–2011).[2]

A **principled state**, by contrast, is one in which the government tries to realize a set of ideals (even if it can do so only imperfectly, given real-world constraints of cost, imperfect knowledge, and, sometimes, flat-out mistakes). This set of ideals constitutes the **political ideology** of the state or government—in other words, the ideals and values surrounding how best to run a country, and how to organize its people and shape their way of life. It seems fair to say that for every unprincipled state out there, there's a principled one trying to give it a go in running society according to some ideals. Let us, therefore, consider the

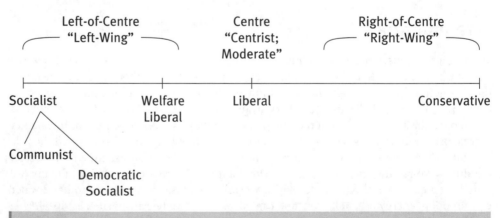

FIGURE 3.1 The Spectrum of Today's Mainstream Political Ideologies

The terms "left," "centre," and "right" all originated during the French Revolution, when they were used to refer to where different groups would sit in the French National Assembly.

most prominent competing political ideologies in the modern world, and how they give rise to very different societies. We'll proceed in order of the chronological appearance of these ideas, and then we'll note which countries best illustrate these different ideas in action, and their importance to international studies. Figure 3.1 offers an overview.[3]

Conservatism

Conservatism—the traditional doctrine of medieval Europe before the liberal revolutions in the United States and France in the 1770s and 1780s—is still the dominant ideology in a number of societies around the world. Conservatism literally implies an aversion to change and a desire to conserve the heritage that has been handed down from previous generations. Conservatives view the past fondly and appreciatively, and wish to transmit the best of the past to future generations. Conservatives have an **organic view of society**: they view society as *greater than* the sum of the individuals who compose it. They see society itself as a kind of living, organic creature, a thing with an internal character or personality, possessing a past, present, and future. The role of government, for conservatives, is to do what it can to further the thriving of this unified, organic thing.[4]

Conservatives see a **positive role for the state**: government should be *actively involved*—in culture, in the economy, in education—directing the society over which it governs. The view is very much "top-down." Conservatives tend to be very *patriotic* and *nationalistic*, feeling a deep attachment to their country and its culture. The old-style element to conservatism, beyond this, is twofold: (1) *often religious*, conservatives tend to believe in a clear and objective moral order; and (2) conservatives maintain an *acceptance of inequality*. They believe that some people simply know better how to run a society, and should therefore be given the preponderance of power. They shouldn't use all that power to benefit themselves, however (as in an unprincipled state); rather, they ought to use their talents on behalf of all, for **the public good** of this greater, organic community in which everyone finds their proper place. This is what the French, during the pre-Revolution *ancien regime*, used to call *noblesse oblige*: the other-serving obligation of the elites towards all of society.[5]

Case Study: Iran's Religious Regime

There are elements of conservatism in all societies. And it's very important to distinguish between *the values of the governing regime* and *the values of the ordinary people*, as these don't always go together. That said, the government of Iran provides one of the clearest examples of conservative ideology in the contemporary world. In 1979, there was a violent revolution in Iran, which resulted in the forceful overthrow of the **shah** (or "king") of Iran, who had been supported internationally by the Americans and British (in exchange for favourable access to Iran's large oil supply).[6] The new government of Iran was a religious government, committed to an extreme version of Islam. In fact, Iran became a kind of **theocracy**: a country in which there is no separation between church and state (as described in Chapter 1), and which is characterized by a deliberate, extensive use of government power to realize a religious vision.

In August 2011, a group of Iranian youths were arrested for taking part in a water fight in the capital's Tehran Square. The arrests were justified on the grounds that the youths involved were disobeying Islamic principles, given that the young men and women involved were not related by blood or marriage. What does the incident tell you about the values of the people versus the values of the state? (© Amir/Demotix/Demotix/Corbis)

Since then, Iran has been governed by a small, elite group of religious figures, who take it as their duty to govern the country in accordance with their own strict interpretation of the **Qur'an**, the holy book of Islam. This group exemplifies all the values of conservatism mentioned above:

- wanting to conserve their heritage (i.e. the religious vision of life, according to Islam);

- having the government intervene extensively in the economy, education, and culture (the Internet, for instance, is heavily censored in Iran); and

- showing a strong sense of patriotism/nationalism (for example, Iran under this regime has gone to war several times, has used force to intervene in other societies like Lebanon and Syria, and is aggressively pursuing the development of nuclear weapons).

A prominent aspect of Iran's conservatism, and one that has become a topic of comment and even debate in the West, is the use of **sharia law**—the official state law, informed by a strict, conservative reading of the Qur'an—and the impact of this law on the rights of the country's citizens. The law is seen as being unequally harsh on women, not just with its stipulation of mandatory, modest public fashion for women but, moreover, with a raft of substantial legal restrictions that add up to a clearly unequal life for the women of that country.[7]

Liberalism

Liberalism began as a reaction against conservatism and, as mentioned, finds its real-world roots in the American (1776–83) and French (1789–1800) revolutions. The core concept of liberalism, clearly, is liberty: *the freedom of the individual.* Liberals view the conservative doctrine as oppressive, and at odds with the personal freedom of people to govern themselves, and to live as they please. There are two kinds of liberalism: classical liberalism and welfare liberalism. **Classical liberalism**—also known as **neo-liberalism**—is the earlier, purer, kind and, as such, must be discussed first. **Welfare liberalism**, the dominant ideology of the developed West nowadays, can be described fully only after discussing socialism, as we'll see below.

Liberals have an **atomistic view of society**, according to which they *reject* the notion that society is a kind of living organism, insisting instead that society is, indeed, nothing more than the individuals it comprises (like a bunch of atoms, or a collection of marbles in a bucket). And liberals see a **negative role for the state**, which is to say that they view government dimly, and minimally. Generally, liberals argue that if one looks at the historical record, one sees that governments often violate personal freedom, and can serve as dangerous threats to civil society. Thus, liberals are keen on keeping government intervention in our lives to an absolute minimum. It is sometimes said they have a **"night-watchman" view of the state**: the state should keep the peace, protect us against thieves and foreign invaders, and uphold our property rights, but otherwise stay out of our lives and, as the saying goes, "let a thousand flowers bloom."[8] That's how liberty will be maximized.

So, a *classical* liberal would be opposed to government funding for healthcare, education, and culture; state intervention in the economy; and, generally, using tax revenues to provide any services beyond the minimal list just mentioned. Critics of this ideology sometimes speak of it conspiratorially as "the neo-liberal agenda." It's important to stress that the terms "conservative" and "liberal" here are being used in their classical, conceptual senses. These terms are often used differently—opportunistically—by political parties. Thus, the Liberal Party of Canada need not be liberal in the classical sense, nor are Canada's big-C Conservatives entirely "conservative" in the classical interpretation of the term.

The one thing liberals *do* share with conservatives is an *acceptance of inequality*. After all, if you let people be free, there's going to be inequality in society, as different people have different interests, talents, work capacities, and competencies. In fact, liberals are *more tolerant than conservatives* regarding social difference of all kinds, including, especially, moral, sexual, and religious difference. Liberals prefer to speak of *different defensible ways of life* than to insist on the supremacy (or moral truth) of one. It follows that liberals are less attached to their own society, and tend to be less patriotic and more **cosmopolitan** (or global) in their outlook and interests—because it's all about *them* and their personal freedom, their pursuit of happiness and well-being, and where they fit in best in the world. These attitudes mean that liberals look *less* towards the past and its preservation and more towards the future and the opportunities it may hold for them.[9]

Case Study: Classical Liberalism in the United States

In terms of examples of classical liberal societies, there really aren't many good ones anymore. Welfare liberalism, and *not* classical liberalism, is the norm today. Still, classical liberal societies *did* exist, with nineteenth-century America being perhaps one of the clearest examples. Before the **Great Depression (1929–39)**—which brought an enormous slowdown in the economy worldwide, creating vast unemployment and poverty—the US government meddled little in the national economy, allowing maximum economic freedom to small and big businesses alike. There was no state-run education or healthcare, or government support of culture, and the frontier experience of settling the Wild West only contributed to the sense of personal freedom and lack of government control.[10]

Today when we speak of classical liberalism, or neo-liberalism, it is much more in terms of political parties (or ideological movements) *within* certain countries, which demand a return to the values of classical liberalism (low taxes, free-market capitalism, strong military and police, and minimal government presence otherwise). Ironically, these parties prefer to label themselves as "Conservative," because of the underlying desire to return to the "good old days" of classical liberalism. Recent world leaders who subscribe to this ideology include British Conservative prime minister Margaret Thatcher (1979–90); American Republican president Ronald Reagan (1981–9); and, perhaps to a lesser extent, Canadian Conservative prime ministers Brian Mulroney (1984–93) and Stephen Harper (2006–present).

When we think today of the US Republican Party—one of that country's big two parties—we note that it is an uneasy mixture of classical liberals (especially on economic issues like taxation and business regulation) and religious conservatives (especially on social issues like education, family, child, and marriage policies). Sometimes, these two groups are at odds with each other, especially over American foreign policy, wherein the classical liberal side of the party wants to stress non-intervention elsewhere and the pursuit of US business and trade opportunities everywhere, whereas the conservative side tends to favour a much more **hawkish** projection of US power around the globe—backed by military strength if need be—with a heavy emphasis on rewarding allies and punishing enemies.[11]

Socialism

Socialism began as a reaction against both classical liberalism and the Industrial Revolution. We saw in Chapter 2 that industrialization, beginning around 1750, sparked urbanization and mass-market manufacturing in factories, using mechanized methods and processes like the steam engine and the assembly line. The Industrial Revolution also generated enormous inequalities, especially in standards of living: factory-owners became as rich as royalty, while their workers laboured all day, in unsafe conditions, for meager wages. But those wages still beat the profits of working on the farm (especially out of season), and so labourers flooded the cities in search of work. Cities exploded in population, and struggled to handle the surge: vast slums developed, where living conditions—and public health conditions—were appalling. Socialists arose together, starting in the 1800s, to resist such realities. Among them were Karl Marx and Friedrich Engels, who noted the growing disparity between those who owned the means of production and those who owned only their ability to work, and foresaw the day when the workers would rise up to protest these realities.[12]

Socialism is, at its core, a rejection of the kind of inequality that conservatives and liberals feel comfortable with. The root of socialism is not just "society"—socialists have an *organic* view of society—but a firm conviction that too much inequality is both wrong in itself and harmful in its consequences. Socialists favour *more political and economic equality*, in particular. They think that "mere" **liberal equality**—that is, non-discrimination and equality of legal rights—is not enough: a wider and deeper *sharing of resources* must happen. And socialists view government as exactly the proper agent for bringing that greater equality about. So, while they have a *positive view of the state*, they certainly don't favour an entrenched elite class (the way conservatives do). And the liberal view strikes socialists as unacceptably selfish: resources and opportunities ought to be shared, and government is just the institution to oversee and enforce their equal distribution. But socialists share with liberals an orientation towards the future. Whereas the conservatives look upon the past with appreciation, socialists look upon it as a place where there was brutality, exclusion, discrimination, lack of opportunity, lack of sharing, and—as a result of these—considerable conflict. The past, for them, is something to be overcome, not cherished and preserved.[13]

Case Study: Socialist Societies, both Moderate and Democratic, and Extreme and Communist

There are two kinds of socialism: democratic socialism and "scientific socialism" (a.k.a. communism). In a system of **democratic socialism**, moderate socialist goals are pursued through democratic means, i.e. by winning free elections and thus a mandate from the people to, for example, raise taxes to pay for publicly funded programs of universal education and healthcare. Democratic socialist leaders prefer to persuade the public of the value of socialist policies, and to demonstrate the benefits of the pursuit of a more equal society, in which there is a broader sharing of resources and a citizenry more committed both to protecting the least well-off and to engaging actively, as a nation, in a robust political partnership. Democratic socialism has had its day in some English-speaking countries, like the UK, where it was the prevailing ideology between the Second World War and the rise of Thatcher's Conservatives. It still exists quite robustly in many parts of the world today (e.g. Scandinavia).[14]

Scientific socialism, by contrast, preferred not to wait, and instead to engage in direct, violent revolution to overthrow existing governments and implement very aggressive socialist measures, such as the abolition of privately owned property and the creation of publicly owned, state-run factories and farms. We saw in Chapter 1 that the communist ideology (with the USSR as its leading world model and champion) was defeated in the Cold War (1945–91) by the forces of liberal capitalism (as led by the US). Almost no countries are truly communist anymore, except perhaps Cuba and North Korea. All other one-time communist states—throughout central and eastern Europe, Latin America, and Southeast Asia—have fallen, replaced over the last 20 years with moderate regimes committed to an ordinary blend of conservative, liberal, and socialist elements. Even though the ruling party of China still calls itself "communist," it does *not* represent a pure form of the doctrine, as it has, for instance, robustly embraced for-profit business growth. China's is a non-democratic, authoritarian government—and one still heavily dependent on control of the military—but it's not a communist one.[15]

Welfare Liberalism

This brings us to the dominant political ideology in the developed world—indeed, probably the whole world—today: welfare liberalism. Essentially, **welfare liberalism** is the attempt to combine liberalism with socialism. So, on the liberalism side, there is *political commitment to democracy*, so that people are free to choose their leaders. There is also an *economic commitment to capitalism* and the free market, as defined in Chapter 1. Finally, there is a *legal and broader social commitment to everyone's human rights*, especially the full set of personal freedoms. Yet, on the socialist side, there is real *concern about inequality*, and a serious attempt to soften the edges of the worst socio-economic inequalities. This is done through the establishment of a **welfare state**: a government with a positive, robust, and intervening role to play, especially with regard to constructing a **social safety net** for the worst off in society. The social safety net is created (at least ideally) by taxing the wealthy and using their resources to provide welfare payments to the very poor and unemployed; the taxation system is also used to create publicly funded infrastructure, such as education and healthcare systems. The welfare state also typically boasts robust anti-discrimination laws as further evidence of the commitment to greater equality, alongside special provisions for such historically disadvantaged groups as women, indigenous populations, and other visible minorities.[16]

Welfare liberalism wasn't merely a response to the socialist critique of classical liberal society and its hands-off, *laissez-faire* (i.e. "let it be" or "leave it alone") approach to governance. It was also a practical, political response to three major historical events:

1. the Great Depression of the 1930s, mentioned above;

2. World War II (1939–45), discussed in Chapter 1; and

3. the return of a huge wave of veteran soldiers after World War II.

In terms of the first, many argued that the economic collapse of the 1930s could have been avoided with the right kind of government intervention. Indeed, Western economies started to grow again only after governments decided to start spending (e.g. on infrastructure projects, such as roads, railways, and electricity grids). In the United States, president Franklin Delano Roosevelt's **New Deal** was one such program, and its perceived success paved the way for positive state intervention in the economy worldwide. (Roosevelt was a Democrat, and since his time in office, the US Democratic Party—the other of the country's big two parties—has been committed to welfare liberalism.)[17]

The second major event, World War II, brought a dramatic increase in state intervention throughout society, by sheer dint of necessity: the need to organize society's diverse resources and direct them effectively towards the one overriding objective of winning the war. When this (eventually) worked (at least for the West), it was only natural to ask, why not apply such powers and energies to other problems, for the sake of creating a better life

Canadian Insights

Canada as a Welfare Liberal Society

Even though Canada has political parties representing every value in the spectrum (Conservatives, Liberals, New Democrats, Greens), it is apparent that, overall, Canada is a welfare liberal society, as defined above. It is a democracy, and its economic system is free-market capitalism. Moreover, there is a clear commitment to securing everyone's human rights, as legally guaranteed in the Canadian Charter of Rights and Freedoms. Every Canadian is entitled to the basic set of human rights, to:

- personal security
- private property ownership
- non-discrimination
- political participation
- a range of **due process** protections in the event of one's arrest and trial (e.g. the right to consult a lawyer)
- recognition as a rights-bearing person before the law.

This is in addition to the many personal liberties Canadians are entitled to, such as freedom of speech, religion, association, conscience, peaceful assembly, movement, occupational choice, whom or whether to marry, and so on. Canada, clearly, is a liberal society, where personal freedom is a cherished value.

But Canada also has clear elements of socialism. There is a robust welfare state—much larger and more intrusive than, say, the American one. Indeed, this is one of the clearest differences between the two North American neighbours: Canada's welfare state is much closer to the European model than to the American. Canada has publicly funded, high-quality universal education at both the primary and the secondary levels. Post-secondary education, and advanced university research, is also subsidized heavily by the government. There is universal, publicly funded healthcare coverage—something noticeably lacking in the United States. The third major social welfare program is unemployment insurance, which is an income safety net for those who lose their jobs and/or are permanently unemployable (e.g. owing to a severe medical condition). Finally, almost all physical infrastructure works are done, or funded, by government.

Government intervention in Canada is not limited to these four pillars of the welfare state: it stretches well beyond and includes such things as government support for the arts and culture, government ownership of media (the CBC on radio, television, and the Internet, for example), government-run transportation systems (e.g. VIA Rail and Ontario's GO Transit), government funding for a whole range of civil society and NGO activities, and government subsidies for corporations, technologies, and industries deemed vital to the Canadian economy and its future.[18]

for us all? Indeed, the soldiers, upon returning in their millions from the battlefields—the third major event—voted overwhelmingly in favour of the welfare state. Having made huge sacrifices in Europe, or in the Far East, they felt they were owed something by the countries they'd fought for—job training, economic security, education for their children, and a better way of life in general. This is important to note, for the development of the welfare state is often portrayed—by classical liberals—as the result of "far-left union activism," or "socialist fans of big government"; in truth—at least in the Western democracies—it was the soldiers and their families who voted it in, and repeatedly so, in the post-war years.[19]

Ideology and National Culture

Let's close this section by restating the importance of political structures and ideologies to culture in general, and to global studies in particular. This importance can be summarized as follows:

- Political structures shape many aspects of life inside a national culture.
- Countries bring their ideologies with them into the global arena, when they interact with other countries. For instance, the socialist countries of Scandinavia are the world's most generous givers of aid to the poor countries of the Global South, which is totally consistent with their values. (More on aid and development in the forthcoming chapter.)
- Generally, we can predict close and friendly relations between countries with similar ideologies (like Canada and the US), and more difficult (or even conflicted) relations between countries with very different political values (like the US and Iran).

RELIGION

By estimated number of adherents, here are the world's top 10 major religious beliefs, in order from top to bottom:[20]

1. Christianity
2. Islam
3. secular/non-religious (atheism, agnosticism, humanism, etc.)
4. Hinduism
5. Chinese folk religion/Confucianism
6. Buddhism
7. indigenous/folk/tribal religions
8. Japanese Shintoism
9. Sikhism
10. Judaism

Figure 3.2 is a map of the general geographical distribution of these religions. (Note how similar this map is to last chapter's map of Huntingdon's world civilizations, illustrating religion's potent historical impact on global culture.)

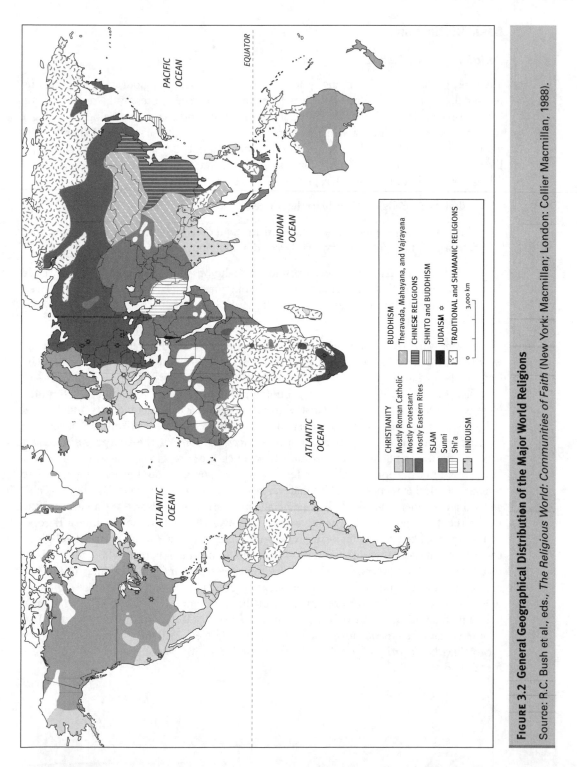

FIGURE 3.2 General Geographical Distribution of the Major World Religions

Source: R.C. Bush et al., eds., *The Religious World: Communities of Faith* (New York: Macmillan; London: Collier Macmillan, 1988).

Basic Distinctions

Religious versus Secular

The most basic distinction among systems of belief is between religious and non-religious (or secular). The word **religion** derives from the Latin *religio*, literally a "re-linking" or "linking back." This refers to the link between humans and the divine being (or beings) who created humankind—and the universe as a whole—in the first place. Different religions, as we'll see below, have quite different views about the nature of the divine, how the universe came to be, and how humans ought to relate to the divine (and among themselves). **Non-religious**, or **secular**, people tend to come in three sorts:

- **atheists** are people who believe that there are no gods

- **agnostics** are people who don't take a firm stand on whether any gods exist, and who are simply not motivated by, or interested in, religious concerns at all

- **secular humanists** prefer to substitute for a religious code their own systematic code of beliefs, a code that refers *not* to the divine but only to humanity, and to the need for human beings to treat each other decently, at minimum by respecting universal human rights.

These three sorts of non-religious people are, when combined, thought to compose the world's third-largest belief system (or attitude towards these kinds of issues). And secularism, while spread worldwide, is represented most strongly in the developed West—in Europe especially—and is seen to be gaining ground, as formerly Christian societies turn increasingly secular. In general, statistics confirm that poor nations tend to be much more religious than rich ones, with the large and important exception of the United States.[21]

Indeed, for all their similarities and connections, one of the sharpest differences between the United States and Canada is how much more religious America is, and how much more like Europe Canada is, in terms of Canadians' attitudes toward religion. There is also statistical evidence that, for whatever reason, Northern peoples tend to be *less religious* than Southern peoples.[22] This principle applies to comparisons of Canada and the US, of the developed and developing worlds, and even of northern and southern Europe. Some experts, like Charles Taylor, even describe contemporary Europe as a **post-religious society**—perhaps the world's first ever—although some Australians might want to claim that title for their country.[23] Now officially, the erstwhile communist regimes of the former USSR and central and eastern Europe, and even the current communist regime of present-day China, were (or are) atheist. But this was more a reflection of official party policy than actual, widespread belief amongst the people. Today, on the other hand, when people speak of countries in Europe—and Australia/New Zealand—being secular, they mean that *the majority of people truly are non-religious* in at least one of the three ways mentioned above.[24]

Monotheistic versus Polytheistic

The second core distinction among belief systems is between monotheistic and polytheistic religions. **Monotheistic religions** believe in one God (*mono* = "one"), whereas **polytheistic religions** believe in many (*poly* = "many"). The three largest monotheistic religions, by population, are Christianity, Islam, and Judaism. Indeed, these three religions—all of which originated in the Middle East—are often categorized as being "**Abrahamic**," since they all share the prophet Abraham as a common figure of both religious and ethnic significance. Abraham, reputed to have lived around 1800 BCE, is thought to have been a descendant of Noah—of Ark and Flood fame—and to have had seven sons. These sons went on to establish a number of family bloodlines crucial to Jewish, Christian, and Islamic communities. Abraham is thought to be the "one common ancestor," distantly related to each of Moses, Jesus, and Mohammed. Historically, Judaism came first, and its origins are recounted in the Hebrew Bible (known to Christians as the Old Testament). Next came Christianity, with its belief in Jesus Christ as the son of God and in the New Testament as further revelation from God. Finally, Islam acknowledges not only Jewish prophets but Jesus, too (yet only as one in a line of respected prophets and teachers). The prophet for **Muslims** (i.e. those who believe in Islam) is Mohammed, who lived about 600 years after Jesus is thought to have died.

This interwoven history, shared by the Abrahamic and monotheistic religions, is an important factor not only in the lives of all these people but also in their politics. For example, when international peace talks are held in a Middle Eastern country, and local countries are represented there, alongside US and sometimes European officials, almost everyone in their speeches will make surprisingly robust reference to "the one true God, uniting us all," in an effort to use cultural similarities as leverage to solve political differences.[25]

Polytheistic religions include Hinduism and the various folk or indigenous religions of various peoples, be they North American or Australian Aboriginal peoples, Chinese, Japanese, or the various peoples of the Caribbean and sub-Saharan Africa. Polytheistic religions recognize many gods or divinities, and typically prefer to talk of an underlying cosmic order, or force, as the all-pervasive context in which all of us—including the various gods—exist. To this extent, a number of polytheistic religions are termed **Dharmic** or **Taoistic**. These terms are *in contrast to* "Abrahamic." Whereas the Abrahamic religions are monotheistic and stress a **personal connection**, or **covenant**, between God and His people, the Dharmic/Taoistic religions do *not* highlight a personal connection between humanity and divinity. There is, rather, an underlying cosmic force or fate—a dharma, kharma, or Tao—that is highly impersonal and absolutely binding on us all—even the lesser gods within the belief system. It is almost like gravity: impersonal and ruling the fate of everything. The aim, then, for adherents of Dharmic or Taoistic religions is to adjust themselves to this underlying, all-pervasive order or structure. This is the route to security and serenity, being utterly aligned with the very cosmos.[26]

Folk versus Non-Folk Religions

Another way of approaching different belief systems is to distinguish between indigenous (or folk) religions and non-folk religions. Essentially, **folk religions** are systems of belief and ritual that are *unique to a people*—in other words, to a coherent nationality or ethnic grouping. Judaism and Hinduism are folk religions in this sense, with the first being the preserve of the Jewish people, both inside Israel and in the Jewish **diaspora** scattered around the world (but especially in Europe and North America). And Hinduism is the preserve of East Indian peoples, both inside India and in the Indian diaspora scattered around the world (but especially in the old British Empire countries of America, Australia, Canada, South Africa, and the UK itself). Shintosim, in Japan, also counts as a folk religion, alongside indigenous faiths like the so-called "tribal" religions of various Aboriginal and African peoples.

Non-folk religions, by contrast, are religions *not limited* to one group, ethnicity, or nationality. Christianity is the clearest example—the world's most diversely spread religion—alongside secular humanism and, perhaps to a lesser extent, Buddhism and Islam. (While Islam is quite concentrated in the Middle East and North Africa, the largest Islamic nation by population is actually Indonesia, which is quite far afield from the Arabian peninsula.)[27]

Fast-Growing versus Slow-Growing

A topical and hotly disputed question among religion researchers concerns which are the fastest-growing religions and which are growing more slowly (or even losing ground). For a while, it was commonly assumed that Islam was the fastest-growing religion, given robust rates of population growth in traditionally Muslim countries. However, recent research, for instance by the PEW Research Center,[28] suggests that Christianity instead merits this title, even in spite of clear trends to the contrary in the developed world, including a decline in church attendance, a decrease in religious school enrolment, and a big rise in secularization. This research suggests that Christianity is spreading rapidly in Russia and former Communist Bloc countries of central and eastern Europe, as well as in sub-Saharan Africa and, especially, China. Some experts have even declared that the fastest-growing religious group in the world—by population over the past several years—is actually Spanish-speaking Catholics throughout Latin America. It needs to be stressed, however, that there are substantial difficulties involved with estimating the numbers of "believers" of any given religion.[29]

Key Elements of the Three Biggest Abrahamic/ Monotheistic Religions[30]

Table 3.1 provides an overview of the main features of the three biggest monotheistic, or Abrahamic, religions: Christianity, Judaism, and Islam.

TABLE 3.1 Key Elements of Christianity, Judaism, and Islam

Religion	Internal Divisions	Sacred Book & Concept of God	Key Figures & Symbols	Religious Temples & Observances	Core Concepts & Basic Duties	Afterlife?
Judaism	Orthodox vs Conservative vs Reform; Orthodox Judaism teaches strict adherence to Jewish law and its traditional observances, including numerous laws governing religious and everyday life; Reform Judaism began as an attempt to adapt to modern changes in social, political, and cultural life; Conservative Judaism, prevalent esp. in North America, attempts to preserve Jewish tradition and ritual but with a more flexible approach than that favoured by Orthodox Judaism.	• *Book*: the Hebrew Bible (known to Christians as the Old Testament), comprising the Law ("Torah"), the Prophets, and the Hagiographa ("Writings"); the *Talmud* and the *Midrash* • *God*: One God, called "Lord" or "God" in English (his name is never spoken in Hebrew); Judaism is strictly monotheistic	• *Figures*: the patriarchs and matriarchs Abraham and Sarah, Isaac and Rebecca, and Jacob and Leah and Rachel; the prophet and lawgiver Moses; other prophets, including Samuel, Isaiah, and Ezekiel; the kings Solomon and David • *Symbols*: the Star of David; the flag of Israel; the menorah; the kippa (skullcap); the tallith (prayer shawl); the shofar (ram's horn)	• *Temple*: Synagogue • *Observances*: weekly Sabbath; Rosh Hashanah (New Year); Yom Kippur (Day of Atonement); Hanukkah (Festival of Lights); Passover (liberation)	• There is a covenant, or contract, between God and the Jews, who are his "chosen people". Those who have faith in God will be rewarded; the Promised Land—the land of Canaan, promised to Abraham and his descendants—is part of this reward. • The principal laws are expressed as the Ten Commandments; Jews must obey these and other of God's laws and follow all the observances. • A goal of Judaism is to keep the faith alive among the Jewish people; Judaism is a "non-proselytizing" faith, i.e. it does not aspire to gain converts.	Jews believe in a messiah who will come and lead them to the promised land, situated in *this* lifetime and *this* world; Judaism does not adopt an institutional belief in the afterlife (i.e. Heaven) the way that Christianity does.

continued

TABLE 3.1 Key Elements of Christianity, Judaism, and Islam *(continued)*

Religion	Internal Divisions	Sacred Book & Concept of God	Key Figures & Symbols	Religious Temples & Observances	Core Concepts & Basic Duties	Afterlife?
Christianity	Catholic vs Protestant vs Eastern Orthodox; the Roman Catholic Church acknowledges the pope as its head; Protestants and Orthodox Christians do not accept the authority of the papacy.	• *Book:* the Bible (comprising the Old Testament and New Testament) • *God:* the Trinity—God, the Father; Christ, the Son; the Holy Spirit—representing a nuanced monotheism	• *Figures:* the patriarchs, prophets, and kings of the Old Testament (as identified above with Judaism); Jesus Christ; the Virgin Mary; Jewish preacher and prophet John the Baptist; the Gospel writers Matthew, Mark, Luke, and John; the apostles, esp. Peter and Paul • *Symbols:* the cross or crucifix; a dove in flight; a fish	• *Temple:* Church • *Observances:* weekly sabbath; Christmas (birth of Jesus); Good Friday (crucifixion of Jesus); Easter Sunday (resurrection of Jesus)	• God became human—as Jesus—to show humans the true path of righteousness. • Jesus was crucified, died, and rose from the dead, proving his divinity. Jesus's life is the model to follow, embodying the qualities of peace, love, forgiveness, and redemption. • Christians ought to obey not just the Old Testament teachings but the New Testament, too, including, especially, the "golden rule" (i.e. do unto others as you would have others do unto you). • A faith open to anyone, Christianity is a proselytizing faith, mandating believers to convert non-believers.	The soul survives death and (in the view of most Christians) one's conduct in life determines its fate: goodness is the path to Heaven; evil is the road to Hell. Some Protestant faiths believe in predestination, the doctrine that all events—including salvation—are foreordained by God.

continued

TABLE 3.1 Key Elements of Christianity, Judaism, and Islam (continued)

Religion	Internal Divisions	Sacred Book & Concept of God	Key Figures & Symbols	Religious Temples & Observances	Core Concepts & Basic Duties	Afterlife?
Islam	Sunni vs Shi'a; Sunnis make up the majority of Muslims and differ from Shi'as in their acceptance of the first three caliphs (leaders) following the death of the prophet Mohammed; Shi'as reject the first three Sunni caliphs.	• *Book*: the Qur'an • *God*: Allah; Islam is strictly monotheistic. Muslims believe Allah to be the same God worshipped by Jews, Christians, and other monotheists.	• *Figures*: the prophet Mohammed; his family. Islam recognizes many of the prophets of Judaism and Christianity (Abraham, Moses, Jesus, etc.) but only as prophets lesser than Mohammed. • *Symbols*: the crescent moon (often with star); the colour green; the kafi (skullcap); the hijab (headscarf)	• *Temple*: Mosque • *Observances*: the "five pillars" of the Qur'an: the profession of faith (shahadah), prayer, almsgiving, the annual ritual of fasting during Ramadan, and pilgrimage to Mecca (the hajj) at least once in one's lifetime; prayer rituals, five times daily	• God revealed the Qur'an to the prophet Mohammed, who spent his life converting his region to Islam by means of a military conquest; the unity of political power and religious doctrine is an enduring theme. • "Islam" means "surrender to God". The will of Allah and the command to follow it are commonly referenced in Islam, which emphasizes, generally, the need to master one's baser desires and put oneself into pure obedience to God. • The "Five Pillars" of the Qur'an stress faith, the observances, and charity to the poor. • Islam, like Christianity, is a proselytizing faith.	As in Christian belief, the soul survives death and is cast by Allah into either Heaven or Hell. Heaven is Paradise, a place of abundance, green fertile lushness, and delight.

Source: See note 30.

Case Study: The Arab–Israeli Conflict

It is a mistake to think of the Arab–Israeli conflict as primarily one of religion, especially since (as noted in Table 3.1) Judaism is a **non-proselytizing faith**, meaning that it does not actively seek out converts. Nevertheless, this is a convenient moment to mention this struggle, a very important and enduring one in modern international politics. And religion is not irrelevant, as we'll see. But, as we'll also see—and as I here stress—this conflict is complex and multifaceted, and has as much to do with territory and the desire of nations for security as it does with spirituality. I should also stress that this is a very controversial subject, about which even the most basic concepts and terms are contested. Still, the subject cannot be ignored.[31]

The Jews originated in the Middle East, probably around Palestine. They grew to have prosperous kingdoms in the area, for instance as governed by King David, succeeded by his son Solomon (both of whom are thought to be ancestors of Jesus through Jesus's earthly father, Joseph). But territorial control became an issue, with the Egyptians and the Romans contesting it, and the Jews lost control over their homeland, beginning between the eighth and sixth centuries BCE and culminating with the sack of Jerusalem in 70 CE. While a number of Jews stayed in the Middle East, many more left for Europe and, later, North America. This is known as the Jewish **diaspora**.

It remained, for centuries, an object of Jewish yearning to re-establish a self-governing Jewish community in Palestine. This yearning came to be called **Zionism** (after Mount Zion, a hill in Palestine, near Jerusalem, where once stood a fortress conquered by King David). At the end of the First World War, in 1918, Palestine was governed by the **Turkish**, or **Ottoman**, **Empire**. This empire—centred around Constantinople (present-day Istanbul)—was Muslim. Palestine itself was inhabited by **Arabs** (an ethnic term referring to those whose ancestors came from the Arabian peninsula, who share certain physical commonalities amongst them, as well as the Arabic language). The Ottoman Empire was on the losing side of World War I, and had only weak control over Palestine to begin with. Jewish leaders lobbied the heads of the victorious **Allied nations** (notably Britain, the US, and the USSR) to support Zionism, which would punish the Ottomans and reward the Jews. The Western powers were willing to do the first but not quite (yet) the second. Britain took over the administration of Palestine but did not cede control of it to the Jewish people. It did, however, vaguely commit in principle to eventual Jewish self-governance via the **Balfour Declaration of 1917**.

At the end of World War II (1945), with the horrors of the Holocaust seemingly providing ample evidence of the need for a self-governed, self-protected Jewish homeland, Jewish leaders *demanded* a follow-through on the promise of the Balfour Declaration. According to their argument, the war had proven that Jews couldn't count on the protection of any nation-state, and thus they needed their own. What better place, then, than the ancient biblical homeland in Palestine? The Allies, especially Britain and the United States, agreed, and they took measures to pave the way for the foundation of the new Jewish state, Israel. The substantial problem, though, was that there were many hundreds of thousands of Palestinian Arabs living on that land. Moreover, these Palestinians, quite plausibly, replied: "Look, we're not the Nazis;

we had nothing to do with the Holocaust. And yet, because of it, we are going to lose *our* land?" The Palestinians had, after all, been living there for centuries.

The formation of Israel went ahead in 1948, to the great joy of many Jews and to the great despair of many Palestinian Arabs, who were coerced by the Allies into vacating their former homes to make way for the Jews (some 700,000 Palestinians were deemed "refugees" by the United Nations, in a 1950 census). Thus began the Arab–Israeli conflict, which endures to this day. The Jews view the creation of Israel as both a necessity for their survival—especially in view of what occurred during the Holocaust—and, perhaps, one step closer to achieving the Jewish Promised Land. But Arabs worldwide view it as the displacement and disenfranchisement of Palestinian Arabs at the hands of both the Israelis and their Western supporters, especially the US. Few things unite **the Arab street**—i.e. public opinion among the majority in the Muslim world—more than sympathy for the Palestinians and anger towards Israel.

Jews view the creation of Israel as both a necessity for their survival and, perhaps, one step closer to achieving the Jewish Promised Land. Arabs worldwide view it as the displacement and disenfranchisement of Palestinian Arabs at the hands of both the Israelis and their Western supporters, especially the US.

When Israel's existence was formally announced, on 14 May 1948, its Arab neighbours immediately declared war: they attacked, trying to strangle the new nation in its infancy. But Israel—with Allied help—fought back, and had actually gained territory by the time a ceasefire was reached in 1949. Since then, Israel has, at one time or another, been at war with every one of its Arab neighbours. It has won every time, and has even expanded its original 1948 territory through some of these wars, especially the **Six Days War** of 1967. Moreover, it has carved out for itself a decent democracy amidst what was—until very recently—a sea of poor and unstable **authoritarian regimes** (i.e. undemocratic governments, ruling by virtue of military force and police control and *not* by virtue of the consent of the people, as determined by free and fair public elections).

This much is to Israel's credit. To the downside, however, Israel must maintain enormous vigilance, and massive military expenditures. (It is helped very substantially, in this regard, by the US in particular, year in and year out.) Every adult Israeli—man or woman—must serve a conscripted term in the **Israeli Defence Forces** (IDF), and everyone knows that Israel has nuclear weapons, even though it has never publicly acknowledged this. Israel's relations with its neighbours are strained at best, ranging from liveable agreements with Egypt and Jordan to outright hostility with Syria and, especially, Iran, whose government is still officially committed to Israel's destruction. Israel's location, hostile neighbours, and small size (population: 7 million) make growing its economy difficult. And then there's the huge remaining issue of the Palestinians.

Displaced in their own land, the Palestinian Arabs have endured a long and varied journey with Israel, starting out as powerless victims and transforming angrily over time—via the **Palestinian Liberation Organization** (PLO)—into an organized political and military movement determined to secure an independent state of Palestine, and fully prepared to use violent force against both Israeli citizens and the IDF in order to achieve it. Recently and thankfully, however, the PLO has laid down its weapons and

FIGURE 3.3 Israel and the Palestinian Territories

*Denotes Israeli-occupied Palestinian territories whose current status is subject to the Israeli–Palestinian Interim Agreement; the permanent status of these territories will be determined through further negotiation.

Source: worldatlas.com

entered the democratic political process. The PLO-led Fatah party currently governs jointly with Hamas, winners of the 2006 parliamentary election but considered by some countries to be a terrorist organization. Together, Fatah and Hamas represent the Palestinian people both within Israel proper and in some of the disputed territories captured by Israel through war, notably the Gaza Strip, the Golan Heights, and the West Bank. The once daily violence between Israel and Palestine has now abated, and movement toward a more enduring solution has been made, focusing on improving, in a concrete way, the daily lives of both Israelis and Palestinians. What this solution will look like is not exactly clear, though often mentioned is the so-called **two-state solution**, wherein there will be separate nation-states, Israel and Palestine, each governing its own people and territory. But drawing the exact lines of that territory, and ensuring for each community security from violence, sufficient water, and a shot at prosperity, is proving extremely complex.

One final word about this issue, and it applies equally to every other religion, too: *there are different kinds of believers for each religion* and, indeed, for almost every kind of belief, especially moral and political opinion. The Arab–Israeli conflict has never been a simple, two-sided conflict. All along, there have been those, in both camps, who have sought peace and accommodation with the other side, just as there have been those of extreme, radical belief, unwilling to compromise at all. For example, in 1995, Israeli prime minister Yitzhak Rabin was assassinated—not by a Palestinian, but by an Israeli extremist who thought Rabin was giving too much away to the Palestinians during peace talks. In general, there is a division within Judaism between **Reform** and **Orthodox** Jews, with the former being more moderate and the latter more strict regarding both the interpretation and the application of God's laws. In Israel, some ultra-orthodox Jews have been firmly opposed to the peace process, and they have taken to becoming settlers in some of the disputed territories, forming residential religious communities on them and standing their ground (which, they are convinced, has been gifted to them by God). On the Palestinian side, there are moderates—indeed, statistics show that the majority, in almost any given religious or political population, are moderates—and extremists, too. For a long time, the extremists in the PLO had the upper hand, and they confronted Israel with indiscriminate armed resistance. Eventually, the moderates prevailed; violence was renounced; the peace process entered; and clear progress was made on making life better. Whenever we discuss these conflicts, and these religions, we must always be mindful of *the spectrum of beliefs*, and especially the omnipresent difference between compromising **moderates** (who reach out to others, and hold their own beliefs more lightly) and uncompromising **extremists** (who turn away from others, and hold their own beliefs more tightly, and who are, generally, willing to act much more radically).

> *Statistics show that the majority, in almost any given religious or political population, are moderates.*

Key Elements of the Three Biggest Eastern/Polytheistic Religions[32]

Table 3.2 provides an overview of the main features of the three biggest Eastern religious traditions: Hinduism, Chinese religions, and Buddhism.

TABLE 3.2 Key Elements of Hinduism, Chinese Folk Religions, and Buddhism

Religion	Internal Divisions	Sacred Book & Concept of God	Key Figures & Symbols	Religious Temples & Observances	Core Concepts & Basic Duties	Afterlife?
Hinduism	There are no formal divisions, though followers often pray more to one god over others.	• *Books:* The Vedas—4 collections of hymns and ritual texts—are the most authoritative texts; the epics (the *Ramayana* and the *Mahabharata,* which includes the *Bhagavad Gita*), the *Puranas* ("Old Tales"), and *Upanishads* (philosophical texts on the nature of knowledge) are also important. • *God:* Hinduism is polytheistic, with many gods; among the most worshipped are the triad of Brahma (the creator), Vishnu (the sustainer), and Shiva (the destroyer).	• *Figures:* All the gods and goddesses (Brahma, Vishnu, Shiva, Devi, Ganesh, etc.); gurus and sages, including Adi Shankara, Ramunja, and Ramananda • *Symbols:* statues of the gods; the lotus flower; the bindi (decorative mark worn in the middle of the forehead by Hindu women)	• various temples and observances devoted to various gods • Major festivals include Holi (in spring) and Maha Shivaratri (in winter), and Divali, the festival of light.	• A folk religion among Indian people, "Hindu" derives from "India" and the river "Indus". • There are many gods, but they and we exist in a universe bound together by a cosmic force (dharma) that is impersonal and all-pervasive. • One must align oneself with this force in both mind and conduct; the "Ten Commitments" are aids in this regard: they include non-harming, not lying or stealing, being clean and self-disciplined, being studious, and obedience to the gods. • A comprehensive philosophical system that blends belief with physical practices (e.g. yoga).	Most Hindus believe the human soul is immortal. Karma—one's good and bad actions—determines the quality of the soul's rebirth in future lives. Eventually the soul will achieve liberation from the shackles of karma and the cycle of reincarnation.

continued

TABLE 3.2 Key Elements of Hinduism, Chinese Folk Religions, and Buddhism (*continued*)

Religion	Internal Divisions	Sacred Book & Concept of God	Key Figures & Symbols	Religious Temples & Observances	Core Concepts & Basic Duties	Afterlife?
Confucianism/ Daoism/ Chinese folk religion	There are no formal divisions, though followers often blend different elements (tai-chi, ancestor worship) in different ways.	• *Book:* The *Analects*, Confucius's ideas about the importance of practical moral values, collected by his disciples; Confucianism is perhaps the least book-bound of all major religions. *Dao De Jing* is fundamental to Daoism. • *God:* There is an all-pervasive Tao, or cosmic order; within it, opposing forces—like yin and yang—exist and compete.	• *Figures:* Confucius, Mencius, and Xunzi; Laozi, the founder of Daoism; one's own ancestors— Chinese religion is more about shared ritual practice than any key figures. • *Symbols:* the yin/yang symbol ☯; various foods (e.g. the mandarin orange) and colours (e.g. red, gold)	• Chinese religions are the least temple-bound of all. • *Observances:* Confucius's birthday; Chinese New Year; Autumn Moon Festival	• A folk religion among Chinese people, it blends various beliefs and practices such as Confucianism, ancestor worship, Chinese medicine, and ritual physical practices like tai-chi and even martial arts. • There is Dao, "the Way", an all-pervasive cosmic order, within which opposing elements— yin and yang—exist. Bringing oneself into harmony with Dao is the most important thing. • Confucius was deeply optimistic and urged excellence both in knowledge/career and morally/socially. • Qi (or chi) is the life force of the universe: one must have it flowing through oneself appropriately. • Individual excellence and social harmony are key values.	Though there is a concept of Heaven ("T'ien"), most of this belief system is focused on living well and successfully in *this* life and *this* world.

continued

TABLE 3.2 Key Elements of Hinduism, Chinese Folk Religions, and Buddhism *(continued)*

Religion	Internal Divisions	Sacred Book & Concept of God	Key Figures & Symbols	Religious Temples & Observances	Core Concepts & Basic Duties	Afterlife?
Buddhism	Theravada vs Mahayana vs Vajrayana. Theravada Buddhism is conservative, and is dominant in Sri Lanka and Southeast Asia; Mahayana Buddhism (or "Zen" Buddhism) is typically concerned with spiritual practice and is dominant in East Asia and Vietnam; Vajrayana Buddhism, dominant in Tibet and the Himalayas, emphasizes ritual.	• *Book:* Zen has no book; however, Theravada does have the *Tripitaka* ("Three Baskets"): *vinaya* (monastic rules), *sutras* (discourses), and *abhidharma* (treatises). Vajrayana has the *Kanjur* (tantric texts) and *Tanjur* (commentaries). • *God:* Zen is often called "atheistic". Theravada believes in an underlying impersonal cosmic order.	• *Figures:* the Buddha (Siddharta Gautama); monks and lamas, esp. the Dalai Lama • *Symbols:* Statues of the Buddha; the lotus flower; the Bodhi Tree; "Zen gardens," distinctive rock gardens found at Buddhist temples; the mandala; the distinctive saffron robes worn by Buddhist monks.	• *Temples:* many monasteries and temples • *Observances:* Buddha's birthday; the day Buddha achieved enlightenment; sometimes blended in with Chinese or Hindu festivals.	• A religion open to all, Buddhism began with the Buddha achieving enlightenment. Formerly a rich prince, the Buddha gave up his privileges to help the needy, found monasteries, and alleviate suffering. He is not venerated as a god but as a fully enlightened human. • The "Three Characteristics of Existence" are suffering, impermanence, and no-self. • The path to enlightenment is to understand and alleviate suffering, through wisdom, compassion, assistance, and meditation. Emphasis on control of the self, letting go of one's ego, and even (with Zen) eliminating the self, as it melts into oneness with the universe.	As in Hinduism, a failure to achieve enlightenment results in rebirth until one does achieve this. Nirvana is the state of bliss associated with final enlightenment.

Source: See note 32.

Case Study: Tibet and China

In the late 1950s, the government of Tibet was overthrown, in war, by the government of China. Tibet was incorporated into China and is now administered as the Tibetan Autonomous Region. During the late 1960s and early 1970s, China experienced a period of political upheaval known as **the Cultural Revolution**. This entailed the systematic killing, exiling, and imprisoning of thousands—perhaps millions—of people, especially intellectuals and cultural and religious figures who did not perfectly fall in line with the atheist ideology of the Chinese Communist Party. As part of this process, nearly all of Tibet's Buddhist monasteries were destroyed, its monks killed or imprisoned. Since the end of the Cultural Revolution, some monks have returned (though the overall number of monks remains strictly controlled), and Buddhist monasteries have begun to resume some of the central cultural functions they used to perform, such as ensuring the protection and survival of the Tibetan language.[33]

Tibet's political status—its very future, in fact—remains controversial. The government position in China may be summarized as follows:

- Tibet is a part of China.

- A number of Tibetan figures are separatists who seek to destabilize China and achieve independence for Tibet. (A **separatist** aspires to have his or her nation released from its existing political arrangements so that it may become an independent nation-state.)

A Chinese tourist takes a photo of Tibetan monks prostrating in front of the Potala palace in Lhasa in the Tibet Autonomous Region, China. Most jurisdictions welcome tourism for its benefits to the local economy. Is tourism good for Lhasa? (© GYI NSEA/iStockphoto)

- Tibet enjoys considerable **autonomy** (i.e. political self-rule) already.
- The harsh measures of the Cultural Revolution are long over—Tibetans have nothing to fear from China.
- China has brought much development assistance into the poor, mountainous area of Tibet.

The counter-perspective, of some Tibetans, is that the so-called "autonomy" is merely a title and *not* a reality; the clampdown on Tibetan Buddhism and broader Tibetan culture (in favour of Chinese culture) remains, and there are allegations that China has encouraged the settlement of non-Tibetans inside Tibet in order to dilute the population of Tibetans and strengthen China's hold on the region. Plus, many Tibetans dispute China's claims over Tibetan territory to begin with. Third-party observers, like the international human rights NGO **Amnesty International**, note that it is very difficult for outsiders to get into Tibet to verify any of these perspectives, and perhaps that fact alone reveals lingering controversies and difficulties. All sides do admit that there was a major uprising in 2008, followed by a violent government crackdown. For its part, the government of China is very thin-skinned when foreign countries, such as Canada and the US, welcome the **Dalai Lama**—the head of Tibetan Buddhism and, prior to the establishment of Chinese rule, Tibet's ruler—into their nations, and extend him high-level meetings with senior government officials.[34]

Studies in Technology

New Media and the Global "Digital Divide"

I don't need to tell you the importance of new media in our lives nowadays. We get up in the morning and, almost immediately, check our cellphone or smartphone for messages. We turn on the computer to scan the latest news headlines and celebrity gossip, access our multiple e-mail accounts, and check up on both friends and "frenemies" on Facebook. We send out texts and tweets, and most of us have our own blogs and/or websites to maintain. Texting is actually changing the way we talk and spell, and even adding new vocabulary to our languages. We rely on these devices and technologies in so many ways throughout our day: GPS for driving to work or to school; iPod for music, to kill the boredom while doing so; laptop with WiFi, just to be able to function at school or work *at all*; Internet for shopping and research of all kinds, not to mention music, TV, YouTube, and other forms of entertainment; social media for our social lives; and the alarm on the smartphone to wake us up in the morning, to start the cycle over again.

Yet the reality is that this speaks to life *only in the developed world*. It is estimated that 88 per cent of all Internet users reside in the developed Western world, or Global North, which, you'll recall from Chapter 1, is home to just a quarter of the world's total population. The latest statistics put global Internet access at around 2 billion people.[35] While this is up (dramatically) from only 1 million Internet users as recently as 1992, that 2 billion figure nevertheless amounts to *less than one-third of the world's population*. Putting these facts together, we arrive at the harsh conclusion that somewhere between 66 and 75 per cent of all of humans—and maybe more—do *not* have access to the Internet and all the latest devices that rely on it.[36] Can you imagine how much their lives differ from yours on a daily basis, and could you imagine your own life bereft of the benefits of such technologies?

The world of Internet-driven gadgets and media is, overwhelmingly, the preserve of upper-income, highly educated, and urban citizens of the democratic countries of the developed West. Some experts, such as Pippa Norris, have thus concluded that there's an emerging global "digital divide" that mirrors, and adds yet another dimension to, the North–South divide that we examined in Chapter 1. The **global digital divide**, Norris writes, refers to "rapidly growing disparities in the utilization, expenditure, and availability of technology between the developed and developing worlds."[37] And yet the potential for the Internet to aid the Global South is immense, through:

- online training and education programs
- **e-medicine** (where people use the Internet to access health information and to consult directly with medical professionals from remote locales)
- **e-government** (where people can access government data needed to apply for government jobs, report crimes, search land ownership titles, etc.)
- international trade, by helping buyers and sellers find each other much more easily and cheaply than through face-to-face interactions
- accessible financial information, on daily banking for instance, to help people earn more and gain wealth
- weather information, which is vital for agriculture
- greater communication in general, to help coordinate behaviour and solve common problems
- all the potential daily lifestyle benefits mentioned above, which we now take for granted.[38]

But there are very substantial obstacles to narrowing the digital divide:

- the costs of building infrastructure, especially in those parts of the developing world that lack basic electrical service
- educational and literacy realities: to benefit from these technologies, one needs to be able to read and type, and yet illiteracy is a major educational challenge in the Global South
- political and cultural realities: some countries—China, Iran, North Korea, Syria—block the Internet, preventing the free flow of information.

There have been serious attempts at bridging this gap. For example, an NGO called One Laptop Per Child is devoted to recycling older computers from the developed world and supplying them to users in the developing world to ease electronic access for the global poor. Norris suggests—vividly—that, at minimum, we now need to think about remote, underdeveloped villages requiring a village computer to serve the needs of the local people just as readily, and vitally, as the village water well. (Much more on helping the Global South will said in Chapter 11, on aid and development.)[39]

CONCLUSION

Culture—as a way of life—permeates all aspects of international affairs and global studies. We've examined culture already, in chapters 1 and 2, and so here in Chapter 3 it fell to us to examine some drivers of culture we had not yet explored. These included political ideology and the structure of the state, religion, and the advent and impact of new media technologies. We looked at case studies, from all around the world, to see how ideologies, religions, and technologies can—in action—produce both progress and regress, both creativity and conflict.

REVIEW QUESTIONS

1. Our opening epigraph came from Camus. Another deep thought he has about culture is this: "Culture: The cry of men in the face of their destiny." Explain what he means by this.

2. In terms of political ideology, if you were forced to choose only one, would you say you were more of a conservative, liberal, or socialist in orientation? Why? (Base your answer on the classical definitions of these terms, not on your preference for any political party that might bear one of these terms in its name.) How does your political ideology affect your attitudes towards other people, and other countries, that have different ideologies? Is it truly possible for us all to get along, in spite of our cultural differences?

3. Offer explanations as to why and how welfare liberalism has come to be the dominant doctrine in the developed West. Can you see any serious challenges to it in the foreseeable future? For example, some think that sizable immigration to the West of people from other cultures will undermine and harm the West's welfare liberal values. Do you agree, or do you think that such arguments are instances of fear-mongering and scapegoating?

4. Offer explanations for why poorer, more southern countries tend to be much more religious than richer, more northern ones. How is this fact of significance to international relations? Why is the US such an exception to this rule?

5. Are you religious? Why, or why not? What role, if any, do you think religion should play in culture in general, and in international affairs in particular? Has religion, historically, been more positive or negative in its effects?

6. If you had to choose to be a member of a world religion *other than your own*, which one would you choose and why? Refer to tables 3.1 and 3.2 as needed.

7. What impact does the Arab–Israeli conflict have on the lives of the people who live in the region? And the rest of the world, more broadly? (Consider, for example, Canadian and American foreign policy decisions, and the West's oil interests in the region.) Do you think a solution is possible?

8. Find out what you can about the conflict between Tibet and China. Chart the extent to which this is (a) a political conflict, between nations; (b) a religious conflict, between Buddhists and atheists; and (c) a cultural conflict, between Tibetan culture and Chinese culture.

9. Can you imagine your life without new media devices? What do they add to your life? Do they detract from your life, as well? Would you choose to be free of them, if you could? How much of your personal culture, and the culture of your friends and family, relies on new technology?

10. Read the benefits of trying to extend technology to the Global South, and the challenges of trying to do so at the same time. Can you think of others, pro or con, not listed? Research "technology transfer" NGOs, like One Laptop Per Child, and read about innovative and inspiring ways people are trying to make a positive difference in the world.

WEBSITES FOR FURTHER RESEARCH

Oxford University's Centre for Political Ideologies http://cpi.politics.ox.ac.uk
– about political ideas

Religion Facts www.religionfacts.com
– especially for factual questions

Ontario Consultants on Religious Tolerance www.religioustolerance.org
– on the tenets of different religions

Council for Secular Humanism www.secularhumanism.org
– on the tenets of secular humanism

Davis Fougler's "Seven Bridges Over the Global Digital Divide"
http://evolutionarymedia.com/papers/digitalDivide.htm

NOTES

1. A. Camus, *The Myth of Sisyphus and Other Essays* (New York: Vintage, 1991), p. 42.
2. T. Abdullah, *A Short History of Iraq* (Toronto: Pearson, 2003); D. Vandewalle, *A History of Modern Libya* (Cambridge: Cambridge University Press, 2006).
3. L. Baradat, *Political Ideologies: Their Origins and Impact* (New York: Prentice Hall, 10th edn, 2008).
4. J. Muller, *Conservatism* (Princeton: Princeton University Press, 1997).
5. Muller, ibid.
6. W.R. Polk, *Understanding Iran* (London: Palgrave Macmillan, 2011).

7. Polk, ibid.
8. This quote is a famous one from Mao Zedong's "Little Red Book." Mao was not a classical liberal but, rather, the brutal communist dictator of China from 1949 until 1976. Still, the quote as stated captures the liberal spirit.
9. J.S. Mill, *On Liberty* (Oxford: Oxford World Classics, 2006); R. Nozick, *Anarchy, State and Utopia* (Cambridge: Harvard University Press, 1974); D. Harvey, *A Brief History of Neoliberalism* (Oxford: Oxford University Press, 2007).
10. W. Barney, *A Companion to 19th Century America* (Oxford: Blackwell, 2006).
11. L. Gould, *Grand Old Party: A History of the Republicans* (New York: Random House, 2003).
12. K. Marx, *Capital: A Critique of Political Economy* (Harmondsworth, UK: Penguin Classics, 1993).
13. M. Newman, *Socialism* (Oxford: Oxford University Press, 2005).
14. M. Harrington, *Socialism: Past and Future* (London: Arcade, 2011).
15. R. Pipes, *Communism: A History* (New York: Modern Library, 2003).
16. J. Rawls, *A Theory of Justice* (Cambridge, MA: Harvard University Press, 1971).
17. J. Witcover, *Party of the People: A History of The Democrats* (New York: Random House, 2003).
18. R. Bothwell, *The Penguin History of Canada* (Toronto: Penguin, 2006).
19. K. McQuaid, *Creating the Welfare State* (New York: Praeger, 2nd edn, 1988); D. Gladstone, *The 20th Century Welfare State* (London: Palgrave, 1999).
20. H. Smith, *The World's Religions* (New York: Harper, 2009).
21. M. Warner, et al., eds, *Varieties of Secularism in a Secular Age* (Cambridge, MA: Harvard University Press, 2010).
22. L. Cody & E. Hurd, eds, *Comparative Secularisms in a Global Age* (London: Palgrave Macmillan, 2010).
23. R.W. Hood, *The Psychology of Religion* (London: The Guilford Press, 4th edn, 2009).
24. C. Taylor, *A Secular Age* (Cambridge, MA: Harvard University Press, 2007).
25. M. Osborne, *One World, Many Religions* (Berlin: DK, 2006).
26. A. Sharma, *Our Religions* (New York: Harper, 1994).
27. M. Coogan, *The Illustrated Guide to the World's Religions* (Oxford: Oxford University Press, 2003).
28. Pew Research Center: www.PewResearch.org (see especially the Pew Forum on Religion and Public Life, and the Pew Global Attitudes Survey).
29. Smith, *The World's Religions* (op. cit., note 20).
30. Content for this chart has been drawn from the sources listed in notes 20–22 and 25–27 above, as well as W.G Oxtoby & A. Hussain, eds, *World Religions: Western Traditions* (Don Mills, ON: Oxford University Press, 3rd edn, 2011).
31. Sources for this case study are: J. Gelvin, *The Modern Middle East* (Oxford: Oxford University Press, 3rd edn, 2011); K. Schulze, *The Arab–Israeli Conflict* (London: Longman, 2nd edn, 2008); J. Gelvin, *The Israel–Palestinian Conflict* (Cambridge: Cambridge University Press, 2007); and W. Laqueur & B. Rubin, eds, *The Israel–Arab Reader* (New York, 7th edn: Penguin, 2008).
32. Content for this chart has been drawn from the sources listed in Notes 20–22 and 25–27 above, as well as W.G. Oxtoby & R.C. Amore, eds, *World Religions: Eastern Traditions* (Don Mills, ON: Oxford University Press, 3rd edn, 2010).
33. P. Clark, *The Chinese Cultural Revolution* (Cambridge: Cambridge University Press, 2008).
34. S. van Schaik, *Tibet: A History* (New Haven, CT: Yale University Press, 2011).
35. J. Margolis, *Stuck in the Shallow End* (Cambridge, MA: MIT Press, 2010).
36. J. Abbate, *Inventing the Internet* (Cambridge, MA: MIT Press, 1999); R. Stross, *Planet Google* (New York: Free Press, 2008).
37. P. Norris, *Digital Divide?* (Cambridge: Cambridge University Press, 2001), p. 11.
38. M. Al-Fahad, *Bridging the Global Digital Divide* (Berlin: VDM Verlag, 2008).
39. Norris, *Digital Divide?* (op. cit., note 37), p. 34; J. James, *Informational Technology and Development* (New York: Routledge, 2004).

II

Core Dynamics:
Nation versus World

4 Foreign Policy and International Politics

"Politics is the art of the possible." —*Otto von Bismarck, (1815–1898)*
First Chancellor of Germany[1]

LEARNING OBJECTIVES

After studying this chapter, you will be able to:

▸ define all the bolded key terms and concepts

▸ know how foreign policy experts see power, in both its hard and soft forms

▸ explain how countries differ based on the kinds of international power they have, and offer contemporary examples of each different kind

▸ discuss whether the US is a rising or a declining power, and offer views on what counts as evidence for such a debate, and what consequences there are for the rest of the world

▸ grasp thoroughly the difference between realism and idealism in foreign policy, and the potential for a middle-road, blended approach that balances the two

▸ understand the four fundamental tools of foreign policy, and offer examples of each

▸ reflect on the accuracy of conventional wisdom regarding Canadian and US foreign policy

▸ come to see how "Can–Am relations" are so successful, and what each country aims for, and offers, regarding the so-called "best foreign policy relationship in the world."

INTRODUCTION

"Policy," generally speaking, comes from the ancient Greek word *polis*, meaning "community." **Policy** can thus be understood as how a community should be run, and why. There's a difference between domestic policy and foreign policy. **Domestic policy** concerns the way one's national community is or should be governed, whereas **foreign policy** concerns the way one's country does or should relate to other countries, and their national governments, around the world. Of special concern in foreign policy, of course, is how one should best relate to one's neighbouring countries, as well as, more generally, to one's friends (allies) and enemies (opponents) around the world.

In this chapter, we will define power, understand different kinds of power, and then consider both the general *goals* and specific *tools* of foreign policy. We'll finish by examining in detail the foreign policy relationship between Canada and the United States.

THE POWERS

Countries are often categorized on the basis of **power**, which is in general terms the ability of a country to get what it wants. As noted in this book's introduction, a distinction is made between "hard" and "soft" power.[2] **Hard power** boils down to "bucks and bullets"—in other words, economic wealth and military capability. According to the UN Statistics Division, the 10 largest national economies in the world, as of 2010, are thought to be:

1. United States
2. China
3. Japan
4. India
5. Germany
6. Britain
7. Russia
8. France
9. Brazil
10. Italy.

Note that these are *national* rankings. Excluded here is the size of the economy of the European Union, or EU, as a whole, which is thought to be either equal to or larger than that of the US. More on the EU below, and in the next chapter. Also note that figures for China are somewhat speculative, as the Chinese government is the sole source for them, and (a) this government is neither public nor democratic in how it handles information, and (b) it may have a vested interest in exaggerating these figures. Clearly, China is a major, and growing, economic power but to which exact degree is another question.[3]

We'll give military capability a closer look in chapters 7 and 8, which deal with war. Military strength is based on a complex set of factors, including war-readiness, military spending, and both the quality and quantity of weaponry and soldiery. It is commonly understood that the United States is the world's dominant military power, but then consensus breaks down after that. The other countries most frequently mentioned (in alphabetical order) include Britain, China, France, Germany, India, Israel, Japan, North Korea, Pakistan, and Russia.[4]

Soft power, in contrast to hard power, refers to one's ability to get others to think the way one does. So, cultural influence and the impact of one's culture and values around the world are crucial here. Think, for example, of the power of Hollywood, or American television, news, and Internet content generally. Think also of the spread of the English, French, and Spanish languages well beyond the borders of their comparatively small home countries, and so on. Now, it is quite controversial to rank countries based on their imagined degree of soft power, but the ones just mentioned now would, I think, rank on anyone's top 10 list. Figure 4.1 represents the continuum of power in international life.

| Great Powers | Middle Powers | Small Powers | Rogue Regimes | Failed States |

FIGURE 4.1 The Continuum of International Power

Great Powers

The **great powers** are those countries with the richest economies *and* the largest armed forces. Their decisions often have a global impact. The great powers would include the US, Britain, China, France, and Russia, which happen to be the five permanent members of the UN Security Council, tasked with maintaining peace and stability around the globe. (More on the UN next chapter.) Other countries may come close, too, such as Germany and Japan. Increasingly, in certain respects, even countries like India and Saudi Arabia may factor in: the latter for its massive oil wealth, the former for its rapid development, huge population size (including diaspora), popular Bollywood culture, and considerable military strength. But, in terms of *both* hard and soft power, and *both* military and economic capability, the first five are the most frequently mentioned as the truly great powers. In fact, as we saw in Chapter 1, it is an open question whether the United States deserves to be lumped into the same category here with, say, France. Many believe that the US deserves its own special category, above and beyond even the other great powers. Whether this special "category of one" should be called a worldwide empire or merely the global hegemon is, of course, something we've seen up for debate.[5]

Middle Powers

Middle powers, obviously, have a level of influence and capability in between that of the great and small powers. Typically, they are Northern/Western, developed, and quite wealthy societies, but they lack the population size, military force, cultural impact, and ambition to become great powers. Examples include Canada, Australia, and Sweden. (Some experts place Germany and Japan in this category, too, since these nations have deliberately restricted their use of military power abroad; others, however, argue that the sheer size of their economies renders them great powers.) The middle powers try to be active and good "international citizens," picking and choosing projects and missions in which they can play a globally constructive role. They tend to be like-minded and mutually supportive, unlike the great powers, which are often rivals and tend to butt heads on a range of issues. The middle powers are among the strongest and most enthusiastic supporters of global co-operation and such international institutions as the United Nations.[6]

Small Powers

Small powers can be either developed or developing, in either the North or the South, and they have only a small degree of impact on international decision-making and global life. Typically, their population, economies, and militaries are simply too tiny for them to exert much influence globally. Examples range from the Czech Republic in Europe to Chile in South America, and from the Caribbean islands to the various island nations in the South Pacific.

Rogue Regimes

Recently, some countries have come to be branded—controversially—as "rogue states" (or "outlaw nations") by political scientists, government foreign ministers, and even the media. **Rogue** is an old-fashioned term for "scoundrel" or "rascal," and it's now sometimes used to characterize undisciplined, irresponsible, or unpredictable actions or actors. The idea here is of a country that is a **bad international citizen**. It refuses to play well with its neighbours, and actively creates trouble and instability on an international scale. It breaks the rules, goes its own way, makes the world worse, and is difficult to rein in. Most simply, rogue regimes are trouble-makers. But note that the "trouble" can actually be very serious and dangerous. For example, some state governments support terrorist groups, either by giving them weapons or safe haven. That is considered rogue state activity and, obviously, makes the world worse off.

The states most frequently mentioned as rogues today include Iran and North Korea. Iran, currently, has a government committed to a quite extreme version of Islam; it supports some terrorist groups, and it is openly pursuing the development of nuclear weapons. North Korea, which already has nuclear weapons, is seen as a rogue because its leadership is very insecure and unpredictable. Two days following the death of its long-time leader Kim Jong-il in December 2011, North Korea set off some of its short-range missiles in a planned test that set anxious neighbours in the region on edge. It also sells weapons to anyone willing to pay, including terrorist groups. From time to time, North Korea will take part in provocative actions, like testing a nuclear bomb or sinking a South Korean ship as it passes, supposedly, in North Korean waters. The international community then has to intercede in an effort to minimize the negative consequences. Often, the North Koreans have been satisfied with the added attention—making them feel like powerful players on the world stage—or else with cash (as North Korea is generally very poor, in spite of its advanced weaponry).[7]

The existence of rogue regimes presents the international community with the challenge of how best to deal with these unpredictable states. The options typically come down to a choice between containment and confrontation. A **containment strategy** is an attempt to handle and control an outlaw country by fencing them in, to minimize the damage they can do. The containment strategy is used either as a first attempt or else if the country in question is simply too strong or too dangerous to confront directly. In the case of North Korea, for example, the US has banded together with the countries neighbouring this rogue regime—South Korea, China, Japan, and Russia—and each of the partners takes its turn to negotiate with, pay off, and otherwise encircle the North Koreans with a set of measures—economic, political—designed to keep the North Koreans under control. A number of classic **positive incentives** are used, including more power, more recognition, and more cash; the classic **negative incentives** include threats to withhold cash or to use military force. If and when these containment measures fail, then—depending on the danger in question—a strategy of direct **confrontation** can be considered. More will be said about such a forceful strategy towards the end of this chapter.

Failed States

Completing our continuum of kinds of country, consider at the end of the spectrum farthest away from a great power the figure of a failed state. A **failed state** is one in which a government exists, but it can no longer effectively govern its people or provide for their basic needs. The state is imploding under its own weight. It fails to do the most basic things people expect from their state: keep the peace, protect them from foreign invasion, enforce law and order, and ensure the most basic social services are provided to the people. Based on these criteria, Somalia is a failed state, and, in fact, many of the states in sub-Saharan Africa are on the verge of earning this designation.[8]

Failed states are often produced by wars, and they often cause wars, too, as groups fight over the state collapsing before their eyes. They can also be caused by desperate poverty, by internal corruption, or, some fear increasingly, by widespread diseases and outbreaks of famine or illness. They are a massive source of international concern and instability. For, failed states produce **refugee flows** across borders, as people, struggling to escape famine, poverty, or bloodshed, flee the failed state for other, safer countries. Failed states can create civil wars, as just noted, or they can become havens for terrorists and criminals (consider the waters off the Somali coast, notoriously aswarm with pirates eager to hijack and loot foreign vessels). The lack of social services in failed states engenders terrible poverty and disease that cry out for international aid and development assistance. More will be said about failed states in Chapter 11, on international development.[9]

EMERGING POWERS

China

Although it does not appear on our continuum of power, another state model is worth mentioning before progressing: the emerging power. An **emerging power** is a country whose economic and/or military stature is increasing, perhaps even to the point of rising from one category on our figure to the next. China is clearly the emerging power of the moment, not so much in terms of its military strength but certainly in terms of its spectacular economic growth over the past 25 years. China's massive, and cheap, labour market is increasingly rendering it *the* hub of global manufacturing. Moreover, as the Chinese economy grows, the average Chinese consumer has more money to spend, with the result that sellers of goods are looking increasingly to sell into the vast Chinese marketplace, the most populous in the world. China is also one of the world's few saver–surplus countries. By contrast, almost all Western countries (notably the US) have borrowed, owe money elsewhere, and are debtor nations. Historically, saver–surplus nations tend to go up in power whereas spender–debtor nations go down.[10]

> Historically, saver–surplus nations tend to go up in power whereas spender–debtor nations go down.

Despite the country's improving financial situation, China has experienced the departure of vast numbers of emigrants to other countries (representing a **diaspora** of Chinese). These emigrants tend to retain close and favourable ties with their families in China. In many cases, Chinese emigrants will send a portion of the wages they earn abroad to parents, spouses, children, and other family members back home. This helps to strengthens China's overall economic position.[11]

Some wonder, though, whether China's economic strength will translate into either global *military* clout or international *soft* power. China is an interesting, inward-looking culture that has, historically, lacked the ambition to spread its values elsewhere, much less engage in conquest or multiple military engagements. With the important exceptions of operations in Nepal, Taiwan, and Tibet, China's military experience tends to revolve around *domestic* conflicts, *internal* revolutions, and *civil* wars rather than wars with foreign powers. The last time China was involved in a war of the latter kind was during World War

II, after Japan had invaded the Chinese province of Manchuria in the early 1930s. Contrast this record with that of the other great powers—the US, Britain, France, and Russia—each of which has been involved in numerous large-scale military conflicts all around the globe since 1945. Other commentators argue that China's non-democratic nature undermines its ability to spread its culture and values globally, as Western countries in particular tend to feel that undemocratic countries lack the moral authority and political legitimacy to teach the rest of the world much about anything, at least in the political realm.[12]

India and Pakistan

India and Pakistan are also emerging powers. They were administered together as a single unit as part of the British Empire until 1947, when they were partitioned and made separate countries by the British as the Empire collapsed following the Second World War. The partition of the two countries was done largely on the basis of religion, as Pakistan is overwhelmingly Muslim whereas India has many religious traditions, the most prevalent of which is Hindu. India and Pakistan have been suspicious, and sometimes bitter, rivals ever since, owing both to religious tensions and to border disputes, especially in the territory of Kashmir, and this accounts, in part, for the fact that over the past 30 years, both countries have become nuclear powers and have grown large military forces. And they both rank among the world's 10 most populous countries.

Pakistan has emerged as a country of real concern to the US in its so-called war on terror. Not only does Pakistan lack political stability, it is also home to many radical Islamic groups (including some that support terrorism), and the border it shares with Afghanistan is one of the world's most dangerous places. Indeed, it was in Pakistan that Osama bin Laden was hiding at the time of his discovery and execution by American forces in 2011. (Sometimes, the "emerging power" designation is a dubious distinction.)[13]

India's population is second only to China's, but unlike China, India is a democracy, making it the world's largest democracy by population. India's economy is starting to grow substantially, and a large middle class of consumers is emerging. It is, as noted earlier, a nuclear power, and like China, it enjoys the financial benefits of having a large diaspora of ethnic Indians around the world who have done well for themselves and are favourably disposed towards "the home country." With nearly one-sixth the world's population, India is clearly a country destined to rise in international importance. To the downside, though, India still suffers from pockets of severe poverty, and it does not have a large territory (relative to its population). Its democracy can become quite chaotic, given its diversity and size. Extremist groups also exist in India, and the country is somewhat "hemmed in and surrounded" by such other major powers as Pakistan to the east, China to the west, and, to the far north, Russia (see Figure 4.2).[14]

Germany

Germany is also an emerging power. The largest nation, by both territory and population, in Europe, it also has Europe's largest national economy, and the fourth-largest economy in the world (behind the US, China, and Japan) based on gross domestic product (GDP). Germany is also increasingly at the heart of decision-making in the European Union. Much more will be said about the EU—its history, function, and effects—in the next chapter. For

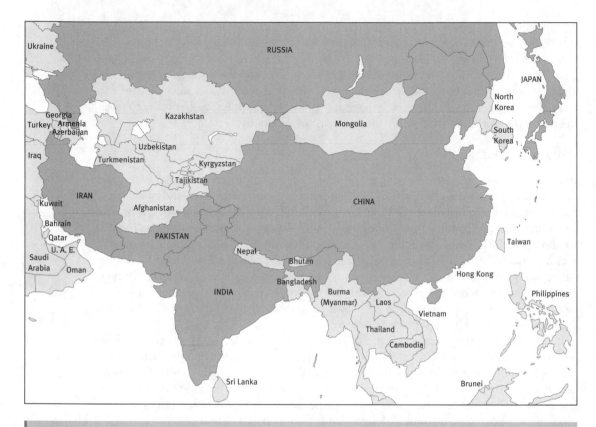

FIGURE 4.2 The Arc of Asia: A Major Emerging Power Bloc

now, we note how the EU grew from early post-war economic agreements between France and Germany in the 1950s to its position today as a political and economic association of European states, from Portugal to Romania and from Sweden to Greece, whose combined population and overall economic size are by most measures comparable to (in fact, slightly greater than) those of the US. There is a common currency (the euro), a central bank, a common passport, a shared legislature, and labour mobility rights throughout the eurozone. Germany's central role in this relatively new, quite successful creation—both politically and economically—render it one of the powers to watch moving forward.[15]

Limits to Germany's growing influence include:

- its lack of military strength (which is deliberate, based on its history);

- its relatively small territory compared with that of great powers like Russia, China, and the US;

- the continued heavy costs of reintegrating and rebuilding the former East Germany;

- the new costs of helping pay down the debts of other EU partners (like Greece); and

- the fact that it must contend with other EU members—notably Britain, France, and Italy—who do not always see things the same way that Germany does.

There is also, and always, Russia to contend with: bad blood has tainted their relationship since the two countries' many gruesome wartime entanglements, especially those fought along the Eastern Front during World War II.[16]

DECLINING POWERS

Russia

Speaking of Russia, if there is a category for emerging powers, we might also recognize a category of **falling**, or **declining**, **powers**. This would include nations whose impact and stature on the world stage are diminishing. The historical reality is that great powers rise and fall: the Egyptians rose and fell, and so did the Vikings; the Greeks and Romans rose and fell; the Portuguese and Spanish rose and fell; the Dutch and Belgians rose and fell; and even the British and French rose and fell (though they do still retain much power and influence). Russia, clearly, is not as influential and dominant as it was during the Cold War (1945–91).[17]

As we saw in Chapter 1, **the Cold War** was the multi-generational global showdown between the US and the USSR (i.e. the Soviet Union, which included Russia and several central Asian republics that are now independent). The United States and Russia were the two biggest winners of the Second World War (1939–45). However, they did not trust each other, and championed completely different social systems: the US, that of free-market, or capitalist, democracy; and Russia, that of police-state, planned- or command-economy communism. The Cold War *was* a war, in that it was very much a struggle between these nations to see whose social system would triumph and survive, and whose would fail and collapse. But the war was *cold*, in that there never was a **hot war** exchange of live-fire hostilities directly between the two powers.[18]

The US eventually won the Cold War, as Russia's command economy could not out-produce America's capitalist one, and Russia went broke trying to keep up with US military spending. As a result, in the 1990s, the Soviet Union broke apart, and Russia's political, economic, and social systems collapsed and had to be reconstructed completely along more Western, free-market, democratic lines. Only recently has Russia achieved political and economic stability, but clearly it has nowhere near the international strength and influence it held when it rivalled the US as the other **superpower** during the Cold War.

> *The historical reality is that great powers rise and fall.*

Yet Russia cannot be counted out, by any means. It has almost the same population as the US and possesses the largest national territory in the world. With such a territory comes a massive wealth of natural resources, including oil and natural gas. Russia is still influential in central and eastern European politics and has one of the largest military forces in the world. Moreover, it retains the second-largest nuclear weapons arsenal, after the US. Russia will always have its sphere of influence, which stretches from Poland to China, and from the Arctic Ocean down towards Iran and India. It has clearly fallen from the lofty position it once held, but if it manages to grow its economy sustainably and to address some of its domestic social problems (such as crime), Russia will continue to be a world power for some time.[19]

America?

What about the Cold War's other superpower? Is the United States, too, a declining power? Have its best days gone by already? Or is it, rather, an emerging power, now that its Cold War rival has been defeated?

During the Cold War, it was said that the world was **bipolar**, with two powerful countries, each dominating its separate sphere of influence, one in the West and one in the East. When the USSR collapsed in the 1990s, there was talk of a **unipolar moment**, a period where there was just one polar power, one centre of global political gravity, so to speak: the US. Where America had once been one of two superpowers, it had now become the one-and-only **hyperpower**, striding the planet like a global colossus, and you will recall, from Chapter 1, our debate regarding "American Empire."

But there are those who think that the only direction for the US to go from here is . . . down. As rich and powerful as America is, it's clear that countries like China, India, and Germany are getting richer, whereas it's unclear whether the same can be said for the US, especially in light of the lingering effects of the global economic meltdown that began in 2008. America is one of the world's biggest spender–debtor countries, and it gets away with this heavy habit of huge spending because countries like China and Japan are willing to lend it plenty of money by buying US government bonds and the like. The United States is also massively reliant on imports of foreign oil, especially from the Middle East, to fuel its economy and consumer lifestyle; indeed, the US now depends on these other countries and regions in ways that it never did before. Similarly, there's no way that the US has the same degree of influence in Europe that it had after World War II and during the Cold War; the success of the European Union has largely driven out American influence in that region. Finally, some argue that American infrastructure, and its education and healthcare systems, are falling behind the average performance levels achieved elsewhere around the world, boding ill for its future achievement. Critics like Morris Berman have taken up the argument in bestselling books with titles like *Why America Failed: The Roots of Imperial Decline* and *Dark Ages America: The Final Phase of Empire*. Even more restrained experts, like Paul Kennedy, have stated that the long view of world history tells us that, just as America rose as a great power, so, too, it must eventually fall.[20]

THE GOALS OF FOREIGN POLICY IN GENERAL

Any country's foreign policy must address two fundamental issues:

1.   What is the goal of its relations with each and any other country?

2.   What are the means it should use to achieve that goal?

In terms of the basic goals of foreign policy, there is a classic, time-honoured split between *realism* and *idealism*.

Realism

Realism is the view that the objective of a country's foreign policy should be to advance its own national interests. **National interests** are those things that benefit or enhance the position of a country; they boil down to the ingredients of hard and soft power. Realism is like a form of national egoism or selfishness: when it comes to dealing with the outside world, or the international community, the motto is, "look out for number one." Do the best you can for your own society, especially in terms of national security and defence; growing the economy, population, and access to natural resources; and augmenting cultural and political influence around the world. Political realism insists that, at minimum, a country must protect what it's already got, and at most, a country should get as much as it can and, in fact (if it's possible), try to re-make the world in its own image. Prominent realist thinkers include the Italian statesman Machiavelli and German-born international relations theorist Hans Morgenthau. Prominent realist politicians include American diplomat Henry Kissinger and former US president Richard Nixon.[21]

Constrained versus Unconstrained Selfishness

Realists don't have to be as crude as they are, at times, made out to be. It all depends how you define "egoistic" or "selfish." There is a difference between what David Gauthier calls "constrained maximization" and "unconstrained maximization." To be an **unconstrained maximizer** (of your own pleasure, benefit, and interest), you must always put your own interests at the forefront in a very obvious, unconcealed, aggressive way. There's no art to it at all: you just demand your way, again and again and again. But others are often turned off by unconstrained maximizers, and they retaliate with selfish, or uncooperative, behaviour of their own. This can actually *decrease* the ability of unconstrained maximizers to get what they want. So, clever realists often suggest—especially when it comes to foreign policy—that the best policy is that of **constrained maximization**, wherein one's motives are still fundamentally selfish, but one hides one's selfishness behind a policy of negotiation, compromise, and reasonableness. One is more artful and tactful about the pursuit of one's self-interest, on the grounds that "honey attracts more flies than vinegar."[22]

The Assurance Problem

One of the most important concepts within the realist worldview is the "assurance problem." The **assurance problem** is this: fundamentally, *countries cannot trust each other*. There are just too many differences between them, in terms of their worldviews, their interests and strategies, and their histories, experiences, and cultures. And there's no effective world government to help them align their policies. In the end, countries have no one to rely upon except themselves.

In this sense, the international arena is completely, and importantly, *different from* the arena in well-ordered national societies like those of Canada or the US. Here in North America, we can (more or less) count on peace and order, civility and good government, on a mostly law-abiding populace, and maybe even a shared, roughly defined worldview. But, internationally, there just isn't that kind of peace and order—much less a good, effective, overarching global government—and there is no guarantee of good behaviour from others. Thus, there's a huge trust (or assurance) problem in international life. The international world is just far more dangerous and unpredictable than life in the developed society we know.

So it is that realists conclude that the only *smart* foreign policy is a *selfish* foreign policy. *Look out for yourself, since no one else will*. Whether that selfishness gets expressed in a constrained or unconstrained way will depend on one's own power and the nature of the situation one is in. Typically, more powerful countries (like the US) are able to be more unconstrained in their foreign policy, whereas less powerful countries (like Canada) need to be more restrained in the pursuit of their national interests.[23]

Idealism

Idealism, by contrast, is the view that your goal as a country, when dealing with others, ought to be to *do your part to make the world a better place*. It's like a form of national altruism or unselfishness. When dealing with the outside world, use your resources and influence to improve the world: make it richer, happier, more secure, and so on. Be a good international citizen. Give a damn, so to speak, and act accordingly. Commonly, idealists tend to divide into those favouring small-scale, concrete, and gradual improvements and those attracted to larger-scale, sweeping, and more sudden shifts in international politics. Prominent idealist thinkers include German philosopher Immanuel Kant, while prominent idealist politicians include former US president Woodrow Wilson.[24]

National Security versus Human Security

A useful illustration of the contrast between realism and idealism is seen in the difference between the time-honoured concept of **national security** and the more recent concern with **human security**. Note, first, the difference between "national" and "human." The former refers only to *one* country and group, and the self-centredness of it is clear. The latter has a totally universal, transnational implication: the concern is for all of humanity and not merely one subgroup within it. You can guess which is of greater interest to the realist and which falls within the purview of the idealist.

Moreover, how the realist and the idealist each perceives the important concept of "security" differs. For realists, national security is about strengthening the nation and providing

New screening measures implemented at airports since 9/11 have put personal security at odds with national security. When national security and human security conflict, which should take precedence? Can you think of other cases where the two are not compatible?
(© Richard Lautens/GetStock.com)

protection for it, and this is done mainly with a strong and capable military force. In fact, realists will often use the terms "national security" and "national defence" interchangeably. (Note, too, the revealing name of the huge domestic law enforcement and anti-terrorist agency in America, created after September 11: The Department of Homeland Security.) But, to have a strong military, you need a strong economy to pay for it, and this requires:

- a huge and smart, healthy, and productive population;
- a pro-business culture; and
- increasing opportunities for your companies to grow and trade abroad.

And so, national security boils down to having hard power: the ultimate sense of protection and well-being for your country comes with being both rich and powerful. On a much smaller scale, national security is very much like the security of well-off North American neighbourhoods: those that are home to the city's wealthier citizens tend to be well taken care of and protected from vandals and burglars, with alarm systems, security cameras, and even private guards standing sentinel at the entrance to gated communities.[25]

The concept of human security not only applies to a different, or much broader and more inclusive, group of people; it also features a different notion of security. Defenders of human security challenge the military implications of national security in particular. They argue that having an abundance of well-armed police and soldiers, supported by high levels of "defence" spending, doesn't really make people secure in their lives. What makes people secure, rather, is having the resources and opportunities to pursue the things they want. With human security, the focus is on things like:

- healthcare spending (hard to feel secure when you're sick);
- education spending (hard to feel secure when you're illiterate, ignorant, or lacking in promising career options); and
- growing a healthy economy to provide for and support these programs.

Importantly, prosperity and economic strength are values shared by both realists and idealists—there *is* some common ground—but the differences, in terms of national versus international, and defence/security versus health/education/well-being, are clear. For the idealist, we all ought to do whatever we can to play our part in augmenting human security around the world, and not retreat—in a sad, even paranoid way—to our posh and protected, gated communities, letting the others to fend for themselves as best they can.[26]

Idealist Multilateralism

The idealist's response to the realist's assurance problem is this: countries should take **multilateral** ("many-sided"), not **unilateral** ("one-sided"), approaches to international problems. In other words, instead of going it on your own, join in with others so that everyone can help each other. Support the UN and international law instead of taking matters into your own hands. This co-operative approach, the idealist argues, is much better than constantly looking over your shoulder to see if anyone is about to undermine your interests and stick it to you. The point here is this: without some idealism, the world would never become a better place. That's actually a nice, sober, realistic thought to keep in mind. The hope that idealists have to offer can generate the energy to improve things, whereas the mistrust and cynicism of the realist can lead to apathy, an acceptance of a sub-optimal status quo, or even a paralyzing and defeatist sense that improvements will be impossible—why even bother trying?[27]

Common Ground Between the Caricatures

This big distinction between realism and idealism is often overplayed and exaggerated, with the two sides becoming caricatures of their actual positions. Idealists tend to portray realists as completely unprincipled, selfish, ruthless, jaded, and cynical. Machiavelli, for instance, was condemned as evil in his day and time (Renaissance Italy). Idealists often argue that if everyone were a realist, the world would be a dreadful place indeed. Realists, for their part, characterize idealists as utterly unrealistic, utopian do-gooders, even to the point of being naive and out of touch with the way the world really is. Realists often view themselves as having superior *factual* knowledge of the many issues in international life, and they view idealists as trying to impose simple, sweeping, *theoretical* beliefs onto a difficult and complex world. The mutual accusations essentially boil down to *excess pessimism* on the part of the realists and *excess optimism* on the part of the idealists.[28]

The good news is that there is, or can be, considerable common ground between the two doctrines:

- As noted, both respect the need for *sustained and reliable economic growth* as a foremost value.

- Often, *ideals and interests can run together*. In other words, following ideals can often be in one's best interests. Consider, as an example, occasions in your personal life when it is in your best interests to treat others in accord with the ideals of honesty and respect.

- For some peoples and nations, advancing their ideals is a fulfillment of self-interested aims. In other words, they define the realization of their ideals *as part of* their national interest. This has clearly been a theme of American history, to cite just one example.

- That some idealism is necessary for the world to improve at all is a neat, and quite possibly true, empirical claim. And, presumably, it is in one's own selfish interests to live in a better world over time; no one, after all, wants to live and attempt to thrive in a dump. (This may seem obvious, but many realists—and I have known many—really seem so pessimistic as to shoot down any reform proposal as being impossible. At their worst, realists can seem more concerned with displaying their own understanding of the world than with actually improving it.)

- Enough common ground exists that, over the years, several experts, such as James Baker, have argued for *a blended approach between these two clashing, classical doctrines*. They have spoken of a "pragmatic idealism," or even of a "visionary realism." The idea is to take the best of both worlds and use it to better *both* oneself (or one's nation) *and* the world at large. Keep the idealist's hope and optimism, and the vision, energy, and willingness to co-operate, but blend it with the realist's emphasis on factual knowledge and the prudent use of money and power (as necessary tools). In other words, in international life or foreign policy, be willing to co-operate and to draw on everyone's best capacities, but also be aware that there can be some bad apples and one must always be willing and able to protect oneself, and one's people, from harm at the hands of these unscrupulous others.[29]

These are five solid points of compromise and wisdom. But a few quick, cautionary points must be made:

- States often pay far more lip service to their ideals than their interests.

- As a result, hard-power interests tend to be a much better indicator of, and predictor for, actual behaviour than spoken ideals.

- Hypocrisy and weakness are very real. Often, peoples and states fail to live up to their own ideals. Or, they say they believe in something, but they actually behave in a way that is inconsistent with those beliefs. We are rarely surprised when we predict people's, and countries', behaviour on the basis of what would best serve their selfish interests rather than their stated ideals.

THE TOOLS OF FOREIGN POLICY

We've seen that a country can choose either realism or idealism—or a blended approach—as its overall foreign policy goal (Table 4.1 provides a summary of these goals). To achieve that goal, you need some tools, or means. Every traditional foreign policy textbook will tell you that there are three basic tools to use: *diplomacy*; *sanctions*; and *force*.[30] I would add a fourth leg to the complete the table, as it were: *economic incentives*.

Diplomacy

Diplomacy is the attempt *to persuade* another country to adopt your view and act accordingly. This persuasion might involve talking, negotiating, lobbying, dealing, rational argument, or positive political incentives. Former British prime minister Winston Churchill once memorably summarized this approach as "jaw jaw" (as opposed to "war

TABLE 4.1 The Goals of Foreign Policy

REALISM		IDEALISM		MIXED/BLENDED	
Unconstrained	**Constrained**	**Small-scale (Gradual)**	**Large-scale (Sweeping)**	**Visionary realism**	**Pragmatic idealism**
• selfish motives are pursued openly • a strategy typical of a great power	• selfish motives are hidden behind negotiation, compromise, and reasonableness • a strategy typical of a small or middle power	• favours the pursuit of small, concrete changes in international politics (e.g. increasing amounts of foreign aid)	• favours large, sudden shifts in international politics (e.g. the formation of the UN)	• as defined on page 110, combining the best of both realism and idealism	

war"). Talk it up, and talk it out. US president Barack Obama recently chimed in on the issue of diplomacy, offering that "Not talking does not work."[31]

Diplomacy goes on every day, and is one of the main functions of consulates and embassies around the world. (An **embassy** is the official residence of a country's **ambassador**, who is in charge of representing the interests of his or her home country in the host country. Technically, a foreign embassy is considered part of the soil of *that* country, and *not* the country in which it is located.) For example, Canada has a massive diplomatic presence in the United States, which is Canada's largest trading partner and, as such, has the greatest effect of any country on the standard of living in Canada. So, the Canadian government has invested massively in a huge diplomatic staff, and not just at the main embassy in Washington. Canada has smaller diplomatic offices (called **consulates**) all around the United States, essentially in every city over a population of 500,000: this adds up to quite a few! The job of Canadian diplomats is to use persuasion, lobbying, and deal-making in representing Canada's national interests to decision-makers in the United States, trying to persuade Americans to adopt Canada's views on certain issues. They also help Canadian businesses that are trying to negotiate deals with American businesses, and they assist Canadians in the US who run into problems—like an expired passport—and need help.[32]

But note, and realize, that diplomacy *isn't always positive* and glowing in its nature, even though it's considered a compliment when we call someone "diplomatic." Diplomacy can involve behind-the-scenes threats or coercion, or even in-front-of-the-camera public criticism. These things are quite common in international relations. The point is that it remains diplomacy as long as it is just *words*. When hostile *actions* start taking place, then we are moving out of the realm of diplomacy and towards the other tools of foreign policy.

Economic Incentives

Economic incentives involve the use of money as either a carrot (**positive incentive**) or a stick (**negative incentive**) in an effort to gain **leverage** on another country and influence them to do what you want. A "carrot" may be a thinly disguised bribe or a more indirect promise of financial gain—for instance, by allowing a country to be able to sell its goods into your country when previously you had forbidden it to do so. Deals to allow for, or to increase, mutually profitable trade between countries are at the very top of the carrot pile. (Trade deals, especially free trade, will be discussed in depth in Chapter 6, on international trade and business.) "Sticks" may be wielded by imposing fines on a country, withholding a historically ongoing payment to that country (e.g. development assistance), refusing to trade with the country, or, in the biggest extreme, imposing economic sanctions.[33]

Sanctions

Imposing sanctions is a way of "stepping it up a notch" in terms of the hostility and displeasure you are willing to show in your relations with another country. It shows that you are prepared to move away from *positive* incentives and mutually beneficial deal-making towards *negative* incentives: threats, non-cooperation, punishment—*deliberate actions that you believe will thwart the interests of the other country*. Sanctions can vary in level, intensity, and effect. Small sanctions include mostly symbolic actions like withdrawing your ambassador from the other country (the "target country"), or even closing your embassy entirely. Or you may expel the target country's diplomats from your own country. You are clearly conveying your displeasure, and punishing that society, but only to a small, mainly symbolic extent and in a way that is very targeted towards the government of that society.

What about economic sanctions? Here we must distinguish between *targeted* and *sweeping* sanctions. **Targeted sanctions** are measures of punishment, non-cooperation, and interest-thwarting that are aimed at hurting only the elite decision-makers in the target country. A recent example occurred in 1994, when the US slapped targeted sanctions on the leaders (and their families) of a military coup in Haiti. The coup leaders had their American bank accounts and assets **frozen**, which is to say that the leaders could not access or sell them—the US government made it illegal for any institution in the United States to let them do that. The coup leaders, and their families, were forbidden from entering the US, and in one case a daughter of one of the coup leaders, attending a US college, had her American visa revoked and was forcibly deported back to Haiti. The goal of such measures is clearly to punish, but *to be discriminate in whom one is punishing*. The punishing country is leaving the common people out of it, concentrating instead on sticking it to the elites (to the extent it can peaceably). Other subjects of targeted sanctions today include Iran and North Korea, who are being punished for their refusal to abandon programs to develop specialized and advanced nuclear weapons.[34]

Sweeping sanctions are measures of punishment and non-cooperation that either deliberately target or at least directly affect the majority of citizens in the target country. Classic examples include complete **embargos on trade**: the refusal to trade at all with any part or person of the target country. This tactic was first used during the Napoleonic Wars of the very early 1800s, when England and France each prohibited *any* economic trade with the other country. These embargos caused more harm to the punishing countries than to the target countries, by preventing much trade and thus *decreasing* wealth and income in both England and France. They also created huge problems for third countries—notably the newly independent US—who were often, as a matter of practice, forced to trade *either* with England *or* with France, and who resented being pressured in that way. A more recent example is the United States' longstanding embargo on trade with Cuba, to oppose Cuban communism and the regime of Fidel Castro. It began in 1962 and continues to this day, although there have been recent relaxations.[35]

The most recent example of such sweeping sanctions deals with those levelled by the international community—particularly the US and the UK—at Iraq following its invasion of Kuwait in 1990. These sanctions were largely maintained after the end of the war in 1991, on grounds they were needed to ensure Iraq's full and continuing compliance with the peace terms of that first war, notably the weapons inspection process. During the 1990s they caused the erosion of many macroeconomic factors: the economy shrank; infant mortality substantially increased; illiteracy increased; rates of easily preventable illness substantially increased; life expectancy decreased; unemployment rates shot up; opportunity went down; and so on. As a result of the severe and sweeping effects of these sanctions, the US lost much international goodwill and co-operation in its dealings with Iraq, notably in 2003, when the US decided to invade the Middle Eastern country. Arab countries especially refused to go along, even though a number of them—Jordan and Saudi Arabia, for instance—had strongly supported America's first war on Iraq in 1991.[36]

There seems to be a pendulum when it comes to sweeping sanctions. Countries sometimes view sanctions quite favourably, usually when relations with the target country are

Studies in Technology

The Wikileaks Scandal

Wikileaks was founded in 2006 as an international, not-for-profit, new media organization. Its mission, as stated on its website, is to "assist people of all regions who wish to reveal unethical behaviour in their governments and corporations." It does this by receiving and then publicly posting on the Internet original documents and videos showing questionable conduct by various people and institutions who, presumably, would not want their conduct publicized. One (in)famous video, now better known as "Collateral Murder," shows gripping, controversial, real-time footage of a US attack helicopter firing at Iraqi civilians in a van in 2007. More recently, between June and December 2010, Wikileaks made public over 100,000 official, classified documents pertaining to the US military and American diplomatic communications around the world. These documents, apparently, were copied by a low-level US soldier, who had downloaded them onto his personal computer by deceptively labelling them as "Lady Gaga Videos." He forwarded the documents to Wikileaks, which then published them. They contain very frank assessments of foreign leaders (and their policies) by US diplomats and ambassadors, as well as confidential discussions of broader US foreign policy strategy. All together, these documents provide a very "warts-and-all," behind-the-scenes look at how diplomats gather information, and how generals plot military strategy, and how both groups send their ideas back to their ruling governments to await debate and further instruction.

The leaks became a major international news story and caused a public sensation, prompting American secretary of state Hillary Clinton to warn that publicizing this classified government material "put people's lives in danger" and even "threatens national security." Robert Gates, former US defence secretary, instead concluded pithily: "Is this embarrassing? Yes. Awkward? Yes. Consequences for US foreign policy? I think fairly modest." (Apparently, a number of governments have responded to the leaks by privately chiding the Americans, and saying: "You should see what we say about *you*, behind *your* back!"[38])

Wikileaks originally swore to continue its unique publishing program, in spite of recent legal troubles for its Australian spokesman, Julian Assange, arising from events in his personal life. Recently, however, Wikileaks has found that lack of money will probably force it to shut down for good.[39]

quite hostile and sanctions seem like a better, more moderate alternative to war. But there is little historical evidence that sanctions work in changing the policy of the target country. For example, the sanctions on Iraq did not affect president Saddam Hussein's grip on power or his attitude towards international weapons inspection. And they often disproportionately hurt innocent civilians—a fact that is largely responsible for the negative attitude

TABLE 4.2 The Tools of Foreign Policy

DIPLOMACY		ECONOMIC INCENTIVES		SANCTIONS		FORCE	
Positive	Negative	Positive	Negative	Targeted	Sweeping	Pinpoint	War
• praise • negotia- tion	• threats • criticism	• cash • trade opportu- nities	• withhold- ing cash • cancel- ling trade	• affects the elites only	• affects the whole society	• targeted force	• wide- spread, direct, "hot" armed conflict

towards them. As a result of the sad Iraq experience in the 1990s, it seems safe to say that, today, the international community definitely frowns upon the use of sweeping sanctions.[37]

Armed Force

When things have completely gotten out of hand, and perhaps when the other three tools of foreign policy have failed, countries sometimes resort to violent force in their relations with each other. This can be small-scale or pinpoint force (or even just "show of force," like a military drill or exercise), or it can be a classic, out-and-out, direct, "hot," shooting war. I shall leave everything about this complex, controversial option for the two forthcoming chapters on war and peace. Table 4.2 provides a summary of the tools of foreign policy we have examined.

Case Study: Can–Am Relations

The following case study examines a unique foreign policy relationship. It is often said that, in terms of foreign policy, Canada and the United States enjoy the very best relationship: a model for the rest of the world to follow. How does this relationship work? Why does it work so well? Before examining the intricate workings of **Can–Am relations**, we'll take a look at the overall foreign policy strategies of the two countries.

The Goals of the Neighbours: Overturning Conventional Wisdom

The conventional wisdom—the clichéd understanding—is that the United States has a *realist* foreign policy (of unconstrained maximization, no less), whereas Canada has an *idealist* foreign policy (of trying to be "a helpful fixer," striving to do what it can to improve the world). The US loves to flex its huge imperial muscles and to bully others into giving it what it wants, which often involves oil or access to new markets for American companies. For the US, it truly is all about maximizing its own hard and soft power. By contrast, Canada, according to common belief, invented peacekeeping and likes to help broker compromises between warring parties. Canada supports the UN vigorously and is a major cheerleader for international law (peacekeeping and

What is the significance of having the world's "longest undefended border"?
(© Francis Vachon/Alamy)

international law are taken up next chapter). Canada strives to make positive contributions around the globe, providing international aid and assistance when called upon. In annual polls carried out by the BBC, *The Economist*, and other media agencies, Canada typically ranks near, or at, the very top of lists of countries with the best global reputation.[40]

All of this amounts to the common perception of the two countries' foreign policy aims. It seems, though, that this conventional wisdom is overblown, and perhaps even quite mistaken. For the United States has been known to have deeply idealistic moments in its foreign policy history, moments in which it has tried very hard to improve the world and to bring better values to an often cynical, power-obsessed international arena. Woodrow Wilson, for example, brought America into the First World War with a promise that this was "a war on behalf of democracy," indeed "the war to end all wars." The US also created the League of Nations and the United Nations, the first ever institutions of global governance (as we'll see in greater detail next chapter). Through a program of financial aid known as the Marshall Plan, the US single-handedly sponsored the redevelopment of Europe—including its arch-enemy Germany—after World War II, and extended additional grants and loans to several Asian countries, including Japan. This is the same approach the US has taken more recently in Afghanistan and Iraq (see Chapter 8 for a discussion of post-war reconstruction). The US gives more than any other country to international aid and development and has done more to promote the ideal of respecting human rights than any other major power.[41]

Canada, for its part, is not quite so "lily white" as its idealistic foreign policy image would have us believe. As mentioned above, by far the greatest portion of its foreign policy resources—actual cash and personnel—is spent *not*, say, on development funds for the Global South but, rather, on *enhancing Canada's power and influence with the United States*, its main trading partner and source of an estimated 30 per cent of Canada's annual GDP (gross domestic product, a measure of the size of a country's national economy). This is a selfish, realistic motive if ever there was one. Also, as often as Canada has been involved as a peacekeeper, it has been involved as a belligerent in war, aligning itself with one side (almost always the US, the UK, or France) aiming at military victory, not just a compromise between the warring parties. For example, Canada fought both in Afghanistan and in Libya, as recently as late 2011, and *not* as a peacekeeper but as part of an alliance seeking to overthrow the ruling political regimes.[42] And while Canada *does* donate to international aid and development, it is *not* an especially generous donor, contributing nowhere close to the percentage of national wealth donated by, for example, the Scandinavian countries. Furthermore, Canada's oil and gas resources, and its desire to sell these to anyone, has led it both to run afoul of international environmental and climate change treaties (e.g. Kyoto, which it has recently backed out of) and to mute its criticism of China's very flawed human rights record, lest China back off buying not only the oil and gas but other valuable commodities that Canada has for sale and that China requires in huge quantities; examples include such natural resource inputs as nickel, coal, potash, platinum, silver, and wheat.[43]

The point is that in judging their respective foreign policy objectives, critics may rush to place the two countries at opposite ends of the ideological spectrum. Closer inspection shows realistic aims behind apparently idealistic motives and vice versa. The discernment of motivations is difficult, and we should, in particular, beware of conventional understandings.

Dealing with Each Other

With some balance now restored to the clichéd views of the foreign policy goals of the North American neighbours, let's now turn to consider how the two nations relate to each other and why they get along so well. We know already that some of this has to do with shared values, as both countries are welfare liberal societies belonging to Western civilization more broadly (as discussed in chapters 1 and 3). But what about the more narrow, neighbourly reasons for the good relations?

Canada's Perspectives and Interests

The United States, as its biggest trading partner, is a massive source of Canada's considerable wealth. As we've already noted, economists suggest that *up to 30 per cent of Canada's national wealth is directly tied to trade with America*, and indirectly, of course, the number would be higher. The US is Canada's *only* geographical neighbour, and it is far more powerful than Canada in terms of its military strength. So, a smart Canada wants an America that is friendly towards it, does not desire to conquer it, and will trade openly with it—and very regularly and profitably. A huge amount of Canada's behind-the-scenes diplomacy goes towards this goal, which some experts argue is actually the

Stephen Harper and Barack Obama, with few problems, lots of smiles, and mutual interests satisfied at the 2010 G20 conference in Toronto. (Official White House Photo by Pete Souza)

largest, and most sensible, goal of Canadian foreign policy. To put it boldly and baldly: Canada's true number one foreign policy goal is not being a co-operative idealist; it is, rather, having a close and profitable relationship with the United States. And note how Canada's public preference for multilateralism and international co-operation actually *plays into* its relations with the United States: after all, Canada wants its southern neighbour to behave in a predictable way, and not throw its enormous weight around unexpectedly or capriciously. It is in Canada's interest that the US engage with multilateral institutions like the UN and behave in a clear, law-governed way. The last thing Canada wants is to wake up one morning to discover that its biggest trading partner has suddenly closed shop, sending its business elsewhere. Thus, whenever it can, Canada urges the US to engage in multilateral, co-operative, outward-looking diplomacy.

> Canada's true number one foreign policy goal is not being a co-operative idealist but having a close and profitable relationship with the United States.

Canada's fundamental foreign policy orientation can thus be seen, arguably, as one of pleasing and supporting the United States. But Canada doesn't want to seem, to the rest of the world, like an American colony or the fifty-first state, so Canada asserts its independence in ways that don't affect relations with America. For instance, it retains its membership in the British Commonwealth and joins La Francophonie (an international organization of French-speaking governments)—groups of which the US is not a member. Canada keeps up its historical and cultural links with the UK and France to give its society a different flavour and reputation. And Canada even asserts its independence in ways that might slightly irritate the US (such as by recognizing and dealing with Cuba), but not so much

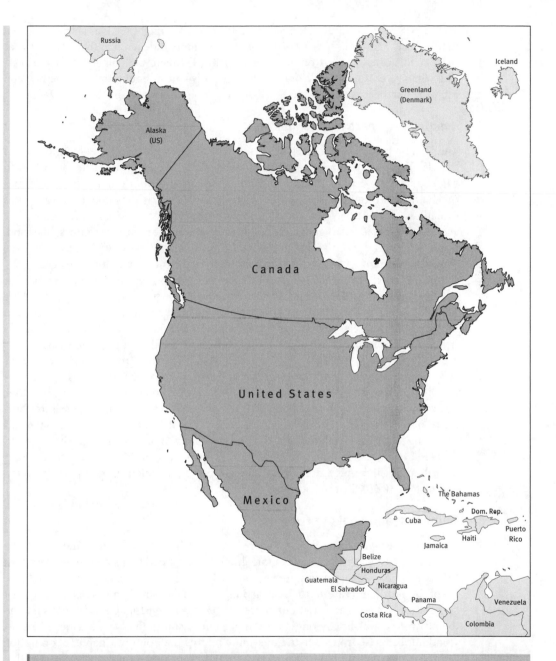

Figure 4.3 North America

North America features two very different borders: the US–Canada border, celebrated as the world's longest undefended border, and the US–Mexico border, criticized (mainly by Americans) for its lack of security and frequent breaches by illegal immigrants and drug smugglers, among others.

that the US would be moved to retaliate. Indeed, the US might see it as being in its own national self-interest to have Canada *appear to be* more independent than it really is, as the Canadian Insights box on page 121 explains. Ultimately, it's all about Canada getting what it wants out of its closest—really, its only—neighbour. It all fits together, and points to a rather smart, yet utterly self-serving, policy of constrained maximization.[44]

America's Perspectives and Interests

The US also has Canada as its largest trading partner, but this is not widely known in the US. Yet, while Canada is America's largest trading partner in terms of total cash value, *only 5 per cent of American wealth comes directly from Canada–US trade*, and maybe not even quite that.[45] So the United States is not as dependent on Canada as Canada is on the US. What America wants from Canada is, first and foremost, free access to its (small) market and especially to its abundant natural resources, like food, water, oil, natural gas, timber, and metals and minerals. The 1989 **Canada–US Free Trade Agreement** (FTA) was in both countries' interests (more on this next chapter).

Americans also want co-operation, help, and support from Canada (small as it is), especially on international issues like the post-9/11 war on terror—issues where Americans feel their vital interests are at stake. (Canada's vintage reply: "We'll help you in Afghanistan [declaration of support] but not in Iraq [assertion of independence].") In the wake of 9/11, the US also very much wants Canada to take action against terrorists and to take greater steps to secure the border so that terrorists cannot have easy access to the US homeland. And that is exactly what Canada has delivered.

So Canada gives Americans what they want: a nice, friendly, co-operative, peaceful, unproblematic neighbour with free markets, who is willing to sell its natural resources in exchange for lots of money. To put it frankly, the United States has much bigger fish to fry than Canada; it is very happy to have such a "boring," secure, peaceful, happy neighbour (unlike Mexico, with the big problems along that border regarding illegal immigration, drug smuggling, and the violence, corruption, poverty, and instability of Mexican society).[46]

Summary, and Looking Forward

So you can see why the foreign policy relations between Canada and America are the way they are today. Each country's foreign policy is guided by its own self-interest. In the case of Can–Am relations, foreign policy is not merely what Bismarck called "the art of the possible" but the true satisfaction of mutual desires. This is not to deny that sometimes problems and frictions come up in the relationship: Canada's refusal to go to war in Iraq was briefly one, for example, and disputes over trade issues like softwood lumber arise from time to time (more on this last point in Chapter 6, on trade). But the problems tend not to be big, and often they just focus on individual issues that can be solved through negotiation. Larger issues might happen in the future—especially over vital commodities like oil and water, and delineating Arctic sovereignty and who exactly owns what way up there in the Far North—but, for now, that remains somewhat speculative.

Canadian Insights

Do the Americans Want Canada To Be More Like Them?

We should elaborate on the observation that the United States actually *wants* Canada to seem independent to the international community.

American leaders know how much Canada has at stake in the "Can–Am" relationship, and they also know that (partly because of this) Canada tends to see the world, and shares many of the same values, as Americans do. The US knows that when push comes to shove, it can almost always count on Canada to be one of—if not *the*—strongest and closest allies to which to turn.

But the US also realizes that Canada's support will mean much more to the rest of the world if Canada is seen as an independent nation with its own perspective and interests—that is, with close ties to Europe and a history of multilateral idealism, and with a more robust welfare state, higher secularism, and so on. For this reason, the Americans are quite comfortable with Canada's taking a whole range of foreign policy decisions that publicly go against the views of the USA.

A small example of this phenomenon at play concerns the **G8**, the Group of Eight largest economies in the world. The G8 holds a diplomatic meeting every year to talk about common economic problems and possible solutions. The group once numbered less than eight, and was essentially the US surrounded by the wealthiest European states (namely, Britain, France and Germany). The Americans got sick of being criticized and told what to do—outnumbered, basically—by the Europeans, particularly the French. So the US insisted on expanding the group to include Canada, which is a country that can speak to the French in their own language, has close historical ties to France, *and yet* sees things more from the American perspective. The expansion happened, much to Canada's benefit—to get to be part of such an exclusive club—but also, as here noted, to America's as well.[47]

CONCLUSION

Foreign policy concerns how countries relate to each other. This chapter has surveyed both the goals and the tools of foreign policy, which countries use to try to advance their power and interests on the international stage. We have looked at the different kinds of power, and how different countries exemplify them and try to use them to gain leverage for themselves and over others. Finally, we took, as an extended case study, the foreign policy relationship between the United States and Canada, in all its forms, to see how the two countries relate, why they relate so well, and what each one is looking for and has to offer.

REVIEW QUESTIONS

1. Explain the full meaning of Bismarck's quote at chapter's start.

2. A big issue right now in American foreign policy is how to contain, or confront, Iran. Research (a) *why* this is so, and (b) *which* options you think are the best for the US at this point. What contributions can the US expect from other nations?

3. History shows that great powers rise and fall. There has been some talk that the United States is declining as a great power, whereas both China and India are emerging. Do you think this is true? Why or why not? How might changes in global wealth and power over the next 50 years personally affect your life?

4. Consider all the countries mentioned in the section on "the powers." Pick three of them, each from a different category of power (e.g. one great power, one middle power, one rogue regime). Research what each one's current major foreign policy goals are. Why do they have these goals, and are they likely to achieve them?

5. Referring to Table 4.1, are you more of a realist or an idealist? Why, and of what kind? What's the importance of this distinction not only to foreign policy but to international studies more broadly?

6. Explain the difference between the concepts of national security and human security. Which do you think is most important to achieve, and why? What actually does make people feel secure? (Further, research why Canada has been one of the main promoters of the idea of human security around the world.)

7. Although there are only four foreign policy tools in general—outlined in Table 4.2—they can be used in a complex combination of ways. Refer back to question 2, and now refine your answer: what is America's best combination of tools for dealing with Iran? Which set of tools is Iran likely to use in reply?

8. Research the Wikileaks scandal. Do you think publicizing the material was a valuable service in the name of democracy and challenging government secrecy? Or, rather, was it reckless, dangerous, even treasonous self-promotion at the expense of national security?

9. Do you agree that the conventional wisdom regarding US and Canadian foreign policy is often mistaken? Or do you think the clichés exist because they are, generally speaking, true? What consequences do such common beliefs (or self-identities) have for the formation of foreign policy itself, and for how citizens push their governments to act on the world stage?

10. It's not all "sunshine and light" between America and Canada. Research some of the enduring, and likely future, problems and irritants in "the world's best relationship." How did, or will, they be solved? Or will they?

WEBSITES FOR FURTHER RESEARCH

Canada's Department of Foreign Affairs and International Trade
www.international.gc.ca

The US Department of State www.state.gov

The US-based Council on Foreign Relations www.cfr.org
– a think-tank on international issues

Foreign Affairs www.foreignaffairs.com
– the CFR's online journal

The Canadian International Council www.onlinecic.org
– a Canadian think-tank on foreign policy

NOTES

1. J. Steinberg, *Bismarck: A Life* (Oxford: Oxford University Press, 2011), p. 4. The quote was uttered by Bismarck in 1867.
2. J. Nye, "Smart Power: In Search of the Balance between Hard and Soft Power," *Democracy* (Fall 2006), pp. 21–46.
3. Material for this, and all subsequent "top 10" factual lists in this chapter, comes from the United Nations Statistics Division, www.unstats.un.org/unsd, and the CIA World Factbook, www.cia.gov/library/publications/the-world-factbook.
4. For all the very latest military rankings—e.g. weapons holdings—the most authoritative primary source is generally considered to be *Jane's Defence Weekly*: www.janes-defence-weekly.com.
5. P. Kennedy, *The Rise and Fall of The Great Powers* (New York: Vintage, 1989).
6. C. Holbraad, *Middle Powers in International Politics* (London: Macmillan, 1984).
7. R. Tanter, *Rogue Regimes: Terrorism and Proliferation* (New York: St Martin's, 1999).
8. A. Ghani & C. Lockhardt, *Fixing Failed States* (Oxford: Oxford University Press, 2008).
9. M. Bukovac, *Failed States: Unstable Countries in the 21st Century* (New York: The Rosen Group, 2011).
10. P. Khanna, *The Second World: How Emerging Powers are Redefining Global Competition in the 21st Century* (New York: Random House, 2008).
11. C-B Tan, *Routledge Handbook of The Chinese Diaspora* (London: Routledge, 2012).
12. E. Vogel, *Deng Xiaoping and The Transformation of China* (Cambridge, MA: Harvard University Press, 2011); H. Kissinger, *On China* (New York: Penguin, 2011); M. Jaques, *When China Rules the World* (New York: Penguin, 2nd edn, 2009).
13. Y. Khan, *The Great Partition: The Making of India and Pakistan* (New Haven, CT: Yale University Press, 2008); O. Bennett-Jones, *Pakistan: Eye of the Storm* (New Haven, CT: Yale University Press, 3rd edn, 2009).
14. J. Keay, *India: A History* (London: Grove, 2011); E. Luce, *In Spite of the Gods: The Rise of Modern India* (London: Anchor, 2008).
15. P. Zelikow & C. Rice, *Germany Unified and Europe Transformed* (Cambridge, MA: Harvard University Press, 1997).
16. P. Wende, *A History of Germany* (London: Palgrave, 2006).
17. P. Kennedy, *The Rise and Fall of The Great Powers* (New York: Vintage, 1989).
18. M. Walker, *The Cold War: A History* (New York: Henry Holt, 1995).

19. M. Goldman, *Petrostate: Putin, Power and the New Russia* (Oxford: Oxford University Press, 2010); P. Longworth, *Russia: The Once and Future Empire* (New York: St Martin's, 2006).

20. Kennedy, *Rise and Fall, passim*; M. Berman, *Dark Ages America: The Final Phase of Empire* (New York: Norton, 2007); M. Berman, *Why America Failed: The Roots of Imperial Decline* (London: Wiley, 2011).

21. N. Machiavelli, *The Prince* (New York: Penguin Classics, 1998); H. Morgenthau, *Politics Among Nations* (New York: Knopf, 5th edn, 1970); H. Kissinger, *Diplomacy* (New York: Harper Collins, 1995).

22. D. Gauthier, *Morals by Agreement* (Oxford: Oxford University Press, 1987).

23. K. Waltz, *Realism and International Politics* (New York: Routledge, 2008).

24. I. Kant, *Perpetual Peace and Other Essays*, trans. T. Humphrey (Indianapolis: Hackett, 1983); M. Price, *The Wilsonian Persuasion in American Foreign Policy* (New York: Cambria, 2007).

25. J. Richards, *A Guide to National Security* (Oxford: Oxford University Press, 2012).

26. M. Kaldor, *Human Security* (London: Polity, 2007).

27. J. Muldoon, *The New Dynamics of Multilateralism* (Boulder, CO: Westview, 2010).

28. M. Walzer, *Just and Unjust Wars* (New York: Basic Books, 1977).

29. James Baker, *The Case for Pragmatic Idealism* (Washington: US Library of Congress, 2008).

30. J. Goldstein & S. Whitworth, *International Relations* (Toronto: Pearson, Cdn edn, 2005).

31. W. Churchill, "Remarks," during White House luncheon, 26 June 1954, from www.bartleby.com & www.brainyquote.com; B. Obama, *Dreams from My Father* (New York: Crown, 2007), p. 40.

32. H. Waller, *Ambassadors and Embassies* (London: Siddharta, 2009).

33. R. Haas & M. O'Sullivan, eds, *Honey and Vinegar: Incentives, Sanctions and Foreign Policy* (Washington, DC: Brookings Institute, 2000).

34. G.C. Hufbauer, et al., *Economic Sanctions Reconsidered* (London: PIIE, 3rd edn, 2009).

35. D. Drezner, *The Sanctions Paradox* (Cambridge: Cambridge University Press, 1999).

36. G. Simons, *The Scourging of Iraq* (London: Macmillan, 2nd edn, 1996).

37. A. Pierce, "Just War Principles and Economic Sanctions", *Ethics and International Affairs* (1996), 99-113.3

38. M. Calabrei, "Wikileaks' War on Secrecy," *Time* (2 Dec. 2010), pp. 18–21.

39. Ibid.

40. See, for example, the CBC report on one of the more recent polls of this kind: www.cbc.ca/news/canada/story/2011/03/06/globescan-canada-poll.html. The BBC, the CBC, *The Economist* magazine, and GlobeScan research partners are among the agencies that carry out such polls.

41. J. Granatstein & D. Oliver, *The Oxford Companion to Canadian Military History* (Oxford: Oxford University Press, 2010).

42. D. Callahan, *Between Two Worlds: Realism, Idealism and American Foreign Policy After the Cold War* (New York: Harper Collins, 1994).

43. D. Bratt & C. Kukucha, eds, *Readings in Canadian Foreign Policy* (Don Mills, ON: Oxford University Press, 2nd edn, 2011); Y. Engler, *The Black Book of Canadian Foreign Policy* (Toronto: Fernwood, 2010).

44. C. Melakopides, *Pragmatic Idealism: Canadian Foreign Policy 1945–1995* (Montreal: McGill–Queen's University Press, 1998).

45. D. Morales & L. Medina, eds., *U.S. Economic and Trade Relationships with Canada and Mexico* (New York: Nova Science, 2011).

46. P. Lennox, *At Home and Abroad: The Canada–US Relationship and Canada's Place in the World* (Vancouver: UBC Press, 2010).

47. J.H. Thompson & S.J. Randall, *Canada and the United States* (Athens, GA: University of Georgia Press, 2008).

5 International Law and Organization

"The security of which we speak is to be attained by the development of international law through an international organization based on the principles of law and justice."[1] —*Ludwig Quidde (1858–1941), winner of the 1927 Nobel Peace Prize*

LEARNING OBJECTIVES

After studying this chapter, you will be able to:

▸ define all bolded key terms and concepts

▸ understand the general goal and function of international law, and its two core principles

▸ grasp the process whereby an international treaty becomes law, and know the different kinds of treaty, the pros and cons of each, and real-world examples of each

▸ discuss the difficulties involved in actually enforcing international law

▸ understand the United Nations—its history, purpose, parts, and functions, its strengths and weaknesses, and its overall role in global governance

▸ appreciate Canada's role inventing UN peacekeeping, and the circumstances of the Suez crisis that led to this

▸ understand the European Union—its history, purpose, parts, and functions, its strengths and weaknesses, and its overall role in furthering international organization

▸ reflect on how the Internet impacts international law and organization, both strengthening and subverting it.

INTRODUCTION

Nation-states, we saw last chapter, are at the core of global affairs and are generally the most powerful actors in the international system. Realists view the international system as an ungoverned anarchy wherein nation-states struggle among themselves for both hard and soft power, whereas idealists urge nation-states to pour their energies instead into a co-operative commitment to improving everyone's lot. We saw possible opportunities for the integration of these theories, and another—very important—one is the subject of this chapter: international law and organization. For even the most hardened realist can admit that nation-states can selfishly benefit from rules and institutions designed to make life easier, more regular, and more profitable for everyone; and idealists in international affairs often have it as a major goal to create and/or grow global organizations that can help solve such common human problems as poverty, disease, and pollution. In this chapter, we will come to understand what international law is, what international institutions do, and how they get made. We will examine their pros and cons, and consider many concrete examples of each, focussing on the United Nations (UN) and the European Union (EU).

Quick Definitions

The **goal of international law** is to order relations between nation-states through *rational, predictable, and mutually beneficial rules of conduct* (rather than through the dominance of a hegemon, the chaos of conflict, or the lawlessness of anarchy). Indeed, we might say that (a) the goal of international law *is* international organization, and (b) specific international institutions get created by countries to help bring this abstract goal into concrete reality.

The institutions created to uphold international law are referred to generally as **international organizations**, or **IOs**. But it's important to distinguish between **IGOs**, or **inter-governmental organizations**, and **NGOs**, or **non-governmental organizations**. The former are the creations *of national governments*, designed to help coordinate behaviour and solve common problems facing modern governments (from trade disputes to cross-border organized crime). The United Nations (UN) is an example of an IO—indeed, an IGO—and much more will be said about it below. International NGOs, by contrast, are *not* created by national governments but, rather, by private individuals or interest groups trying to improve international life in some specific way. Among the most prominent are the International Red Cross and Red Crescent (providing humanitarian relief efforts, especially in war), Amnesty International (promoting human rights), Greenpeace (championing environmental causes), and Doctors without Borders (or *Médecins Sans Frontières*, concerned with global public health). In this chapter, we are concerned with IGOs, as they are the creations of international law and are specifically designed to serve international organization.

INTERNATIONAL LAW

Origins of International Law

As we saw briefly in Chapter 1, most experts claim that international law has a specific birth date: 1648, when the **Treaty of Westphalia** was signed. This treaty, we know, was the peace treaty that brought to an end the Thirty Years War (1618–48), a battle over religion between European Catholics and Protestants. After three decades of savage violence, the European leaders got together to make a deal for peace. The deal came with the mutual acknowledgement that neither side in the religious conflict could fully "kill off" the other, and an agreement that it should be left up to the government of each country to decide which religion would prevail in its own state. No one would again try to convert the people of another country by force of arms. It was an agreement to lay down arms, and to live and let live. It was also the earliest expression and affirmation of the two most important and foundational principles of international law: political sovereignty and territorial integrity.[2]

The Two Core Principles of International Law

Political sovereignty is the right of a group of people to rule themselves. "Political" refers to power or to *polis*—the ancient Greek term for a group of people living together as an ongoing community. "Sovereignty" means the authority of a sovereign, such as a king or queen—in other words, the entitlement to rule. To be sovereign is to be self-ruling, acknowledging no higher authority over oneself. More fully, then, political sovereignty is the most basic right of a country in modern international law: the right of a country to make its own laws and to govern itself, *provided*—crucially—that it respects the right of all other countries to do the same. Every country on Earth jealously guards, and is proud of, its national or state sovereignty.

But this sovereignty must be exercised *somewhere*. To be real, the abstract right of political sovereignty must imply some secure space in which to live, and in which to enjoy self-rule. Hence, the right to **territorial integrity**. A country has a right to some liveable territory and is considered to be the general "owner" of all the natural resources on, under, or above its land. That's the "territorial" part; the "integrity" part refers to that group's right not to have other countries invade its territory and try to take its resources. A community not only needs *to have* territory and resources; it needs to be able *to count on having* such resources moving forward, if it is to remain—as Aristotle said in *The Politics*—an ongoing partnership formed for the general good of its members. Thus, the most basic and central value—the primordial premise—of international law is this: within a clearly defined territory, with resources seen as its own, a people or nation ought to be able to govern itself as it best sees fit, provided that it respects the rights of all other peoples and nations to do the same.[3]

> *Within a clearly defined territory, with resources seen as its own, a people or nation ought to be able to govern itself as it sees fit, provided that it respects the rights of all other peoples and nations to do the same.*

International Law, Defined

International law comprises all the agreements and undertakings that different peoples or nations make between themselves, presumably for mutual benefit. International law is, essentially, the sum of all treaties between countries. A **treaty** is a contractual deal between countries. It's a promise to do something, and countries make such promises with the expectation of benefit. So, international law is made by national governments seeking to make their lives easier: once more, we see how so much of everything in international life has its origins *within* the borders of the nation-state.[4]

Technically, there are some sources of international law other than treaties. However, experts concur that the vast majority of the pieces that make up international law *are* treaties, and that treaties form the strongest and clearest expression of international law. The other sources are:

- custom
- general principles of law
- international legal decisions
- international law scholarship.

Custom refers to habitual practice. If countries have behaved in a certain way X for a long time, it's considered reasonable to conclude that they are accepting a law-like rule to adhere to X. Custom has been important in a body of international law known as **the laws of the sea**, which regulate shipping across oceans and such.

General principles of law refer to the most elemental rules contained in national or domestic legal systems the world over. Such principles would include, for example, rules against theft and murder. Since these principles are present everywhere *nationally*, it's thought reasonable to infer they must be present *internationally*, too. So, for instance, when Iraq invaded Kuwait in 1990 to steal the latter's land and oil, everyone agreed that it was a violation of international law. There are also international courts (more below) that make **decisions on international cases** brought before them. These decisions become part of international law and help shape future decisions, ensuring consistency and predictability in the rules.

Finally, learned lawyers, judges, and professors of international law write **expert, peer-approved articles and books** on various aspects of international law. With enough reference and influence, these, too, can be thought of as forming, or at least informing, part of international law.[5]

Treaties, though, remain the gold standard of international law, as they are self-made and self-affirmed agreements as to how sovereign states promise to behave. Countries themselves freely pledge to adhere to certain rules, and thus holding them accountable to those rules seems completely reasonable. There are tens of thousands of treaties, on tens of hundreds of subjects. Before we mention some of the most prominent kinds, further explanation of how international law gets made will be of interest.

THE PROCESS OF TREATY-MAKING

Like most laws, a treaty tends to find its origin in a problem. There's a dispute between two or more countries, and they are looking for a solution. But it's not a small or one-time dispute; at the least, it promises to be an ongoing issue, thus requiring an enduring solution or framework of understanding. Say, for example, that there is a lake between countries *A* and *B* (much like the Great Lakes between the United States and Canada). The lakes aren't going anywhere, and neither are all the people living around them, and together they create all kinds of problems and opportunities between the neighbouring countries, such as:

- Where exactly is the border between the two countries on the surface of the lakes?
- How much drinking water should each country be allowed to take out, and why?
- How much pollution should each country be allowed to put in, and why? Who's responsible for cleaning up excessive pollution? And who's going to be responsible for monitoring these matters?
- How should boaters on the lakes be monitored and policed?
- Who "owns" the natural resources in, or under, the lakes, especially when they—like fish—might move (i.e. swim) back and forth across the border?

The list, obviously, goes on and on. And it cries out for a detailed deal, some sort of contractual arrangement, between Canada and the US. This deal becomes a clearly worded treaty (and in this particular case, there is *The Boundary Waters Treaty* of 1909[6]). It is usually produced after years of negotiation, fact-finding, deal-making, and treaty-drafting back and forth between lower-level officials, civil servants, and experts from both countries. There can be guidance from more powerful officials, and sometimes the top-most officials—senior cabinet secretaries and ministers, or even presidents and prime ministers—are required to step in to break an impasse or re-energize a negotiation.

The leaders of Abkhazia, Russia, and South Ossetia shake hands after signing a Friendship Treaty in Moscow's Kremlin. Why is this kind of ceremony—essentially a photo op— **important?** (© ITAR-TASS Photo Agency/Alamy)

Once a deal has been made and agreed upon behind the scenes by the countries involved, the treaty is drafted and approved by international lawyers from both societies. There is then often a **formal signing ceremony**, especially if the treaty is on an important topic. This ceremony is a public, political event—great photo opportunity, with everyone smiling and shaking hands—highlighted by the moment when the heads of state put their signatures on the treaty. The signature represents the head of state's promise to take this treaty back to his or her country and then either treat it like law straight away or, more commonly in a democracy, introduce that treaty as a bill that needs to be turned into a law under the country's national or domestic constitutional procedure for turning a bill into a law. Once that long process has been completed, the international treaty has been turned into a law in that society, the same as (and just as real as) any other piece of legislation in that country, and just as enforceable by the police and the civil service.

Generally, then, that's how a treaty gets made and then becomes law, both nationally and internationally. When a treaty has been turned into a law in country *A*, we say that *A* has **ratified** the treaty. Once the treaty has been ratified by the **signatories** (i.e. the countries that have signed the treaty), there is usually a **grace period** to allow the various societies to make whatever changes they need to make in order to bring their countries in line with the promises sworn to in the treaty. These may include budgetary changes, creating a new government department to monitor or enforce something, and so on. After that grace period ends, though, the treaty is now said to be **in force**, i.e. full-blown, actual, enforceable law, the violation of which can result in penalties, sanctions, and lawsuits. The process is summarized in Figure 5.1.[7]

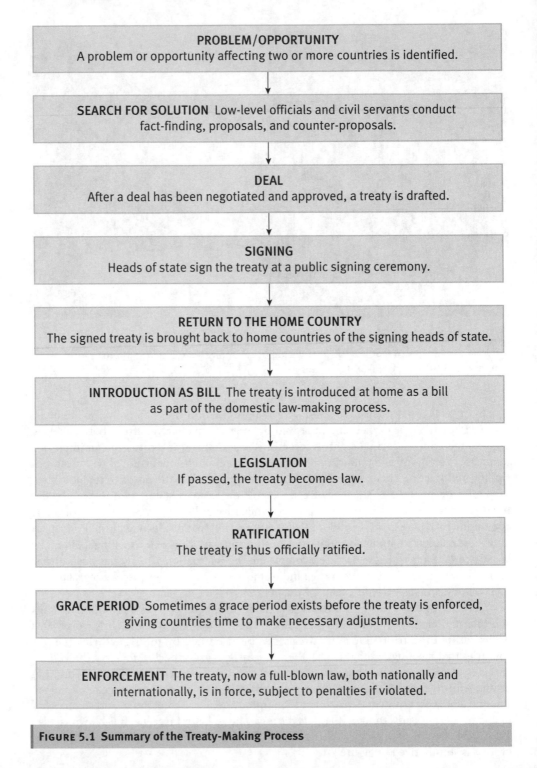

PROBLEM/OPPORTUNITY
A problem or opportunity affecting two or more countries is identified.

SEARCH FOR SOLUTION Low-level officials and civil servants conduct
fact-finding, proposals, and counter-proposals.

DEAL
After a deal has been negotiated and approved, a treaty is drafted.

SIGNING
Heads of state sign the treaty at a public signing ceremony.

RETURN TO THE HOME COUNTRY
The signed treaty is brought back to home countries of the signing heads of state.

INTRODUCTION AS BILL The treaty is introduced at home as a bill
as part of the domestic law-making process.

LEGISLATION
If passed, the treaty becomes law.

RATIFICATION
The treaty is thus officially ratified.

GRACE PERIOD Sometimes a grace period exists before the treaty is enforced,
giving countries time to make necessary adjustments.

ENFORCEMENT The treaty, now a full-blown law, both nationally and
internationally, is in force, subject to penalties if violated.

FIGURE 5.1 Summary of the Treaty-Making Process

Kinds of Treaty

There are two kinds of treaty: *bilateral* and *multilateral*. **Bilateral** means "two-sided," and it denotes a treaty between two countries. **Multilateral** means "many-sided" and refers to any agreement between three or more countries. Multilateral treaties, in turn, are of two kinds: *regional* or *global*. A **regional multilateral treaty** has been negotiated by at least three countries in a close, coherent, geographical region, whereas a **global multilateral treaty** has been negotiated by all, or almost all, countries in the world. Examples?

- The **Canada–US Free Trade Agreement** (or FTA) of 1989 is an example of a *bilateral treaty*, dealing with the trade of goods and services across the Canada–US border. (More about the FTA in the chapter that follows, on international trade.) Another bilateral treaty between these same countries, in 1958, created NORAD, the North American Aerospace Defense Command (designed to monitor North American airspace and defend it from foreign invasion). The United States has many bilateral treaties with Russia, most aimed at arms control and limiting the number of (especially nuclear) weapons each country has. Some of the most important of these treaties are the Anti-Ballistic Missile (or ABM) treaty of 1972, the Strategic Arms Limitation Talks (or SALT) treaty of 1972, the Strategic Arms Reduction Talks (or START) treaty of 1991, and the Comprehensive Test Ban Treaty of 1996.[8]

- Signed in 1994, the **North American Free Trade Agreement** (or NAFTA) is an example of a *regional multilateral treaty* between Canada, the United States, and Mexico, again on the flow of goods and services between these three countries. (NAFTA grew out of, and extended, the FTA.) The 1648 Treaty of Westphalia, mentioned above, would also fall into this category, as would the many treaties founding, creating, and extending the **European Union** (EU)—such as the Treaty of Maastricht, 1991—signed by most of the countries of Europe but no countries outside of that region. Also relevant here is the 1949 treaty that created **NATO**, the North Atlantic Treaty Organization, which is probably the most important military alliance of our time. Composed of the US, Canada, and the nations first of western Europe and now of central and eastern Europe, too, NATO is an alliance dedicated to mutual defence, or **collective security**, in the event any one of its members is attacked. It was founded especially with an eye to protecting western Europe from a ground invasion by the Soviet Union (Russia) during the Cold War but has since survived the end of that conflict. Currently, NATO forces have been, since the September 11 attacks, in action in Afghanistan.[9]

- *Global multilateral treaties* are harder to come by, as there are more differences of opinion and varied circumstances across the planet. But the **Charter of the United Nations** (1945)—the deal founding the United Nations and detailing its branches and how they should work—is one such example. (The UN's structure and function will be detailed below.) Some of the human rights treaties also belong here, and they will be discussed in Chapter 9, on human rights.

Technical versus Economic versus Political Treaties

In spite of this reference to difficulty, there actually *are* a number of global treaties, both bilateral and multilateral, that have enjoyed great success. But many of them are known as "technical treaties." **Technical treaties** are those that deal with practical issues of very little political controversy. Technical treaties address such things as how mail gets transported across borders, how luggage is handled on international flights, how radio waves should be distributed, how telephone (or, in the past, telegraph) lines ought to be laid across the ocean floor, and so on. You can see how it would be pretty easy to get strong, even worldwide, consensus on such targeted, precise, and practical issues, because (1) they are very detailed, (2) they are of little political controversy, and (3) they pertain to matters that everyone has a clear interest in seeing run smoothly and efficiently.

Political treaties are much more controversial, since they have deeper implications for how a society runs itself. So, for example, the international human rights treaties are much more contentious and hard to negotiate successfully than, say, the postal or telephone treaties because the human rights treaties are promises by governments about how they are going to treat their own people. Governments, especially non-democratic ones, can be prickly about the subject of the rights of their citizens, viewing the matter as their sovereign privilege—and none of the rest of the world's business. There are *some* global human rights treaties, as stated above, but they were much harder to come by than the radio wave treaties, and they are *not*, to say the least, perfectly realized in the actual world.

Economic treaties, such as trade agreements, are in between, in terms of controversy. On the one hand, they *are* contentious because they can have implications for how a government collects taxes, and what kinds of goods can be sold to its people. (For example, initially, the Canada–US Free Trade Agreement was controversial, as people in certain industries on both sides of the border feared they would be put out of business by competitors in the other country.) On the other hand, if every country can come to see that they will benefit in some concrete way from a deal, common sense and rationality will typically win the day; and so there are thousands of commercial treaties in place around the world. It's easier to show countries that they stand to make some money, whereas it's much harder to show countries that they should change the way they run their society, which is why political treaties are the most difficult, rare, and contentious of the three types presented here (and summarized in Table 5.1).[10]

TABLE 5.1 Typical Subject Matter of Three Kinds of Treaty

Technical	Economic/Commercial	Political
• international mail • organized crime • telephone/telegraph/ radio waves • international flights and luggage	• natural resources (e.g. air, water) • trade, free trade • intellectual property (e.g. inventions, copyright law) • international taxation (e.g. when resident of country A earns income in country B) • regulation of multinational corporations	• regional governance (e.g. EU) • global governance (e.g. UN) • war and peace • borders • human rights • refugees • climate change

Enforcement of Treaties

Enforcing international law can be problematic. Some scholars actually think that international law doesn't even deserve the term "law," as there is no effective world government to back it up and enforce it, the way there is in a developed national society.[11] While this is true, and while there have been shocking, saddening cases of non-enforcement of international law, as happened during the Rwandan genocide in 1994,[12] by and large international law *does* go observed. In fact, the regard for and observance of international law is getting stronger over time. Why?

- Countries have a substantial self-interest in keeping the promises they make. If they don't, they get a reputation for defaulting on their commitments, and other countries refuse to deal with them, limiting the power and benefits accessible to them.

- Generally, countries want to deal with each other in rational, predictable ways. This requires less effort overall and allows them to focus on more profitable or urgent matters. International law creates this kind of stable order, and most countries see the benefit in that.

- When confronted with a law-breaker, countries often join together to issue a collective response that penalizes the law-breaker. These responses, we've seen last chapter, include criticism, refusal to engage, sanctions, and armed force.

- Increasingly, international institutions are being created by treaties to monitor, police, and enforce the terms of a treaty. IOs make co-operation easier, ongoing, and more concrete, and thus make non-compliance harder to achieve and benefit from.

International law is not perfect, though. Particular problems come, on the one hand, from determined rogue regimes and, on the other, from great powers who do not wish to sign on to, or agree with, a treaty the rest of the world wants. As we saw in the discussion of the environment in Chapter 2, the recent efforts to forge an effective global treaty on climate change—one that would have signatories commit to reducing the carbon emissions thought to cause global warming—have run afoul of countries like China, the US, and (with its recent withdrawal from the Kyoto agreement) Canada. The result has been a standstill—perhaps even a step back—in this regard.[13]

INTERNATIONAL ORGANIZATION

The League of Nations

In 1919, following World War I, the League of Nations—one of the very first IOs, and IGOs—was founded. It was the first serious attempt at true global governance, and was the pet project of the American president Woodrow Wilson (who is, as we saw last chapter, one of history's biggest international idealists). Wilson hoped the League of Nations would move humanity towards coordinated, worldwide solutions to international problems. But the League was seriously hampered right from the start, when (ironically) the US refused to join. (Republican Party senators refused to ratify the treaty crafted by Wilson, who was a Democrat.) Then, when the League publicly condemned fascist Germany and imperial Japan for their various aggressive invasions throughout the 1930s, those countries withdrew

> We know, from experience, that international institutions do not work well without the support of great powers.

from the League. We now know, partly from this experience, that international institutions do not work well without the support of great powers. And so, once the Second World War started in 1939, the League collapsed and the world's first attempt at global governance ended in failure.[14]

The United Nations

After the Second World War, US Democratic presidents Franklin Roosevelt and Harry Truman tried again to create an international body charged with global governance: the result was the United Nations. Founded in San Francisco in 1945, the UN was headquartered in New York, where, it was thought, it stood the best chance of securing the continuing support and interest of the American people. This worked, and the UN officially came into being the following year. The UN Charter, which details the aims and structure of the organization, is one of the most successful global multilateral treaties, and almost every country in the world is a UN member. (Only national governments may become UN members: no individuals, NGOs, corporations, or any other kind of organization may join the UN.)[15]

While the UN *does* advance global governance in a range of meaningful ways, it is crucial to note that it is *not* a world government. The United Nations—as the name shows—is an international organization created by nation-states to help them solve problems and to realize mutual gains. The UN does not *rule over* the countries of the world, the way the Canadian federal government rules over the various provincial governments. The UN, rather, is a creature of sovereign states—a worldwide *volunteer club* of national governments—and thus can be and is limited by those states in a range of ways. The entire UN budget, for example, comes from the donations (or "contributions") of national governments. (And to put the size of the UN's budget in perspective, consider that it is only about one-one hundredth of what gets spent, every year, by the world's national governments *on their militaries alone*.) Furthermore, all UN peacekeepers are supplied on a temporary basis as a loan, so to speak, from various national armed forces. In short, everything the UN has is supplied to it by national governments. This reveals the true realities of power internationally, and sometimes the UN suffers from the wrath of disapproving governments. For instance, the United States owes the UN a bunch of money (though not as much as it used to). The US is thus **in arrears** on its UN contributions—and deliberately so, to show occasional displeasure and perhaps just generally to keep the UN in its place. But it must be noted, to be fair, that even in spite of this fact, the US is by far the UN's single largest contributor country, and always has been.[16]

New York City was chosen as the site for the UN's headquarters in part to get greater support from the American people. Do you think it's still the most appropriate site?
(© Jeremy Edwards/iStockphoto)

Goals of the UN

The aims and functions of the UN range from the sublimely ideal to the tangibly practical. The most important include the following:

- to prevent war and secure peace
- to help realize everyone's human rights
- to serve as a symbol of our common and evolving humanity
- to aid in the development of the Global South
- to serve as a forum where the world's nations can share their views and seek to coordinate behaviour that can solve shared problems
- to gather, and make available, information about international life and global affairs (e.g. data about worldwide economic growth or the cross-border spread of a disease).

The UN's Parts and Functions

The General Assembly (GA)

The General Assembly (GA) is the heart of the UN. Every member nation (all 192, as of writing) is a GA member. Every one gets exactly one vote; majority rules on votes taken, and no one gets a veto. The GA is thus a very *inclusive* club, and equality here shines forth, as the smallest country's vote counts the same as that of a great power. While it is true that resolutions passed by the GA are generally **non-binding** (i.e. not mandatory) on member-states, the General Assembly does (a) raise and allocate the UN's budget, and (b) remain broadly accountable for the overall aim and direction of the UN. The General Assembly may thus be seen as something like the **legislative branch** of the UN. It meets regularly—with the heaviest schedule usually being in late fall every year—and is often

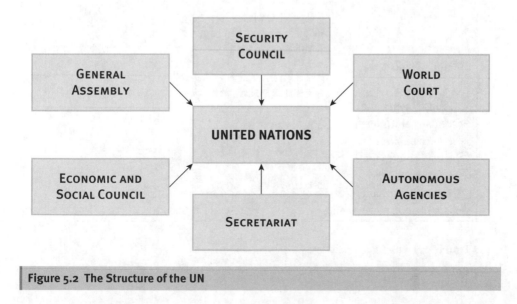

Figure 5.2 The Structure of the UN

Canadian Insights

Canada and Peacekeeping

Canada is widely credited with creating the UN peacekeeping role during the 1956 Suez Crisis. Cutting across the Sinai Peninsula between Egypt and Israel, the Suez Canal is a vital shipping route linking the Mediterranean Sea to the Red Sea and Persian Gulf (see Figure 5.3). It was under British control when the Egyptian government of the day, headed by Gamal Abdal Nasser, "nationalized" (effectively took over) the strategically and commercially important waterway. The governments of Britain, France, and Israel responded by going to war with Egypt in an effort to keep the canal as an international waterway. The three countries wanted to preserve quick and easy shipping access to the huge Middle Eastern oil fields, whereas Nasser wanted a cut of the profits from all that oil flowing through the Suez.

When the war broke out, everyone around the world wanted the fighting to stop immediately. The country of Israel had been founded only recently—in 1948, as we saw in Chapter 3, on comparative culture—and the wounds from that event were still raw. Furthermore, it was a tense time during the

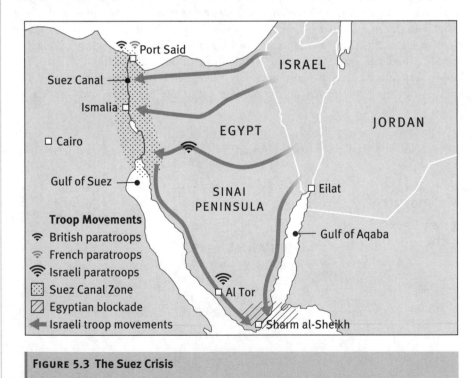

FIGURE 5.3 The Suez Crisis

Source: Based on http://news.bbc.co.uk/2/hi/middle_east/5195068.stm

Cold War, and no one wanted either the US or the USSR to get involved in the fighting. The UN demanded the belligerents declare an immediate ceasefire and withdraw their forces. The governments of the invading armies complied and agreed to talk peace, but they needed a neutral force to separate their armies and ensure that fighting would not re-erupt during negotiations. Canada, forgoing its traditional support for Britain and allying itself with one of the war's most outspoken critics, the US, had denounced the conflict, and it was Canada's Minister for External Affairs, Lester B. Pearson, who lobbied for the creation of the UN Emergency Force (UNEF) to keep the combatants at arm's length from each other. Because Canada was viewed as an acceptable neutral party, the international peacekeeping contingent was made up largely of Canadians and was led by a Canadian general.

And so the UNEF kept the peace while the belligerents agreed to a deal: the Suez would be kept international and open, but the government of Egypt would now receive some royalties from each ship passing through. Pearson was awarded the Nobel Peace Prize in 1957 and went on, six years later, to become prime minister of Canada.[17]

formally addressed by the world's leaders. The GA is one of a very few international institutions wherein the countries of the Global South have the majority say.

The Security Council (UNSC)

In contrast to the General Assembly stands the UN Security Council (UNSC), which—as the name shows—is tasked with maintaining international peace and security. Resolutions passed by the UNSC are generally **binding** (i.e. mandatory) on all member-states, and the UNSC has the power to both (a) declare a threat to international peace and security, and (b) structure a response to it. A possible response would be to mandate that all UN members impose sanctions on the threatening country (this was done with Iraq, following its invasion of Kuwait in 1990). Another would be to authorize a **peace-making mission**, designed to impose a peace on a warring nation (as the UN tried to do in the early 1990s during the civil war in the former Yugoslavia—see Chapter 7 for more on this). Finally, the response might involve authorizing **a peacekeeping mission**, wherein the opposing sides have already halted hostilities but require a neutral body to separate their forces and keep the peace while they negotiate the terms of a final ceasefire and broader peace agreement.

UN *peacekeeping* has been much more successful than UN *peace-making* over the years, which is no surprise when one considers that the difference between them is that, in the first instance, a peace of sorts *has already been achieved* by the sides in question, whereas in the second, the UN must intervene in a hot war and try to force a settlement to which at least one side—or possibly all—disagrees. When the UN failed to make peace in Yugoslavia, NATO took over, imposing a peace on the warring sides via the Dayton Accords of 1995. But the UN has succeeded in some peacekeeping missions, notably in the Middle East and in Southeast Asia. UN peacekeepers collectively won the Nobel Peace Prize in 1988.[18]

As noted, the UN has no permanent military force of its own: the UN asks member countries to make armed forces available to it, and it either clothes them in distinctive powder-blue UN helmets or else leaves them under national command but tasks them with achieving UNSC resolutions. The UN has authorized scores of peacekeeping and peace-making missions, all around the world, since the start of the concept at Suez. The UN's record, as noted, has been mixed. Success has depended on the quality and funding of UN forces but, above all, on the local situation and whether the belligerent sides could them-selves agree on a peace. As of writing, there are 16 ongoing UN military missions, with over 102,000 uniformed personnel, contributed by over 115 countries.[19]

The UNSC meets only when there seems to be a threat to international peace and security. It has 15 members, and 9 votes are needed for a resolution to pass. Plus, there must be no vetoes. Only the **five permanent members** of the UNSC hold vetoes, and they form perhaps the world's most exclusive political club. They are (1) Britain, (2) China, (3) France, (4) Russia, and (5) the United States (i.e. the major winning powers of the Second World War). Nothing gets passed by the UNSC without all five essentially giving their support. (Sometimes, instead of vetoing a resolution, a permanent member will instead indicate its displeasure by **abstaining**, i.e. by refusing either to vote or to veto. China does this somewhat often.) The other 10, non-permanent members of the UNSC hold two-year terms, and they run for election within the General Assembly. (Canada has held six terms since the UNSC was founded, one of the best records in this regard.)

The severe exclusivity of the UNSC has made it the subject of regular calls for reform. Germany and Japan, for example, are near-great powers and generous UN funders, yet have been denied permanent seats. (As a result, Japan in the early 2000s cut its annual contribution to the UN by 25 per cent.) India, an emerging power, a nuclear power, and the world's second-most populous country, is a developing society, and some experts find it a scandal that, amongst current UNSC permanent members, only China is a developing nation; all the rest are developed, Northern, Western, Caucasian, Christian, and European (or European-derived) societies. Other critics feel at least one Islamic country should be a permanent member, whereas others have proposed that the UNSC be expanded so that every continent have at least one country as a permanent UNSC member (the Australians, in particular, love this idea). During the 1990s there was a concerted Brazilian effort to pass a reform measure that would have seen the following countries become new, permanent UNSC members with vetoes: Brazil, Germany, Egypt, Japan, Indonesia, and Nigeria. The proposal got some support but then ultimately failed.

The huge problem with reforming the UNSC is that any of the five permanent members are entitled to veto any proposed changes, and, usually, one or all have serious problems with reform proposals, not the least of which being that expanding the UNSC means dimin-ishing their own power. Why should they agree to that? Thus, realism tells us not to expect UNSC reform any time soon, regardless of our idealistic hopes.[20]

The Secretariat

If there is an "executive branch" of the UN, it is a combination of the UNSC and the Secretariat. The UNSC, as we have seen, is the branch of the UN that can deploy armed force, and its resolutions are mandatory. But the Secretariat has executive functions, too. The Secretariat comprises all the employees and civil servants in the UN system, which totals over 63,000 worldwide. (Their salaries are paid in tax-free US dollars, so it's nice work if you can get it!) UN offices are spread out globally, but there are denser concentra-tions of UN staff in New York, Geneva, and Paris.

At the head of the UN organization is the **secretary-general** (SG). The SG is the chief executive officer of the UN system, responsible for running the UN on a daily basis and for personnel and bureaucratic decisions. Sometimes known as "the world's top diplomat," the SG is frequently called upon to help nations use the UN system to help solve their problems. The SG is nominated by the UNSC, and thus the "permanent five" must all support him (and so far, historically, all SGs *have* been "hims"). Once he is approved by majority vote in the General Assembly, he holds office for five years, a term that may be renewed (and often is). As of writing, the secretary-general is Ban Ki-Moon, of South Korea. He took over from Ghana's Kofi Annan, who had held the office from 1997 until 2007.

When it comes to international crises, there is little the SG can do if nations are not willing to submit their disputes to the UN. But the SG does occupy a high-profile position, which allows him to publicize problems and use **moral suasion** to try and persuade leaders to be constructive. Failing that, the SG *does* have the legal power to force the UNSC to meet *to discuss* a problem—but he cannot force the UNSC even to vote on a resolution, much less to act in a substantive way.[21]

The World Court

The judicial branch of the UN is the world court, better known as the **International Court of Justice (ICJ)**, located in the Dutch city The Hague (long a site of importance to international law). The ICJ is composed of 15 judges, who serve nine-year terms and must be approved by both the UN Security Council and the General Assembly. By tradition, five of these judges are from the five permanent member countries of the UNSC. The ICJ hears cases brought to it *voluntarily* by member states, which typically come to it looking for a neutral expert opinion on a complex issue contested between two states. (And *only* state governments—not individuals, groups, or corporations—can bring suits to the ICJ.) For example, in 1992, the ICJ settled a longstanding border dispute between El Salvador and Honduras, drawing the border definitively and thereby settling a bitter division that had lasted for over a hundred years (and had even triggered war in 1969).

The ICJ lacks any enforcement power, and can only issue decisions. The decisions *do* have some moral authority—especially since the countries that are parties in the lawsuit voluntarily agreed to submit the dispute to the court in the first place—but no effectual authority beyond that. In 2004, for instance, the ICJ ruled that Israel's security wall in the West Bank—constructed to keep terrorists out of Israel—violated international law. But Israel immediately announced it would ignore the ruling and maintain the wall, which it argues has been successful in achieving its purpose, greatly reducing the number of terrorist suicide bombings since its construction. Or consider the 1986 decision in the case of *Nicaragua v. The United States*, wherein Nicaragua argued that the US government—via the CIA—had blown up the harbours of its capital city, Managua. This would be seen as a very serious act of war, one the Americans might have engaged in as part of the Cold War fight against communism, since Nicaragua's government of the day was quite left-leaning—almost Cuba-esque. The ICJ found in favour of Nicaragua, but the US suffered nothing more than public embarrassment for its actions.

The ICJ is not often used. Countries, after all, prefer to negotiate their problems directly between themselves, and so, on average, only a dozen cases are heard per year. This may increase with the new branch of the ICJ, the **International Criminal Court (ICC)**, founded in 1998 via the Treaty of Rome to try individuals accused of war crimes and other crimes against humanity. (More will be said about the ICC in Chapter 8, on post-war reconstruction.)[22]

The Economic and Social Council (ECOSOC)

This branch of the UN is in charge of helping to co-ordinate economic and social policies among the member countries of the UN, to the benefit of all. There are 54 members of the Economic and Social Council, and each one has a vote but no veto. The members of ECOSOC serve three-year terms and are elected for membership within the General Assembly.

ECOSOC is actually a very effective and powerful part of the UN system, and the UN has seen some of its greatest successes come out of this branch. Why? Think back to the whole issue of "technical versus political versus economic" treaties. Many of the issues that ECOSOC deals with are focused, concrete, practical, and technical—involving such matters as trade disputes, child welfare, access to food, narcotics control, the plight of refugees—and these issues tend to get greater co-operation than, say, war and peace or border disputes. We must be mindful of the fact that for every high-profile failure of the UN, there are many small-scale successes that it has had through ECOSOC, improving the lives of some of the world's most vulnerable people.[23]

The Autonomous Agencies

The autonomous agencies ultimately report, through ECOSOC, back to the General Assembly. But conceptually, it makes sense to consider them separately, as there are so many of them, and, on a daily basis, they are expert organizations with highly specific mandates. They, too, focus on achieving concrete progress, in measurable ways, on issues of little political controversy and with clear practical relevance. There are scores of these agencies, and they range from perhaps the world's two oldest IOs, the International Labour Organization (ILO) and the Universal Postal Union (UPU), to such powerful and successful agencies as the World Health Organization (WHO), the World Trade Organization (WTO), and the International Monetary Fund (IMF). More will be said about these latter agencies in chapters to follow.

The Trusteeship Council

This last branch of the UN has now closed shop. It was set up in 1946 to aid **European decolonization** throughout Africa, Asia, and Latin America. It became defunct in 1994, after Namibia became independent. Namibia was called "the world's last colony."[24]

UN: Pros and Cons

Before moving on, we need to review the strengths and weaknesses of the UN in general.

To the plus side, the UN has had some amazing practical and technical success stories, especially through ECOSOC and the autonomous agencies. Because of them, children have become literate and educated, refugees saved from starvation, people inoculated against terrible diseases, and international trade has increased and grown wealth worldwide. Also, the UN is as close to genuinely global governance as we currently have and can expect—thus it seems to fill a needed niche. On the other hand, the UN is a slave to the sovereign states which compose it, and generally it only works well when the great powers—especially America—want it to work. There are also controversies about exclusivity, big power dominance, and the need for structural reform. And, on the big-ticket, big-picture, blue-sky political goals—of the realization of human rights, and the prevention of armed conflict—the UN's record of achievement is, shall we say, far from flawless.

The European Union (EU)

An international institution with a clearer record of success is the **European Union**: a regional, multilateral organization centred in Europe and held together with an amazing array of treaties, organizations, and, increasingly, shared beliefs and practices. Because of the breadth, depth, and overall success of the integration it has brought about between the

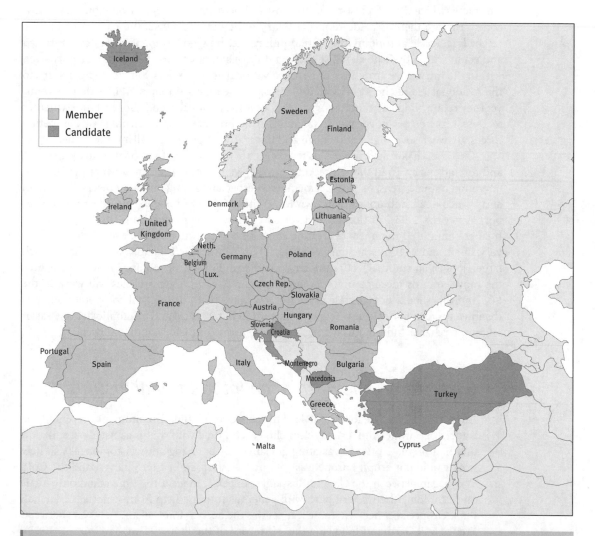

FIGURE 5.4 EU Member States and Current Candidates

Source: US Central Intelligence Agency, Perry-Castañeda Library Map Collection. Courtesy of the University of Texas Libraries, The University of Texas at Austin

nations of Europe, the EU is sometimes called a **trans-national** or even **supra-national institution**. In other words, although it *began* as a voluntary club of nations (like the UN), the EU now has, in many ways, transcended its member nations and rules over them from an effective and substantial—not merely symbolic—new and higher level of governance.

EU member states have a combined population of over 500 million, who make up the largest or second-largest economy in the world (depending on the source and how it compares the EU to the United States), and the largest trading partner of both China and India. The EU is made up of 27 countries speaking 23 languages. Sixteen of the countries use one common currency (the **euro**) and share a common central bank, based in Frankfurt, Germany, which sets interest rates (the cost of borrowing money) throughout the "euro-zone." Though there is a common **monetary policy** in this sense, the nations of Europe retain large-scale autonomy over **fiscal policy** (i.e. how government revenues are raised and spent within their borders), so there is still considerable nation-state sovereignty, even within the integrative structures of Europe. National governments contribute huge sums to the headquarters of the EU—located in Brussels, Belgium—to enable EU-wide programs, yet they retain budgetary control over their domestic political agenda, for instance, whether to raise taxes or cut government spending. This produces some tensions, or competing forces, between sovereign nationalism and integrative supra-nationalism in Europe.[25]

The other major field where this tension is obvious is that of national security, defence, and foreign policy. Even though recent treaties have committed EU members to greater co-operation in these areas, in practice, members—especially strong military powers like Britain and France—can, and do, go their own way. Witness, for example, Britain's decision to support America's 2003 invasion of Iraq versus France's strong criticism of the same. Recent treaties commit EU members to creating some kind of common military force, yet it will be very small, and NATO—which unites western Europe with the US and Canada—has a much larger, longer, and more effective military presence in Europe. So, no one knows exactly how the move towards more common security structures and foreign policies will work in the EU. And this should not surprise us, as we now know that it is political co-operation that is the most difficult to achieve, whereas co-operation in technical and economic fields is easier and more reliable. Indeed, this truth is driven home by the history of the EU itself.

Case Study: The Birth of an International Institution

After World War II ended in 1945, Europe stood in ruin. The moment presented the leaders of Europe with a stark, clear choice: continue with things as usual—a situation that had produced two devastating global wars—or change things completely, so new wars would not erupt. Europe was split into western and eastern halves, and the Cold War began between the US and Russia. European leaders at the time could only focus on re-building the western part, with generous funding help from America's Marshall Plan. Of special concern to these leaders was the need to forestall any new wars between France and Germany, following the sad record of the Franco–Prussian War (1870–1), the First World War (1914–18) and the Second World War (1939–45). They did not want yet another generation to suffer the terrible effects of this bitter and bloody rivalry in the heart of Europe, especially now that atomic weapons had been invented. But the leaders of these European nations—like French diplomat Jean Monnet and French prime minister Robert Schuman—were smart enough to know that in the immediate post-war environment, the people of France and Germany would be hostile to plans for robust co-operation with each other, much less integration. Yet Monnet and Schuman dreamed of tying the economies of France and Germany so closely together that for either country to go to war against the other would result in economic suicide—and so no rational future leader would ever again go down that path.[26]

The solution to the problem—the practical way to try to achieve this ideal—was to take baby steps. More precisely, it was to focus on small, concrete, technical issues,

TABLE 5.2 Members of the European Union

Country	Year of Admission	Euro Currency? (Yes/No)
Austria	1995	Yes
Belgium	1951	Yes
Bulgaria	2007	No
Cyprus	2004	Yes
Czech Republic	2004	No
Denmark	1973	No
Estonia	2004	No
Finland	1995	Yes
France	1951	Yes
Germany	1951	Yes
Greece	1981	Yes
Hungary	2004	No
Ireland	1973	Yes
Italy	1951	Yes
Latvia	2004	No
Lithuania	2004	No
Luxembourg	1951	Yes
Malta	2004	Yes
Netherlands	1951	Yes
Poland	2004	No
Portugal	1986	Yes
Romania	2007	No
Slovakia	2004	Yes
Slovenia	2004	Yes
Spain	1986	Yes
Sweden	1995	No
United Kingdom	1973	No

Source: www.europa.eu

and then, after seeing successes there, to build momentum toward pursuing bigger, bolder forms of economic and political co-operation. So the EU found its birth in one tiny treaty in 1950, committing France and Germany to co-operation in the steel and coal industries. Monnet and Schuman knew this would work—a common, mutually advantageous industrial policy—and that it would be more important than people realized, as steel and coal were vital to the enormous post-war rebuilding task. In 1951 the two countries were joined by Belgium, the Netherlands, Italy, and Luxembourg as the founding nations of the European Coal and Steel Community.

The plan worked: first, focus on targeted, technical, non-controversial issues and opportunities; then, forge co-operation and integration, yielding tangible benefits. Ensure, and wait for, success, and then move forward more ambitiously to deeper and wider political and economic integration. Don't push too fast: letting the successes speak for themselves will enhance the benefits of European integration in the minds of the people, and ease the minds of national leaders fearful both of both losing sovereignty and of backing an ambitious, untried, grand schema for integration. The Treaty of Rome was signed in 1957, moving the process forward, followed by the Merger Treaty of 1967, which renamed the project the European Community (to show things had advanced beyond mere coal and steel).

The first wave of growth came in 1973, when Britain, Denmark, and Ireland joined, and there have been several waves of growth since then—in the 1980s, and then again especially in 2004, when a large number of formerly communist countries of central and eastern Europe joined, following the end of the Cold War and their own internal reform (see Table 5.2). No one has ever dropped out of the EU, and perhaps that is the simplest and strongest indicator of success.[27]

Membership Criteria and "The Five Pillars"

It is important and revealing to consider the **Copenhagen criteria** for becoming a member of the EU. To become eligible, a country must be *European*, and have *a free-market economy* (i.e. one that allows for entrepreneurship, the ownership of private property, and open business competition). The candidate country must also, politically, be *a stable democracy*, with regular, free, fair, and public elections of the government. The country's legal system must be committed to *the rule of law* and respecting and realizing everyone's basic *human rights* (to life, liberty, and the pursuit of happiness, as well as to security, equality, political participation, and due process). The country must also, of course, be willing to accept all the obligations that becoming an EU member entails—agreeing to obey all EU laws—and, moreover, must meet technical criteria (e.g. about the size of its national debt), showing that it has *the financial fitness* and general potential to participate in, and compete within, the EU. The most recent members are Bulgaria and Romania, admitted in 2007. Several countries are up for membership or are about to apply; these include, perhaps most controversially, Serbia and Turkey.[28]

Probably the most important treaties in the European integration process are the Single Europe Act (1985) and the seminal Treaty of Maastricht (1991), and yet the process of treaty-making continues apace, most recently with the Treaty of Lisbon (2009). The various treaties have helped to create a Europe that looks like this:

- In the first instance, the EU is an economic system designed to generate, through co-operation and integration, wealth far beyond what each country could achieve on its own via competition. The EU does this through a **free-trade area**, which allows for the tariff-free (or tax-free) exchange of goods and services across the national borders of all member-states.

- Second, the EU is a **customs union**: while there is free trade *internally* within the EU, all EU members agree to keep identical tariffs or taxes on goods and services traded with non-member countries, like Canada and China.

- Third, the EU is a **common market**, allowing both labour (i.e. workers) and capital (i.e. cash for investment) to flow freely within the Union. For example, a person born in England can get a job in Italy and move there without any special visa; and an investor in Germany wanting to build a tourist hotel in Greece can likewise do so with ease, just as if the hotel were being built in Germany itself.

- Finally, there is both a currency and a central bank shared by most EU members. The **one currency** eliminates the inefficiency of working with multiple currencies, and the **one central bank** keeps borrowing costs level and predictable across the whole zone. Businesses in particular love both measures.

As a result of these "five pillars of Europe," the EU has essentially become a single market, functioning as a cohesive economic entity, and a very successful one, too—either first or second in the world, with the US and China rounding out the top three.[29]

But the EU has moved beyond economic, towards political, integration. There is *a common passport* issued to all EU citizens, and passport controls have been abolished

The headquarters of the EU in Brussels. (© Ziutograf/iStockphoto)

within the Union, easing the flow of people around the continent. In other words, once you pass one passport entry point in the EU, you're in, and you don't have to keep lining up every time you pass an international border. (This is totally *unlike* how it used to be.) EU members also commit to common policies on such issues as environmental protection, trade with non-members, fisheries and energy, and criminal justice. Two issues in particular are worth highlighting: agriculture and regional development.

The EU is committed to a kind of equalization formula regarding standard of living and quality of life across the Union. This means that poorer member states, and poorer regions within member states, receive funds from the centre to invest in projects that will promote prosperity and trade. These projects tend to focus on **physical infrastructure**—roads, bridges, railways—and on so-called **human infrastructure**, like education and healthcare. But other projects that might qualify for funding include modernizing a tourist site to make it more attractive for, say, North American and Japanese tourists. The policy has already provided huge benefits to many poorer regions of Europe, but it is also one reason why considerable care is taken with allowing new member countries into the EU, lest the demands of the poorer regions swamp the centre.

Meanwhile, the Union's **Common Agriculture Policy** (or **CAP**) provides subsidies and other financial support to farmers. The CAP says that, whatever subsidy one government offers to its farmers *must* be matched by all other countries (but with EU money). So EU farmers enjoy EU-wide support and protection in terms of loans, tax benefits, price supports, and protection from cheap competing imports. This last issue has caused a substantial problem in international trade, angering both the US (which sees the CAP as socialist-style protectionism) and the Global South (who wish to sell their lower-cost produce into Europe but get prevented from doing so by the tariffs on non-members imposed by the CAP). More will be said on this important issue in Chapter 6, on international trade.[30]

Structure of the EU

A bit on the complex political structuring of the EU is in order (see Figure 5.5). There is a **European Parliament**, which sits in Strasbourg, France (right on the border with Germany). European parliamentarians are elected by the people every five years, and they are typically affiliated with Europe-wide parties (such as the Christian Democrats); they do *not* sit as representatives of countries. The parliament is weak, though, and mainly acts as a kind of democratic watch-dog overseeing the other institutions within the EU. There is a **European Court of Justice**, in Luxembourg, which is the judicial arm of Europe and is much stronger than the parliament in terms of its function. The ECJ has real teeth, interpreting and enforcing EU law, and it has declared null and void national laws of member states that conflict with EU law.

The body tasked principally with governance of the EU is the **European Commission**, in Brussels. It both proposes new laws and measures, and executes them. It has been the active, daily hub of the growth and success of Europe from the get-go. The Commission has had the reputation for being somewhat remote, bureaucratic, and **technocratic** (i.e. operating within a demanding environment of technological skill and expertise). But it does report both to parliament and to the **European Council**, another oversight body composed of a president and one person (usually the head of state or head of government) from each member country.[31]

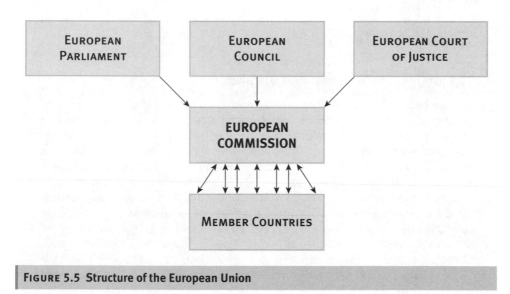

FIGURE 5.5 Structure of the European Union

Summary Reflections

Europe has been an amazing success story, especially given the continent's war-soaked history. It just keeps growing and growing, with no one quitting, and with more and more countries clamouring for entry into the club. It is, indeed, a model for modern international governance and for innovative political problem-solving and the creation of institutions. The EU has improved national economies, and millions of individual lives, across the whole of Europe. To that extent, idealists dream of the day when the successful model designed for the EU can be implemented in other regions of the world, or even in the UN itself. If there is ever to be an effective world government, it would seem as though the EU provides the framework for one that is efficient, rational, democratic, prosperous, and rights-respecting. Hard to beat that.

At the same time, Europe is small geographically and sports among its people many shared values that unite the continent and make international governance there possible; the world, by contrast, is far bigger, with sharper and more serious problems and with deeper divisions on things like beliefs and values. (The issue of world government will be rejoined in this book's conclusion.) Europe is not perfect, having its substantial share of problems. These include tensions between national sovereignty and supra-nationalism; between local democracy and remote, expert, un-elected bureaucracy; and between the older and more core members of the Union and the newer, less involved, "fringe" members. Finally, there is real tension between the richer members, such as Germany, and the poorer members, such as Greece—tension that has been heightened in recent years as Greece has taken on more and more national debt, violating the EU's technical rules for what is allowed (noted above) and forcing wealthier countries like Germany to bail it out by paying off Greece's debt. This creates bad feelings and certainly can't be sustained indefinitely: if every EU country were like Greece, then the EU would go bankrupt. These **sovereign debt problems** aren't limited to Greece: other EU countries, such as Ireland, Spain, and Portugal, are facing them, too. Even Italy is thought to be on the verge of real trouble. As of writing, the solution to this problem remains unclear and elusive.[32]

Studies in Technology

The Internet and International Distance

International institutions like the UN and EU face political and economic problems as a result of their substantial distance from ordinary citizens and taxpayers. It's safe to say, for example, that the average American or Canadian does *not* feel close to the UN, would *not* agree with the statement: "The UN is my government, too." And this is true even though (a) the United States has always been the UN's biggest funder, by far, and (b) Canada is widely seen, around the world, as one of the UN's strongest and most consistent supporters. (Many UN staffers, incidentally, are Canadian: that kind of support, together with Canadians' bilingualism and typically decent education and awareness of the outside world, pays dividends in this regard.) And we've seen, in the case of the EU, that this tension between *local* government and *national* identities, on the one hand, and the *supra-national* needs of Europe as a whole has been a big issue. (Governing 500 million people does, after all, demand some impersonal administration, and considerable technical expertise.) The international institutions can thus suffer from **legitimacy issues**: are these organizations worthy of the average citizen's support and tax dollars? By what right do these organizations regulate international issues that affect individual citizens?

To try to combat this distance—or **democratic deficit**—between citizen and international institution, many of these organizations have developed robust websites and online services, providing a clear rationale for *why* they exist and *how* they benefit millions of people, as well as an easy route to practical, and sometimes quite valuable, information on how ordinary people can access data and knowledge that can empower them, services that can ease their lives, and even employment and funding opportunities.

Global governance institutions aren't alone in this regard, of course. It's still a brave new world for us all, in terms of communications technology. The pace and depth of change over the past 25 years has been mind-boggling. Experts are not quite sure how these new technologies will affect international law and global governance, but it's clear that they can be used either (a) to *support* status quo institutions (usually by those very institutions themselves, as just explained), or (b) to *challenge* those institutions (as witnessed last chapter, regarding Wikileaks). The spread of these technologies makes it much harder for governments to control the flow of information, and that can be good when, say, an undemocratic government is using violence against its own people and trying to hide the fact. People, via their cellphone cameras and postings on websites, let the world know the truth. Yet such technologies can also be used to aid bad causes, such as when terrorist groups or drug- and people-smugglers use quick codeword tweets on Twitter to plot more efficiently their brutal attacks or illicit transactions. The global communications revolution both serves and subverts ongoing processes of national and international governance.[33]

REVIEW QUESTIONS

1. Define international law, its two core principles, and its goal or function in international life.

2. Research a prominent recent treaty between your country and another. What's it about? Why did your country sign it? What changes will the treaty bring about in your country?

3. People often proclaim frustration that the political treaties—for instance, the human rights treaties—are neither as many nor as successful as the technical or economic treaties. My reply to them is that the facts show that the political treaties should be made as much like the technical treaties as possible in order to succeed. What do I mean by this, and do you think this would be a good strategy? Why or why not?

4. Would you—and *how* would you—reform the UN Security Council?

5. Reading the section on the structure and function of the UN, did anything surprise or inform you? How is the reality of the UN different from what you expected or previously believed? Is the UN a worthwhile institution? How might it be improved?

6. Consider the EU membership criteria. What do you think of them? Are they too demanding, or not demanding enough? Some have suggested establishing more rigorous criteria for membership in the UN: what might be the pros and cons? Indeed, to what extent can the EU serve as a model for the UN, or for such other regions of the world as Africa, Asia, or Latin America?

7. Why would the admission of Serbia and Turkey into the EU be controversial? Research this, and opine whether these two countries will ever, or should ever, be admitted.

8. There are many, many other international organizations—e.g. the African Union, the Arab League, the Organization of American States, The Asia–Pacific Economic Co-operation Forum (APEC), and so on. Quickly research these to get a flavour of what they try to do, and how successful they are.

9. George Orwell, in his classic novel *1984*, wrote of a world divided into three massive, fiercely competitive, social, political, and economic blocs. Some have felt that this is exactly what is now happening in the real world, with the rise and congealing of Europe, China, and North America. Does this picture seem true? In what sense? What about the Islamic world, or Africa, or India? Any chance of real co-operation, or even integration, between "The Big Three" of North America, China, and Europe?

10. Research the very recent sovereign debt problems, both in the EU and in the US, and explain how they could have serious consequences, both internally and around the world.

WEBSITES FOR FURTHER RESEARCH

American Society of International Law www.asil.org

United Nations www.un.org

International Court of Justice www.icj-cij.org

International Criminal Court www.icc-cpi.int

European Union www.europa.eu

NOTES

1. K. Holl, *Ludwig Quidde* (Frankfurt: Doste Verlag, 2007), p. 625.
2. J.L. Brierly, *The Law of Nations* (New York: Waldock, 6th edn, 1963); P. Wilson, *The Thirty Years' War: Europe's Tragedy* (Cambridge, MA: Harvard University Press, 2008); L. Henkin, *How Nations Behave: Law and Foreign Policy* (New York: Columbia University Press, 2nd edn, 1979).
3. H. Kelsen, *Principles of International Law* (New York: Holt, Rinehart and Winston, 1966); Aristotle, *The Politics*, trans. C. Lord (Chicago: University of Chicago Press, 1985).
4. H.C. Black, *Black's Law Dictionary* (St Paul's, MN: West Legal Press, 6th edn, 1990).
5. T. Buergenthal & H. Maier, *Public International Law* (St Paul, MN: West Legal Press, 1990).
6. International Joint Commission, *The International Joint Commission and The Boundary Waters Treaty of 1909* (Washington, DC: IJC, 1998); see also www.oursharedwaters.com.
7. A. Cassese, *International Law* (Oxford: Oxford University Press, 2nd edn, 2005); M. Shaw, *International Law* (Cambridge: Cambridge University Press, 2008).
8. J. Schott & M. Smiths, eds, *The Canada–US Free Trade Agreement* (Washington, DC: Institute for International Economics, 1988); J. Larsen & J. Smith, *Historical Dictionary of Arms Control and Disarmament* (Lanham, MD: Rowman & Littlefield, 2005).
9. G. Hufbauer & J. Schott, *NAFTA Revisited: Achievements and Challenges* (Washington, DC: Institute for International Economics, 2005); P. Duignan, *NATO: Its Past, Present and Future* (Stanford: Hoover Institute, 2000).
10. Shaw, *International Law* (op. cit., note 7), *passim*.
11. J. Goldsmith & E. Posner, *The Limits of International Law* (Oxford: Oxford University Press, 2005).
12. B. Orend, *The Morality of War* (Peterborough, ON: Broadview, 2006); 68–105; G. Prunier, *Rwanda: History of a Genocide* (New York: Columbia University Press, 2005).
13. M. Noortman, *Enforcing International Law* (London: Routledge, 2005).
14. M. Housden, *The League of Nations and The Organization of Peace* (London: Longmans, 2011).
15. S. Schlesinger, *Act of Creation: The Founding of the United Nations* (New York: Basic, 2004).
16. J. Goldstein & S. Whitworth, *International Relations* (Toronto: Pearson, Cdn edn, 2005).
17. A. Gorst & L. Johnman, *The Suez Crisis* (London: Routledge, 1997); M. Carroll & R. Bothwell, *Pearson's Peace-keepers* (Vancouver: University of British Columbia Press, 2009); J. English, *The Worldly Years: The Life of Lester B. Pearson, 1949–72* (Toronto: Knopf, 1992).
18. W. Durch, *The Evolution of UN Peace-keeping* (London: Palgrave Macmillan, 1993).
19. *The United Nations Today* (New York: UN Publications Office, 2008). For this, and the entire "UN Parts and Structure" section, see also www.un.org
20. E. Luck, *United Nations Security Council: Practice and Promise* (London: Routledge, 2006); B. Cronin, *The United Nations Security Council and The Politics of International Authority* (London: Routledge, 2008).

21. S. Chesterman, *Secretary or General? The United Nations' Secretary-General in World Politics* (Cambridge: Cambridge University Press, 2007).

22. H. Meyer, *The World Court in Action: Judging Among the Nations* (Lanham, MD: Rowman Littlefield, 2001).

23. United Nations, *Basic Facts About the UN* (New York: United Nations Press, 2011).

24. T.G. Weiss & S. Daws, eds, *The Oxford Handbook on the UN* (Oxford: Oxford University Press, 2009).

25. A.M. El-Agraa, *The European Union: Economics and Policies* (Cambridge: Cambridge University Press, 8th edn, 2007).

26. M. Dedman, *The Origins and Development of the European Union, 1945–2008* (London: Routledge, 2nd edn, 2009). The EU's official website, which provides a wonder of information about the organization's history, structure, and function, is www.europa.eu

27. A. Warliegh, *European Union: The Basics* (London: Taylor and Francis, 2008).

28. J. Pinder, *The European Union* (Oxford: Oxford University Press, 2nd edn, 2008).

29. C. Archer, *The European Union* (London: Taylor and Francis, 2008).

30. D. Dinan, *Ever Closer Union: An Introduction to European Integration* (London: Lynne Rienner, 4th edn, 2010).

31. Archer, *The European Union* (op. cit., note 29), *passim*.

32. S.P. McGiffen, *The European Union: A Critical Guide* (London: Pluto, 2005).

33. M. Franda, *Launching into Cyberspace: Internet Development and Politics in Five World Regions* (London: Lynne Rienner, 2002); J. Erikksson & G. Giacomello, *International Relations and Security in the Digital Age* (London: Routledge, 2007); J. Gainous, *Rebooting American Politics: The Internet Revolution* (New York: Rowman Littlefield, 2011); E. Morozov, *The Net Delusion: The Dark Side of Internet Freedom* (Washington, DC: Public Affairs, 2012).

III

Traditional Issues of Hard Power: Bucks and Bullets

6 International Trade and Business

"It's The Economy, Stupid!"[1] —*Slogan from the 1992 election campaign of Bill Clinton (b. 1946), US president 1993–2001*

LEARNING OBJECTIVES

After studying this chapter, you will be able to:

‣ define all the bolded key terms and concepts

‣ understand the "big picture basics" of how a national economy works, including the GDP equation, the business cycle, and the foundations for economic growth

‣ explain why countries trade at all, and what the doctrine of comparative advantage entails

‣ be aware of the world's most valued traded goods, the most active trading nations, and Canada's particular interests and status in international trade

‣ grasp the three basic policy options countries have when it comes to international trade—offering examples of each—and understand how each option employs protectionist tools to some extent

‣ reflect on the nature of globalization, and understand the many obstacles that stand in the way both of its further development and of heightened volumes of international trade

‣ appreciate the differences regarding cross-cultural business conventions and practices

‣ know the pros and cons of MNC activity, especially in the developing world

‣ become familiar with the emerging industry practice of fair trade, and how it links into global aid and development.

INTRODUCTION

The previous two chapters examined the complex, inescapable, enormously important interaction between nation and world—specifically, between the realism of a self-concerned state and the idealism of an international order concerned for all. This chapter sets us out on a new section, one concerned with examining in detail the **two pillars of hard power**: (1) military strength, and (2) financial wealth. Our focus this chapter is on trade, the economy, and international business.

Now, we've already discussed a great number of things about **economics**, that is, how goods and services are produced, distributed, and used. In Chapter 1, for instance, we defined the essential features of free-market capitalism, the prevailing economic system of our time. In Chapter 2, we discussed natural resources—a prime component of national wealth—alongside resource-related problems, such as food and water scarcity, peak oil theory, and the sometimes uncertain supply of energy. In Chapter 3, we explained the rise of the welfare state in the West, and how welfare liberalism has now become the international norm, blending for-profit, free-market capitalism with not-for-profit government intervention designed to protect and provide for the least well-off. In Chapter 4, we examined the two major economic tools of foreign policy: positive incentives (including cash and aid) and negative sanctions (whether targeted or sweeping). We also saw, generally, how support for increasing national wealth, and growing economic resources, united both realists and idealists. Finally, in Chapter 5, we looked at international commercial laws, including, especially, various free trade treaties, as well as the details of the dynamic economic structures of the European Union (EU). All of this demonstrates the extent to which economics play an integral role in many aspects of international relations.

Throughout the first two parts of this book, we've touched on and explained such history-changing economic events as the Industrial Revolution, the Great Depression, the rise of the welfare state, the Green Revolution, and the OPEC oil shocks. We've even peered into the future to consider the claims of those neo-Malthusians who predict economic ruin, in contrast to the views of those optimists confident of technological salvation. And, on that note, our recurring feature Studies in Technology has highlighted the impact of technological change on our lives, and on how we organize our economies. So, we need not repeat such things here. Then what's left, you might ask? Two big things:

1. a sustained look at international trade

2. a glimpse into international business practice, first as carried out by multinational corporations (MNCs), and then as evident in different forms of international business dealings, which will also serve as a further study in comparative culture.

SUMMARIZING THE DRIVERS OF ECONOMIC GROWTH

Fundamentals

There are many factors that drive the growth of a national economy. We've already mentioned **natural resource endowments**. But **human resource endowments** are just as critical, perhaps even more so. The size and quality of labour power obviously affects what one can do with the territory and natural resource endowments at one's disposal. By *quality* of labour power we mean the extent to which one's workforce is hard-working and well educated. These two qualities help to maximize **productivity**, which is defined as economic output per worker. Another huge factor affecting productivity and the potential for economic growth is **technological development and innovation**. Machines help us save our time for critical "human-only" tasks, like strategy and invention, and make repetitive tasks—like calculations or assembly-line manufacture—so much easier and, generally, of much higher quality.

But these ingredients aren't enough to guarantee the economic well-being of a country. As we'll see further in Chapter 11, on aid and development, we now know that the set of basic social institutions that a society establishes has a huge impact on the level of wealth that it can generate. If a nation opts for political and economic systems rooted in communism rather than capitalism, for example, we can safely predict that this will drag down the nation's economic growth and potential, as the absence of a profit motive will dampen productivity. (Economists are fond of touting the need for "**the right incentives**" to encourage the right kind—the productive kind—of behavior; few things motivate productive activity more than money.) So, certain abstract items provided by a nation's institutions—like **freedom**, a **well-functioning legal system**, **decent and widely available education**, and **general social peace**—matter importantly to the economy, too. So does the **health status** of the population, as we'll understand further in our chapter on global public health. (Sick people, after all, can't work and contribute to the economy.)[2]

The GDP Equation

In addition to depending on the prerequisites for a strong economy (summarized in Figure 6.1), it is often said that at any given time, the state of an economy is determined by the following simple equation:

$$C + I + G + (X - M) = GDP$$

where:

- GDP is the **gross domestic product**, the total value of goods produced and services provided in a country in one year (used as a measure of the strength of a nation's economy).

- **C** stands for **consumer spending**. Consumer spending is thought to make up between one-half and two-thirds of most national economies. Of particular interest to experts are (a) the amount of spending on **durables** (long-lasting, expensive goods, like houses and cars), and (b) the level of **consumer confidence**, taken as an

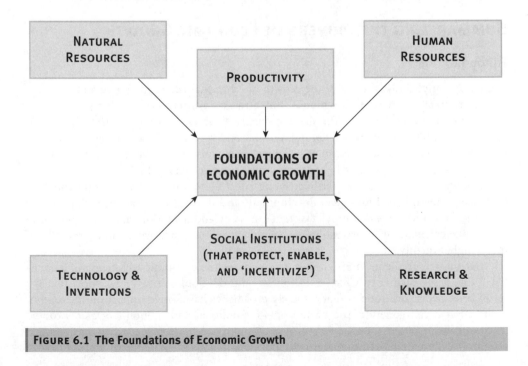

FIGURE 6.1 The Foundations of Economic Growth

indication of how financially secure and optimistic consumers are feeling, based on the degree to which they're willing to spend.

- **I** stands for **business investment**. Businesses spend on all kinds of things, notably land/office space, natural resources (or other inputs required for production), technology, research and development (or **R&D**, an investment in future products), and employee wages. **Business confidence**, like consumer confidence, is viewed by economists as a valuable indicator of the health of the economy.

- **G** stands for **government spending**. Governments spend on physical infrastructure (e.g. roads and sewers), the military, education and healthcare systems, social programs (e.g. employment insurance), and wages for their own workforce of civil servants.

- **X** stands for **exports**, goods produced for sale to another country. Exports increase economic growth because when a foreign customer buys your good, his or her money comes into your pocket, adding to your own national economy.

- **M** stands for **imports**, goods produced in another country and purchased in your country. Imports *decrease* economic growth, because when you buy the foreign-made good, your money leaves your national economy and goes into the pockets of the foreign producer. This is the lone variable in the equation that has a **negative relationship** with GDP: a rise in imports contributes negatively to your GDP. Everything else above is in a **positive relationship** with GDP, meaning that as they go up, GDP goes up as well; when they go down, GDP follows.

When GDP goes up, the economy is in an **expansion phase**, i.e. a growing phase; when GDP goes down, the economy is in a **contraction phase**: a period of **recession** or shrinking economic growth. Almost all economies experience this so-called **business cycle**, characterized by alternating periods of economic expansion and contraction (or "boom and bust"), as depicted in Figure 6.2.

Our focus in this chapter is on exports and imports, together known as the **foreign trade sector** of a national economy. But before turning to them, we must explore two other major factors affecting economic growth: (1) interest rates, and (2) the value of a national currency.[3]

Interest Rates

Interest rates represent the price of money. They are what banks, or other lenders, charge when they lend you money, such as to buy a house or a car. When interest rates go up, money becomes more expensive. This effectively decreases demand for it, which translates into decreased spending in the economy by consumers and businesses, and a shrinking of the economy. Conversely, when interest rates go down, the price of money falls, and so more people "buy" more of it (i.e. they take out more loans), thereby growing the economy. If you want to stimulate the economy, lower interest rates so that people will be more inclined to borrow money to spend on new cars, condos, home renovations, and so on.

Who controls interest rates? The answer is complicated. All we need to know here is that nearly every country has a **central bank**. This is a public institution—like the Federal Reserve of the United States, or the Bank of Canada—that is in charge of (a) printing the

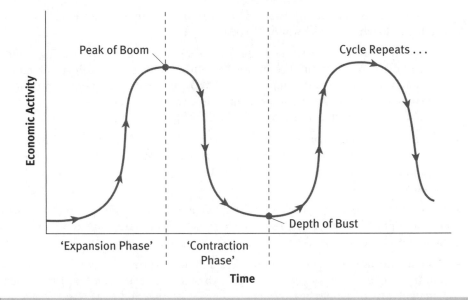

FIGURE 6.2 The Business Cycle

The welfare state is expected to engage in "counter-cyclical activity" to smooth out the business cycle. For example, the government is supposed to increase spending during a contraction to hasten an expansion.

national currency, and (b) managing interest rates. Together, these two things determine **the money supply** in a given country. (Central banks manage just the leading national interest rate—often called the **overnight rate**—which sets the tone for all other lending institutions inside that country.)

The central bank is usually **semi-autonomous**, meaning that it is set at arm's length from the (elected) national government, so that the passions of party politics don't inter-fere with the serious, sober, difficult, technical business of setting interest rates, which in many ways set the tone for the whole economy. The difference between fiscal and monetary policy is vital here. **Monetary policy** is as just described: control of the money supply by a semi-autonomous central bank, aloof from party politics. **Fiscal policy**, by contrast, refers to how governments spend money; it is reflected in the official budget, the rate of taxa-tion, new spending measures, and so on. Fiscal policy *is* in the direct daily control of the (elected) government; monetary policy is *not*.[4]

When a central bank sets its interest rate, what does it take into account? What's the main objective? Overall, it's to help ensure the long-term health of the national economy. In the shorter term, though, it's the rate of inflation that is the central concern. **Inflation** is the overall increase in the price of goods and services in an economy over time. If, for example, the annual rate of inflation is 5 per cent, then a loaf of bread that cost $2.00 last year now costs $2.10. Most central banks aim for *a very modest and controlled rate of inflation*, roughly between 1 per cent and 3 per cent per year. The average annual rate of inflation in the US between 2005 and 2010 was 2.87 per cent; in Canada it was 1.78 per cent.

High inflation, above the desirable **target band**, is thought to be destabilizing, perhaps leading to **hyperinflation**—very rapid and unpredictable price increases. High inflation is bad for the economy because it prevents consumers from planning their purchases, and the constant rise of prices means they can afford less and less as time goes on (unless their incomes rise very rapidly, too, which usually doesn't happen). Generally, inflation rates are much higher in developing societies than in developed ones. For instance, the average annual rate of inflation in India, 2005–10, was 10.35 per cent; in Russia, 12.54 per cent. In Africa, they don't have reliable figures, but the rate can rise by hundreds of percentage points per year (!).

The converse problem is that of **deflation**, which is a downward spiral of falling prices and falling asset values, which encourages saving instead of spending (as people wait for prices to fall even further). Deflation causes the economy to shrink. (Japan has had recent problems with deflation, with its average annual inflation rate, 2005–10, being −0.39 per cent.) Ideally, as a central bank, you want your country's asset values (such as real estate) to *increase*, and the economy to *grow*; at the same time, you do *not* want prices to skyrocket, especially on consumer staples like bread, clothing, and gasoline. Hence, the ideal 1–3 per cent inflation target band.[5]

Currency

Now, who or what determines the relative value of a nation's currency? As with interest rates, the answer is complex, but the big, sweeping answer is that the world demand for your currency, by and large, determines its value. When the world wants to invest in your country, when it wants to buy your goods and services, it must buy your national currency in quantities sufficient to pay for those things; this drives the value of your currency up (your currency thus **appreciates**). When the reverse things are true, your currency falls (or **depreciates**). Much has to do with (a) the way the world sees your economy in the future, and (b) the value of the things your country produces and trades. For example, over the past 20 years, the Canadian dollar has gone from being worth about 75 cents US to being about equal in value to one US dollar. This is so because international investors have confidence in Canada's future (i.e. they believe that it has a well-managed national economy) and because the demand for the natural resource commodities that Canada has in abundance—oil and gas, potash, coal, steel, nickel, silver, and wheat—is skyrocketing, especially from such newly industrializing giants as China and India.

The world's most important, and frequently traded, currencies are:

- the US dollar
- the EU's euro
- China's yuan
- Japan's yen
- the British pound
- India's rupee
- Russia's ruble
- the Swiss franc
- the Canadian and Australian dollars.[6]

Since World War II, the US dollar has been far and away the biggest and strongest national currency, the benchmark against which all other currencies are measured, and the principal **reserve currency** (a currency that central banks of other countries are comfortable holding as part of their foreign exchange reserves). Under the terms of the Bretton Woods agreement, signed in 1944, the value of the US dollar became **fixed**—tied to the price of gold. This meant that other countries holding reserves of US dollars in their central banks could convert their American currency to gold at a fixed rate (of 35 US dollars per ounce of gold). In the early 1970s, when American gold reserves were running low, US president Richard Nixon put an end to the **gold standard**. Since then, all major currencies have been **floating**—based on their value relative to other world currencies and to world demand, *not* on the possession of any kind of **hard asset**, such as gold.

When the value of one country's currency drops relative to the value of another country's currency, the first country's goods and services become cheaper, and the second country becomes tempted to buy more of them. Consider an example: when the value of the Canadian dollar falls, Americans buy more Canadian products (like lumber, salmon, wheat, and oil and gas) because now the US dollar buys more Canadian goods. (When Americans—be they large retailers or individual consumers— buy Canadian goods for import, they must pay in Canadian dollars, and vice versa.) Conversely, when the Canadian dollar goes up vis-à-vis the US dollar, Canadian goods become more expensive, and Americans buy less of them: they don't take summer vacations in Canada, and they switch to buying their apples from Washington State and not from BC. And Canadians, for their part, take advantage of their own rising currency to import American goods, or to go on cross-border shopping trips to Bellingham, Grand Forks, Buffalo and other American cities along the border, because now those things are cheaper for them. The key fact is this: when your nation's currency falls in value, this actually stimulates export growth and thus expands your economy, whereas when your nation's currency rises in value, this stimulates import growth and shrinks your economy.[7]

> When your nation's currency falls in value, it stimulates export growth and expands your economy; when your nation's currency rises, it stimulates import growth and shrinks your economy.

INTERNATIONAL TRADE

Why Trade at All?

International trade is the movement of goods and services across national borders in exchange for money. Why trade at all? Several reasons:

- Some goods and services just *can't* be produced at home, for instance, because of climate. If you live in Iceland and you love oranges, the only way your love can be satisfied is by shipping in some citrus from, say, Spain or Florida. That's *importing*.

- You might want to expand the market for your product. Let's say you make an excellent product, but you want to make more money than you're currently making selling it at home. In that case, you might want to consider selling not just to customers in your own country but to paying customers in other countries, too. That's *exporting*.

- The theory, and reality, of **comparative advantage**, the idea that *when we trade, we benefit.* Think of an analogy to personal life. Imagine if all of us, as individuals, had to produce *everything* we needed and wanted for ourselves: we had to grow our own crops, milk our own cows, sew our own clothes, build our own cellphones, manufacture our own cars, and so on. We couldn't do it, of course, and it would be exhausting and impoverishing merely to try. Indeed, our ancient ancestors had to do just that (minus the cars and cellphones, of course!), and it was a very tough life, until someone clever said: "I'm only really good at growing corn, so I'm going to grow *a ton* of it—way more than I need. Then I'll take some of the surplus to Sam, who'll give me surplus milk from his cows. And I'll take some more surplus corn and give it to Jenny, who in exchange will make some clothes for me—she's good at that. *I'll specialize in what I do best, produce a surplus, and trade that surplus for all the other things I want and need.*" This principle is known as **the division of labour**, and it amounts to specializing in one's comparative advantage (i.e. do what you do best) and then trading one's surplus for the surplus of others who've done the same thing. On the basis of this principle the modern global economy was built, with all its dazzling variety, complexity, and wealth-generating capacity.

- Countries are like the individuals described above: some are better suited to doing, producing, or providing some things than others are (thanks either to natural endowments or to how history has situated them). Want a sunny, beachfront vacation in January? Then head for the Caribbean, and not the shores of, say, Churchill, Manitoba. But, want to see polar bears, beluga whales, and northern lights? Reverse the order. Or, want a huge supply of oil? Then head to Saudi Arabia—and not Japan. But if you're looking for the glitziest electronics and some of the best-produced cars in the world, reverse the order. Finally, want the latest and greatest software, military technology, or Hollywood blockbuster? Go to the States—and not Africa. But if you want to see the Pyramids or Victoria Falls, or go on a wild animal safari . . . you get the idea. Countries have comparative advantages, and the prevailing theory is that they, like people, ought to stick to what they do best, produce it in abundance, and trade the surplus to other countries with something different to offer. The net result is that we all save time and effort, we all get to experience a greater diversity of things, we can access some of the world's (and not merely just our nation's) best products and services, and our lives will be improved as a result. International trade makes for better lives and higher average standards of living. Indeed, trade is a significant and growing contributor to global wealth, accounting for between 16 and 22 per cent of overall global economic activity. This is to say, loosely, that without international trade, we'd all be nearly 20 per cent *poorer* than we are. That, in a nutshell, is the value of engaging in international trade.[8]

Fun Facts: Trading Nations, Traded Goods

An important concept for any country it its **current account balance**. This is, roughly, a country's exports minus its imports. A country that exports more than it imports has a **trade surplus**, which we know *grows* its economy; a country that imports more than it exports has a **trade deficit**, which *drags down* its economy. The top 10 trade surplus countries, as of 2009, are:

1. China
2. Japan
3. Germany
4. Saudi Arabia
5. Russia
6. Iran
7. Norway
8. the Netherlands
9. Kuwait
10. Singapore.

Canada ranks number 22 on this list, while the USA sits at number . . . 181. Indeed, the United States has *the world's largest trade deficit*. With a population of over 310 million, the US has the biggest trade deficit because it must import so many things, worth so much money, from other countries to meet its enormous domestic demand for consumer goods, for oil and gas, and for the supplies—natural and human-made—that American businesses need to manufacture their own products. (Some people cite this fact when arguing that America is a declining power rather than a rising one.)[9]

Some nations are much more active traders than others. By US dollar value of trade, the world's top 10 trading economies—i.e. those most actively involved in international trade—are:

1. the European Union (considered as a whole)
2. the United States
3. China
4. Germany
5. Japan
6. France
7. the United Kingdom
8. the Netherlands
9. Italy
10. South Korea and Canada (tied).

And some economies are, of course, much more dependent on international trade for their national wealth. (This can be either good or bad, depending on the circumstances: good insofar as it helps that economy grow way beyond its borders, but potentially bad in that it also introduces clear aspects of dependence on other countries.) By percentage of their national GDP, the 10 most trade-reliant nations are:

1. Belgium
2. Taiwan
3. the Netherlands
4. South Korea
5. Saudi Arabia
6. Switzerland
7. Sweden
8. Poland
9. Austria
10. Germany.

On this list, Canada is thirteenth; the US, thirtieth.[10]

Finally, it may be of interest to note that the world's 10 most actively traded goods, by dollar value, are:

1. oil and gas

2. electrical/electronic equipment (e.g. switches, wiring, lights, consumer electronics)

3. heavy machinery (e.g. for factories and construction)

4. vehicles (i.e., cars and trucks)

5. medicines and pharmaceuticals

6. optical aids and apparatuses (i.e. contact lenses and glasses)

7. plastics

8. precious metals (gold, silver, etc.)

9. chemicals

10. iron, coal, and steel.

You may find it surprising that consumer staples—food, beverages, clothing, and so on—are not on this list. They *are* in the top 20, though, and surely the *volume* of trade in such goods is enormous. However, (1) many of these necessities are produced locally rather than imported, and (2) they are clearly *not* worth as much, in terms of dollar value, as cars, heavy machinery, or precious metals. Note, too, the world's most valuable traded good and consider how much it helps many of the countries on the list of those with the biggest trade surpluses. It's amazing how vital oil is to so many countries, and to the world economy generally.[11]

Trade Policies

There are three basic policy orientations that countries can take towards international trade: autarchy, free trade, and export-led development. Let's consider each in turn.

Autarchy/Mercantilism

Autarchy is a policy of determined self-sufficiency in economic matters. An effort at being "beholden to none," autarchy is the drive for a nation to provide as much as it can for itself, and to minimize any dependency on foreign relations or trade. The related doctrine of **mercantilism** sees the national government playing the leading role in economic policy, trying to do the absolute best it can for its country and its people by maximizing their resources and using them to further develop and strengthen the nation.

As economic policies, autarchy and mercantilism are viewed today as dated doctrines that are *not* good for the wealth of the people. First, think of the 20 per cent pay cut mentioned above: opting out of trade is costly. Second, consider how countries that try to follow this policy—like Albania and North Korea—are very much impoverished outsiders on the margins of the world economy. Think, too, of what such policies condemn their citizens to: poverty, invasive government control, lack of diversity, and shoddy products manufactured by local businesses that know their goods don't have to compete with foreign ones. Finally,

Canadian Insights

Canada's Vital Economic & Trade Statistics

Population: 34 million (81 per cent urban; 19 per cent rural)

Total GDP: US$1.5 trillion/year (10th–15th largest economy in world, depending on the measuring tool used)

GDP per capita: US$40,000/per person/year (again, 10th–15th highest)

Composition of Economy (by labour force, estimated): 70 per cent **services**; 25 per cent **industry** (manufacturing/construction); 5 per cent **primary sector** (i.e. agriculture & natural resource extraction)

Economic Growth (2005–10 average): 1 per cent/year (lower than the historical, post–World War II norm of 3 per cent/year, owing largely to the recent recession of 2008–9)

Currency: Canadian dollar ("the Loonie") (currently around par [+/– 3 cents] with the US dollar)

Inflation Rate (2005–10 average): 1.78 per cent/year

Unemployment Rate (2005–10 average): 7.75 per cent/year

Trade Surplus/Deficit: Consistently a **trade surplus** country (currently number 22 in world)

Trade Dependency: Canada ranks number 13 among the most trade-dependent nations in the world: an estimated 36–42 per cent of Canada's GDP comes from its very active involvement in international trade.

American Dependency: the US takes 75 per cent of all Canada's exports, and is the source of 50 per cent of all Canada's imports.

Top Five Trading Partners (as of 2010):

1. USA
2. EU
3. China
4. Japan
5. Mexico.

(To illustrate Canada's dependency on the US, note that the US is the destination for 75 per cent of Canada's exports; the EU, second on the list, receives just 10.5 per cent of Canada's exports. The US is the source of 50 per cent of Canada's imports; number 2 on that list is China, which provides Canada with just 11 per cent of its total imports.)

Free Trade Treaties: (1) with the United States, the Canada–US Free Trade Agreement (FTA), 1989; (2) with the US and Mexico, the North American Free Trade Agreement (NAFTA), 2004. Lesser, more limited agreements exist with Israel, various Caribbean and Latin American countries, and, in 2010, the EU.

Top Traded Goods:

A. Exports

- oil and gas
- uranium and aluminum
- timber and wood pulp
- electric power
- cars and parts
- industrial machinery
- telecommunications equipment
- chemicals and plastics

B. Imports

- industrial machinery
- vehicles
- electronics
- consumer durables and retail goods.

Source: Statistics Canada, www.statscan.gc.ca; United Nations Statistics Division, www.unstats.un.org/unsd; CIA World Factbook, www.cia.gov/library/publications/the-world-factbook.

when you think about it, you can see how, historically, mercantilism was a recipe for war. All the European empires used to be run on mercantilist lines: maximize self-sufficiency and minimize dependency and connections with other empires. Such an attitude fuelled imperial drives towards colonialism—since the more land, resources, and people you had under your imperial roof, the more self-reliant you could be, right? But that brought empires into direct competition and conflict for those resources, causing many a horrible war. And that, we saw in Chapter 5, is why the founders of the EU in 1950 went the other way: *away from* autarchy, mercantilism, colonialism, and imperial rivalry, *towards* linking economies together, forging robust trading relations, and creating many, and deep, social interconnections.[12]

Free Trade/Internationalism

With the demise of historical mercantilism, the tide has turned towards the second kind of trade policy: free trade and **internationalism** (i.e. being a fully interconnected participant in the global economy). Most countries now realize the benefits to be had from trade—the 20 per cent pay raise, as it were—and have gladly shrugged off the silly and inefficient burdens of trying to produce everything for themselves. They have embraced the "trade" part, but what about the "free" part?

Free trade refers to the exchange of goods and services between countries that elect *not* to use any protectionist measures (defined below) against each other. Free trade is international commerce that is tariff-free, quota-free, ban-free, and subsidy-free: what gets traded—and at what price and quantity—is determined *solely* by the market forces of supply and demand, *not* by any government regulation or intervention.

The facts show that, historically, the freer the trade, the greater the wealth that is created. Today it is all the rage for countries to enter into either bilateral or multilateral free trade agreements, and there are now hundreds of these agreements in place around the world. We saw in Chapter 5 how the Canada–US Free Trade Agreement was created in 1989 as a bilateral (i.e. two-sided) free trade agreement between the two countries. The signing of the North American Free Trade Agreement in 1994 brought Mexico into the treaty, making it a multilateral (i.e. many-sided) deal. Other important free trade deals and regions include:

- the EU (western and central Europe)
- APEC (the Asia–Pacific region)
- CARICOM (the Caribbean islands)
- MERCOSUR (South America)
- CAFTA (Central America).

Currently Russia is trying to negotiate such a deal with its ex–Soviet Union partners in central Asia and eastern Europe. There is even talk of some deal between the so-called **BRIC countries** (Brazil, Russia, India, and China), who have recently begun to meet annually to (a) draw world attention to their emerging status as major economic and political powers, and (b) advance their claims for "a multi-polar world order" to replace the two-dimensional view that considers only the developed West, on the one hand, and the Global South on the other.[13]

That said, it must be admitted—and stressed—that *nowhere does pure free trade exist*. It is an ideal that exists to varying degrees in various places, but even countries that are clearly committed to the ideal of free trade have been known to take **protectionist** measures. These are hurdles or obstacles imposed by national governments on certain imported goods in order to protect domestic goods or industries. The most common protectionist measure is the **tariff**, a tax on foreign, imported goods, which increases the price of these goods, making them more unattractive to consumers (relative to competing local or domestic goods). The US, for example, levies tariffs on Canadian softwood lumber to protect American lumber companies that would otherwise lose out on sales to customers at home in the US.

Other protectionist measures include quotas, product bans, and government subsidies. **Quotas** are limits a country places on the number of foreign-produced goods that it's willing to allow to be imported for sale into its country. Japan, for instance, limits the number of North American–made cars it's willing to allow for sale in Japan. Outright **product bans** are used to totally prohibit certain goods from entering a country; product bans usually exist in connection with agricultural goods. The US bans citrus fruit imports from any other country, and Canada bans the import of fresh milk from any non-Canadian source. This protects both the orange groves of Florida and the dairy farmers of Canada. **Government subsidies** are investments made by national governments (using domestic taxpayer dollars) into a domestic company or industry, with the goal of giving it a "leg up" on foreign competitors and create jobs at home. Almost every government does this in some way: Canada gives government subsidies to the transport supply company Bombardier, which manufactures planes, subways, and other large transportation vehicles. The US subsidizes almost its entire weapons industry. (Cynics note that Bombardier is located in vote-rich Montreal; and many defence industry companies are in vote-rich California. Should we consider these subsidies genuinely economic or, rather, political?)[14]

MERCOSUR
- Argentina
- Brazil
- Paraguay
- Uruguay

DAFTA
- US
- Costa Rica
- Dominican Republic
- El Salvador
- Guatemala
- Honduras
- Nicaragua

CARICOM
- Antigua and Barbuda
- Bahamas
- Barbados
- Belize
- Dominica
- Grenada
- Guyana
- Haiti
- Jamaica
- Montserrat
- St Lucia
- St Kitts and Nevis
- St Vincent and the Grenadines
- Suriname
- Trinidad and Tobago

(ASSOCIATE MEMBERS)
- Anguilla
- Bermuda
- British Virgin Islands
- Cayman Islands
- Turks & Caicos Islands

FIGURE 6.3 Free Trade Regions in Central and South America

Not to be outdone by the EU, China, and North America, such regions as the Caribbean and Latin America have recently developed a taste for free trade deals.

Source: US Central Intelligence Agency, Perry-Castañeda Library Map Collection. Courtesy of the University of Texas Libraries, The University of Texas at Austin

Export-Led Development

This third policy represents something of a blended approach between autarchy and internationalism. The goal of **export-led development** is to use the tools of mercantilism and protectionism to grow select local industries until they are strong enough to compete on the world stage. At that point, you can aggressively engage in free trade and earn lots of money off your exports, and then use that money to develop your society further, making it richer and more sophisticated.

Case Study: Asia and Export-Led Development

The most successful model of export-led development in modern history is post–World War II Japan, and now many other nations throughout Asia are trying to copy that success. When South Korea decided to jump-start its economic development during the

FIGURE 6.4 Free Trade Regions in Asia

The "Asian Tigers/Dragons": China, Singapore, South Korea, Hong Kong, and Taiwan, all following in the footsteps of Japan.

Source: www.taiwandocuments.org/map01.htm

1960s and 1970s, it did so by trying to grow a local car and electronics manufacturing industry (modelled after Japan's). To nurture these industries, the government gave Korean auto-makers and electronics-makers taxpayer dollars (subsidies) and placed quotas on imported foreign cars and electronics equipment so as to build local Korean demand for both. After a couple of decades, once quality had substantially improved, the South Koreans were confident that their cars and electronics could compete on the world market. As a result, both the subsidies and the quotas were substantially relaxed, and South Korean cars like Hyundai and Kia and electronics like Samsung and LG are now sold very successfully around the world. This success allowed South Korea, in 2009–10, to sign free trade deals both with the European Union and the United States, and the country, as we saw above, is now one of the most actively engaged trading nations on Earth.

Adopting a policy of export-led development—beginning with mercantilism, then free trade, and then using the profits to grow richer—has allowed South Korea to substantially increase its GDP, and it has worked very well for the other so-called **Asian Dragons**, or **Asian Tigers**: China, Japan, Singapore, and Taiwan. Whether it can work elsewhere, like the Global South, is something we'll address in Chapter 11, on aid and development.[15]

Globalization and International Trade Institutions

International trade has skyrocketed since the mid-twentieth century. Both The Great Depression of the 1930s and World War II in the 1940s were blamed on autarchy, mercantilism, and the lack of trade and economic co-operation between countries. Following the war, the EU countries, as we've seen, sought to grow trade and interconnection among themselves on a *regional*, multilateral basis. But the Americans went one step further, pushing the cause of free trade on a truly *global*, multilateral basis. They did this by using their position as a superpower (in the wake of the war) to create some global economic institutions. We shall consider the World Bank and International Monetary Fund in future chapters, as their mandate is to aid the development of the Global South. Here, we will discuss the **General Agreement on Tariffs and Trade** (GATT) and its successor institution, the **World Trade Organization** (WTO).

Founded in 1947, GATT was the focal point for several huge—i.e. truly global—rounds of multilateral negotiations on reducing tariffs (on manufactured goods, in particular). These negotiations were very successful, resulting in a substantial, mutual lowering of tariffs around the world. The results were exactly as economists predicted—much more trade, and much richer economies. Contemporary globalization, with the United States as its driving force, had begun.[16]

In 1995, the GATT became the WTO, headquartered in Geneva. It is a *permanent* institution, a watchdog of sorts, with powers of oversight, mediation, and enforcement in particular. The oversight is needed to ensure that countries keep their promises about reducing tariffs. Mediation has to be available so that if two countries are having a trade dispute (these tend to focus on whether government subsidies are unfair and violate free trade), they can appeal their case to the WTO, which investigates, hears both sides, and then issues a neutral, third-party ruling. Canada and the US, for example, have had to do this with the issue of Canada's export of softwood lumber into the United States. The US alleges that this industry is indirectly and unfairly subsidized by the Canadian government; Canada denies the claim, counter-arguing that American tariffs on Canadian lumber violate free trade and are simply America's way of protecting its own domestic lumber industry. The WTO has issued a number of rulings in the ongoing trade dispute, most of them in Canada's favour. Which brings us to *enforcement*. The WTO is empowered to levy fines when it determines that a trade deal has been violated or that unfair subsidization has occurred. Alternatively, the WTO allows the victimized countries to retaliate with tariffs or subsidies of their own. In 2000, the WTO allowed Canada to slap $345 million worth of tariffs and sanctions on Brazil, as a result of the latter's heavily subsidizing its aircraft industry, which has caused Canadian companies like Bombardier to lose valuable contracts. Such "tit-for-tat" measures, when authorized globally by the WTO, are accepted by the international community as a legitimate way to (a) level the playing field, ensuring fairness and reciprocity, and (b) avoid **trade wars** between countries. A trade war is characterized by a downward spiral of mutual tariffs, quotas, non-engagement, and even sanctions between the disputing countries; it can create much ill will, cost the people of the two countries substantially, and lead to further bad feelings that, at worst, might spark an armed conflict.[17]

So the recent expansion of international trade has brought about new levels of economic development and created considerable wealth. And the institutions are now in place to drive and enforce the continued growth of trade on both a regional and global basis. Does it follow that, as they say, we are now on "auto-pilot to the moon"? Have we reached the nirvana of globalization, or is it, at least, just around the corner?

Globalization *has* begun, and it *is* a clear trend (there's no denying it), evident perhaps more clearly in the realm of trade than in any other. There are now wide and deep interconnections between economies that a few decades ago had nothing to do with each other. More production is global in scale; more sales and marketing are global; the horizons of businesspeople are global; communications technology has allowed for unprecedented global information-sharing and increasingly tight cultural interconnectivity; and there is a global hegemon (i.e. the US) that is generally supportive of free—or, at least, freer—trade in respects of most goods. In spite of all this, the answer must be that there are potential problems with the status quo of trade and globalization moving forward.[18]

Problems with the Status Quo

A Cautionary Reminder from History

Free trade, internationalism, and globalization clearly *are* trends, and vital features, of the era in which we live. However, history tells us that there's nothing guaranteed about the continuance of these trends. There have been previous eras of relative globalization and freer trade—going all the way back to the Roman Empire—and they all, eventually, came to an end. It's important to keep perspective and appreciate historical cycles. The most relevant historical epoch, for our purposes here, was from about 1850 to 1914, when there was another global hegemon—Great Britain—that favoured the free trade of British goods throughout not just its worldwide empire but the rest of the world as well. It supported trade vigorously with its Royal Navy and its excellent system of railroads. Moreover, its hegemony secured stability and relative peace while deterring

> There have been previous eras of relative globalization and freer trade, and they all, eventually, came to an end.

major wars. It was also a time of amazing new inventions—railways, electricity, automobiles—as well as a revolution in communications technology, with the introduction of mass newspapers and radio, and the first experiments with television. Sound familiar? Change the hegemon from the UK to the USA and the technology innovations from the list above to today's high-tech gadgets, and you have something a lot like our time. But that era came to an end once Germany decided to challenge Britain (and France) for supremacy. These poisonous national rivalries kicked off a series of events that eventually sparked the two biggest wars the world has yet seen. People, and nations, don't always make choices based on the ideals of pure economic rationality—and sobering facts like that undermine our confidence in predicting the ever-upward progress of free trade and globalization.[19]

Trade Rivalries between Big Regional Blocs?

Some experts, like Harold James, see the unfolding facts of free trade and globalization more gloomily still.[20] Instead of a relentless, American-led march to global free trade, these observers see the creation of several huge **trading blocs**: grouped countries that practise free trade *internally* with each other but that are fiercely protectionist *externally* towards non-members and other blocs. The blocs most frequently identified are Europe, North America, and the Pacific Rim with China at its centre. While these *are* the "big three" economic units right now, and while they *do* have many trade disagreements between them, and while such a dystopian future *may* unfold, for now we should note—to balance the ledger—the many interconnections that nevertheless exist between these huge groupings. The EU, for instance, is both China's and India's largest trading partner. North America has many historical ties of immigration with all these regions, and the US, moreover, has a complex *interdependence*—not just a rivalry—with China. China very much wants to sell its goods into the vast and wealthy US marketplace, and the American consumer certainly wants China's inexpensive goods. China is a saver–surplus nation that likes to invest in American real estate and American companies that, in turn, are grateful for the cash (the US being the top spender–debtor nation). So, in spite of grim, Orwellian predictions about huge rival trading blocs going to war against each other—a situation akin to a return to mercantilism, on a much larger scale—we must note the existence of other, more peaceful possibilities.[21]

Winners and Losers

Even when trade *is* mutually beneficial, which it very often is, it does *not* follow that all parties benefit to the same degree. This has to do with the **distribution of benefits**, and it creates a divide between (relative) winners and losers. Consider the following example. A company in China and another in the US strike a deal: the Chinese company makes chairs, and the American company imports them into the States for sale to American furniture retailers. The deal might create profit for both companies, yet the US company might enjoy $12 million worth of profits from the deal, whereas the Chinese company may only profit to the tune of $5 million.

Much worse than that is a case of **outright loss from trade**. For example, the United States used to have its own flourishing sector of furniture manufacturing. Today, many of the country's furniture manufacturers have gone bankrupt, unable to compete with the incredibly low costs of production—especially labour costs—enjoyed by their global

Studies in Technology

The Pains of Global Interconnection

This criticism of the status quo in international trade hinges on the question of whether globalized interconnections—technological and otherwise—really bring unqualified benefits to all parties involved.

On the one hand, globalization has brought such undeniable rewards as the enrichment that comes with experiencing the cuisine, entertainment, and other cultural contributions of societies very distant and different from our own. Advances in global technology and new media facilitate this sharing and mean that we can communicate with almost anyone almost anywhere in the world.

On the other hand, interconnectedness means that when problems hit one part of the world, we can no longer isolate ourselves from it, or protect ourselves from its negative consequences. This has been made most apparent over the last 20 years in the case of financial markets, which have become almost totally global and totally high-tech. Like never before, the banking and financial sector, alongside the insurance industry and the stock, bond, and currency markets, is global in nature. Huge banks in America and Europe have massive financial interests around the globe, as do the governments of China, Japan, Russia, and Saudi Arabia. Behemoth insurance companies in New York and London provide insurance to homeowners, vehicle owners, and businesses all over the world, exposing them to worldwide risk.

This Indian man might be going online to see how his Apple stock is doing today. How has technology united world financial markets like never before? (© nullplus/iStockphoto)

Everyone seems to have their hands in everyone else's pockets, so to speak. This might be fine when things are going well: "a rising tide lifts all ships," as they say. But it can become a big problem when someone goes under, and suddenly everyone is at risk of drowning. Given the rapid speed of worldwide information-sharing via the Internet, combined with these many and deep financial interconnections, it's nearly automatic that when problems hit one region, the rest of the world suffers, perhaps quite needlessly. And the effects are immediate, given instantaneous high-tech trading.[22] There are two recent examples worth considering.

The first is the 2006–8 US mortgage crisis, which threatened almost the entire banking system in the developed world and is widely credited with creating the most recent, nearly worldwide recession. **The mortgage crisis** began when bankers in the US loaned too much money to people who used it to buy expensive homes they couldn't really afford. The bankers did this because (a) it was legal, and (b) the bankers themselves got paid on the basis of *how many* mortgage deals they signed, and *not* on whether those signing customers could keep making their mortgage payments into the future. It was a case of a short-term obsession trumping sound long-term planning. So, when interest rates went up, raising mortgage rates with them, many homeowners couldn't afford their mortgage payments anymore, which meant they had to give up, and move out of, their homes. With a glut of homes lost to foreclosure suddenly on the market, house prices

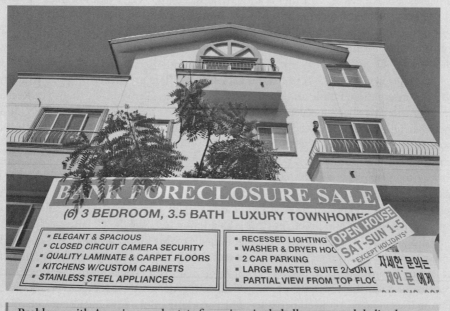

Problems with American real estate financing rippled all over our globalized world, causing recession nearly everywhere in 2007–9. (© GYI NSEA/iStockphoto)

crashed, saddling banks with a lot of properties they couldn't sell and debts they couldn't collect, causing them huge losses. Banks became much pickier when it came to deciding to whom they were willing to lend money. Result: US banks lending much less; much less money going around; much less consumer spending; recession. And almost worldwide, too, for—as they say—when the US consumer substantially cuts back, everyone around the world (trying to sell to them) substantially feels it.[23]

The second example of the pains of global interconnection, still ongoing, is the sovereign debt crisis in Europe. As we saw last chapter, debtor countries like Greece and Italy have enormous public debts, and surplus countries like the Netherlands and Germany are sick of bailing them out. The rich EU members are pushing the have-nots to get their financial houses in order, darkly suggesting the country's EU membership is at stake (though revoking EU membership is an untested process that might not be possible). This serious instability within the world's largest (or second-largest) economic unit has caused stock markets around the world to draw back and lose much value, uncertain of how this will affect the entire world economy and its prospects for growth moving forward.[24]

competitors, China in particular. When trade with China opened up, the American labourers who used to work in that industry lost their jobs, and the business owners lost their businesses. So, American consumers in general *did* gain, as did Chinese factory owners and workers, but *specific* American owners and workers in the same field *lost* when the recent wave of US–China trade took off. Trade can create *both* mutual benefits *and* winners and losers, owing to the number of people—and the different groups of people—who are affected.[25]

Examples like the one above help to explain why there are groups of people out there who *resist* international trade and the growth of trade organizations like the WTO. Recently, whenever there has been a meeting of the World Trade Organization or the **G8/G20** (i.e. either the eight or the twenty countries with the largest economies), there have been large groups of protesters—in fact, since the early 1990s, these groups have been fixtures at such events. Often, these protesters, who typically come from labour, environmental, human rights, and anti-poverty groups, claim to be acting in the interests of the global poor and unskilled—those most vulnerable to outright losses from international trade. Trade deals often include an agreement on certain standards that all signing parties must observe, such as specific labour laws and practices. This is an attempt to "level the playing field" and make the trading fair. There is a fear, though, that in deals of this kind, the lower, less demanding standard will prevail, as it is likely to be the least costly to business interests. Protesters fear that labour arrangements signed as part of trade deals will always be maximally advantageous to for-profit businesses and very disadvantageous to the average working person, bringing lower wages, reduced benefits, longer working hours, fewer safety standards, and fewer pollution controls—all in the name of competing with countries like China (where, incidentally, workers work for peanuts in often unhealthy and unsafe conditions, where pollution is a terrible problem, and where striking for better conditions is *not* an option).

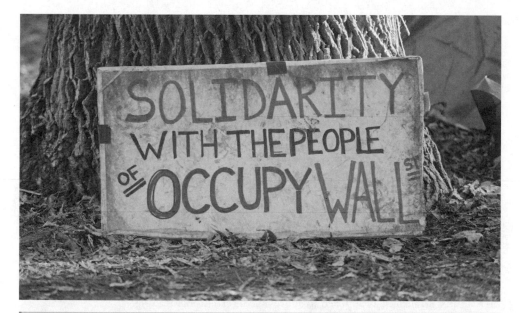

A sign in St James Park, the main site of Toronto's Occupy movement. Globalization certainly brought about the interconnection of the world's financial systems, but it also enabled this protest movement—one hatched in Vancouver and begun in New York—to spread globally with unprecedented speed and effectiveness. (© Jen Grantham/iStockphoto)

Thankfully, these fears *haven't* been realized on a mass scale. For example, NAFTA has been in place since 1994, and wages and working conditions in the US and Canada haven't collapsed to Mexican levels. As it turns out, there are *other* factors that businesses care about, such as the education and skill level of their workers—fields where the developed world scores very highly. Transportation costs are relevant, too, as is the existence of a stable and effective legal and political framework within which to conduct business. But it does seem, *generally*, true to say that the rise of free trade and globalization has accelerated the trend of developing countries getting more and more low-cost, labour-intensive, goods-producing employment while developed societies are growing more and more in terms of highly skilled, service-based employment (like research, education, law, finance, accounting, engineering, management, design, and civil service). Thus, low-skilled, goods-producing workers in developed societies—think of workers on the assembly line at an American furniture company—are facing an increasingly bleak future in a globalized, free trade world. Even in a globalized Utopia, there will still be winners and losers.[26]

Participants versus Non-participants

It can be argued that not everyone benefits *enough* from the rise in trade and the growth of globalization. Certainly there are countries like North Korea, wilful non-participants in the global economy, who miss out on some of the benefits of globalization. But there is also the more disturbing problem of those who *wish* to participate in global trade but *can't*, owing to their poverty or lack of tradeable goods, or to other barriers. The clear majority—about two-thirds—of all international trade is conducted either *within* the developed Northern economies or *between* the Northern economies and (a) the powerhouse emerging economies of China and India, or (b) the oil-producing states like Saudi Arabia and Kuwait. Other economies in the Global South simply *aren't* players in international trade—and they suffer from it.[27]

North versus South

How to explain such a discrepancy in trade activity between North and South? Several reasons come to mind. First, there is the issue of *quality of goods*. Many facilities in the South simply aren't advanced enough to produce the kind and quality of good—especially manufactured good—to compete in the global marketplace. Second, trying to overcome that quality gap takes an investment of *time* and *considerable resources*: think back to the decades it took South Korea to build globally competitive automotive and electronics sectors. Many countries, especially in Africa, simply do *not* have the capital savings to invest in such an intensive program of manufacturing-based, export-led development, owing to their poverty. Third, in many developing societies—following the end of European colonialism—there has, until very recently, been a general bias *away from* international trade and *towards nationalist ideals* of self-sufficiency. This created a governance style closer to mercantilist strategies, as opposed to aggressive international trading.

Finally, it's not just *internal* reasons that explain why the South lags behind in international trade. The most recent round of global, multilateral tariff negotiations ended in failure over fundamental disagreements between North and South. Agriculture was, and remains, a big sticking point. The North—Europe in particular—heavily subsidizes its farmers and protects their wares from the global competition of fully free trade. This is so because farmers are well-organized politically and simply demand the subsidies, but also because there exist legitimate *raisons d'état* (i.e., "reasons of state"): food and agriculture are vital for any society, and retaining some self-sufficiency in this field is sensible. It's too risky for America, say, to start importing all its wheat from Russia, lest one day the Cold War return and thus expose the US to hostility, and leverage, from the Russians on something so central as a major food staple.

The Global South, for its part, views this as unprincipled, self-regarding behaviour by the North. The South's argument would run along these lines: "Look, here is one area where we can truly compete on a global basis: we have tons of fertile land, an abundance of cheap labour, and a warm climate fit to grow lots of high-quality agricultural products. Give us free trade here, and you will truly help us trade and develop. Plus, your own consumers back home will enjoy better selection at lower prices. But you refuse to do this out of hypocrisy: you favour free trade only when you know you'll win. If it looks as though *we* might win, then you retreat—in a completely unprincipled way—behind the wall of protectionism." Until this huge issue of trade in agricultural goods is settled, it's hard to see the South making significant gains in global trade.

And the North has issues of its own with the South. The North wants freer trade in such services as insurance and banking, so that its huge financial companies can have access to new markets. The North also wants Southern governments to better protect **intellectual property**, that is, ownership rights, held by creators and inventors, to the products of intellectual creativity, such as books, software, music, TV programs, video games, and Hollywood movies. Right now, these products get copied illegally and sold with abandon, especially in such huge markets as China and India, robbing their creators of any profit from their own creation. A related point, relevant to global public health, is that Northern pharmaceutical companies want similar protections, and assurances of profit before making their drugs and medicines widely available throughout the Global South (which very much needs them). The South, for its part, has little appetite for making any such reforms, linking progress here to reductions in Northern agricultural barriers. And the North, of course, prefers the deal the other way around: no reduction in agricultural barriers until there's progress on IP protection and freer trade in financial services. This has created a **stalemate**, and it's unclear how things will move, regarding North–South trade, in the future.[28]

INTERNATIONAL BUSINESS

This section, on international business, consists of three parts, dealing with three important subjects:

- a generalized, cross-cultural look at how standard business practices and conventions differ across major world regions (Table 6.1)

- a critical examination of the role of multinational corporations (MNCs) in international trade and business

- a closing look at the new industry of fair trade and its connection to international development.

MNCs: Pros and Cons

The principal players in international trade are **multinational corporations**, or MNCs: large, for-profit business enterprises with offices, branches, or outlets in many countries. The list of largest MNCs changes from year to year, but the following are regularly counted among the top 20:

- Wal-Mart (retailer)
- HSBC (bank)
- Exxon (oil producer)
- General Electric (**conglomerate** [i.e. combined business] of manufacturing and finance)
- Shell (oil producer)
- Bank of America (bank)
- British Petroleum (oil producer)
- J.P. Morgan Chase (bank)
- Apple (software, computers, and telecommunications equipment)
- Saudi Aramco (oil producer)
- Toyota (auto maker)
- ING (bank)
- Sinopec (oil producer).

Note that the world's very top MNCs specialize in only four areas: oil, money, manufacturing, and consumer retailing.[29]

Table 6.1 Cross-cultural Business Practices

Business Convention	Cultural Region					
	English/ Germanic Societies	East Asia	Romance-speaking Europe & Latin America	Southeast Asia	Eastern Europe	Middle East
Physical & Eye Contact	Body contact (e.g. handshakes, hugs) and eye contact are **welcome.**	Body contact and eye contact are **avoided** as sign of respect.	Body contact (e.g. hug, cheek kiss)is **expected.** Eye contact is **avoided** as a sign of respect.	Body contact is **avoided** unless it is initiated by another. Eye contact is **fine.**	Handshakes and eye contact are **expected.**	Handshakes and eye contact are **expected.** Body contact with members of the opposite sex are **avoided** unless it is initiated by another.
Attitude Toward Innovation in Business Practices	Moderately strong tendency to **welcome** new ideas and change.	Strong tendency to **resist** change and hold on to old traditions.	Strong tendency to **welcome** new ideas and change	Strong tendency to **welcome** new ideas while being skeptical of their benefits.	Strong tendency to **resist** new ideas and change.	Moderately strong tendency to **resist** new ideas and change.
Prevailing Leadership Style*	• Performance-oriented • Autonomous	• Team-oriented • Group-protective • Autonomous	• Performance-oriented • Group-protective	• Team-oriented • Group-protective	• Autonomous • Team-Oriented	• Team-oriented • Group-protective
Decision-Making	**High tolerance** for uncertainty, meaning fewer rules and laws exist to control outcomes.	**Medium tolerance** for uncertainty, meaning a moderate number of enacted laws and regulations exist.	**Low tolerance** for uncertainty, meaning stringent laws, policies, and regulations exist.	**High tolerance** for uncertainty, meaning fewer rules and laws exist to control outcomes.	**Low tolerance** for uncertainty, meaning stringent laws, policies, and regulations exist.	**Low tolerance** for uncertainty, meaning stringent laws, policies, and regulations exist.

continued

TABLE 6.1 Cross-cultural Business Practices (continued)

Business Convention	Cultural Region					
	English/Germanic Societies	East Asia	Romance-speaking Europe & Latin America	Southeast Asia	Eastern Europe	Middle East
Legal/Contractual (i.e. To what extent does business depend on legal contracts?)	Business relationships are **heavily dependent** on extensive contract clauses.	Legal documents in business are viewed as **peripheral** to the relationship itself.	Legal documents in business are viewed as **peripheral** to the relationship itself.	Legal documents in business are viewed as **peripheral** to the relationship itself.	Legal documents in business are viewed as **peripheral** to the relationship itself.	Legal documents in business are viewed as **peripheral** to the relationship itself.
Social Inequality (i.e. To what extent do political, social, and economic inequalities exist?)	**Moderate** power and wealth disparity in society.	**Large** power and wealth disparity in society, which is the accepted norm.	**Moderate** power and wealth disparity in Romance Europe. Large disparity in Latin America.	**Large** power and wealth disparity in society, which is the accepted norm.	**Large** power and wealth disparity in society, but it is not widely accepted.	**Large** power and wealth disparity in society, which is the accepted norm.

Notes: "English/Germanic Societies" includes Australia, Canada, Germany, Scandinavia, the UK, and the US. "Romance Europe" includes esp. France, Italy, Portugal, Moldova, and Spain.

Source: Material for this table comes from the following sources: www.executiveplanet.com; N. Dresser, *Multicultural Manners* (Toronto: Wiley & Sons, 2005); R.J. House, et al., eds, *Culture, Leadership and Organizations* (New York: Sage, 2004); G. Hofstede, *Culture's Consequences* (New York: Sage, 2001). **Table co-authored with Deanna Qi, whose research was funded partially by the University of Waterloo's Accounting and Financial Management Program.**

Leadership Styles

- *Autonomous:* characterized by an independent, individualistic, self-centred approach to business leadership.
- *Group-protective:* emphasizing procedural, status-conscious, and 'face-saving' behaviours; focusing on the safety and security of the group and its members.
- *Performance-oriented:* stressing high standards, decisiveness, and innovation; seeking to inspire people around a vision while instilling in them a passion to perform.
- *Team-oriented:* fostering pride, loyalty, and collaboration among organization members; placing value on team cohesiveness and a common purpose.

Increasingly, there is talk of other leadership styles, especially among high-tech companies of the 'new economy' and not-for-profit organizations. These include *participative leadership*, which emphasizes equality, supports delegation of responsibilities, and encourages input from others in decision-making and implementation; and *humane leadership*, which stresses compassion, generosity, and patience, support for others, and concern with their well-being.

The vast majority of MNCs started out and are headquartered in the global North. Some critics view this fact dimly, suggesting that the direct, state-sponsored colonialism of history has been replaced with an *indirect* colonialism in which big businesses call the shots. Indeed, many large multinational corporations have far more resources than the governments of the developing societies in which they operate.[30] But the criticism of MNCs doesn't end there. The critics' chief concerns can be summarized in five arguments:

1. Multinational corporations have, in the past, often co-operated with and supported distasteful, even repressive, regimes, as long as those regimes have granted them access to their markets and allowed them to carry on their business in a profitable way. Classic examples include the huge oil companies operating in such non-democratic Middle Eastern countries as Kuwait and Saudi Arabia.

2. MNCs have, at times, engaged in employment practices that the rest of the world views as distasteful, often by taking advantage of lax employment standards and regulations. Examples: the use of child labour (e.g. by the sugar industry in Central America, and by the cocoa industry in West Africa); the dumping of garbage and pollution in Africa; the use of **sweat-shop manufacturing** (characterized by very low pay, very long hours, demanding physical work, and unsafe, cramped conditions) by the clothing industry in Central America and Southeast Asia.

3. MNCs contribute to uneven development in underdeveloped societies, focusing attention and resources on a precious few goods and commodities, not on the broad-based development that needs to occur. Consider: the Ivory Coast in West Africa provides between 40 and 50 per cent of the world's cocoa beans (for chocolate), and local statistics indicate that about 70 per cent of the population is involved in the agricultural production of cocoa and coffee beans. Tying the country's whole economy to the agricultural production of two beans is risky, sub-optimal, and even dangerous.[31]

4. MNCs create inequalities within developing societies, as they and the local workers they hire tend to make profits and wages superior to what is earned by local businesses and the rest of the local population. The well-paid employees of these MNCs also tend to coalesce together, coming to form, over time, isolated and protected pockets of relative wealth and privilege, quite detached from the rest of the society. In a sense, the MNCs and their workers come to form "gated communities" within these societies.

5. MNCs exploit the relative neediness of developing societies, especially in terms of labour. Many multinationals set up shop in the Global South because of the attraction of cheap land, cheap labour, minimal (if any) obligation to pay healthcare costs for their workers, minimal (if any) safety regulations, and a minimized tax burden. Critics stress the issue of wages especially, pointing out the huge disparities between what MNCs pay their workers in the developed world and what they pay them in the developing world. The differences can be shocking: mere *dollars a day* for tough, physical labour in the factories and fields of the Global South versus *millions of dollars a year* for the executives managing the MNC from the comfort of the North.[32]

Needless to say, multinational corporations and their defenders refute these allegations. They respond to the charges with the following counter-arguments:

- Governments are to blame for historical injustices associated with colonialism and imperialism; it's unfair to tar today's multinational corporations with the same brush.

- MNCs do *not* support repressive regimes. They are businesses, after all, and as such they are obliged to pay taxes to the governments of the jurisdictions within which they operate. An MNC is *not* a political agency or a civil society institution with a political agenda. It's simply *not* an MNC's job to agitate for broad-based political change in a society.

- Broad-based development is the proper ambit of governments, not of any given MNC. MNC activity *does* help develop the economy of the land in which it operates—that is, at least, better than nothing. Indeed, what is the practical alternative to multinational-led business ventures in these societies: no economic activity there at all?

- MNCs do not exploit the local residents of the societies in which they operate. The wages they pay their workers are typically superior to those earned by other locals doing comparable work: how can that be exploitation? MNCs create jobs and income; they pay tax revenues to the government; they develop the skills of their employees; often, they pay for infrastructure—like roads and water treatment near and around their factories—creating more jobs as well as amenities that local communities benefit from. In short, they help develop the local economy and tie it to the global one. These are all to the plus side of the equation, and they must be weighed against the occasional "bad apple" business ethics horror story that gets held up as the example when it is really the exception to the rule.[33]

Fair Trade

Fair trade is a recent topic that blends the issues of free trade and multinational corporations. Small farmers and producers in the developing world often fear that they simply cannot compete against the huge MNCs that operate in their territory. Consider an independent farmer trying to grow and sell pineapples; then think of how hard a time he would have competing against the massive multinational fruit company Dole, with its huge market share, its thousands of acres of land filled with pineapples (grown with the best technology), and its thousands of workers devoted to growing, selling, and distributing them. It's like David versus Goliath, these solitary local farmers versus some of the world's biggest food MNCs, such as Nestle, PepsiCo, Unilever, Tyson, Archer Daniels Midland and General Mills.

To try to even the odds a bit in the marketplace for such goods as coffee, cocoa, sugar, tea, cotton, honey, bananas, chocolate, wine, and flowers, many of these independent Southern farmers have joined together since the 1960s as part of the fair trade movement. Their aim is to appeal to consumers *not*

Where does your coffee come from? Increasingly "fair trade" signs are popping up in coffee shops and stores of the Global North. Do they factor into your buying decisions? (© ranplett/iStockphoto)

on the basis of free trade price but on the basis of quality and the importance of supporting independent local farmers—everywhere, but especially in developing societies—by purchasing the produce they grow. As a result, the prices charged for most fair trade goods are typically higher than those of mass-market, free trade goods, because they are calculated to provide these independent farmers with a **living wage** (i.e. an income consistent with the standard of living, one that will actually pay the bills). Fair trade supporters claim that what you get in exchange for those premium prices is not only a product of a better quality, produced with small-scale, environmentally friendly growing techniques, but the knowledge that you're helping poor independent farmers in the Global South survive, rather than fattening the profits of a few mega-food MNCs headquartered in the North.

The fair trade movement has come a long way since its beginnings. The value of annual fair trade sales worldwide is now in the billions of US dollars. In some countries, in connection with some of these goods, it is estimated that fair trade options might account for as much as 5 to 8 per cent of the total market for that good. That might not seem like much, but then fair trade market share was 0 per cent not that long ago. Witness, too, the number of specialty shops selling only fair trade goods—something unheard of 30 years ago.

The higher prices *have* attracted some criticisms from staunch supporters of free trade,[34] who firmly believe—as a matter of principle—that the combination of lowest price and highest quality ought always to win in the global marketplace. To support fair trade is, for them, *not* economically rational and rewards inefficient producers. Yet because they believe in freedom, these free trade supporters can hardly deny consumers the right to support causes they find worthwhile, such as that of the local farmer. (The rural poor—i.e., agricultural labourers—are thought to form the clear majority of the population in the Global South.)

Fair trade also gets criticized from the other side of the political spectrum, by those who think it doesn't really challenge the free trade system and the dominance of the North and West in that system. Fair trade is just a sideshow, rewarding a few Southern farmers. The movement's energies ought to be put instead into reforming the international trading system (for instance, by eliminating Northern agricultural subsidies to their own farmers, and/or by increasing the prices of those commodities most important to the Global South, like sugar, tea, coffee, cotton, fruit, and cocoa). The reply of fair trade supporters is that such sweeping, systemic transformation is much easier said than done, at least in the foreseeable future. What, then, is wrong with supporting the fair trade system as one way of actually improving the lives and economies of some of those living in the Global South? Fair trade is real; wholesale trade system reform and perfect equality are merely (as yet) hoped-for ideals.[35]

CONCLUSION

In this chapter, we examined international trade and then international business. We learned how a national economy works, and why nations trade with each other. We grasped the three basic policy options on trade, and came to understand many facts about today's trading world, including who are the most active participants, and what products are most traded and valued. We defined globalization, and surveyed the many obstacles that could hinder its further progress. We then extended our knowledge of comparative culture by looking at how international business practices differ from culture to culture. Finally, we considered the role of multinational corporations in the world, alongside fair trade. Fair trade ties into aid and development, which is the subject of Chapter 11. For now, having looked long and hard at the economy, and how nations try to grow their economic strength, we must turn to the other pillar of hard power in our world: military force.

REVIEW QUESTIONS

1. Research the comparative advantages of your country. How have these shaped your society?

2. Research your country's top five trading partners, both by dollar value of trade and by volume of trade. Anything surprise you? List some of the mutual benefits enjoyed by your country and these five partners.

3. Research the current and forward-looking trade strategies of your federal government. Why are these ones the priorities? What is the overall, long-term strategy? What's a problem, or weakness, the government wishes to overcome? What strength does the government wish to develop further?

4. Trade can also happen by mistake. What seemed like a good, mutually beneficial deal might turn out to be not so great after all, leaving one or both sides feeling considerable regret. Can you think of some examples in the history of international relations?

5. Research a trade dispute your country is currently having. Outline the relevant facts and show that you understand both positions. If you were a judge at the WTO, in whose favour would you rule and why?

6. Research why Japan has struggled with deflation recently, and what it has meant for that society. Then, research a country where inflation is severe (i.e. at least 20 per cent a year) and discover both the explanation for its cause and the costs and consequences of it.

7. As noted, there is a severe clash between North and South about freer trade moving forward. I outlined the major sticking points on both sides. Can you see a possible compromise that might break the present stalemate?

8. As we've seen, the world's most valuable commodity and most highly prized traded good is oil. Why is oil so valued? By whom? Who benefits from the high values? Who pays the costs? List some pros and cons of the exalted position oil enjoys in our world.

9. Show research of one case where an MNC had a clearly positive effect on the developing society in which it operated, or still operates, and another where it had a clearly negative impact. Can we generalize about the overall effects of MNCs, or are we limited to case-by-case judgments?

10. History quite reliably shows that things tend to cycle. Right now, free trade, internationalism, and globalization are dominant. Can you imagine any circumstances—say, another September 11—that might trigger the rise once more of mercantilism, tough border controls, and a collapse in international trade?

WEBSITES FOR FURTHER RESEARCH

DFAIT (Department of Foreign Affairs and International Trade Canada)
www.international.gc.ca

Executive Planet (for comparative business practices worldwide)
www.executiveplanet.com

Fair Trade International www.fairtrade.net

NAFTA Secretariat www.nafta-sec-alena.org

World Trade Organization (WTO) www.wto.org

NOTES

1. W.J. Clinton, *My Life* (New York: Vintage, 2004).
2. P. Dasgupta, *Economics: A Very Short Introduction* (Oxford: Oxford University Press, 2007); A. Sen, *Development as Freedom* (New York: Anchor, 2000).
3. Material for this section was drawn from C. McConnell, et al., *Macroeconomics* (New York: McGraw Hill, 18th edn, 2008).
4. N. Goodwin, et al., *Macroeconomics in Context* (London: M.E. Sharpe, 2008).
5. G. Skene, *Cycles of Inflation and Deflation* (New York: Praeger, 1992). Country-specific statistics compiled from the United Nations Statistics Division, www.unstats.un.org/unsd, and the CIA World Factbook, www.cia.gov/library/publications/the-world-factbook.
6. B. Graham, *World Commodities and World Currencies* (New York: Martino, 2010).
7. C. McConnell & S. Brue, *Economics* (New York: McGraw Hill, 17th edn, 2008); H.-P. Spahn, *From Gold to Euro* (New York: Springer, 2010); E. Helleiner, *Towards North American Monetary Union?* (Montreal: McGill–Queen's University Press, 2006).
8. R. Feenstra, *International Trade* (London: Worth, 2007).
9. P. Krugman, et al., *International Economics* (New York: Prentice Hall, 9th edn, 2011).
10. Krugman, et al., ibid. Country-specific statistics compiled from the United Nations Statistics Division, www.unstats.un.org/unsd, and the CIA World Factbook, www.cia.gov/library/publications/the-world-factbook.
11. Krugman, et al., ibid.
12. I. Wallserstein, *The Modern World-System II: Mercantilism and The Consolidation of the European–World Economy* (Berkeley, CA: University of California Press, 2011).
13. D. Lynch, *Trade and Globalization: An Introduction to Regional Trade Agreements* (New York: Rowman and Littlefield, 2010).
14. J. Bhagwati, *Protectionism* (Boston: MIT Press, 1989).

15. H. Schonberger, *Aftermath of War: Americans and The Remaking of Japan* (Ohio: Kent State University, 1989); E.M. Kim, ed., *The Four Asian Tigers: Economic Development and Global Political Economy* (London: Emerald, 1999).

16. W. Bernstein, *A Splendid Exchange: How Trade Shaped the World* (London: Grove, 2009).

17. A. Narlikar, *The World Trade Organization* (Oxford: Oxford University Press, 2005).

18. M. Steger, *Globalization* (Oxford: Oxford University Press, 2nd edn, 2009); J. Bagwati, *In Defence of Globalization* (Oxford: Oxford University Press, 2007).

19. N. Ferguson, *Empire: The Rise and Demise of The British World Order and The Lessons for Global Power* (New York: Basic, 2005).

20. H. James, *The Creation and Destruction of Value: The Globalization Cycle* (Cambridge, MA: Harvard University Press, 2009).

21. J.A. Frankel, et al., *Regional Trading Blocs in the World Economic System* (London: IIE, 2007); R. Findlay & K. O'Rourke, *Power and Plenty* (Princeton: Princeton University Press, 2009).

22. J. Stiglitz, *Globalization and Its Discontents* (New York: WW Norton, 2003).

23. B. McClean & J. Nocera, *All The Devils are Here* (New York: Portfolio, 2011); G. Morgenson & J. Rosner, *Reckless Endangerment* (New York: Times Books, 2011).

24. M. Lynn, *Bust: Greece, The Euro, and The Sovereign Debt Crisis* (New York: Bloomberg Press, 2010).

25. Feenstra, *International Trade* (op. cit., note 8).

26. Stiglitz, *Globalization and Its Discontents* (op. cit., note 22); J. Stiglitz, *Making Globalization Work* (New York: WW Norton, 2007).

27. Krugman, et al., *International Economics* (op. cit., note 9).

28. A. Wood, *North–South Trade, Employment and Inequality* (Oxford: Oxford University Press, 1995); R. Gilpin & J. Gilpin, *Global Political Economy* (Princeton: Princeton University Press, 2001); J. Bhagwati, *Termites in the Trading System* (Oxford: Oxford University Press, 2008).

29. M. Peng, *Global Business* (Los Angeles: Southwestern College Press, 2nd edn, 2010).

30. A. Chandler & B. Mazlish, eds, *Leviathans: Multinational Corporations and the New Global History* (Cambridge: Cambridge University Press, 2005).

31. C. Off, *Bitter Chocolate: The Dark Side of the World's Most Seductive Sweet* (Toronto: New Press, 2008).

32. Material for the above five points is drawn from N. Jensen, *Nation-states and Multinational Corporations* (Princeton: Princeton University Press, 2008); S. Cohen, *Multinational Corporations and Foreign Direct Investment* (Oxford: Oxford University Press, 2007); and J. Dunning & S. Lundan, *Multinational Enterprises and The Global Economy* (London: Elgar, 2nd edn, 2009).

33. Ibid.

34. D. Henderson, "Fair Trade is Counter-Productive and Unfair," *Economic Affairs* (2008), pp. 61–72.

35. J. DeCaralo, *Fair Trade* (London: Oneworld, 2007); J. Bowes, ed., *The Fair Trade Revolution* (London: Pluto Press, 2011); J. Stiglitz & A. Charlton, *Fair Trade for All: How Trade Can Promote Development* (Oxford: Oxford University Press, 2007).

7 Armed Conflict, Part 1: Causes and Outbreak

> "War is the continuation of politics by other means."[1] —*Carl von Clausewitz (1780–1831), author of* On War

LEARNING OBJECTIVES

After studying this chapter, you will be able to:

▸ define all the bolded key terms and concepts

▸ enumerate the costs and casualties of war, and to reflect on whether or when they are worth it

▸ know the major theories regarding the causes of war and the various proposals to solve it

▸ understand the international laws for resorting to armed force

▸ discuss several recent examples of major wars and their significance to international studies

▸ appreciate the need for, and the evolution of, the new "R2P" doctrine regarding armed humanitarian intervention

▸ be familiar with the "brave new world" of cyberwarfare: its basic terms, techniques, examples, and concerns of the future.

INTRODUCTION

Military capability, the use of armed force, and war all have massive impacts on society, both domestic and global. Alongside national wealth (i.e. GDP), they constitute the other "pillar of hard power," one of the most potent means—at least in the short term—of protecting oneself and advancing one's national interests on the international stage. This is not to say that the use of armed conflict is problem-free—far from it—but merely to note its historical force, and the degree to which violence is one of humanity's most familiar tools of attempted interpersonal leverage.

Owing to its overarching impact on world affairs, we've already—inescapably—discussed a number of important things about armed conflict. In Chapter 1, we saw the centrality of the use of force in establishing and keeping an empire. We witnessed the enormous impact that war has had on the world since the start of the twentieth century, notably with World War I (1914–18), World War II (1939–45), the Cold War (1945–91), and then the post-9/11 war on terror (2001–present). In chapters 2 and 3 we encountered two frequent causes of warfare: respectively, the competition for critical natural resources—notably territory and oil—and the clash of cultural values between different civilizations (such as the Arab–Israeli conflict, or China's difficulties with Tibet).

Chapter 4 introduced armed force as one of the four basic tools of foreign policy, and we shall revisit this subject in detail throughout the next two chapters: its nature as a foreign policy tool; its cost; its likelihood of success; its pros and cons; and so on. Indeed, we saw that military power is a vital part of what separates a great power from the middle powers. We also examined the role of armed force in the concept of national security (as favoured by the realists) over the concept of human security (favoured by the idealists). Realists insist that, in an insecure and untrustworthy world, every country must retain the ability to defend its interests by armed force if necessary.

In Chapter 5, we saw that international law itself was born in a peace treaty—the Treaty of Westphalia—that in 1648 brought to an end the Thirty Years War and laid the basic contours of state-centric international law for centuries to follow. We also saw that the world's first two attempts at global governance—the League of Nations and the United Nations (UN)—were likewise born in the aftermath of war. The avoidance of war and the preservation of peace remain major objectives of the UN, even if success has proved fleeting in this regard. We distinguished between UN Security Council peace-*making* and peace*keeping*, and examined Canada's seminal role in the creation of the latter as a new kind of armed force.

Finally, last chapter, we saw how the trade policies of autarchy and mercantilism proved, historically, to be recipes for war, whereas—thus far—the growth of free trade, interconnection, and internationalism has presented a clear **disincentive** (i.e. a strong reason not) to resort to armed violence. We came to understand how previous periods of globalization, trade, and technological progress—whether under the Romans or under the British—were always secured with the prevailing military force of a dominant empire or hegemon, and we noted clear parallels to today's era of American hegemony.

What remains to be done, over the next two chapters, is to delve more deeply into the outbreak of war, its methods, and its aftermath. Given the magnitude of war's impact, this sustained, two-chapter focus seems entirely proper, and many fascinating case studies that are especially relevant to our times will serve as illustrations of different aspects of warfare. In this chapter, we consider the origins of war, the rules of international law designed to regulate the outbreak of war, and a variety of graphic examples illustrating each.

> *There have been over 200 wars in the last 100 years alone, meaning that on average, there are 2 new wars every year.*

WAR DEFINED

War is well defined as an actual, intentional, and widespread armed conflict between groups of people. This is true whether these groups are *within* one country (**civil war**) or in *different* countries (**classic international warfare**). **Armed conflict** is the use of weapons and physical violence with the intention of inflicting damage and harm upon people in an effort to get them to do what you want. As Clausewitz said, war is "an act of violence, intended to compel our opponent to fulfil our will." War is like a duel, he concluded, "only on an extensive scale." There have been over 200 wars (thus defined, and with a minimum of 1,000 battlefield deaths) in the last 100 years alone. So, on average, there are 2 new wars every year. As of writing, there seem to be, around the world, about 12 armed conflicts ongoing.[2]

WAR'S COSTS AND CASUALTIES

Given that there are so many wars, we must be mindful of the deep impact they have on the societies they affect, particularly (but not solely) in terms of the amount of death and destruction they bring. Table 7.1 shows the casualties (deaths and serious injuries) from major conflicts of the twentieth century.[3] Table 7.2 shows the financial cost to the United

TABLE 7.1 War's Massive Casualties

War	Total Estimated Deaths*
Greater Wars of the 20th & 21st Centuries (more than 500,000 people killed)	
World War I (1914–18)	20 million
Spanish Civil War (1936–9)	500,000–1 million
World War II (1939–45)	50 million–72 million
Korean War (1950–3)	2.5 million–3.5 million
Vietnam War (1954–74)	2.3 million–3.5 million
Eritrean War of Independence (1961–91)	600,000
Nigerian Civil War (1967–70)	1 million
Bangladesh Liberation War (1971)	1 million
Angolan Civil War (1975–2002)	500,000
Mozambican Civil War (1977–93)	1 million
Soviet War in Afghanistan (1979–89)	1 million–1.5 million
Ugandan Bush War (1981–6)	500,000
Iran–Iraq War (1980–9)	1 million
Second Sudanese Civil War (1983–2005)	1 million
Somali Civil War (1988–present)	500,000
Afghan Civil War (1989–2001)	1.5 million–2 million
First Congo War (1991–7)	800,000
Rwandan Civil War/Genocide (1994)	800,000
Second Congo War (1998–present)	3.8 million–5.5 million
Lesser Wars of the 20th & 21st Centuries (fewer than 500,000 people killed)	
Persian Gulf War (1991)	100,000
Bosnian Civil War (1991–5)	97,000
War in Afghanistan (2001–present)	13,000–35,000
War in Iraq (2003–present)	100,000–135,000
Darfur Genocide (2003–present)	300,000

*Includes both military and civilian deaths, and includes direct killing as well as deaths related to illness, injury, and starvation.

Note: All estimates are quite contested, especially for ongoing conflicts.

Sources: Based on C. Gelpi, et al., *Paying the Human Costs of War* (Princeton: Princeton University Press, 2009); J. Denson, *A Century of War* (Washington, DC: Ludwig von Mises Institute, 2006).

TABLE 7.2 War's Massive Costs

Major US Wars since WWI	Costs in Constant 2008 US Dollars
World War I (1917–18)*	$253 billion
World War II (1941–5)*	$4,114 billion
Korean War (1950–3)	$320 billion
Vietnam War (1954–74)	$686 billion
Persian Gulf War (1991)	$96 billion
War in Afghanistan (2001–present)	$171 billion
War in Iraq (2003–present)	$805 billion
War on Terror**	$987 billion

*American participation in these wars started later than that of most other belligerents (e.g. Canada and the UK fought in World War I from 1914 and in World War II from 1939).
**Includes all post-9/11 enhanced security as well as the wars in Afghanistan and Iraq.

Sources: Based on: S. Daggett, *CRS Report for Congress: Costs of Major US Wars* (Washington, DC: Congressional Research Service, Order Code RS22926, 24 July 2008); J. Denson, *The Costs of War* (New York: Transaction, 2nd edn, 1999).

These costs represent only those of American military contributions as paid out by US Congress. Imagine the worldwide totals.

States of the twentieth-century wars it has been involved in.[4] (US figures are used here for the sole reason that they are the best researched and the most publicly verified.)

We should add here further reflections on the interconnection between the military and the economy, beyond the obvious—yet still striking—point regarding just how much war costs (as illustrated in Table 7.2). First, a strong economy is clearly needed to fund a strong military: technology, transportation, weaponry, and personnel all cost a tremendous amount of money. Second, military technology has often become a big part of the civilian economy. Prominent examples include the Internet (as we saw in Chapter 1), the helicopter, and satellites, all of which began as tools to support the military. Finally, some argue that having a strong military is essential to having a strong economy. Consider what happened in the aftermath of September 11: immediately after the terrorist attacks, authorities in the US essentially shut down the economy—or, at least, the international, trading part of the economy—as they made sure new attacks were not forthcoming, and that new border controls and air security controls were put in place. The shutdown lasted over a week. Some, such as Wesley Clark, have suggested that such a dramatic incident shows that unless you have reliable security to guard against such violent attacks, you cannot get on with the business of growing the economy and improving everyone's living standards.[5]

WHAT CAUSES WAR, AND IS THERE A SOLUTION?

There are various influential theories, backed by evidence, about what causes war. These are outlined in Figure 7.1 and explained below. Special attention is given to what each theory

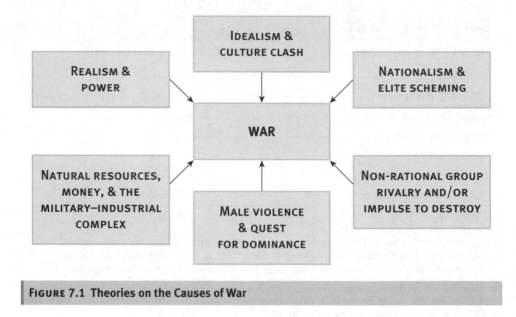

FIGURE 7.1 Theories on the Causes of War

has to say about how to solve the problem of war, given that we would, obviously, prefer to do without something so costly and destructive if we could. Note that no one theory is completely satisfying, and several (or all) may figure into the explanation of any given war.

Realism and The Quest for Power

We've already discussed, in Chapter 4, the realist worldview. According to the realist, war is all about power, with military force one of the most potent means of getting others to comply with one's will. War is about the use of violence to exert control, whether domestically over one's own people or internationally over foreigners. A variant of this account is the **hegemony/backlash theory of armed conflict**, according to which wars are produced by one power's pursuit of hegemony and/or by those resisting such aggrandizement. This is a popular explanation for many recent European wars—especially the world wars, sparked by Germany's quest for hegemony—and for many of America's recent wars, from Vietnam to Iraq.[6]

It is interesting to note that even though the realist view seems quite bleak, there is actually a hint regarding a possible solution to the problem of war. The essence of the assurance problem, for realists, is the lack of world government. Thus, if a truly effective world government could be established—one that could settle disputes between nations the way effective police and court systems settle disputes between individuals in well-run national societies—then we could have something like a reliable solution to the problem of war. The sizable difficulty with this idea, however, is the matter of creating such an institution—a topic to which we shall return in the conclusion to this book.[7]

Idealism and the Clash of Values

We need not say much about this theory, as it was explained in Chapter 1, under the heading of Huntingdon's "Clash of Civilizations." Huntingdon, you'll recall, is skeptical of claims that war is about power over others, and especially the claim (discussed below) that war is about gaining natural resources. He argues, instead, that war is created and fuelled by a profound disagreement over ideals—in particular, competing cultural values about justice and how best to run a society. Using these ideas, Huntingdon predicted—following the end of the Cold War—that the next major armed conflict would be between Western civilization and Islamic civilization.

Suffice it to say, the only way to imagine a solution to war on these grounds would be if there came to be substantial worldwide agreement on basic values. Historically, this is *not* to be expected, though some truly universal norms *might* be emerging, such as the "soft power" values associated with individual well-being, like human rights. More on this in the next chapter.[8]

Nationalism and Elite Manipulation

This theory hinges on the notion that wars are waged between groups of people, and usually—in the modern world—these groups are nations. We saw in Chapter 1 how potent nationalism and a sense of national belonging are to so many people in modern history. Given the power of the nation-state over so many aspects of social life, we have all been deeply shaped by the ideals and interests of our country. Thus, it's very plausible to suppose that such a strong identification with one's group plays a huge role in the outbreak of warfare, and in the ability of a government to sustain a war over time.

That adds a further dimension. This theory actually has two parts:

1. That national identification—i.e. **patriotism**—is a common, powerful reason why *ordinary people* agree to fund and fight wars.

2. That *ruling elites* use, or manipulate, this prevailing sense of patriotism for their own self-interest.

This theory is thus a blend (of a kind) between realism and idealism: the people fight for their ideals, whereas the rulers orchestrate the fight for their own benefit. Many a ruler has, historically, found war with a foreign power a quite convenient way of distracting his people from a problem at home. Consider, for example, Saddam Hussein's 1990 decision to invade Kuwait. He drew heavily upon Iraqi nationalism, claiming that Kuwait was properly part of Iraq. The reality was that he had just finished a terrible 10-year war with Iran, which had left Iraq enormously in debt. Moreover, he had a huge, restless, embittered army on his hands—an army that historically has determined who rules Iraq. The perfect solution for him: invade Kuwait. This would keep his army busy and off his back, and it would give him Kuwait's oil wealth, which he could use to pay down Iraq's debt. (He did not expect the US would care enough to get involved, and thus began his severe miscalculations.)[9]

Money and Materialism

Vladimir Lenin, leader of the world's first communist revolution—in Russia, in 1917—argued in favour of this theory. As soon as his communists prevailed in the revolution, creating the Russian Soviet Socialist Republic, he pulled that country out of World War I, leaving the others to fight it out. For him, countries fight over the means of economic production, specifically land and all the natural resources it contains, both on top and underneath: people, animals, timber, crops, water, oil, gold, silver, coal, diamonds—you name it. Lenin argued that as long as you have an economic system based on free-market capitalism (as described in chapters 1, 2, and 6), wars will break out, sparked by greed and competition over these material resources. He blamed pretty much the whole history of European colonialism and imperialism on this fact.

Lenin thought the only solution to the problem of war was to transform the economic system itself, from one driven by for-profit, private greed, to one driven by common, public, state-run ownership of the means of economic production. Everyone should create and *contribute what they can*; and in return, everyone should *receive only what they truly need*. Take away the private profit motive, Lenin thought, and you'd take away the reason for wanting to capture and steal resources by force.[10]

You don't have to be a communist radical to agree with this general thesis about money and material gain being the real reasons behind war. Critics like Stephen Pelletiere and William Clark have argued that America's recent wars in the Middle East—the two Iraq wars, in particular—have been, above all, about securing supplies of oil and gas to satisfy the vast American consumer appetite for fuel.[11] And no less a conservative, establishment figure than Dwight Eisenhower publicly endorsed this general thesis in his famous 1960 "Farewell Address." (Eisenhower had been Supreme Commander of Allied Forces in the Second World War, and a two-term Republican president of the United States in the 1950s.) In his much cited address, he warned Americans about the suspect, growing influence of the **military–industrial complex**. He was referring to a group of people and companies—both inside and outside of the military—with a greedy, vested interest in the business of war. He warned even further about how these companies—weapons manufacturers, in particular—donate heavily to the political campaigns of politicians who support them, creating an insidious **military–industrial–congressional triangle**, each side of which has its own selfish interest in big military spending, and in selling weapons around the world. You can't fight a war without weapons, right?[12] One stunning fact is this: total annual military spending worldwide is at least US$800 billion, one-third of which is spent by the United States alone. (The US is, by far, the world's biggest military spender, followed distantly by Russia, Japan, China, France, Britain, and Germany.)[13]

The upshot is that there is an elite, wealthy group of people with a selfish interest in violence and war—*the business of war*—and they are often well connected to high-ranking officials with decision-making power in wartime. Critics of the George W. Bush administration (2001–9) called attention to the close personal connections between such high-ranking members as Dick Cheney (vice-president) and Donald Rumsfeld (Defense secretary), and various oil and gas companies, weapons companies, and so-called **private military companies** (or **PMCs**). A PMC is a for-profit company that provides military or military-like services to a client country for a hefty fee. Often staffed with former soldiers and ex-military officials looking for higher wages, these self-styled "security solutions providers" (like Academi, better known by its former name, Blackwater) have come under criticism for being **mercenaries** (professional soldiers hired to fight wars for money) and/ or for usurping the truly public, defence-related function of a legitimate national military. Representatives of these companies reply that they are merely delivering services that national governments require and are willing to pay for, such as providing security for a town in Iraq so that the national army is free to go and fight battles with the enemy.[14]

Another thing to note about the military–industrial complex, and of particular relevance to international studies, is the North–South dimension of the weapons trade. This is to say that the majority of arms manufacturers are from the developed North, and they sell weapons into the underdeveloped South, enabling wars in the developing world. (The US is the world's leading arms seller, accounting for half of all global sales, followed by Russia and France.) Critics find this exploitative and sad, and even point to instances in which this has come back to haunt the selling country. An example: the United States in the 1980s provided extensive weapons, military training, and guidance to Afghan rebel fighters, who were resisting the invasion and occupation of their country by America's Cold War nemesis, the USSR. A number of those "allied" Afghan fighters of the 1980s went on to become "enemy" terrorists of the 1990s and 2000s, using their weapons and training against the US itself.[15]

Perhaps a quick further comment on the connection between military spending and the economy is relevant. Experts agree that in the short term, increased military spending *benefits* economic growth, as governments pour money into their economy with the purchase of domestic-made weapons and the like. But it is thought that in the long term, excessive military spending *hurts* economic growth, as it forces government to grow and "crowd out" the more productive private sector. It has often been argued that, more than anything, this is why the USSR lost the Cold War: it went broke spending all its money on its ferocious military machine, leaving other sectors of society—basic infrastructure, schools, hospitals, research—to fall apart. Development economists like Amartya Sen sometimes use the following logic to argue that military spending is a lousy way to make your economy more advanced. Think of weaponry: it either gets used, or it doesn't. If it *doesn't*, then it just sits uselessly in a storage facility—a poor investment. If it *does* get used, the result is death and destruction. Either way, such is clearly *not* the best way to invest for sustainable economic growth. Military spending is, then, at best a necessary evil, for defence-related purposes.[16]

A Feminist Analysis

Feminist thinkers like Susan Faludi have argued that men are the main cause behind war, and that, for this reason, any solution to the problem of war must involve deep, systemic, and widespread promotion of women into positions of power and influence around the world.[17]

Different feminists stress different reasons why men are behind war. Some of the most common among them include the following:

- *Biochemistry*. Men have more testosterone, which has been linked to greater degrees of violence and risk-taking. Men are simply more aggressive than women are. Combine that with male social power, and you have a recipe for the war-soaked social history that we have suffered through as a species.

- *Competitiveness*. Men are said to be more competitive than women, and frequently, when their competition cannot be contained, it spills over into violent conflict. The implication is that men are worse than women are at resolving conflicts peacefully.

- *Co-relation*. This argument infers male guilt for war from a host of damning co-relations. War is present throughout human history, and men have held the clear preponderance of power throughout history: coincidence? Feminists think not. And who are the main leaders during war? Men. The vast majority of soldiers? Men. The main heroes and war criminals? Men. The principal CEOs of weapons companies? Men. The chief scientists and engineers behind weapons development? Men. The primary audience for the seemingly endless parade of movies, books, video games, TV shows, and documentaries about war? Men. Add up all these co-relations, and a clear picture emerges of a profound male fascination with, and complicity in, warfare in all its forms.[18]

- *The assertion and expression of social power.* Feminists like Susan Faludi argue that war is just another expression of everyday, and historical, male dominance. An even shrewder argument is that war itself is a tool for ensuring male dominance over women. Faludi has argued that war is rooted in (a) a male myth about needing to protect women from other men, and (b) a male fantasy about being heralded as the mighty hero of his tribe. These two primordial psychological drives explain male propensity to go to war. Further, men have parlayed their success in war into stronger social control more broadly, and over women in particular. For instance, war heroes win political power; war profiteers make lots of money; the fortunes of war determine the fates of nations; and women and children often form the majority of civilians impacted by military activity, especially in the developing world.[19]

War as an Irrational Impulse to Destroy

What all the theories above share in common is a conviction that war has a *rational* explanation, a goal-oriented causation, as it were: war is about getting power, or money; or it's about men or a national culture seeking dominance; and so on. But others have theorized that war has a darker, more intractable dimension, one that bodes very ill for any supposed

Do you believe that war is a man's game? (© Luis Sandoval Mandujano/iStockphoto)

attempt to "solve the problem of war." In 1920, famed psychologist Sigmund Freud wrote *Civilization and Its Discontents*. At the time, just after World War I, people wondered how such a brutal, pointless war could have followed a sustained period of peace, progress, and economic and technological growth. How, when things were going so well, could they have ended up so badly?

Freud's answer was that humans have two basic and innate drives: for creation and for destruction. (These are further linked, for Freud, to the one, omnipresent, foundational human drive: the selfish pursuit of sexual pleasure.) We are driven to create, and we are driven to destroy—and not always for good reasons. Think of a child who spends a day at the beach, building a sand castle. There's all that wonderful, careful creation—with great pride upon completion. Yet many of us have known children—or *were* such children ourselves—who, when sunset falls and it's time to go, have taken an equal joy in smashing apart their own creation in a fit of destruction. There's not much rationale to it, just an impulse to wreck. As the child goes, so goes civilization, Freud concluded: we alternate between periods of peace and progress, on the one hand, and war, disease, and destruction on the other. It doesn't make much sense—there's no overall, rational story or **narrative**—but it's the fate of humanity. War is part of who we are: war and humankind will forever walk on together.[20]

Regulating the Outbreak of War

Thus far, of course, there's been no solution to the problem of war. The international community has responded by agreeing that until such a solution is found, it shall try to regulate and control warfare, since it is so destructive and impactful. As a result, there are many **international laws of armed conflict** designed to try to do this. They don't always succeed in controlling countries, of course—just like, say, the criminal laws of a domestic legal system do not always control or prevent criminal activities. But these **laws of war** are still very instructive—both when they are upheld and when they are broken—for what they reveal about armed conflict in our time. For our purposes in this chapter, focussed as we are on the outbreak of war, the relevant pieces of international law are the Charter of the United Nations (1945) and, to a lesser extent, the Hague Conventions (1899–1909). These are global, multilateral treaties regulating war, in the sense explained in Chapter 5. The more famous Geneva Conventions (1949) deal with conduct during war, and will be discussed next chapter.[21]

What does international law say about the legitimacy and permissibility of starting a war? This is the topic of what international lawyers call ***jus ad bellum***, Latin for "the justice of war." When, if ever, may states fight?

The answer is that states may fight *only* if *all* of the following criteria (summarized in Figure 7.2) are met:

- just cause

- proportionality

- public declaration of war by a proper authority

- last resort.

A head of state must ensure that these criteria have been satisfied before embarking on war; otherwise, he or she may wind up charged with war crimes after the armed conflict.[22]

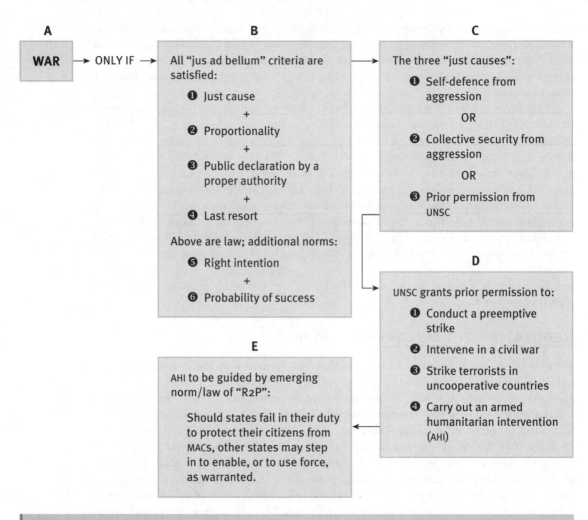

Figure 7.2 Resorting to Force

Just Cause

Most experts agree that, when it comes to a just cause for war, international law recognizes three general principles:

1. All countries have the inherent, "natural" right to go to war in **self-defence** when facing aggression. **Aggression** is defined as the use of force against another country. Any armed attack that crosses an international border constitutes aggression and is a ***casus belli***, i.e. "a cause for war." Put otherwise, aggression is the use of armed force to violate the two core rights that any legitimate, recognized country enjoys under international law: political sovereignty and territorial integrity. We saw the full meaning of these rights in Chapter 5, on international law.

2. All countries have, in addition, the inherent, "natural" right of **other-defence**—otherwise known as **collective security**—to go to war as an act of aid to *any* country victimized by aggression.

3. *Any other use of force*, such as a pre-emptive strike or an armed humanitarian intervention (or AHI, explained in the Canadian Insights box on pages 206–8), is *not* an inherent, "natural" right of states. Any country wishing to engage in this kind of force must get the prior approval of the UN Security Council (UNSC), whose structure and function we detailed in Chapter 5. Failing to receive prior authorization renders any such use of force illegal, itself an act of aggression.

So if Country *A* commits an armed attack against Country *B* (without prior approval of the UNSC), then *B* (and any other country, *C*, *D*, or *Z*) is entitled to go to war against *A* as an act of *defence from*, *resistance to*, and *punishment of*, aggression. Aggression is seen as a wrong so severe that war is a fitting response, based on the fact that aggression violates the most basic rights of groups and individuals to life and security, and to freedom and well-being—that is, to go about their lives peacefully on a territory where their people reside. Classic examples of international aggression include the following:

- Imperial Germany's invasion of Belgium in 1914, which sparked World War I
- Nazi Germany's invasion of Poland in 1939, which instigated World War II
- Japan's invasion of China in 1937, and its attack on the US at Pearl Harbor in 1941, triggering the Pacific War during World War II
- the Soviet Union's invasion of Afghanistan in 1979
- Iraq's invasion of Kuwait in 1990, which touched off the Persian Gulf War.

There are actually thousands of historical examples of international aggression.[23]

Proportionality

In every kind of law, there is supposed to be a **proportion**, or balance, between problem and solution (or between violation and response), which is to say that international law commands that the problem in question be serious enough that war is a proper reply. Since war is so costly, bloody, and unpredictable, it follows that only a very few problems in international life are truly so bad that war will be a proportionate response. The function of this rule is to get those with the power to go to war to consider again, deeply, whether there isn't some other thing to be tried—say, one of the other foreign policy tools—before resorting to force.

What, if anything, might be a problem truly so severe that war is a proportionate response? International law's answer, for reasons stated above, is *aggression*. When confronted with an aggressive invader—like Nazi Germany, Imperial Japan, or the Soviet Union—that is intent on conquering and essentially enslaving other nations, it's deemed reasonable to stand up to such a dark threat to life and liberty and to resist it, beat it back, with force if need be. Just as dangerous criminals must be resisted and prevented from getting away with their crimes, countries are entitled to stand up to aggressors, and to defeat them.[24]

Studies in Technology

Cyberwarfare

Cyberwarfare is a cutting-edge topic in armed conflict studies. It can be defined as attempting to use the Internet and related computer technologies to substantially harm the national interests of a political community. This can take one of the following forms:

- **espionage**, involving the use of computer technology (especially the Internet) to gather information that a country has taken steps to protect as a matter of national security, such as secret, confidential, or classified information;
- **the spread of disinformation**, via computer technology, in a manner that harms the security interests of the target country; and/or
- **sabotage**, involving the use of computer technology to destroy or impair the operation of various systems that are integral to the national interest of a political community. Systems vulnerable to sabotage include electricity and power; water and fuel distribution; computerized parts of manufacturing facilities; transportation systems, such as air or rail; banking and the stock market; and even the Internet itself, or at least the most commonly used websites, Internet service providers, and most basic operating systems.[25]

Cyberwarfare is not science fiction but a reality. However, owing to the newness of the technology, it is widely misunderstood. Indeed, the current state of cyberwarfare seems much like the state of play immediately after atomic weapons were invented in 1945: there's an important, brand-new technology; there's widespread ignorance and fear about it, some of it voiced with apocalyptic overtones; there's no law to regulate it whatsoever; and many nations are aggressively experimenting with it to see how this new technology can be incorporated into their means and methods of warfare. It's like a classic **weapons-testing/arms-race scenario**: who can come up with the best technology and be the first to use it effectively? The countries most frequently mentioned in connection with cyberwar technology include the United States, Britain, China, France, India, Israel, Pakistan, and Russia.[26]

So how does this misunderstood tactic of cyberwarfare actually work? Here are a few examples of actual cases:

- In 1982, at the height of the Cold War, a Canadian oil and gas company believed they had a Soviet spy in their midst. They contacted American military officials. Together the Canadian and American parties hatched a plan: they would let the presumed spy steal what he was after—a computerized control system for regulating the flow of oil and gas (which the Russians wanted supposedly to modernize their pipeline system in Siberia). But American intelligence personnel programmed the computer system with "a logic bomb," designed to make the pipelines malfunction and eventually explode after the system was implemented. This is exactly what happened, causing some loss of life and a substantial setback for a key sector of the Soviet economy.[27]

- In 2007, Russia and one of its neighbouring countries, Estonia, became embroiled in a dispute over the latter's relocation of a Soviet-era war memorial in Tallinn, Estonia. Many Estonians regarded the monument—ostensibly a memorial to soldiers who died during the Second World War—as a symbol of Soviet oppression of Estonians following the war. When the Estonian government, facing angry protests about the monument's future, had the memorial moved, Russia responded with a crippling **cyber-attack** that targeted the websites of the Estonian government, national media outlets, and the country's most powerful banks. For nearly a week, these institutions could not conduct any business online.[28]
- In 2010, Iran was attacked by a computer virus (nicknamed "Stuxnet") commonly believed to have been a joint creation of the United States and Israel. A piece of **malware** (i.e. malicious software), this very sophisticated computer virus was planted in a German-made component of one of Iran's nuclear reactors. When it was activated, the virus disabled the reactor, forcing it to shut down for an unspecified time. The goal, reputedly, was to set back Iran's progress towards developing nuclear weapons.[29]
- The country most associated with cyber-attacks today is China. But unlike American and Russian attacks, which have tended to feature sabotage of the sort just described, Chinese attacks tend to involve espionage, of both the commercial and the political variety. Many of the top US high-tech firms, such as Google, Microsoft, and various weapons companies, have complained of Chinese cyber-espionage attacks, which have been used to access extremely sensitive, high-security information, including, especially, information on product design and patents. The companies have pressed the US government to respond, but to date the only official response has taken the form of verbal warnings by American secretary of state Hillary Clinton.[30]

The British government reports that its government systems are targeted 1,000 times each month in cyber-attacks, carried out by attackers ranging from petty criminals and amateur hackers to rogue regimes. The US Pentagon has admitted publicly that in the first half of 2009 alone, it spent over US$100 million "responding to, and repairing damage from, cyber-attacks." The Pentagon has even described the cyberworld as "the fifth domain of warfare," after land, water, air, and space. It has, accordingly, created a new military department, USCYBERCOM, to defend American security interests in the cyberworld.[31]

Clearly the stakes are high, and there is substantial concern regarding the threat of malign regimes, terrorist groups, and outlaw individuals using cyber-expertise in a very damaging way. How to secure the cyberworld, and the physical world, against cyberwarfare is a subject whose importance is only going to increase with time. For their part, government officials from the US, China, and Russia have met to discuss the possibility of a treaty regulating the technology of cyberwarfare. Apparently, talks have broken down amid bitter mutual accusations. And so, for now, every country on Earth has stated publicly that it will treat any substantial cyber-attack against it to be a *casus belli*—a reason (or just cause) for it to go to war.[32]

Public Declaration of War by a Proper Authority

War is supposed to be declared out in the open, officially and honestly, by the individual or government department with the authority for doing so. In every country, some branch of government has **the war power**: the authority to order the use of force and warfare. In Canada, the war power rests with Parliament; in the United States, the war power likewise rests with the legislature (i.e. Congress). But the American president, as commander-in-chief of the Armed Forces, has enormous factual power to order the American military into action. As a result, many experts argue that the war power in the US is actually split—in classic American "checks-and-balances" style—between the legislative and executive branches of government. This arrangement produced a struggle between the branches during both the Korean War (1950–3) and, especially, the Vietnam War (1954–74), when Congress felt successive presidents were running a *de facto* war without actually declaring it and getting *de jure* (i.e. legitimate) authority for doing so from Congress.[33]

Generally speaking, in most democracies, the legislature has the war power, whereas in most non-democratic societies, it's the executive—the president or dictator—who has the authority to order war. We have seen, further, how in all cases where non-defensive armed force is being considered, the UNSC must also approve of the action beforehand. This is to say that, with non-defensive war, both domestic and international authorization must be satisfied.[34]

Last Resort

State governments are only supposed to go to war as a **last resort**, only after all other reasonable means of problem-solving have been tried, and failed. Recall that, from our foreign policy chapter, it's said that countries have four tools in their foreign policy toolbox: diplomacy, economic incentives, sanctions, and force. We have already discussed the first three of these and are in the middle of discussing the fourth one now. Obviously, you want to exhaust all other means of problem-solving before engaging in something as expensive, bloody, and risky as war.

A useful illustration of this principle in action happened during the run-up to the Persian Gulf War of 1991. We've mentioned already that in August 1990, Saddam Hussein's Iraq invaded its tiny neighbour Kuwait. International allies, led by the US and Britain, tried to talk to Saddam Hussein. They tried to negotiate with him, and then they tried threatening him, to no avail. They slapped sweeping sanctions on him, and got most of his neighbours to agree to put pressure on Iraq. Still nothing. As a result, the international community felt the decision to go to war to push Saddam out of Kuwait and back into his own borders was, indeed, a last resort. This they did, within 2 months, in early 1991.[35]

Case Study: A Tale of Two Recent Wars: Afghanistan and Iraq

Using these rules of international law, let's consider as case studies America's invasion of Afghanistan in 2001 and its invasion of Iraq in 2003. The analysis will show that international law probably supported the former but not the latter.

Afghanistan, 2001

This case begins on 11 September 2001, with the attack on the United States by the terrorist group al-Qaeda. What is terrorism? Terrorism is a tactic; it is *not* itself an actual, full-blown "ism"—i.e. a coherent, developed political ideology with a systematic view of how social institutions should be structured (like liberalism, or other ideologies we examined in Chapter 3). **Terrorism** is the use of random violence—especially killing force—against civilians with the intent of spreading fear throughout a population, hoping that this fear will advance a political objective. Crucial to terrorism is not just the deed itself but also what some have called **the propaganda of the deed**. Since terrorists want to spread fear, it's vital that their acts be not just terrible but *so terrible* that they will be covered by the media, so that word and image about the act become disseminated throughout the population, escalating the perceived threat of future strikes. The 9/11 attacks were clearly motivated not just by the desire to kill civilians but also by the drive to maximize the propaganda value of these high-profile attacks.[36]

What kind of "ism" was served by al-Qaeda's September 11 terrorist attacks? The answer is **radical Islamic extremism**. Radical Islamic extremists are a very small minority of believers in Islam (see Chapter 3), and they have a very narrow, aggressive, and unpopular agenda: they wish to install strict Islamic theocracies throughout traditional Muslim lands. A **theocracy** is a regime where the state uses its power to realize and enforce a religious vision: there is an explicit attempt to blend church and state. Islamic extremists—like the members of al-Qaeda—want all traditional Muslim lands throughout the Middle East and North Africa to have such a government, devoted to realizing their own, very strict and fundamentalist, interpretation of the Qur'an.[37]

The reason there has been conflict between radical Islamic extremists and Western civilization is that the extremists view the West, especially the US, as a major obstacle in the way of their goal. For the West supports numerous Arab governments—of Egypt, of Kuwait, of Pakistan, of Saudi Arabia—and this frustrates the extremists' agenda of toppling these governments. The West, and the US in particular, also supports Israel, a nation the Islamic radicals view as occupying traditional Arab land. So the extremists decided to commit large-scale terrorism against the United States, hoping that this would (or will) create enough pain and fear among the American people that *they* will force the US government to withdraw from the Middle East.[38]

Just Cause

The 9/11 attacks, carried out by radical Islamic extremists in **al-Qaeda,** were a clear instance of aggression. They involved the use of armed force, first to hijack the planes and then to use the planes themselves as high-powered missiles, not only destroying property but killing over 3,000 people in the process. The terrorists violated America's right to territorial integrity, in that they penetrated American airspace and made their lethal attacks on American soil. And they violated America's right of political sovereignty, by attempting to force serious foreign policy changes upon a freely choosing population. So 9/11 was an act of aggression, very reminiscent of Japan's strike on Pearl Harbor in 1941, just as it was obviously meant to be ("propaganda of the deed" and all). And aggression, as explained above, justifies a defensive war in response.

A glaring difference between the attack on Pearl Harbor by Japan and the 9/11 attack by al-Qaeda is that al-Qaeda is not a state with established territory that can be the target of a retaliatory strike. How do you go to war with a group that does not have its own territory? The connection of all this to Afghanistan came to light immediately following the September 11 strikes, when it was revealed that al-Qaeda was receiving substantial and knowing support from the then-government of Afghanistan, known as the Taliban. A militant Islamist political organization, the **Taliban** had used military force to take control of many Afghan provinces and the capital city, Kabul, in 1995–6. Embodying strict fundamentalist principles, the Taliban found common cause with al-Qaeda's terrorist objectives, in particular the desire to spread strict Islamic theocracies throughout traditional Muslim lands. So the Taliban allowed al-Qaeda refuge within Afghanistan, knowing full well that al-Qaeda was running terrorist training camps with the objective of committing terrorism around the world. In doing so, the Taliban made itself a legitimate target in the US's war on terror following the 9/11 attacks. Since al-Qaeda committed aggression, and the Taliban government in Afghanistan made it possible for them to do so, the Taliban was *a material part* of al-Qaeda's aggression—in other words, the Taliban (and Afghanistan by extension) was a co-conspirator, an enabling accomplice. The term most often applied to states that sponsor terrorism, as we saw in Chapter 4, is "rogue regimes" or "outlaw states." These are defined as states disobedient to international law and moral custom in such a flagrant way that they reveal themselves as dangerous threats.[39]

FIGURE 7.3 Taliban Presence in Afghanistan (2009)

In sum, it's commonly agreed that in the run-up to America's November 2001 invasion of Afghanistan, the US had a just cause for going to war: having been attacked two months earlier, it had the right of self-defence to strike back. And 28 other allied countries exercised their right of other-defence, or collective security, by joining in. Within two months, the Taliban was removed from power, and an uneasy process of post-war reconstruction began. It continues to this day and will be discussed further in the next chapter.[40]

Proportionality

But was the armed attack on Afghanistan a *proportionate* response? Arguably so, when one considers that the terrorist strikes on September 11 killed 3,000 people (all civilians), caused massive property damage, and negatively affected the lives of nearly everyone in North America, given the substantial new security restrictions, especially at airports, put in place afterwards. The defensive retaliation on Afghanistan lasted for only six weeks, and it focused on legitimate government and military targets. It toppled a terrorist-sponsoring rogue regime and started a rebuilding process in Afghanistan. And the important general principle remains that, once you've been aggressed against, you really ought to respond with defensive force, lest others take your non-response as weakness, which could result in further attacks upon your country and people. In the rough-and-tumble world of international politics, the projection of strength and the punishment of aggression are deemed vital.[41]

Public Declaration of War by a Proper Authority

Since the aggression here involved a direct attack on the United States, the UN Security Council need not have been consulted, and thus the only proper authority in this matter was the federal government of the United States. In the wake of 9/11, the US Congress empowered the president with sweeping authority for launching whichever armed strikes he deemed necessary to protect the United States and to punish terrorist aggression. So this condition was also satisfied.[42]

Last Resort

Once you've actually been attacked, the rule of last resort can seem almost beside the point. Or, more accurately, it has clearly and quickly been fulfilled, as the aggression has happened and a response is in order. The American government did, however, publicly call on the Taliban government to (a) hand over those members of al-Qaeda receiving safe harbour in Afghanistan, and (b) dismantle terrorist bases and training camps on its soil (and allow inspectors in to verify that this dismantling had taken place). This is, arguably, going to the maximum in terms of one last warning. When the Taliban failed to comply, or even reply, the last resort condition was met.

Since all the conditions for a legitimate use of force were satisfied in the case of Afghanistan, the US received widespread support from the international community—support that continues to this day, during the difficult post-war reconstruction of Afghanistan.[43]

A brief comment is warranted on two additional—not legal, but moral or customary—rules regarding the resort to force. These are right intention and probability of success. The rule of **right intention** is supposed to ensure purity of motive and

The Canadian government backed the US invasion of Afghanistan but not the Allied attack on Iraq. Research and explain Canada's position on these two conflicts. Do you think the positions were justified?

(© Oleg Zabielin/iStockphoto)

clarity of mind: that one goes to war for *the sole purpose of achieving the just cause* (and not, say, for some seedy ulterior motive, like commercial gain). And the rule of **probability of success** is designed to rule out a resort to force that is doomed to fail. In the case of the Afghanistan invasion, it seems that America's actions were well grounded in terms of these two additional rules: clearly, the main initial intention of the action was to topple the Taliban government and to capture, punish, or eliminate the aggressors; and, given the relative strengths of the United States and Afghanistan, the US had probability of success on its side with regard to achieving these objectives.[44]

Iraq, 2003

In May 2003, the United States and Britain launched a pre-emptive strike against Iraq, resulting in the overthrow and eventual execution of Saddam Hussein, who had been the dictator of that country for over 25 years. The move generated much controversy as Iraq had attacked no one in the run-up to the war. Thus, the principles of self-defence and other-defence (or collective security) seemed unsatisfied. We know that, in such a case, prior UNSC authorization is required before war can be launched legally. The US initially sought such authorization but then withdrew its request when it became clear that France and Russia would veto. As a result, many international law experts argued that the resulting war was illegal and unjust, as it did not have proper prior authorization from the United Nations. They also argued that the war was neither a last resort nor a proportionate response to the problems of friction and non-cooperation that Iraq represented to the international community.[45] What were America's perspective and reply?

Having failed to gain a vote of authorization from the UNSC, the US argued that they didn't really require approval, for two reasons. First, the UN's authorization for the 2003 strike was already granted in the UNSC resolution ending the 1991 Persian Gulf War. There, it clearly stated that the US reserved the right to resume hostilities should Iraq fail to comply fully with the terms of peace. Was this American claim true? Arguably yes, as, for instance, Iraq had received food aid money for its people throughout the 1990s and yet had not spent the money on that humanitarian purpose. Moreover, Iraq had repeatedly breached the "no fly zones" imposed on it by the peace treaty. And, finally, Iraq had kicked out UN weapons inspectors, who were in the country to find and dismantle Iraq's **weapons of mass destruction** (WMDs): nuclear, chemical, and biological (NBC) weapons capable of large-scale destruction of life and property. From 1991 to 1998, UN inspectors had found numerous stores of prohibited weapons in Iraq. When Saddam expelled the inspectors in 1998 (declaring,

"You found them all"), the US claimed that the UN officials had only just begun to find the most serious things, including the makings of a possible start-up nuclear weapons program. Historically, it has been commonly understood that a serious breach of the terms of a peace treaty gives grounds for the resumption of war.[46]

The second—more controversial and more emphatically expressed—reason the US offered for the 2003 attack on Iraq linked these Iraqi WMDs and the September 11 terrorist attacks to a different concept of defence, namely **pre-emptive self-defence**, which would *not* require UNSC authorization. Now, in international law, *defence* is clearly defined in strict and reactive terms: unless the UNSC says otherwise, you must wait until you've been attacked. You *cannot* attack first and *not* be the aggressor. The administration of George W. Bush claimed that Iraq both had weapons of mass destruction and, moreover, was plotting to give some of them to al-Qaeda for use in another large-scale

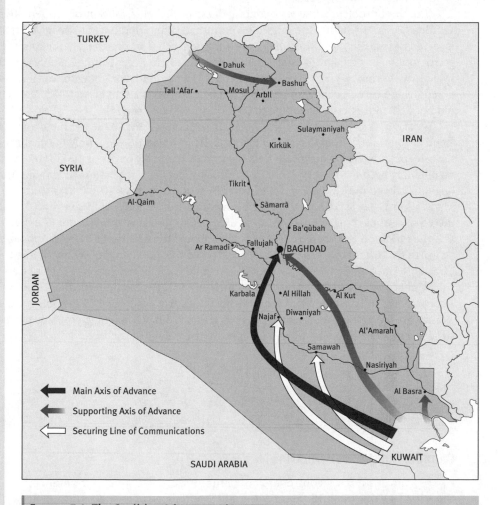

FIGURE 7.4 The Coalition Advance on Iraq, 2003

terrorist strike on the US. The United States thus re-defined "defence" proactively, arguing that, as the saying goes, the best defence is a good offence, and that the old rules had become outdated in the post-9/11 era. As it declared in its 2002 *National Security Strategy*: "The greater the threat, the greater is the risk of inaction—and the more compelling the case for taking anticipatory action to defend ourselves, even if uncertainty remains as to the time and place of the enemy's attack. To forestall or prevent such hostile acts by our adversaries, the United States will, if necessary, act preemptively."[47]

There were, or have turned out to be, three big problems with this high-profile American argument. First, having invaded and toppled the Iraqi government in June 2003, the US could in fact find no remaining weapons of mass destruction. Second, according to the US's own *Congressional Commission Report on the Attacks of 9/11*, released in 2004, the US could find no evidence of any links or collaboration between Saddam Hussein and al-Qaeda.

The third problem is the very contestedness of this new concept of "pre-emptive self-defence" and whether it ought to be permitted in international affairs, given that it seems to *broaden and loosen* the reasons for going to war, presumably making *war easier and more frequent*. It is a principle that seems to accept things like fear and insecurity (in this case, US fears of another 9/11) as grounds for going to war instead of requiring a certain quality of evidence of a true plot or intent to harm (evidence that did not exist in this case, according to the *Congressional Report*).[48]

Most countries did not buy these American arguments, and so the war hung under a cloud of controversy from the moment it began. Many questioned not only the quality of the evidence provided as justification for the strike but also the purity of the US's motives, highlighting both the issue of oil (a matter of considerable concern to the US) and the ongoing grudge the US had with Saddam Hussein dating back to the first Gulf War. Many argued that Saddam could have been contained without being confronted, that there was a whole range of options to be tried before resorting to measures as extreme as armed invasion and coercive regime change. Could the results of such a war possibly be worth the costs? For given that Iraq had attacked no one when the war began, the US invasion seemed at least disproportionate, and quite possibly a violation of the just cause rule. Unlike the war in Afghanistan, which received widespread international support, America's war in Iraq proceeded substantially on its own (with the UK providing some assistance). Since 2003, the United States has found it difficult to guide post-war reconstruction in Iraq, something we will examine more carefully next chapter.[49]

Canadian Insights

Canada and the R2P Doctrine

Apart from America's controversial claims of "pre-emptive self-defence," there has in the past 15 years emerged *another* strong challenge to the **aggression/defence paradigm** described above as the status quo regarding the international laws of armed conflict. This is the **Responsibility to Protect doctrine**, or R2P for short. Canada has been at the forefront of the movement to establish this doctrine as a norm (though not yet a law) for states to follow in international affairs.

The issue here concerns when, if ever, states may intervene with armed force in the internal crises of another country. Typically, this is referred to as an **armed humanitarian intervention** (or AHI). Supporters of R2P fear that international law shows too much respect for state sovereignty, and that, as a result, the criteria for carrying out an armed attack are really relevant only to wars between countries. But when it comes to civil wars and/or so-called "mass atrocity crimes" (MACS) within a state, when, if ever, may other countries intervene with armed force?

The Canadian government came to believe that it's not enough to reply, as international law does: "whenever the UNSC says so." Their reason: the UN Security Council can sometimes fail completely in this regard. The most searing recent example of this—in which Canada played an important part—was the 1994 genocide in the African country Rwanda. (**Genocide** is committed when an entire group or population is targeted for murder, as the European Jews were under the German Nazis during the Holocaust. The term *genocide* means literally "the killing of a whole people.")

Rwanda, during its colonial days under Belgian rule, was dominated by a minority group, the Tutsi. The majority group, the Hutu, resented being dominated, and when the country gained its independence from Belgium in 1959, the Hutu turned the tables and seized control. Relations between the two groups were always tense, and armed conflict at times broke out between the Hutu-dominated Rwandan army and the Tutsi-dominated rebel force, the Rwandan Patriotic Front (RPF). In 1993, after several years of fighting, the two sides reached a peace accord and power-sharing arrangement. However, before they could be implemented, Hutu extremists formed private **militias** (small, non-state, private military groups) to carry out an audacious and murderous plan designed not just to derail the peace accords but to eliminate altogether the Tutsi and any moderate Hutu who supported peace with the Tutsi. Genocide was truly on their minds: they aimed to eradicate the Tutsi people.

These Hutu extremists seized power in a coup in early 1994, killing members of the moderate Hutu leadership. While the UN did have a peacekeeping force already in place in Rwanda, the UN Security Council, as soon as some of the UN's (Belgian) officials were killed in the coup's early days, ordered a complete withdrawal—in spite of the pleas of the peacekeeping unit's own commanding officer, Canada's Roméo Dallaire. He knew what was going to happen and presented the UN with evidence of a genocidal plot. The UN ignored him, and all Western troops left the country, taking their own nationals with them. They even closed their embassies. The Hutu extremists had free rein to execute their horrible plan and, by April, had killed about 800,000 people, both Tutsi and Hutu. Most were butchered brutally with machetes, or shot at point-blank range with small guns. *Fully one-third of all Tutsi on Earth were murdered.* France, alone among Western countries, re-intervened late in June and helped re-establish some sanity (though some say France allowed the principal perpetrators of the genocide to escape the country as well). It was only then that the UNSC voted to return "peacekeeping" forces back to Rwanda.[50]

In 2000, Canada—feeling its peacekeepers in Rwanda had been betrayed by the UNSC—convened the International Commission on Intervention and State Sovereignty (ICISS) to draft a set of guidelines for the UNSC to follow when deciding whether or not to authorize an armed humanitarian intervention. The R2P doctrine, which is outlined in the ICISS report, *The Duty to Protect*, asserts that:

1. All states have the responsibility to protect their own people from such **mass atrocity crimes (MACS)** as genocide, war crimes, crimes against humanity, and ethnic cleansing. (A **war crime** is a violation of the laws of war as described in this and the next chapter. **Crimes against humanity** include war crimes as well as violations of basic human rights, as described in Chapter 9. **Ethnic cleansing** was discussed in Chapter 2, in connection to the situation in Darfur, Sudan; it occurs when an ethnic group is driven from their home territory to make way for another group to come in and occupy that territory.)

2. If a state *fails* in this responsibility, then other states have *the duty* to step in (a) to aid if it is somehow incapable of meeting this responsibility, or (b) to intervene with armed force, if the issue is that the state itself has turned murderously against its own people.[51]

Though the relatively new doctrine of R2P is considered only a norm and not an actual law, some experts have argued that it is well on its way to becoming the latter. After all, in the unanimous outcome document released following its 2005 World Summit, the UN General Assembly gave R2P a ringing endorsement. More to the point, the UN Security Council itself has endorsed Responsibility to Protect in principle on at least two occasions: in 2006, following the World Summit, and in 2011, when it authorized an AHI in Libya—a military action that Canada participated in.

Fighting broke out in Libya in late 2010 as part of the **Arab Spring** uprising (discussed at length in Chapter 9, on human rights). The belligerents eventually coalesced into two groups: one supportive of dictator Mu'ammar Gaddafi and one devoted to his overthrow. When Gaddafi loyalists turned violently against not just the rebel groups but also unarmed civilians and even whole towns deemed to be "enemies," NATO—led by France and Italy, which have historical ties to Libya—sought authorization from the UN Security Council to intervene with armed force. In March 2011, the UNSC gave its approval, citing the R2P doctrine as rationale. Between March and October 2011, NATO forces provided aid to the rebels and performed many direct strikes—especially air strikes—of their own against Gaddafi's forces. Canada was a robust participant in this action, which ended when Gaddafi was killed in October. The NATO mandate ended in November 2011, and Libya is currently in a state of transition.[52]

CONCLUSION

War has world-shaping significance. In this chapter, we have defined it, seen its costs and casualties, and reflected on whether these financial and human costs can ever be justified. We've studied various theories as to why war breaks out, and corresponding theories of how it might be prevented. With no solution imminent, we turned our attention to current attempts to regulate warfare through international law. After exploring these laws in detail, we applied them to the cases of Afghanistan and Iraq, noting the differences in how each war met the internationally recognized criteria for going to war. We then looked at the growth of the emerging R2P humanitarian doctrine, noting especially Canada's role in promoting and applying it. The chapter also featured an examination of the latest developments in cyberwarfare.

Having discussed the origins and causes of war, we must now turn our attention to the equally important issues of how wars get fought, and how wars end.

REVIEW QUESTIONS

1. List the many ways in which war impacts people's lives, and how it drives and shapes so many aspects of international studies. How has war impacted your life personally (whether directly or indirectly), and the history of your nation?

2. Look at Tables 7.1 and Table 7.2, noting the (partial) costs and (estimated) casualties of the major wars since World War I. Nowadays, total global military spending, every year, is at least US$800 *billion*. What else could society spend all that money and manpower on? Is that simply the cost of national security in the modern world, or is it a tragic waste of resources?

3. If you had to pick only one, which of the theories of war presented in this chapter provides the best overall account of why wars break out? Explain the strengths of this theory in contrast to the weaknesses of the others.

4. Do you believe that we'll eventually solve the problem of war? Why or why not? If yes, how (generally speaking) do you suppose this can, and will, be achieved?

5. We saw that it can be legal and permissible to go to war. Pacifists, though, dispute this on ethical grounds. What arguments might they give to justify their belief that war is *never* permissible? (Consult the online Stanford article noted below for help.) Do you accept these arguments, or do you believe they are trumped by other concerns?

6. Did the start of the recent wars in Afghanistan and Iraq fully satisfy the rules of *jus ad bellum*? Explain, and be sure you can back up (with references) any factual claims you make.

7. Should pre-emptive self-defence, otherwise known as "anticipatory attack," be permitted *without* prior authorization from the UN Security Council? Why or why not?

8. How would you describe the course of the so-called war on terror since it began after 9/11? What have been its successes and failures? Its costs and benefits? Is it, overall, a justified war or not?

9. Do you agree with the emerging R2P doctrine? Or do you find it an excessive interference with state sovereignty? An invitation to violate international law? Before you answer, watch the documentary *Shake Hands With the Devil*, which catalogues Canadian lieutenant-general Roméo Dallaire's experience during the Rwandan genocide.

10. Recently, theorists have spoken of the potential for state-sponsored **cyber-aggression**, in which one country (say, China) unleashes a massive computer-based attack (like a software virus) on some of the vital social systems (e.g. banking) of another country (for instance, the US or Canada). Would such an assault count as aggression in your eyes, perhaps even justifying an armed response?

WEBSITES FOR FURTHER RESEARCH

Avalon Project at Yale Law School http://Avalon.law.yale.edu
– for primary, treaty sources on the laws of war

Infowar Monitor: Tracking Cyberpower www.infowar-monitor.net
– for cyberwarfare

International Coalition for the Responsibility to Protect
www.responsibilitytoprotect.org

'War' in the Stanford Encyclopedia of Philosophy
http://plato.stanford.edu/entries/war
– for the ethics of war and peace

United Nations Security Council www.un.org/Docs/sc

NOTES

1. C. Von Clausewitz, *On War*, trans. A. Rapoport (Harmondsworth, UK: Penguin Classics, 1995), p. 101.
2. B. Orend, *The Morality of War* (Peterborough, ON: Broadview Press, 2006); direct quotes from Clausewitz, ibid., pp. 10–11; war frequency statistics from the Nobel Prize Organization, www.nobelprize.org.
3. C. Gelpi, et al., *Paying the Human Costs of War* (Princeton: Princeton University Press, 2009); J. Denson, *A Century of War* (Washington, DC: Ludwig von Mises Institute, 2006).
4. S. Daggett, *CRS Report for Congress: Costs of Major US Wars* (Washington, DC: Congressional Research Service, Order Code RS22926, 24 July 2008); J. Denson, *The Costs of War* (New York: Transaction, 2nd edn, 1999).
5. Der Spiegel, *Inside 9/11: What Really Happened* (New York: St Martin's, 2002); M. Ignatieff, *The Lesser Evil: Political Ethics in an Age of Terror* (Princeton: Princeton University Press, 2004); W. Clark, *Waging Modern War* (Washington, DC: Public Affairs, 2002).

6. J. Joseph, *Hegemony: A Realist Analysis* (London: Routledge, 2007).

7. Famed British philosopher and pacifist Bertrand Russell, for one, thought this was the only possible solution to the problem of war. See his *New Hopes for a Changing World* (London: Allen & Unwin, 1936).

8. S. Huntingdon, *The Clash of Civilizations and The Remaking of World Order* (New York: Simon & Schuster, 1996); B. Orend, *Human Rights: Concept and Context* (Peterborough, ON: Broadview Press, 2002).

9. E. Gellner, *Nations and Nationalisms* (Ithaca, NY: Cornell University Press, 2nd edn, 2009); W. Danspeckgruber & C. Tripp, eds, *The Iraqi Aggression Against Kuwait* (Boulder, CO: Westview, 1996).

10. V. Lenin & N. Bukharin, *Imperialism and War* (London: Haymarket, 2010); F. Firet, *The Passing of an Illusion* (Cambridge, MA: Harvard University Press, 1999).

11. S. Pelletiere, *Iraq and The International Oil System: Why America Went to War in the Gulf* (London: Maisonneuve, 2nd edn, 2004); W.R. Clark, *Petrodollar Warfare: Oil, Iraq and the Future of the Dollar* (London: New Society, 2005).

12. J. Ledbetter, *Unwarranted Influence: Dwight Eisenhower and The Military–Industrial Complex* (New Haven, CT: Yale University Press, 2011); W. Hartung, *Prophets of War* (New York: Nation, 2010); N. Turse, *The Complex: How The Military Invades Our Everyday Lives* (New York: Metropolitan, 2009).

13. J. Goldstein & S. Whitworth, *International Relations* (Toronto: Pearson, 2005), pp. 202–5; SIPRI, *SIPRI Yearbook 2010* (Stockholm: SIPRI, 2011).

14. S.M. Pavelec, ed., *The Military–Industrial Complex and American Society* (New York: ABC-CLIO, 2010); P.W. Singer, *Corporate Warriors* (Ithaca, NY: Cornell University Press, 2008); J. Scahill, *Blackwater* (Washington, DC: Nation, 2008).

15. SIPRI (op. cit., note 13); G. Crile, *Charlie Wilson's War* (London: Grove, 2007); S. Tanner, *Afghanistan: A Military History* (New York: De Capo, 2009).

16. Amartya Sen, *Development as Freedom* (Oxford: Clarendon, 1981). M. Walker, *The Cold War: A History* (New York: Henry Holt, 1995); J. Payne & A. Sahu, eds, *Defence Spending and Economic Growth* (Boulder, CO: Westview, 1993).

17. K. Alexander & M. Hawkesworth, eds, *War and Terror: Feminist Perspectives* (Chicago: University of Chicago Press, 2008); S. Faludi, *The Terror Dream* (New York: Metropolitan Books, 2007).

18. J. Meyer, *Men of War* (London: Palgrave Macmillan, 2012).

19. Faludi, *Terror Dream* (op. cit., note 17).

20. S. Freud, *Civilization and Its Discontents* (New York: Norton, 2005); J. Keegan, *A History of Warfare* (New York: Vintage, 1994); B. Orend, *On War: A Dialogue* (New York: Rowman & Littlefield, 2009).

21. W. Reisman & C. Antoniou, eds, *The Laws of War* (New York: Vintage, 1994); A. Roberts & R. Guelff, eds, *The Laws of War* (Oxford: Oxford University Press, 1999); H. Lauterpacht, *International Law, vols 3 & 4: The Law of War and Peace* (Cambridge: Cambridge University Press, 1978).

22. The laws of armed conflict grew out of just war theory, among other things. Just war theory levels two further *jus ad bellum* rules: right intention; and probability of success. See Orend, *The Morality of War* (op. cit., note 2) and M. Walzer, *Just and Unjust Wars* (New York: Basic, 1977).

23. Lauterpacht, *International Law* (op. cit., note 21); Walzer, ibid.; J. Keegan, *A History of Warfare* (New York: Vintage, 1993).

24. Orend, *The Morality of War* (op. cit., note 2), pp. 59–61.

25. R. Clark, *Cyberwar* (New York: Harper Collins, 2010); D. Ventre, *Information Warfare* (London: Wiley, 2009).

26. D. Ventre, *Cyberguerre* (Paris: Hermes-Lavoisier, 2010); D. Ventre, *Cyberespace et actueurs du cyberconflict* (Paris: Hermes-Lavoisier, 2011).

27. The Economist, "Special Report on Cyberwar: War in The Fifth Domain," *The Economist* (1 July 2010), pp. 18–26.

28. J. Carr, *Inside Cyber Warfare* (London: O'Reilly, 2010).

29. M. Gross, "The Stuxnet Cyber-Weapon," *Vanity Fair* (April 2011), pp. 152–98.

30. M. Gross, "Enter the Cyber-Dragon," *Vanity Fair* (Sept. 2011), pp. 220–34.

31. S. Brenner, *Cyber Threats* (Oxford: Oxford University Press, 2009). See also the influential "Lipman Report" at www.guardsmark.com

32. R. Dipert, "The Probable Impact of Future Cyberwarfare," paper delivered at The First International Workshop on "The Ethics of Informational Warfare," University of Hertfordshire (UK), 1 July 2011.

33. R. Regan, *Just War: Principles and Cases* (Washington, DC: Catholic University Press of America, 1996).

34. Orend, *The Morality of War* (op. cit., note 2), pp. 50–7.

35. J.T. Johnson & G. Weigel, eds, *Just War and Gulf War* (Washington: University Press of America, 1991).

36. W. Laqueur, *New Terrorism* (Oxford: Oxford University Press, 1999); Jim Sterba, ed., *Terrorism and International Justice* (Oxford: Oxford University Press, 2003).

37. J. Corbin, *Al-Qaeda* (New York: Nation, 2002); R. Gunaratna, *Inside al-Qaeda* (New York: Berkley Group, 2003).

38. J. Hughes, *Islamic Extremism and The War of Ideas* (Washington, DC: Hoover Institute, 2010); M. Palmer, *Islamic Extremism* (New York: Rowman & Littlefield, 2008).

39. A. Rashid, *Taliban* (New Haven, CT: Yale University Press, 2001); M.T. Klare, *Rogue States and Nuclear Outlaws* (New York: Hill and Wang, 1996).

40. T. Barfield, *Afghanistan: A Cultural and Political History* (Princeton: Princeton University Press, 2009).

41. S. Tanner, *Afghanistan: A Military History* (New York: DaCapo, 2nd edn, 2009).

42. J. Hoge & G. Rose, eds, *Understanding the War on Terror* (New York: Foreign Affairs, 2005).

43. S. Jones, *In the Graveyard of Empires: America's War in Afghanistan* (New York: Norton, 2010).

44. Orend, *The Morality of War* (op. cit., note 2), pp. 70–82.

45. D. McGoldick, *From "9/11" to "Iraq War 2003": International Law in an Age of Complexity* (London: Hart, 2004); M. Sifry & C. Cerf, *The Iraq War Reader* (New York: Touchstone, 2003); M. Byers, *War Law* (Toronto: Douglas & McIntyre, 2005).

46. S. Ritter, *War on Iraq* (New York: Profile, 2002); B. Woodward, *Plan of Attack* (New York: Simon & Schuster, 2004).

47. *The National Security Strategy of the United States of America*, September 2002, available at www.whitehouse.gov/nsc/nss.pdf, p. 15

48. *The Congressional Commission Report on the Attacks of 9/11* (Washington, DC: US Congress, 2004); R. Scarborough, *Rumsfeld's War* (New York: Regnery, 2004).

49. W. Murray & R. Scales, *The Iraq War* (Cambridge, MA: Harvard University Press, 2003); T. Dodge, *Inventing Iraq* (New York: Columbia University Press, 2003).

50. G. Prunier, *Rwanda: History of a Genocide* (New York: Columbia University Press, 1995); M. Barnett, *Eyewitness to a Genocide: The UN and Rwanda* (Ithaca, NY: Cornell University Press, 2003); L. Melvern, *A People Betrayed: The Role of The West in Rwanda's Genocide* (New York: Zed, 2000); R. Dallaire, *Shake Hands with the Devil* (New York: Random House, 2004).

51. The International Commission on Intervention and State Sovereignty, *Report: The Responsibility to Protect* (Ottawa: International Development Research Centre, 2002).

52. A. Bellamy, *Responsibility to Protect* (London: Polity, 2009); G. Evans, *The Responsibility to Protect: Ending Mass Atrocity Crimes Once and For All* (Washington, DC: Brookings Institute, 2009); N. Gvosdev, *R2P: Sovereignty and Intervention after Libya* (London: World Politics Review, 2011).

8 Armed Conflict, Part 2: Methods and Aftermaths

"The object in war is a better state of peace."[1] —*B.H. Liddell Hart (1895–1970), British soldier & military historian*

LEARNING OBJECTIVES

After studying this chapter, you will be able to:

▸ define all the bolded key terms and concepts

▸ identify the world's major military powers, the characteristics that make them so, and their policies regarding the use of force

▸ grasp the latest high-tech weaponry, alongside concerns about its use

▸ understand the *jus in bello* laws of armed conflict, their rationale, and real-world examples of each law

▸ become familiar with the two major, contrasting policies on post-war reconstruction, and the case studies that illustrate each in action

▸ reflect, overall, on the significance of armed conflict to international studies, to the interstate system, and to our attempts to forge a better world.

INTRODUCTION

Once wars begin, they get fought, and then eventually, they come to an end. Having examined war's beginning in the last chapter, we must now turn our attention to war's middle and its aftermath. Such is this chapter's two-fold objective. Before that, we'll quickly define some basic military concepts—such as *capability, strategy,* and *tactics*—in order to better our bearings.

DEFINING SOME MILITARY TERMS

It makes sense, before talking about the ways in which wars are fought, to offer an overview of the elements that contribute to a country's military capability. **Military capability** refers to the resources a country has to deploy armed force. Most countries have an army, a navy, and an air force, each using its own kind of weaponry.

An **army** is a ground-based force, composed of soldiers and the officers who command them. An army's most basic function is to secure and hold a given piece of territory. Since so much of warfare has, historically, revolved around the control of territory, the army has always been the core and largest component of military capability.

A **navy** is a water-based force, composed of ships and submarines, and the sailors who operate them. The navy's goal is to secure and hold a given waterway or sea route. The

marines make up a versatile water-and-land–based force, originating historically in the corps of brave souls who were the first to disembark from ships and fight their way onto shore (hence the marines' reputation for extreme toughness).

Finally, the **air force** is composed of pilots and their gunners or bombers, and the different kinds of planes and helicopters they fly. Its basic function is to control and secure a given airspace.

When working together during wartime, a nation's military forces aim to control the air, water, and land of a given region. This would give them **maximum leverage** to inflict their will upon that region's population: the hardest of hard power. Table 8.1 below summarizes the general military capabilities of some select nations, focusing on the great powers.[2] Compare this breakdown of different countries' military capability with the comparative data presented on the website GlobalFirepower.com, which ranks the overall top 10 military powers, in descending order, as follows:

1. United States
2. China
3. Russia
4. India
5. Britain
6. France
7. Germany
8. Brazil
9. Japan
10. Turkey.

Two further aspects of military capability must be stressed. The first is **logistics**, which concerns the ability of a country to supply its armed forces with everything they need to fight, which ranges well beyond weapons to include such things as food, clothing, medicine, and gasoline. Supporting an army is a massive effort of resources, planning, and organization. Historically, it has often been as damaging to strike an enemy's **supply chain** as to strike directly at its armed forces. Both Alexander the Great (356–323 BCE) and Napoleon (1769–1821) had to give up their campaigns of conquest because of severe logistical problems. The second aspect is **intelligence**, which entails the gathering and analysis of data about the enemy: its weapons and capabilities, its plans and intentions, its most vulnerable or most strategic targets, and so on. Most countries have some kind of intelligence agency to serve this function. In the US, for example, it's the **Central Intelligence Agency (CIA)**; in Canada, the **Canadian Security Intelligence Service (CSIS)**.[3]

Weapons

Modern armed forces are amazingly expensive, both to assemble and to maintain. All the soldiers and sailors, and all the pilots and marines, must be fed, clothed, housed, and trained; all the weapons must be built and kept battle-ready, and then replaced after they break down or become **obsolete** (i.e. out of date and inferior). Transporting troops and their weapons is difficult and costly, too, and the technology for doing so can range from simple Jeeps and Humvees to naval aircraft carriers, nuclear-powered submarines, cargo planes, and **stealth bombers** (which can avoid radar detection). And when it comes to weaponry, no one wants to be caught using yesterday's technology, which means that countries are continually paying to upgrade their equipment. Consider advances in the manufacture

TABLE 8.1 Some Core Capabilities of Select Military Powers

Country	Military Spending (billions of dollars)*	Active Personnel	Tanks	Warships & Submarines	Combat Aircraft	Nuclear Weapons**
Canada	16	67,000	200	75	200	0
China	64–122	3,500,000	8,000+	320	2,000	250
France	53	260,000	400	90	350	300
India	25	1,800,000	3,000+	120	800	75
Israel	12	177,000	3,000+	85	370	200
Japan	43	240,000	1,000	59	300	0
Pakistan	4	650,000	1,500	35	210	80
Russia	38–70	1,000,000	3,000–10,000	400	2,000	12,000
UK	57	240,000	400	90	350	200
US	610	1,500,000	8,000	325	3,500	10,000

*For the 2008 fiscal year, in constant 2005 US dollars. The numbers for China and Russia are disputed, as there is no true public scrutiny of them.

Russia and the United States have mutually agreed to deploy only 6,000 nuclear weapons and to **decommission (or dismantle) the rest. The numbers for *all* the equipment and weapons do *not* reveal the age of these weapons, nor their true quality or **battle-readiness**.

Source: All numbers in Table 8.1 are author's best estimates, drawing from the following sources: Carnegie Endowment for International Peace, www.ceip.org; Stockholm International Peace Research Institute, www.sipri.org; Global Issues, www.globalissues.org.

of missiles, which are used to strike at one's enemy from afar, minimizing risk to oneself. Improvements in technology have made missiles more accurate and more powerful in units that range from shoulder-fired, anti-aircraft or anti-tank missiles to ship-fired, guided **cruise missiles** capable of destroying buildings a thousand kilometres away. Cruise missiles were first extensively used by the United States during the Persian Gulf War in 1991. The biggest missiles are intercontinental ballistic missiles, or **ICBMs**, which are capable of flying into near-space and then dropping nuclear bombs on targets *over 8,000 kilometres from the launch site*, destroying whole cities or even entire regions. And yet, for all the cost of developing, building, and acquiring these nuclear missiles, ICBMs have never actually been used in battle. In fact, the only time atomic bombs have been dropped in wartime was in August 1945 at the very end of World War II, when the US dropped bombs on Japan, destroying the cities of Hiroshima and Nagasaki and killing at least 250,000 people.[4]

An American Titan intercontinental ballistic missile at a launching silo in Arizona. The Titan family of ICBMs were developed during the Cold War, but they were used for a host of non-military purposes, including launching weather satellites and interplanetary space probes for NASA. Does this help to justify the cost of developing an expensive piece of weaponry that was never actually used in battle? (© LOU OATES/iStockphoto)

Studies in Technology

New Weapons Technologies

Four **emerging military technologies** (EMTs) are especially prominent today:

Cyberwarfare

Studied in detail last chapter, this is the use of advanced computer-based and Internet-based technologies for:

- **espionage** (i.e. data-gathering).
- spreading **disinformation** (i.e. damaging, embarrassing lies), and
- **sabotage** (i.e. destruction of computer networks).

Non-lethal Weapons

These are otherwise known as **incapacitating agents**. Today's militaries are anxious to keep the body count low in war, as the public—especially in voting democracies—doesn't like to see large numbers of casualties. Incapacitating agents range from such everyday tools of law enforcement as pepper spray and Taser electric-shock guns to sophisticated, military-scale weaponry. The US military, for example, possesses a weapon designed to cause permanent blindness to anyone within a certain distance of its deployment unless they are wearing specially fitted eye-gear. It is an intensely bright laser discharge that essentially fries the rods and cones of everyone within eyesight unless they are wearing specially calibrated eye shields. The thinking is that enemies incapacitated in this way would promptly surrender, and have their lives—though not their eyesight—saved.[5]

Soldier Enhancements

Militaries know that they are limited, significantly, by the limits of the human body. This is especially true for the land-based army. Military officials are thus keenly interested in anything that will enhance soldier performance on patrol and, especially, in battle. Thus, technologies for providing enhanced vision, hearing, and even smell are constantly being improved upon. Of special interest are drug-related enhancements designed to minimize the need for rest and sleep and to maximize battle-readiness, alertness, and energy. The US military has developed (but does not use) a "souped-up" cocktail (containing, among other ingredients, forms of cocaine, adrenaline, and testosterone) that allows some soldiers to maintain battle-ready energy, with no sleep, for 72 hours—three days!—straight.[6]

Unmanned Systems

"Unmanned systems" are robots and drones. Voting publics also don't like losing their own soldiers, so militaries are increasingly using weapons systems that are either piloted by robots or operated from a distance by remote control using satellites and GPS technology. The unmanned systems with the highest profile are **drones**, which are small planes that can often be flown remotely and without enemy radar detection, and that can be used either for espionage and surveillance or else for dropping bombs and shooting missiles. The US military has rapidly escalated its use of drone technology over the past 10 years, especially for surveying rogue regimes and attacking terrorist bases, particularly in the Middle East, as part of the war on terror.[7]

Strategy versus Tactics

Like weapons technology itself, the study of how best to fight different kinds of enemy is constantly evolving. Military planners distinguish between strategy and tactics. **Strategy** refers to the big-picture plan of how to defeat an enemy, whereas **tactics** refers specifically to how one should fight particular battles *as pieces in* the overall strategy. A rough example: during World War II, the Allied *strategy* for beating Hitler was to surround him with overwhelming force—Soviets/Russians from the east; the British and their empire from the north and west; the Americans from the south and west—in order to draw an ever-tightening circle around him. The *tactics* for carrying out this strategy varied from battle

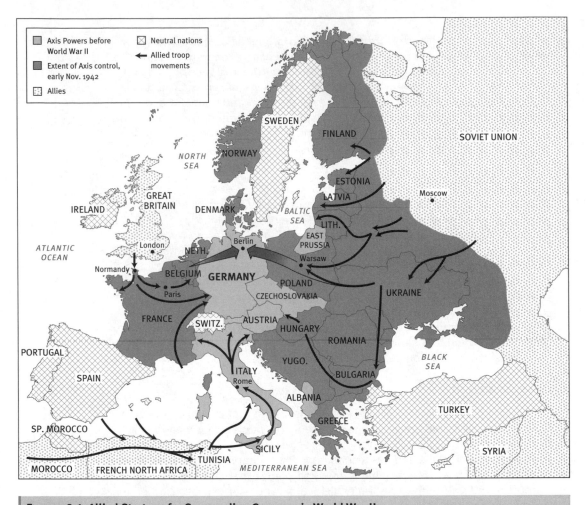

FIGURE 8.1 Allied Strategy for Surrounding Germany in World War II

Source: Based on http://dsf.chesco.org/heroes/images/europe_nafrica.jpg

to battle, culminating with the planning and execution of the successful D-day invasion of Normandy in 1944.[8]

Wealthy nations have enormous advantage when it comes to armed force, owing to the immense costs (discussed above) of military planning, weapons research, and technological growth. But two things to note: first, as mentioned last chapter, too much military spending is bad for a country's economic growth over the long term (as the Soviets discovered); and second, enemies using unpredictable, low-level, counter-conventional **guerrilla tactics** can be capable of inflicting surprisingly large damage even on the richest and most powerful countries (witness the 9/11 attacks on America). Recently, experts have distinguished between **conventional** (or **symmetrical**) **warfare**, which is classical, open,

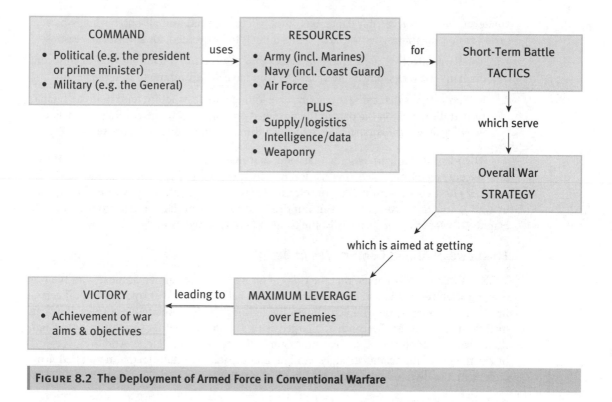

Figure 8.2 The Deployment of Armed Force in Conventional Warfare

direct warfare between states or between evenly matched sides, and **asymmetrical warfare**, which is warfare pitting a state government on one side against a non-state actor (like a terrorist or insurgent group) on the other. Obviously, the strategy and tactics deployed will vary substantially, depending on which kind of war, and which kind of adversary, one is fighting. Figure 8.2 shows how tactics fit into a country's approach to war.[9]

Fighting a War

Realism versus Idealism, Redux

The realist's way of thinking about the conduct of war is this: once you have made the grave and dramatic decision to go to war (based on a calculus of national self-interest, of course), the most important thing to do is . . . win it. The losers of war suffer terribly, history tells us, and so a smart country ought to do whatever it deems necessary to win its wars. There are no restraints, for the realist; there are only results, and the only one acceptable in wartime is victory.

There are no restraints for the realist; there are only results, and the only one acceptable in wartime is victory.

This might sound obvious—that the goal of war is to win it—but there are alternatives to the realist's win-at-all-costs approach. The idealist's perspective of international law is one such alternative. The idealist believes that to let countries involved in war do whatever they want is terribly dangerous, for it will create **total war**: all-out, no-holds-barred, unrestrained, anything-goes warfare. Such a thing is to be avoided, for at least two reasons:

1.   Total war involves *indiscriminate killing and destruction*, including that of innocent civilians (such as women and children) who have done nothing to deserve death.

2.   Military strikes that cause indiscriminate killing and destruction tend to invite retaliation and revenge on the part of the outraged enemy, causing the conflict to escalate to *even higher levels of destruction*, which is ultimately in no one's rational self-interest.

The idealist is a firm believer that, odd as it may sound, war ought to be fought in a fair, decent, restrained way. How is decency in war measured in international law? The rules of good conduct in battle are referred to by the Latin phrase *jus in bello* ("justice in war"), and they are contained in hundreds of treaties, perhaps most prominently the Hague (1899–1909) and, especially, the Geneva (1949) conventions.[10]

The Laws of Armed Conflict: *Jus in Bello*

Whereas we saw, last chapter, that the rules of *jus ad bellum* are aimed at those with the war power (often the head of state), the rules of *jus in bello* are aimed at soldiers and officers—in other words, at those who actually do the fighting. If they violate these rules, they can find themselves, after the conflict, charged with war crimes, either domestically through their own military justice system or internationally through The Hague. And in this regard, by far the most important, strongly worded, and repeatedly mentioned and codified principle is that of discrimination and non-combatant immunity.

Discrimination and Non-Combatant Immunity

Discrimination here means the need for fighters to distinguish, or discriminate, between legitimate and illegitimate targets, and to take aim only at the former. A **legitimate target** is anyone, or anything, that is part of the war machine of the enemy society. (The **war machine** refers to the military–industrial–political complex that guides the war and fights it.) Loosely speaking, it is anything that is a source of potential physical harm to oneself. Specific examples of legitimate targets include the following:

- soldiers, sailors, marines, pilots, and their officers
- their weapons and equipment
- their barracks and training areas
- their means of transportation
- their supply and communications lines
- the industrial sites where their supplies, weapons, etc. are stored or produced.

Core political and bureaucratic institutions are also legitimate objects of attack, in particular things like the building housing a country's defence department or ministry.
    Illegitimate targets include the following:

- residential areas
- schools

- hospitals
- farms
- churches
- cultural institutions
- non-military industrial sites.

In general, anyone or anything not demonstrably engaged in military supply or military activity is out of bounds and should be immune from direct, intentional attack. Thus, **non-combatants** (i.e. unarmed civilians) are considered immune from intentional attack. It is for this reason that the intentional killing of civilians is seen as probably the worst war crime.[11] Consider the following, infamous case.

Case Study: The My Lai Massacre

Capitalist America fought the Communist Viet Cong during the Vietnam War (1954–74), one of the largest and lengthiest armed conflicts that occurred during the Cold War. The Viet Cong refused to fight the Americans in the open, lest they be blown away by superior US firepower. Instead, the Viet Cong used guerrilla tactics: hiding, and then striking quickly and unpredictably, before fading back either into the jungle or into small villages, where they would then blend in with the local population, much to the frustration of American soldiers and strategists.

On 16 March 1968, a unit of the US Army commanded by William Calley entered the village of **My Lai** (pronounced "me-LIE") and rounded up everyone—man, woman, and child. When the villagers refused to identify the Viet Cong soldiers in their midst, Calley ordered the immediate and systematic execution of everyone. Between 350 and 500 people died, the vast majority of them thought to be completely innocent. Many were women, children, and elderly citizens. Calley—but only Calley—was later tried and convicted of war crimes by the American military justice system.[12]

Minimizing Civilian Casualties

One of the bitter ironies of the rule of non-combatant immunity is that, on the one hand, it is the most frequently and forcefully *mentioned* principle in the laws of armed conflict, while on the other, it is probably the most frequently *violated* principle as well. For civilian casualties have outnumbered military casualties in every known major war since World War I, and often by an enormous margin.[13] How can this grim fact be true if the nations of the world truly care so much about the safety of civilians? A few possibilities to consider:

> *Civilian casualties have outnumbered military casualties in every known major war since World War I.*

- Not all regimes care about civilian safety. In particular, **non-democratic regimes**, which are typically propped up with the help of the military (rather than the popular support of the people), have less reason to care about minimizing civilian casualties.

- The rules of international law, while they may be compelling, are abstract and ideal, and thus very difficult to uphold.

- Many civilians who die in major wars do not die directly from military attack but, rather, from the indirect consequences of military activity. Many, for instance, die from starvation and illness when food supply routes and basic social infrastructure (e.g. water supplies, hospitals, etc.) are destroyed by military activity.

- The non-combatant immunity principle does not make it illegal for civilians to die in wartime. What is illegal is *taking deliberate and intentional aim* at civilians with armed force. If a fighting side has taken every reasonable effort to avoid and minimize civilian casualties, then the death of some civilians by accidental or indirect means is *not* a war crime. Civilian casualties under these circumstances are viewed as **collateral damage**—accidental, unintended victims of the fighting. For example, if during an air-bombing raid on an enemy's industrial sites a few bombs accidentally go astray, hitting a nearby residential area and wounding and killing some civilians, these civilians would be considered collateral damage.

So civilians are entitled *only* to "due care" from fighters; they are *not* entitled to absolute and fail-safe immunity from warfare. What does **due care** include? It includes serious and sustained efforts, from the top of the military chain of command down to the bottom, to protect civilian lives as much as possible under the difficult circumstances of war. So, for example, strategists must make their plans with an eye to minimizing civilian casualties; intelligence needs to be gathered and analyzed to determine which targets are permissible; soldiers need to be trained exhaustively in proper (i.e. restrained, discriminating) ways of fighting; and any rough treatment of civilians needs to be investigated and punished.[14]

What about so-called **dual-use targets**? These are targets—mostly pieces of infrastructure—that are used *both* by the military and by civilians during war: roads, bridges, radio and television networks and transmitters, railway lines, harbours, airports, and so on. International law forbids these to be targeted, but in reality, they often are, as they are vitally important in helping military planners communicate with their troops and to move them around to where they can fight. More controversial, and thus more criticized, is targeting basic infrastructure, like farms, food supply, sewers, water treatment plants, irrigation systems, water pipelines, oil and gas pipelines, electricity generators, and power and telephone lines. The civilian population pays a huge price for any damage inflicted on such vital social infrastructure, and so it seems to violate civilian immunity to make them targets. The United States has done this twice recently. During the opening days of both the 1999 Kosovo War, and the 2003 Iraq attack, the US conducted a **"shock and awe" campaign**, relying on air power, bombing raids, and cruise missiles to inflict heavy damage on basic infrastructure (especially communications and electricity lines) in Serbia and Baghdad, respectively. The military goal of such a strike is to hit the enemy as fast and furiously as possible, dazing them, and "softening them up" for a subsequent ground invasion by army soldiers. It is also to shock the civilians in that society into putting pressure on their regime to give up and surrender quickly.[15]

Case Study: Child Soldiers

An issue of grave concern connected to non-combatant immunity is that of child soldiers. Child soldiers are not unknown in history—Hitler notoriously conscripted German boys during the final, losing days of the Second World War, desperate as he was for any kind of manpower—but the modern concern revolves around Africa. In the early 1980s, rebels in Mozambique fought a civil war against government forces. Outnumbered, the rebels tried to even the odds by kidnapping boys—some as young as 8!—from their parents, conscripting them into the rebel cause. The rebels would brainwash the boys, train them, abuse them, arm them, and then unleash them on government forces. Some of the tactics used to manipulate the child soldiers included threats and coercion, the administering of drugs or alcohol, and fabrication, including telling the boys that the whole thing was a giant game.

Since that time, child soldiers have been used extensively in conflicts throughout Africa, and even in Asia. In March 2012, a prominent example leapt into public consciousness when an Internet video went viral. The video depicted the actions of the Ugandan rebel group The Lord's Resistance Army (LRA), led by Joseph Kony. Since 1986, the LRA has abducted over 60,000 children and forced them to fight against the Ugandan government.[16] It is estimated that over 250,000 child soldiers have been used in Africa alone since 1980. Child soldiers, *as soldiers*, remain legitimate targets in wartime, but there is a serious movement to get the use of child soldiers to be declared a war crime, punishable against those adult leaders brutal enough to use them. (Kony, for example, has been indicted for war crimes by the International Criminal Court at The Hague: see more below.) There are also necessary, encouraging efforts by such NGOs as Save the Children to help rehabilitate former child soldiers and ease them back into productive life once the war has ended or they have been liberated from the fighting.[17]

POWs, Benevolent Quarantine, and Torturing Terrorists

It follows from the idea of non-combatant immunity that should enemy soldiers cease to be a source of harm during war (i.e. by laying down their weapons and surrendering), then they cannot be targeted with lethal force after that point. In fact, any enemy soldiers who surrender are to become **prisoners-of-war** (or **POWs**): they are to be offered "benevolent quarantine" for the duration of the war, and then returned to their home country in exchange for one's own POWs. **Benevolent quarantine** means that captured enemy soldiers can be stripped of their weapons, incarcerated with their fellows, and questioned verbally for information. They cannot be tortured during questioning, nor can they be beaten, starved, or somehow medically experimented on. They cannot be used as human shields between one's own fighters and the opposing side; the understanding is that captured enemy soldiers are to be incarcerated far away from the front lines of combat. Very basic medical and hygienic treatment is supposed to be offered—things like pain medication, soap, water, and toothbrushes—and, while making captives engage in work projects is permitted, the Geneva Conventions actually require that, under those circumstances, captives be paid a modest salary for their labour. This last condition is rarely met in the real world, but it is quite common for combatants to disarm, house, and feed their captives, keeping them out of harm's way and ensuring their basic needs are met until the war ends. After all, one hopes one's own POWs are being treated as well by the other side.[18]

Two points remain controversial here:

1. At what point does aggressive questioning become a form of torture?

2. Do non-state actors (like terrorists) who are taken prisoner deserve the same quality of treatment as state captives?

There's a sense that a soldier fighting for his community deserves better treatment than a terrorist fighting for his cause. This distinction can be difficult to sustain, though, and courts worldwide have found that, generally, non-state actors brought into capture should be accorded the same rights as captured enemy soldiers. After all, if soldiers fighting for an *unjust* cause deserve fair treatment, then surely so do terrorists—whose method, if not their cause, is likewise unjust. In other words, if it's wrong to torture Nazi soldiers—whose cause was heinous and irredeemable—then it's wrong to torture radical Islamic terrorists (much less mere suspects).[19]

This topic was recently highlighted and became a point of debate during America's roundup of alleged terrorists in Guantanamo Bay, Cuba. The incidents in Abu-Ghraib prison, in Iraq, also come to mind. In the late spring of 2004, the world saw some shocking photos depicting the conduct of American military prison guards in that jail. Iraqi prisoners—captured during the war and subsequent insurgency—were subjected to questionable treatment. Some of it—like deliberate, prolonged sleep deprivation, and using dogs to attack or threaten already vulnerable people, prone and naked—clearly violated the Geneva Conventions. Other acts might have been visually disturbing but don't obviously count as human rights violations; examples including forcing prisoners to wear dog collars, or having American women ridicule their private parts, or putting female panties on the faces of some prisoners. When these various acts are considered all together, they seem to constitute a violation of both the letter and the spirit of the principle of benevolent quarantine. Some of the US soldiers involved have since been charged, tried, and sentenced in the American military justice system.[20]

Now, questioning is permitted under the Geneva Conventions. But the infliction of physical harm cannot be, even if it supposedly serves the questioning process. Why? Because it's impossible to square the infliction of *physical harm* with the concept of *benevolent quarantine*. Benevolent quarantine may not mean actually being nice to your prisoners, but it cannot, logically, include things the Geneva Conventions define as torture: prolonged sleep deprivation; starvation; slapping, punching, biting, or strangling; the breaking or severing of limbs or digits; urging or allowing an animal to attack; any kind of drowning-based (e.g. **waterboarding**) or electrocution-based session; sexual assault or rape; poisoning or medical experimentation; shooting; and so on. These things are simply prohibited. In domestic society, we do not permit prison guards to torture *anyone*—even those convicted of the very *worst* crimes. So why should we allow it in international society? The answer is, we shouldn't, and we don't. The thing to do with terrorist suspects, it seems, is to question them within the rules, prosecute them for their crimes, and upon conviction, send them to jail.[21]

Proportionality

The *jus in bello* version of **proportionality** mandates that soldiers deploy only proportionate force against legitimate targets. The rule is *not* about the war as a whole; it is about tactics *within* the war. Be sure, the rule commands, that the destruction needed to carry out a goal is proportional to the good of achieving it. The crude version of this rule is, don't squash a squirrel with a tank, or shoot a fly with cannon; *use force appropriate to the target.*

The rule of proportionality is designed to prohibit excessive harm and purposeless violence during war. One case in which this rule might have been breached occurred toward the end of the Persian Gulf War. During the war's final days, in early 1991, there was a headlong retreat of Iraqi troops from Kuwait along a road subsequently dubbed "The Highway of Death." When American forces descended upon the road, it was so congested that retreating soldiers were easy targets for American fire. The result was a bloodbath that was afterwards much photographed and publicized. The controversy of the case surrounds the fact that although the Iraqi soldiers did not surrender, and thus remained legitimate targets, the killing was, as experts like Michael Walzer have suggested, "too easy." The battle degenerated into a "**turkey shoot**"—a conflict in which one side has an overwhelming advantage—and the force deployed seemed disproportionate. It could be argued that Saddam Hussein, in the same war, was likewise guilty of breaking the rule of proportionality when he used oil spills and oil fires, with reckless disregard of the environmental damage, as a supposed means of defence against a feared amphibious invasion of Kuwait by the Allies.[22]

No Prohibited Weapons

Aside from the canonical Hague and Geneva conventions, there are many conventions and legal treaties on the issue of prohibited weapons, such as those banning the use of chemical (1925), biological (1972), and "excessively injurious" (1980) weapons. Also relevant are the conventions against genocide (1948), against "methods of warfare which alter the natural environment" (1977), and banning land mines (1997). Prohibiting certain categories of weapons puts an added restriction on belligerents and, as such, is consistent with the deepest aim of *jus in bello*, namely, to limit war's destruction.[23]

Weapons of mass destruction (WMDs) fall under the category of prohibited weapons. As we saw last chapter, WMDs are capable of generating unusually large casualties and property destruction. They are also known as NBC **weapons**, because they typically contain a *nuclear*, *biological*, or *chemical* agent. Yet although some of the prohibited WMDs contain a nuclear agent, **nuclear weapons**, as a category unto itself, have not yet been outlawed by treaty, because the major nuclear powers have blocked any such move (even as they move to prevent or deter other nations—especially rogue states like Iran—from acquiring or developing their own nuclear weapons). Nuclear weapons unleash an atomic explosion, causing devastation to physical structures and radiation poisoning in people. They are, to date, the most destructive weapons yet invented. As mentioned, they have been used in battle just twice in all of world history, and it is worth noting that the current generation of nuclear weapons is much, much more powerful than those that destroyed Hiroshima and Nagasaki. The list of countries that have admitted to, or are suspected of, possessing nuclear weapons includes the following:

- Britain
- China
- France
- Israel
- India
- North Korea
- Pakistan
- Russia
- United States.

Germany and Japan, together with such wealthy middle-power countries as Canada, are thought to be capable of building such weapons, but they have decided not to, for reasons of history or conviction. Other states are suspected of wanting very much to develop their own nuclear weapons, notably Iran. The move to prevent the spread of weaponry throughout the international community is known as **non-proliferation**.[24]

Both chemical and biological weapons have been outlawed by treaty, but research on chemical and biological weaponry and stockpiling these for purely defensive and deterrent purposes are either permitted or at least allowed to go unpunished. Dozens of nations have, or could have, these devastating weapons. **Chemical weapons** unleash a gas, or some other chemical, that kills or harms those exposed to it. Mustard gas, for example, was used by both sides during the First World War (1914–18) and the Iran–Iraq War (1979–89). **Biological weapons** release a living organism—usually a virus or bacteria—capable of harming or killing those exposed to it. These are widely dreaded for their unpredictable side effects, but this hasn't stopped biological weapons from being used in battle—such as by the Japanese against China in the late 1930s.[25]

Two soldiers wear protection during a chemical weapons test. Can you defend the right of a country to develop and stockpile chemical weapons even though their use is prohibited by international treaty? (© Ivan Tykhyi/iStockphoto)

Canadian Insights

The Ottawa Treaty Banning Land Mines

Last chapter, we discussed Canada's pivotal role in the development and promulgation of "R2P," the Responsibility to Protect doctrine. Previously, we mentioned Canada's support for the idealistic concept of human security, in contrast to realism's support for national security. In keeping with this cluster of concepts and values, Canada during the 1990s provided governmental support to a civil society, NGO-based movement to ban land mines.

The movement to ban land mines, otherwise known as **anti-personnel mines**, arose in the 1980s and 1990s. Laid either on or just below the surface of the ground, these armaments are cheap, destructive, and very effective: one wrong step will cause them to blow up, producing loss of life or very serious injury. However, they often remain active and in the ground even long after a war has been settled, posing considerable risk to unsuspecting civilians. Children are especially vulnerable, as they frequently play in mine fields without realizing that these are the sites of former battlefields; the result may be lifelong, catastrophic injury or death. Land mines are also despised by soldiers, who view them as cowardly, unbecoming weapons, given that they can easily be used by anyone and require no fighting skill to be deployed. For these reasons, a number of international NGOs, collectively called the International Campaign to Ban Landmines (ICBL), joined together to persuade national governments to prohibit the use of these weapons. The campaign was organized by American educator and aid worker Jody Williams (who received the 1997 Nobel Peace Prize jointly with the ICBL for her efforts) and received diplomatic and political support from Canadian Foreign Affairs minister Lloyd Axworthy. The movement garnered extensive media coverage when Diana, the late Princess of Wales, campaigned on behalf of the cause.

The result of the ICBL's efforts was the Convention on the Prohibition of the Use, Stockpiling, Production and Transfer of Anti-Personnel Mines and on their Destruction, otherwise known as the Ottawa Treaty. It was signed in 1997 and entered into force in 1999. Over 160 states have ratified the treaty, but over 35 have not. Among the hold-outs are such great powers as the US, China, and Russia, alongside such other nations as India, Israel, Pakistan, and the two Koreas. (The hold-outs view land mines as essential ingredients in the defence of their territory and/or that of their close allies.) The treaty commits signatories to destroying and ceasing to use land mines, save for such legitimate training purposes as mine detection. Over 86 countries have thus far completed this process, resulting in the worldwide destruction of over 44 million mines.[26]

No "Means Mala in Se"

There is a traditional ban on **means *mala in se***, or "methods evil in themselves." The impre-
cise yet interesting idea here is that some weapons and means of war are forbidden not so
much because of the badness of the *consequences* they inflict but because they themselves
are intrinsically awful. Using rape as a tool of warfare—for instance, to drive a population
off a territory, or to reward one's troops after battle—is a clear example. Rape is ruled out
not so much because of all the pain it produces, or because it is aimed at civilians, but
because the act itself is rights-violating, a disgusting disregard for the humanity of the
woman raped: a coercive violation of her bodily integrity and her entitlement to choose
her own sex partner(s). Rape has been used as a tool of war both in the Bosnian Civil War
(1991–5) and in the ongoing fighting in the Democratic Republic of the Congo. Campaigns
of genocide, ethnic cleansing, and torture also fall under this category of means *mala in se*.[27]

No Reprisals

Finally, **reprisals**—acts of retaliation on an aggressor, typically by the same means used in
the original attack—are not permitted in the laws of armed conflict. At the same time, they
have been used historically, and they are rather frequently threatened during wartime. Let's
examine the controversy.

The **reprisal doctrine** permits a violation of *jus in bello* rules but *only* in response to a
prior violation by the opposing side. Walzer offers an example of what he labels a justified
reprisal, and it focuses on proportionality and prohibited weapons. He claims that Winston
Churchill was "entirely justified when he warned the German government early in World
War II that the use of [poison] gas by its army would bring an immediate Allied reprisal."
In other words, in Walzer's view, the Allies would have been warranted in using poison gas
had the Germans used it first.[28]

Such threats by heads of state have become rather commonplace. In 1991, American
president George Bush, Sr, warned Iraq that, should it deploy chemical weapons on the
battlefield, the United States would reserve the right to deploy its own WMDs, up to and
including nuclear armaments. International law, for its part, disallows any reprisals, on
grounds that—more often than not—they will lead to a serious escalation in violence. One
is supposed to win well, so to speak: the pursuit of victory, but within the rules.[29]

JUS POST BELLUM: AFTERMATH

So far we have seen that in an armed conflict, belligerents need to:

- distinguish between legitimate and illegitimate targets;
- respect non-combatant immunity and minimize civilian casualties;
- offer benevolent quarantine to POWs;
- refrain from using banned weapons, reprisals, or means *mala in se*; and
- use only proportionate, effective tactics to secure their overall strategy.

But what happens if you have done all of this, and done it well, and now it is clear that you
are about to win the war in question? What do you do then?

There is, perhaps surprisingly, very little international law regulating matters in this regard. The preference, historically, has been for the winner to "enjoy the spoils of war"—in other words, for the winner to impose whichever terms of peace it prefers upon the loser.[30] Generally, one of two approaches tends to be followed in this regard: retribution or rehabilitation.

The Clash of Post-War Policies: Retribution versus Rehabilitation

Retribution

According to the **retribution** model, the basic aspects of a decent post-war peace are these (and, crucially, they assume that "the good side" won, and that the aggressive side lost).[31]

Public Peace Treaty

While it does not need to be finely detailed, a peace agreement, or its basic elements, should be written down and publicly proclaimed so that everyone's expectations are clear, everyone knows the war is over, and everyone has an idea of what the general framework of the new post-war era will be. (Sometimes, by contrast—such as in medieval Europe—the most crucial parts of a peace treaty were kept secret from the public.)

Exchange of POWs

At war's end, all sides—winner and loser—must exchange all prisoners of war taken during the armed conflict.

Apology from the Aggressor

The aggressor in war, like the criminal in domestic society, needs to admit fault and guilt for causing the war by committing aggression. (And aggression, we've seen last chapter, is the first use of armed force across an international border, thus violating the rights of political sovereignty and territorial integrity that all recognized countries enjoy.) This may seem quaint and elemental, yet in practice, it can be quite controversial. For example, Germany has offered many, and profuse, official apologies for its part in World War II and, especially, the Holocaust. (To this day, Germany still pays an annual reparations fee to Israel for the latter—an arrangement that will be discussed next chapter.) By contrast, Japan has been nowhere near as forthcoming with a meaningful, official apology for its role in the Second World War (perhaps feeling that the bombings of Hiroshima and Nagasaki constitute retribution so severe that no further justice can be served with an apology). This reticence enrages particularly the Chinese, who suffered mightily from Japanese aggression and expansion in the 1930s.[32]

War Crimes Trials for those Responsible

The world's first post-war international war crimes trials were held in 1945–6, after World War II, in both Nuremberg and Tokyo. The vast majority of those tried were soldiers and officers charged with *jus in bello* violations, like torturing POWs and targeting civilians. But a handful of senior Nazis were also charged with the *jus ad bellum* violation of "committing crimes against peace," that is, of launching an aggressive war. In 1998, the international community passed the **Treaty of Rome**, creating the world's first *permanent* international war crimes tribunal. Sitting mainly in The Hague, in the Netherlands, the tribunal's ambitious mandate is to prosecute *all* war crimes, committed by *all* sides in *all* wars, and to do so using lawyers and judges from countries that were *not* part of the war in question (a procedure that was not followed in Nuremberg and Tokyo). Recently, this new court has heard many cases from the Bosnian Civil War and from various African wars. It has even put on trial former heads of state, and not just ordinary soldiers: Slobodan Milošević of Serbia (until his death in 2006); and Jean Kambanda, who was prime minister of Rwanda during the 1994 genocide.[33]

Aggressor to Give Up Any Gains

There is a strong belief that the aggressor in war, as the wrongdoer, cannot be rewarded for its aggression by being allowed to keep any gains it may have won for itself during its aggression. For instance, during its initial campaign in 1992–4, the Serbian side in the Bosnian Civil War conquered 70 per cent of Bosnia, a figure far exceeding the area traditionally occupied by ethnic Serbs. During negotiations on the Dayton Agreement (1995), designed to bring peace to the region following the conflict, Bosnian Serbs were pressured to surrender some of the territory they had gained during the fighting. More dramatically, during the Blitzkrieg of 1939–40, Hitler's Germany conquered Austria, Czechoslovakia, France, Poland, and the Scandinavian countries. These were considered unjust gains that, as the aggressor, Germany was forced to cede after losing the war.[34]

Aggressor Must Be Demilitarized

Since the aggressor broke international trust by committing aggression, it *cannot* be trusted *not* to commit aggression again—certainly not in the short term, and not without a change in government. And the international community is entitled to the security of knowing that there will not be a repeat of the aggression. Therefore, the tools the aggressor has to commit aggression must thus be taken away from it, in a process known as **demilitarization**. Essentially, the defeated aggressor loses many of its military assets and weapons capabilities, and has caps or limits placed on its ability to rebuild its armed forces over time.

Aggressor Must Suffer Further Losses

What makes this model one of retribution is the conviction that it is *not enough* for the defeated aggressor merely to give up what it wrongly took (i.e. territory), plus some weapons. The view here is that the aggressor must be made worse off than it was prior to the war. Why? The defenders of this model suggest several reasons. First is the belief that justice itself demands retribution of this nature: the aggressor must be made to feel the wrongness, and sting, of the war that it unjustly began. Second, consider an analogy to an individual criminal. In domestic society, when a thief has stolen a diamond ring, we don't just make him return the ring and surrender his thieving tools; we also make him pay a fine or serve a prison sentence to impress upon him the wrongness of his conduct. And this ties into the third reason: by punishing the aggressor, we hope to deter or prevent future aggression, both by him (so to speak) and by any others who might be entertaining similar ideas.

But what will make the aggressor worse off? Demilitarization, sure. But two further penalties are often applied: *reparations payments* to the victims of the aggressor, and *sanctions* slapped onto the aggressor as a whole. These are the post-war equivalent of fines levied on the whole society of the aggressor nation. **Reparations payments** are due, in the first instance, to the countries victimized by the aggressor's aggression and then, secondly, to the broader international community. The reparations payments are *backward-looking* in that sense, whereas the **sanctions** (as discussed in Chapter 4, on foreign policy) are more *forward-looking* in the sense that they are designed to hurt and curb the aggressor's future opportunities for economic growth, at least for a period of time (like a period of probation) and especially in connection with any goods and services that might enable the aggressor to commit aggression again.[35]

Case Study: Two Examples of the Retribution Model

Two of the most obvious, and infamous, historical examples of the retribution model in action came with the settlements of World War I and the Persian Gulf War.

World War I and the Treaty of Versailles

The **Treaty of Versailles** (1919) ended the First World War, and is widely considered a controversial failure that actually contributed to the conditions that gave rise to World War II. The First World War was a disaster for all of the belligerents, with the possible exception of the United States. It cost far more, and lasted much longer, than anyone had predicted; indeed, it came to an end, with victory for the Allied side, only when the US intervened in 1917. Because of all the cost and misery, the European powers were determined to punish Germany for invading Belgium and sparking the war to begin with. So Germany was extensively demilitarized, had all its war gains taken away, and, furthermore, lost some valuable territory of its own as part of its punishment. The international community also levied crushing reparations payments on Germany, a penalty that would have lasted into the 1980s (!) had the peace terms stuck.

But they didn't, because these fines essentially bankrupted Germany within just a few years, causing massive economic dislocation, hardship, and eventually, civil unrest. The victorious powers tried to force elections on Germany, but the only result was that German citizens came to associate democracy with their economic problems, and they began to turn to radical, non-democratic parties promising simple solutions in a time of complex crisis. It was in this environment that Hitler was able to come to power: he stopped all reparations payments; he cancelled all elections and named himself dictator; and he rebuilt the German war machine—growing the economy in the short term—and promised to get back all of lands lost as part of the Versailles settlement. His efforts to do so sparked the Second World War.[36]

The Persian Gulf War

The 1991 treaty ending the Persian Gulf War was similarly punitive and likewise paved the way to a second war. The treaty called upon Saddam Hussein's Iraq to give up any claims on Kuwait, to officially apologize for the aggression, and to surrender all POWs. Saddam was left in power, though, and no attempt was made either to change his regime or to bring anyone to trial on war crimes charges. But Iraq *was* to be extensively demilitarized: it lost many weapons, and had strict caps put on any re-building.

It also had **no-fly zones** (NFZs) imposed on it, both in the north (to protect the minority Kurdish population, which had been the target of a genocidal campaign carried out by the Iraqi government between 1986 and 1989) and in the south (to protect the Shi'ites, who made up the majority of Iraqi Muslims but who were often oppressed by the Sunni-led government).

Saddam also had to agree to a rigorous, UN-sponsored process for conducting periodic weapons inspections. The inspections occurred between 1991 and 1998, and uncovered literally tons of illegal weapons, including chemical and biological agents, which were subsequently destroyed. But when Saddam kicked out the inspectors, in 1998, he touched off a major international crisis that contributed directly to war in 2003. Saddam's move effectively confirmed, for many American officials, the view that Iraq still had WMDs and, moreover, was plotting to give some to al-Qaeda to enable another 9/11-style terrorist strike on the US.

Finally, Iraq had to pay financial reparations to Kuwait for the aggressive invasion in 1990 and, moreover, had to suffer continuing sweeping sanctions on its economy, especially on its ability to sell oil. These sanctions devastated Iraqi civilians while doing very little to hurt Saddam. In fact, there is evidence that the sanctions only *cemented* Saddam's grip on Iraq, as increasingly impoverished citizens grew more and more dependent on favours from Saddam's government in order to survive.[37]

The Rehabilitation Model

There is no sharp split between the retribution and rehabilitation models. They share commitment to the following aspects of a proper post-war settlement:

- the need for a public peace treaty
- official apologies
- exchange of POWs
- trials for war criminals
- some demilitarization
- the surrender, by the aggressor, of any unjust gains.

However, the models differ over three major issues. First, the rehabilitation model *rejects sanctions*, especially on grounds that they have been shown, historically, to harm civilians. Second, the rehabilitation model *rejects compensation payments*, for the same reason. In fact, the model favours *investing in* a defeated aggressor, to help it rebuild and to help smooth over the wounds of war. Finally, the rehabilitation model *favours forcing regime change*, whereas the retribution model views that as too risky and costly. Indeed, enforcing this condition might be costly, but those who favour the rehabilitative model believe it can be worth it over the long term, by enabling the creation of a new, non-aggressive, and even progressive member of the international community. To those who scoff that such deep-rooted transformation simply can't be achieved, supporters of the rehabilitative model reply that, not only *can* it be done, it *has* been done. The two leading examples are West Germany and Japan after WWII.[38]

Case Study: Reconstructing Germany and Japan

The settlement of the Second World War was not contained in a detailed, legalistic peace treaty like the Treaty of Versailles that ended World War I. This was, partly, because Germany and Japan—the conquered aggressors—were so thoroughly crushed that they had very little leverage. But World War II's settlement was sweeping and profound, with immense effects on world history. It was worked out, essentially, between the United States and the Soviet Union at meetings in Tehran and Yalta, but with participation from Britain, France, China, and other of the "lesser" Allies. Both Britain and France kept control over their colonies, but everyone knew that powerful forces of anti-colonialism—abetted by the exhaustion of England and France—would soon cause those old empires to crumble. As for the new empires, it was understood that the USSR would hold sway in eastern Europe, ostensibly to serve as a barrier between itself and Germany, preventing another Nazi-style invasion. (It also, though, provided for the export and spread of communism in the other direction.) The US, by contrast, would get Hawaii, a number of Pacific Islands, and total sway over the reconstruction of Japan. As for Germany, it was agreed that it would be split into eastern and western halves, with the eastern territory administered by the Soviets and the western side governed jointly by the US, Britain, and France. Ditto for the German capital of Berlin (which was otherwise within the eastern, i.e. Soviet, territory; see Figure 8.3).

Within the Soviet sphere, police-state communism came to dominate as readily as it did in Russia. But within the West, there was a concerted effort to establish a genuine free-market, rights-respecting democracy. In Japan, the same experiment was undertaken, but there the US military, under the firm leadership of Douglas MacArthur, held more direct control, for longer, than it did in West Germany.[39]

The Allies, working with nationals in both countries—more so in West Germany than in Japan, perhaps—first undertook a purging process, which in West Germany came to be known **as de-nazi-fication**. All signs, symbols, buildings, literature, and other items directly associated with the Nazis were destroyed utterly. The Nazi party itself was abolished and declared illegal. Surviving ex-Nazis—but not all of them— were put on trial, put in jail, or otherwise punished and prohibited from political participation. The militaries of both West Germany and Japan were completely disbanded, and for years the Allied military became *the* military, and the direct ruler, of both West Germany and Japan.

After completing the negative purging process, the Allies in both countries established written constitutions, known by the term "Basic Law." These constitutions, after the period of direct military rule ended, provided for bills and charters of human rights, eventual democratic elections, and above all, the "checks and balances" featured so prominently in the American system. Since government had grown so huge and tyrannical in both Germany and Japan during the 1930s, the Allies decided that it had to be shrunk down and then broken into pieces, with each piece authorized to handle only its own business. Independent judiciaries and completely reconstituted police forces were an important part of this, and they went a long way to re-establishing the *impersonal* rule of law over the *personal* whims of former fascists. The executive

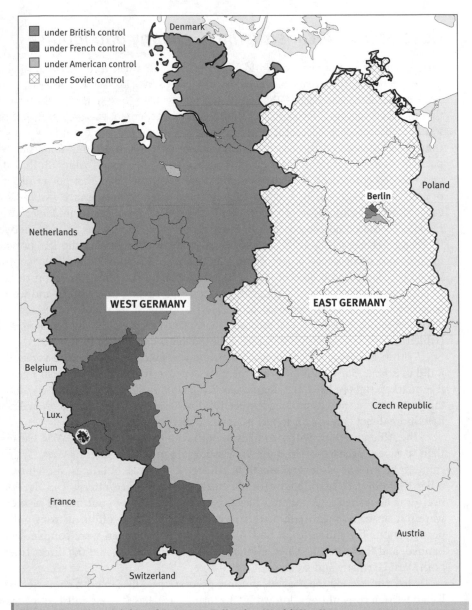

FIGURE 8.3 The Division of Germany Following World War II

branches, much more so than in the American system, were made more accountable and closely tied to the legislative branch. The goal, of course, was to ensure that the executive couldn't grow into another dictator. By design, there were to be no strong presidents. So West Germany and Japan became true *parliamentary* democracies, more in the European than in the American style.

Western-style liberal democracy was not the only change forcibly implemented. The education systems of both West Germany and Japan were overhauled, since they had played a huge role in spreading propaganda for both regimes, with curriculums filled with racism, ultra-nationalism, and distorted, ignorant views of the outside world. Western experts redesigned these systems to impart the concrete skills needed to participate in reconstruction, as well as to stress a more objective content favouring the basic cognitive functions (the "three Rs": reading, writing, and arithmetic) as well as critical thinking and, especially, science and technology. The course curriculums were stripped of political content, though of course some lessons on the new social institutions and their principles had to be included.

The Americans quickly saw that their sweeping legal, constitutional, social, and educational reforms would lack stability unless they could stimulate the West German and Japanese economies. The people had vital needs to be met in the present, and hopes to be raised for the future. For without some sense that, concretely, the future would get better, the people might revolt, and the reforms fail. Instead of making the World War I mistake of *sucking money out* of these ruined countries through mandatory reparations payments, the Americans *poured money into* West Germany and Japan. The United States shunned

An American truck patrols a ruined Germany after World War II. US reconstruction efforts in Germany and Japan are generally considered a success. What kind of forcible changes might not have succeeded? What changes could have adversely affected either country's "national character"? (© Kevin Russ/iStockphoto)

the retribution paradigm and embraced the rehabilitative one. It was a staggering sum of money, too, provided via a US-sponsored program known as the **Marshall Plan**. West Germany and Japan needed money to buy essentials and to clear away all the rubble and ruined infrastructure. They also needed it just to circulate, to get their citizens used to free-market trading. Jobs were plentiful, as entire systems of infrastructure—transportation, water, sewage, electricity, agriculture, finance—had to be rebuilt. Since jobs paid wages, thanks to the Marshall Plan, the people's lives improved and the free-market system took hold. But it wasn't just money that made a difference to the recovery. American management experts poured into West Germany and Japan, showing them the very latest, and most efficient, means of production. Within 30 years, not only had Germany and Japan rebounded economically, but they had the two strongest economies in the world after the US itself, based especially on the quality of their high-tech manufacturing (of automobiles, for instance).

The post-war reconstructions of West Germany and Japan easily count as the most impressive post-war rehabilitations in modern history, rivalled perhaps only by

America's rebuilding of its own South after the US Civil War (1861–5). Germany and Japan, today, have massive free-market economies, and politically, they remain peaceful, stable, and decent democracies—good citizens on the global stage. In addition, these countries are by no means "clones" (much less colonies) of the US: each has gone its own way, shaping its economy around the resources—physical and human—available within its borders and pursuing political paths quite distinct from those that most interest the United States. Consider especially West Germany's journey, which went on to involve reunification with the former East Germany in 1990, and then the absolutely central role that the new Germany has carved out for itself—politically, economically—within the European Union.

FIGURE 8.4 Japan

Fans of the rehabilitation model of post-war reconstruction point to Japan as an example of what can be achieved in the best-case scenario.

So we have clear evidence that even massive and forcible post-war changes need *not* threaten a nation's character, or what makes it unique and special to its people. But such success *did* come at a huge cost in terms of time and treasure: it cost trillions of dollars, it took trillions of human hours in work and expertise, it took decades of real time, and it took the co-operation of most of the German and Japanese people. Above all, it took the will of the United States to see it through. It was American money, American security, American know-how, American patience, and American generosity that brought it all into being.

The 10 Principles of Rehabilitation

Based on these best-case practices, supporters of rehabilitation have devised their own list of desirable elements during the post-war period. Explained above in connection with Germany and Japan, the principles are listed in Table 8.2. Figure 8.5 summarizes the differences and overlap between the retribution and rehabilitation models of post-war settlement.

TABLE 8.2 The 10 Principles of Rehabilitation

The occupying war winner, during post-war reconstruction, ought to:

1. Adhere strictly to the laws of war during the regime take-down and occupation.

2. Purge most figures, symbols, and other items associated with the old regime, and prosecute its war criminals.

3. Disarm and demilitarize the society.

But then

4. Provide effective military and police security for the whole country.

5. Work with a cross-section of local citizens on a new, rights-respecting constitution that features checks and balances.

6. Allow other, non-state associations (i.e. "civil society") to flourish.

7. Forgo demanding compensation, and imposing sanctions, in favour of investing in and re-building the economy.

8. If necessary, revamp educational curriculums to purge earlier propaganda and cement new values.

9. Ensure that the benefits of the new order will be (a) concrete, and (b) widely, not narrowly, distributed.

10. Follow an orderly, not-too-hasty "exit strategy" when the new regime can stand on its own two feet.

Sources: J. Dobbins, et al., *America's Role in Nation-Building: From Germany to Iraq* (Washington, DC: RAND, 2003); J. Dobbins & S. Jones, eds, *The United Nations' Role in Nation-Building* (Washington, DC: RAND, 2007); B. Orend, *The Morality of War* (Peterborough, ON: Broadview Press, 2006).

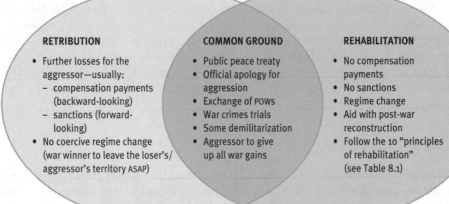

RETRIBUTION

- Further losses for the aggressor—usually:
  - compensation payments (backward-looking)
  - sanctions (forward-looking)
- No coercive regime change (war winner to leave the loser's/ aggressor's territory ASAP)

COMMON GROUND

- Public peace treaty
- Official apology for aggression
- Exchange of POWs
- War crimes trials
- Some demilitarization
- Aggressor to give up all war gains

REHABILITATION

- No compensation payments
- No sanctions
- Regime change
- Aid with post-war reconstruction
- Follow the 10 "principles of rehabilitation" (see Table 8.1)

FIGURE 8.5 Consensus and Contrast Regarding War Termination Policies

Case Study: Reconstruction Models Applied to Afghanistan and Iraq

Let's return to our contemporary cases from last chapter. Afghanistan has been in a period of post-war reconstruction since early 2002; Iraq, since mid-2003. (These dates refer to when the regime fell in each society, as a result of American invasion and leading then to US military **occupation**.[40]) It seems true that in each of the two cases, the international community, as led by the US, has been trying to implement the 10-step "rehabilitation recipe" set out above in Table 8.2. Indeed, it has been a very difficult process, in both countries, and has seen a mixture of both successes and failures.

Successes

The major post-war successes, in both nations, have been the replacement of aggressive, rogue regimes with new governments. The old regimes have been purged, and the new governments enjoy democratic legitimacy—through multiple elections, in both countries (most recently in 2010)—and are based on written constitutions crafted by locals. Civil society, compared with what it was under Saddam Hussein or the Taliban, has now blossomed. The gains in terms of personal freedom, in both societies, have been huge, and Afghanistan has seen sizable gains in terms of gender equality, with the international community (including Canada) building and staffing many new schools for girls and women.[41]

The problem, though, is that the evidence suggests that it's *not* things like individual liberty and gender equality that matter most when it comes to the success and durability of post-war reconstruction. The historical data suggest, rather, that the most important things are physical security (i.e. personal safety) and economic growth. Jim

A mountainside village in Afghanistan. It's said that villages such as this one must have their "hearts and minds" won over for post-war reconstruction to succeed. If you were a US officer tasked with this objective, how would you try to achieve it?
(© Mie Ahmt/iStockphoto)

Dobbins, probably the leading scholar on the issue, has distilled all this data into one crystal-clear rule of thumb regarding post-war success: the war-winning occupier and the new local regime have about 10 years to form an effective partnership and to make the average person in that society feel better off—more secure and more prosperous, especially—than they were prior to the outbreak of the war. If they can do this, they will probably make a success of post-war reconstruction; if not, there will be failure, and a serious risk of back-sliding into armed conflict.[42]

Using this rule of thumb, we note that the approximate deadline for achieving this goal in Afghanistan would be 2012, and in Iraq, 2013. The US occupation of Iraq has been declared officially over as of December 2011, but a number of American troops remain indefinitely to help train the new Iraqi army, and to protect Iraqi oil infrastructure.[43] Meanwhile, NATO troops have committed to remain in Afghanistan until 2014. The question is, can physical security and economic improvement be achieved in the time remaining?

Challenges

Security

While the capital of Afghanistan, Kabul, *is* quite secure, the same *cannot* be said for the rest of the nation. In fact, there is a deep urban–rural split when it comes to security. Afghanistan is a highly

The evidence suggests that it's not things like individual liberty and gender equality that matter most when it comes to the success and durability of post-war reconstruction; rather, that the most important things are physical security and economic growth.

"weaponized" society, with nearly all men owning guns and with local tribal leaders protecting their families' farms and crops with their own armed militias. The Taliban is making a comeback in rural areas, by clamping down on these local tribal warlords and promising a return to the very strict (religious) law-and-order state they feel they achieved when in power. So, would the *average* Afghan feel more secure now than when the Taliban was in power? Maybe not, and this is one reason why US president Barack Obama has ordered a new surge of American troops deployed into Afghanistan over the next few years. The move is designed to bring security, turn the tide against a resurgent Taliban, deal more effectively with the border area, ensuring that radical Islamic extremists don't use it to rebuild their forces and strike America once more.[44]

In Iraq, meanwhile, the security situation was so bad in 2005–6 that experts spoke openly of there being a civil war involving the three main groups: the Kurdish people, Sunni Muslims, and Shi'a Muslims. At the time, US president George W. Bush ordered more troops into Iraq, and they have succeeded beyond anyone's expectations in cutting down group-on-group violence and in keeping the peace. (This success is what inspired President Obama to order the same for Afghanistan.) But is it enough? Dobbins would remind us that an increase in security over 2006 levels is not the same as having more security than when Saddam was in power in 2003. The former Iraqi ruler was a brutal tyrant, but he did keep law and order. Would the average Iraqi today feel safer and more secure than before the war? It's hard to say, and the answer might depend on which group one is speaking to: the Kurds and Shi'ites might well say yes, whereas the minority Sunni population—well represented in government during Saddam's regime—might say no. While there have been clear gains since 2006, all the groups are concerned about what might happen once the US pulls out entirely.[45]

Economy

Would the average Afghan or Iraqi today feel more prosperous than prior to the war? Thankfully, the Americans did not implement the retribution model in either case, and instead have sent investment flowing into both countries. Iraq is probably in the better position economically as it has large reserves of oil and gas, as well as a large and reasonably well-educated workforce (see Table 8.3). Yet huge challenges remain. The near-constant war since 1979, plus the effects of the sanctions imposed from 1991 to 2003, devastated Iraq's basic infrastructure and well-being. So much rebuilding needs to be done, and unemployment remains a terrible problem. A solution that could address both matters would be to pay the unemployed to perform all the rebuilding, but the costs would be enormous—in the dozens of billions, or more—and the US has been reluctant to foot the bill all on its own. Other countries, for their part, reply that it was America's war, and so America needs to pay the price.[46]

Afghanistan, in contrast, is one of the world's poorest countries, with two-thirds of the population living on just two dollars per day (US). The same proportion of the population is thought to be functionally illiterate, and unemployment is thought to afflict half the workforce. Afghanistan, like Iraq, faces issues of ruined infrastructure and the brutal consequences that constant warfare has inflicted on the economy. (These consequences can be condensed as follows: *would you open a business in a war zone?*) Afghanistan's economy is a toxic mixture of war and drugs. Poppies grow well there, and it is estimated

TABLE 8.3 Substantial Difficulties in Post-War Afghanistan and Iraq

Country	Domestic War Casualties since 2002	Average Life Expectancy	Average Per Capita Annual Income (in 2008 US dollars)	Estimated Unemployment (as percentage of workforce)	Illiteracy (as percentage of population)	Primary School Enrolment (as percentage of population)
Afghanistan	13,000–35,000	44	$250	50	72	60
Iraq	100,000–135,000	68	$2,200	30	26	86

Source: Data from UNICEF, www.unicef.org.

that one-third of Afghanistan's economy comes from growing this one plant. After all, farmers can earn much more growing these illegal crops—produced for the heroin and opium trade—than legal crops like wheat or corn. Transforming Afghanistan's economy from one based on war and drugs to a peaceful and legal economy rooted in broad-based, healthy economic growth is proving terribly hard. It remains unclear whether success will ever be achieved on this front, but at least in Afghanistan the Americans can count on international support, as all of NATO is involved. Britain, for instance, is thinking of buying Afghanistan's poppies and using them for medical-grade opiates (i.e. painkillers) in Western hospitals. Canada and Germany are heavily involved in building and running schools for Afghan children. Even Russia, in 2010, signed an agreement to help stop the narcotics trade, given that many of Afghanistan's drugs wind up on the streets of Moscow, the closest metropolitan city.[47]

Summary

It is clear that if post-war reconstruction "succeeds" in Iraq and Afghanistan, it won't be anywhere near the same degree of success achieved in Japan and Germany in the ten years following the end of the Second World War. This won't necessarily make these recent cases "failures," as Japan and Germany represent the gold standard of post-war reconstruction—it's hard to beat, or match, the very best. What these complex, mixed, imperfect, contemporary cases *do* mean—for the Middle East, and the rest of the world—is, as yet, deeply unclear.[48]

CONCLUSION

In this chapter, we concluded our look at armed conflict, which is quite pervasive in the international arena. We familiarized ourselves with key military terms, alongside the key concepts, resources, and general strategies that commanders and military strategists use in pursuit of victory. We gave special attention to weaponry, especially the latest high-tech forms. We then canvassed the laws of armed conflict to understand how countries are allowed to use armed force, looking at many relevant examples along the way. We also used a number of case studies to examine post-war reconstruction, comparing and contrasting the two main post-war policies of retribution and rehabilitation.

REVIEW QUESTIONS

1. Pick a country at random from your atlas and research its position, neighbours, and general recent history. In light of these factors, which set of military capabilities would you most want to have, as that country's president/prime minister, and why? Keep in mind not just ideals but costs, too.

2. Look at Table 8.1, on comparative military capabilities. Does anything surprise you about it? Do some countries have less, or more, than what you expected?

3. Look at Figure 8.2, the flow chart showing how commanders make use of resources in pursuit of military victory. Then, go online and research, in summary, a major war you've always interested in but have never really known a lot about. See how the leaders in that war followed the components of the Figure 8.2 flow chart in their quest for leverage.

4. The war on terror has rightly been described as asymmetrical warfare. Historically, even the most powerful and resourceful societies have had difficulty dealing effectively with this kind of war. This may explain why, for example, the US could defeat both Nazi Germany and Soviet Russia—ferocious, well-armed states—but then experience such problems and frustrations confronting non-state terrorist organizations. Explain this difference, and then research recent successes with US General David Petraeus's acclaimed "counter-insurgency strategy."

5. Is it fair that nuclear countries try to prevent other countries from acquiring nuclear weapons? Why or why not? Cast yourself into the mindset of national leaders on both sides of the debate.

6. Do you agree, or disagree, that torturing terrorists—in the hopes of getting information useful in preventing future terrorist attacks—is justified? Why?

7. After reading the *jus in bello* rules, do you find they still make sense? Are they full of good, detailed guidance? Or are you now inclined to agree with the realists that these rules are too much trouble, and belligerents should just fight as best they see fit?

8. For you, which is the superior model of post-war reconstruction, and why: retribution, or rehabilitation? Or perhaps we should just stick with the very thin common ground, or "overlapping consensus" between them? Consult Figure 8.2 for your answer.

9. We all hope that post-war reconstruction can work in Afghanistan and Iraq. But do you think it will, say, looking back from 2020? If you had to bet your

own money, would it be on success or failure? What lessons should be taken from these experiences into future post-war situations?

10. Refer to all the photos in the two war chapters. Also, if interested, research "war photojournalism" online and examine some of the images that turn up in your results. What is your reaction to these images, knowing that they depict real events, which actually happened to real people? What thoughts about war in general do such images provoke?

WEBSITES FOR FURTHER RESEARCH

Global Firepower www.globalfirepower.com
– for assets and rankings of military powers

International Criminal Court (ICC) www.icc-cpi.int/Menus/ICC
– for information on ongoing war crimes trials

Stanford Encyclopedia of Philosophy http://plato.stanford.edu/entries/war
– for the ethics of war and peace

YouTube www.youtube.com/watch?v=YfSAfltVXUk (part 1)
www.youtube.com/watch?v=UJoEsWpkotw (part 2)
– speech on post-war reconstruction, given in an address at the Stockdale Center, US Naval Academy

US Strategic Command www.stratcom.mil
– information on high-tech warfare

NOTES

1. B.H. Liddell Hart, *Strategy* (London: Faber & Faber, 3rd edn, 1954), p. 8.
2. J. Keegan, *A History of Warfare* (New York: Vintage, 1994).
3. R.G. Grant, *Battle* (London: DK, 2005); US Central Intelligence Agency, www.cia.gov; Canadian Security Intelligence Service, www.csis-scrs.gc.ca
4. R. O'Connell, *Of Arms and Men: A History of War, Weapons and Aggression* (Oxford: Oxford University Press, 1990).
5. Human Rights Watch, *Report on US Blinding Laser Weapons* (New York: Human Rights Watch, 1995).
6. K. Dockery, *Future Weapons* (New York: Berkley, 2007).
7. P. Singer, *Wired for War* (New York: Penguin, 2009); M. Martin & C. Sasser, *Predator: The Remote-Control Air-War over Iraq and Afghanistan* (New York: Zenith, 2010).
8. Hart, *Strategy* (op. cit., note 1).
9. R. Thornton, *Asymmetric Warfare* (London: Polity, 2007).
10. W. Reisman & C. Antoniou, eds, *The Laws of War: A Comprehensive Collection of Primary Documents on International Laws Governing Armed Conflict* (New York: Vintage, 1994); A. Roberts & R. Guelff, eds, *Documents on the Laws of War* (New York: Oxford University Press,

3rd edn, 2000); H. Lauterpacht, *International Law, Vols 3 & 4: The Law of War and Peace* (Cambridge: Cambridge University Press, 1978).

11. M. Walzer, *Just and Unjust Wars* (New York: Basic Books, 4th edn, 2006).

12. J. Olsen & R. Roberts, eds, *My Lai: A Brief History with Documents* (London: Palgrave Macmillan, 1998).

13. Keegan, *A History of Warfare* (op. cit., note 2), pp. 16–18.

14. Walzer, *Just and Unjust Wars* (op. cit., note 11), pp. 40–156.

15. W. Clark, *Waging Modern War* (New York: Public Affairs, 2002); M. Ignatieff, *Virtual War: Kosovo and Beyond* (London: Picador, 2001); B. Orend, "Crisis in Kosovo: A Just Use of Force?" *Politics* 19 (1999), pp. 125–30.

16. M. Green, *The Wizard of The Nile* (London: Portobello, 2008). The video is "The Invisible Children," available through many online portals, such as YouTube (search: "Kony video").

17. P. Singer, *Children at War* (Berkeley, CA: University of California Press, 2006); R. Dallaire, *They Fight Like Soldiers, They Die Like Children* (Toronto: Vintage Canada, 2011).

18. B. Orend, *The Morality of War* (Peterborough, ON: Broadview Press, 2006), pp. 105–59.

19. E. Saar, *Inside the Wire* (New York: Penguin, 2005).

20. M. Ratner & E. Ray, *Guantanamo: What the World Should Know* (New York: Chelsea Green Books, 2004); S. Hersh, *Chain of Command: The Road from 9/11 to Abu-Ghraib* (New York: Harper Collins, 2004).

21. M. Danner, *Torture and Truth: America, Abu-Ghraib and The War on Terror* (New York: New York Review of Books, 2004). The claim that torture is justified because it gets access to vital information is at odds with the truth. Under torture, people are willing to say anything—even making up lies they think will please the torturer—to get the pain to stop. For this reason, torture is not a reliable information-gathering technique. See B. Innes, *The History of Torture* (New York: St Martin's, 1998).

22. Walzer, *Just and Unjust Wars* (op. cit., note 11), p. 129.

23. Reisman & Antoniou, *The Laws of War* (op. cit., note 10).

24. J. Cirincione, et al., *Deadly Arsenals* (New York: Carnegie Endowment for International Peace, 2nd edn, 2005); N. Busch, *Combating WMDs: The Future of Nonproliferation* (Atlanta: University of Georgia Press, 2009).

25. F. Schreier, *WMD Proliferation: Reforming the Security Sector to Meet the Threat* (Washington, DC: Potomac Press, 2009).

26. J. Williams, et al., *Banning Land Mines* (New York: Rowman & Littlefield, 2008).

27. A. Stigylmayer, et al., *Mass Rape* (Omaha, NE: University of Nebraska Press, 1994); B. Allen, *Rape Warfare* (Minneapolis, MN: University of Minnesota Press, 1996).

28. Walzer, *Just and Unjust Wars* (op. cit., note 11), p. 207.

29. R. Regan, *Just War: Principles and Cases* (Washington, DC: Catholic University Press of America, 1996), 172–8.

30. Reisman & Antoniou, *The Laws of War* (op. cit., note 10); B. Orend, *War and International Justice: A Kantian Perspective* (Waterloo, ON: Wilfrid Laurier University Press, 2000), 217–67.

31. Of course, this doesn't always happen as a matter of fact. These are abstract models as to what states *ideally try to achieve* in the post-war period.

32. J. Keegan, *The Second World War* (New York: Vintage, 1990).

33. J. Persico, *Nuremburg: Infamy on Trial* (New York: Penguin, 1995); T. Maya, *Judgment at Tokyo* (Lexington, KY: University of Kentucky Press, 2001); W. Schabas, *An Introduction to the International Criminal Court* (Cambridge, UK: Cambridge University Press, 2001).

34. D. Reiff, *Slaughterhouse: Bosnia and The Failure of the West* (New York: Simon & Schuster, 1995); Keegan, *The Second World War* (op. cit., note 32).

35. B. Orend, "Justice After War," *Ethics and International Affairs* (2002), pp. 43–56.

36. M. Boemeke, ed., *The Treaty of Versailles* (Cambridge, UK: Cambridge University Press, 1998); M. MacMillan, *Paris 1919: Six Months that Changed the World* (New York: Random House, 2003).

37. W. Danspeckgruber & C. Tripp, eds, *The Iraqi Aggression Against Kuwait* (Boulder, CO: Westview, 1996); G. Simons, *The Scourging of Iraq* (New York: Macmillan, 2nd edn, 1996).

38. Orend, *The Morality of War* (op. cit., note 18), pp. 190–220.

39. Material for this section on post-war reconstruction in Germany and Japan draws upon the following sources: L.V. Segal, *Fighting to the Finish: The Politics of War Termination in America and Japan* (Ithaca, NY: Cornell University Press, 1989); H. Schonberger, *Aftermath of War: Americans and the Remaking of Japan* (Kent, OH: Kent State University Press, 1989); J. Dobbins, et al., *America's Role in Nation-Building: From Germany to Iraq* (Washington, DC: RAND, 2003); and E. Davidson, *The Death and Life of Germany: An Account of the American Occupation* (St Louis, MO: University of Missouri Press, 1999).

40. E. Carlton, *Occupation: The Policies and Practices of Military Conquerors* (London: Routledge, 1995).

41. M. Tondini, *Statebuilding and Justice Reform: Post-Conflict Reconstruction in Afghanistan* (New York: Routledge, 2010); US Government Accountability Office (GOA), *Afghanistan Reconstruction: Despite Some Progress, Deteriorating Security and Other Obstacles Threaten Achievement of US Goals* (Washington, DC: Books LLC, 2011); M. Lamani & B. Momani, *From Desolation to Reconstruction: Iraq's Troubled Journey* (Waterloo, ON: CIGI, 2010).

42. Dobbins, *America's Role in Nation-Building* (op. cit., note 38); Dobbins & Jones, *The United Nations' Role in Nation-Building* (op. cit., note 39).

43. This was widely reported in December 2011 by Associated Press, together with the following figures: Iraq War lasted 9 years (2003–11), costing over US$800 billion and with 4,500 US military dead and 32,000 US military wounded.

44. GOA, *Afghanistan Reconstruction* (op. cit., note 41); D. Zakheim, *A Vulcan's Tale: How the Bush Administration Mismanaged the Reconstruction of Afghanistan* (Washington, DC: Brookings Institute, 2011).

45. US Special Inspector General, *Hard Lessons: The Iraq Reconstruction Experience* (Washington, DC: US Independent Agencies and Commissions, 2009).

46. Lamani & Momani, *From Desolation to Reconstruction* (op. cit., note 41).

47. Zakheim, *A Vulcan's Tale* (op. cit., note 45).

48. J. Bridoux, *American Foreign Policy and Post-War Reconstruction: Comparing Japan and Iraq* (New York: Routledge, 2012).

IV

Newer Issues of Soft Power: Improving Well-Being

9 Human Rights

"Everyone is entitled to a social and international order in which the rights and freedoms set forth in this Declaration can be fully realized." —Article 28, of the UN's Universal Declaration of Human Rights (1948)[1]

LEARNING OBJECTIVES

After studying this chapter, you will be able to:

▸ define all the bolded key terms and concepts

▸ discuss the recent history of the human rights movement: how it began as a reaction to the Holocaust and has grown enormously from there

▸ articulate the basic values behind human rights, as well as the ultimate goal and function of human rights

▸ describe how human rights make claims on all of us as well as on the basic structure of social institutions

▸ understand the development of international human rights law, both globally and regionally

▸ appreciate the limits of such law, and explain how other tools are used to realize human rights, too: diplomacy; economic incentives; armed force; and NGO activity

▸ reflect on the significance of topical case studies on the Arab Spring, women's rights, the Internet, and Canada's human rights record.

INTRODUCTION

In Part Three, we discussed in detail the "hard power" issues of armed force and economic wealth. These state-centric concerns traditionally dominate international affairs. Recently, however, there has emerged growing interest in "soft power," accompanied by a move away from the focus on states (and their interests) towards concern for individual persons (and their well-being). This is the subject matter of this, the final, section. First up: human rights. It's a nice starting point, as it contrasts sharply with realist obsessions with military strength and the growth of national economies, highlighting instead idealistic hopes for a better world. What better place to start than with an improved treatment of persons?

RECENT HUMAN RIGHTS HISTORY

The Holocaust

The contemporary human rights movement begins with, and was powerfully motivated by, **the Holocaust**, one of human history's most appalling and atrocious acts of mass murder, which saw the complete violation and degradation of the human rights of its *approximately six million* victims. Although the Holocaust was a complex event that developed over the course of several years, with many contributing factors, it is rightly understood by most people as Nazi Germany's systematic persecution, and then mass slaughter, of about six million people—mainly Jewish people, but also mentally and physically challenged people, homosexuals, political radicals (especially communists), and persons of Slavic origin.[2]

It's hard to date the start of the Holocaust exactly, as discriminatory measures against Jewish people began in Germany at least as early as 1933, when the Nazis first gained some power. But it definitely ends in 1945, when Nazi Germany surrendered unconditionally at the end of World War II, and the Allies discover the concentration camps, the gas chambers, and then the ovens and mass graves. The Nazis, fanatically committed to a twisted ideology of "the supremacy of the Aryan race," had begun, systematically, by first identifying those who didn't fit their ethnic "ideal," then limiting the work options and voting rights of these people, and then confiscating their money and property. Once the war broke out in 1939, the Nazis used the cover of war with *external* powers to step up their campaign of *internal* rights violation. (This is a common tactic of **rights-violating regimes**, defined more thoroughly below.) People were rounded up, had everything taken from them, and then were shipped off to labour camps to work, under hellish conditions, on the Nazi war effort (weapons manufacturing, especially). Once they were completely exhausted and "used up" in terms of their productive potential for the Nazi war machine, they were killed in the gas chambers—asphyxiated by nerve gas, hundreds at a time; then their bodies were incinerated to ashes in the mass ovens, or else were dumped and buried, by the truck-full, in mass graves dug to hold thousands. This was Hitler's **"final solution"** to what the Nazis felt was a dreadful problem: simply put, that there were so many Jews—and Slavs and socialists, and gays and physically challenged people—running around free in Europe. For the Nazis, their world was all about domination and subjugation, violence and persecution, intolerance and hatred, and rabid, warmongering mania.[3]

When the war ended and people began to discover the horrifying extent of the Nazi treatment of so many Jews and others, there rose a cry that "never again" would such brutal and depraved treatment of human beings be tolerated. Indeed, one of the particularly shocking aspects of the Holocaust was how it blended, in a single process, white-hot, irrational emotions (e.g. hatred) with detached, rational planning (e.g. the sophisticated set-up for exploiting prisoners in the labour camps, and then transferring them to the death camps). The utter lack of regard for human life, and the mechanization of mass murder, had to be challenged and torn down,

Inmates of the Buchenwald concentration camp, near Weimar, Germany. Has humankind succeeded in ensuring that "never again" would an episode like the Holocaust be allowed to occur? (© World History Archive/Alamy)

and then principles and laws put into place to enshrine a totally different set of values. These would become core values of the modern human rights movement.

A Different Set of Values

Indeed, a simple yet effective way of understanding the beliefs and values of the human rights movement is to take everything the Nazis stood for, plus how they acted, and turn it on its head and negate it.

- The Nazis cared only about the German nation—or, at most, the "Aryan race"— whereas human rights defenders are concerned about everyone. It's about *the rights of humans everywhere*, not just those of a single ethnic group or nation. This is the principle of **universality**, as opposed to national **partiality**.

- The Nazis wanted full rights for only themselves, and they moved to deny rights to others; their intolerance of difference produced discrimination and violent brutality. The human rights ideal, by contrast, believes in equal rights for all, and urges instead a tolerance (even celebration) of difference. The goal is to end discrimination, and to swap for violent brutality *a non-violent respect for all persons*.

- The Nazis denied their victims freedom—locking them up in camps—and then inflicted horrible sufferings, and eventually killing, upon them. The human rights ideal endorses everyone's right to be free and to enjoy personal liberties, as well as to live and be secure in their own persons from the assaults and violent designs of both criminal individuals and wicked governments.

- The Nazis stole personal property, and then nearly starved to death those they worked to the bone in factories, whereas the human rights ideal respects the individual right to own one's private property and the greater responsibility to ensure for everyone at least a subsistence living wherein they have enough food and water, and can pursue a profession of their own choosing.

The human rights ideal believes in equal rights for all, and urges a tolerance (even celebration) of difference

- Finally, the Nazis radically distinguished between a favoured "in group" and all other, disfavoured "outsiders." They didn't recognize the outsiders as equals, as members of their country, or indeed, even as human beings. They certainly didn't let the outsiders vote or participate in their own governance. The human rights ideal believes in democracy and political participation, and insists that everyone has the right to social recognition—at the very least, as a rights-bearing member of humankind.[4]

These contrasts are summarized in Table 9.1 below.

The Universal Declaration of Human Rights (UDHR)

Proclaimed as a unanimous declaration by the United Nations' General Assembly in 1948—just three years after the discovery of the Holocaust—the Universal Declaration of Human Rights (UDHR) was crafted by representatives from Britain, Canada, Chile, China, France, Egypt, India, Iran, Lebanon, Panama, the Philippines, Russia, the United States, and Uruguay—quite an international, and cross-cultural, representation of countries. But

TABLE 9.1 Understanding Human Rights Values through Historical Comparison

Nazi Values	Human Rights Values
National/racial partiality	Universality
Inequality, discrimination	Equality, non-discrimination
Violent brutality	Physical security of the person/self Non-violent respect for others
Deprivation of freedom	Individual liberty
Theft, starvation	Private property rights Material subsistence for all
Denial of social recognition to "outsiders"	Social recognition of others "Everyone inside the tent"
No democracy (authoritarian regime)	Democracy (political participation for all)

it's fair to say that a special impetus for the UDHR came from Eleanor Roosevelt, a former first lady, the wife of US president Franklin Roosevelt, who during his presidency had guided America through both the Great Depression and the Second World War (but who had died in 1945, before war's end).[5]

The UDHR, quoted at the very start of the chapter, has *no legal weight*: it is a **political proclamation** (i.e. a grand, popular statement of intent and principle) of the General Assembly. In spite of that fact, most experts consider the UDHR the most influential and inspiring human rights document of our time.[6]

COMPLETING THE VALUES PICTURE: THE POINT OF HUMAN RIGHTS

The overall goal of the human rights movement is to secure for everyone a **minimally decent life**. The objects of human rights listed above in Table 9.1—security, liberty, and so on—are vital human needs, often referred to together as "the all-purpose means of human action." Jim Nickel elaborates, cleverly, that human rights are "what you want, no matter what you want." In other words, whatever goals you have in life (e.g. to become rich and famous, to get married, to buy a house, etc.), you need the objects of human rights beforehand. You can't get married if you're dead, after all, nor choose a lucrative career without freedom, nor buy a house if you're so poor that you're starving. And, since we all have goals in life, we all have the strongest possible reasons (of self-interested personal prudence) to claim human rights.[7]

Though the idea of human rights originates in Western civilization, it is imagined, by its supporters, to have *genuinely universal* appeal and application.[8] After all, who doesn't have goals and desires? And who doesn't want the objects needed to pursue them? And so we all want to claim security, subsistence, liberty, etc., for ourselves. But, why should we acknowledge and respect the human rights claims *of others*? For several strong reasons:

- Generally, as Jan Narveson says, it's the *prudent* thing to do. After all, we all want others to respect our own rights claims, and as they say, "what goes around, comes around."[9]

- Also, as John Rawls says, it's the *fair* thing to do: it's only fair that if we get our human rights, then others should get theirs, too.[10]

- All around the world, there's an emerging, *overwhelming social consensus* in favour of human rights, as Michael Walzer has noted.[11] Evidence of this is plain in the number of cross-cultural legal documents described later in the chapter.

- Since human rights are designed to protect what everyone vitally needs for a minimally decent life, it follows that to disrespect or violate someone's human rights is to do them serious harm. And every major civilization has it, as a foundational moral duty, not to inflict serious harm on other human beings. As Thomas Pogge concludes, *there's a powerful negative duty not to harm*.[12]

- Human rights aren't just about avoiding the bad but also about achieving the good. John Stuart Mill argued, long ago, that respecting and realizing human rights will *create a better world*.[13] And modern studies show, time and again, that both *objective* quality-of-life measures (lifespan, income, health, educational attainment, etc.) and *subjective* measures of life satisfaction (i.e. personal happiness) are much higher, on average, in human rights–respecting societies than in countries where human rights are not respected.[14]

These justifications for human rights, as well as the aims of human rights, are summarized below in Figure 9.1.

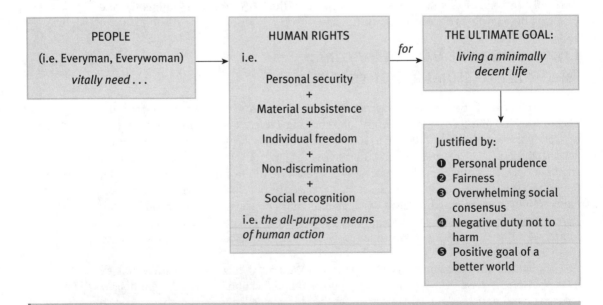

FIGURE 9.1 People, Their Human Rights, and the Ultimate Goal

Realizing Human Rights

Moral or Legal?

Are human rights *moral* or *legal*? The answer is both. Human rights *began* as a *moral* idea, crafted by ethical activists, thinkers, and social reformers who wanted to improve the way people treat each other and how they are treated by government. Over time, the human rights idea gained widespread acceptance, and thus social pressure was brought to bear on governments and international organizations to change their laws to include human rights. These changes were carried out at both the *national* level (e.g. the US Bill of Rights, 1789, and the Canadian Charter of Rights and Freedoms, 1982) and the *international* level (discussed below).

A **legal right** is a right that has been **codified**: this means it has been written into the law, and there exists a concrete **remedy** (such as a fine) for cases in which it is violated. But legal rights are *not always morally correct*—consider, for example, the rights of slave-owning families in pre–Civil War America, or the rights of white people during South Africa's **Apartheid** era, when whites were systematically separated from non-white people, with the latter, majority group being treated in a clearly inferior and discriminatory way.[15] As a result, human rights will forever remain a moral ideal in the first instance.

At the same time, human rights activists often have it as a major goal *to translate the abstract moral values of human rights into actual, concrete law*. That said, to be effective, the law in question must be real and it must be enforced. This is to avoid the phenomenon known as trophy law. A **trophy law** is a law that has been written and passed but it does *not* get enforced and does *not* reflect the reality on the ground; it has been created essentially for show. An example is the constitution of the Soviet Union, drafted during the Cold War. It is a document that aims to portray the USSR as a blissful utopia, not the bleak military dictatorship it actually was. Environmental legislation, as passed in many countries, can include aspects of trophy law, and, I'm sorry to say, so can human rights law, both national and international. But human rights defenders know this, and so rarely are they content simply with the passing of new laws. Remember, the goal is to make sure that people have the objects of their human rights, that is, that they actually enjoy secure possession of those things to which they have human rights claims or entitlements (be it, say, security or liberty).

So, the human right to property, for example, is **realized** (literally "made real") when the right-holder actually enjoys secure possession of his or her property. This can happen only when both individuals and social institutions perform the duties or tasks they must in connection with human rights. As individuals, we're duty-bound *not* to steal the right-holder's property. But sometimes, we know, individuals fail in that duty. Because of that, social institutions must be structured to help minimize the likelihood of rights violations (such as thievery) and to maximize the chances of either restoring the property to the property-owner or, at least, compensating the property-owner for his or her loss. This involves the construction of a strong system of law and order in that society.

Generally speaking, then, we, as individuals, are all duty-bound:

1. not to violate another person's rights ourselves; and

2. to support the formation and maintenance of those social institutions needed to minimize the chance of rights violation and to maximize the chance of right-holders having secure possession of the objects of their rights.

The most important social institutions shape the overall conditions within which we live our lives; they exert profound influence over the social context in which we freely make our choices and forge lives for ourselves.

We "support" such institutions by doing things like paying our taxes and voting in appropriate ways. But which are the relevant social institutions?[16]

The Basic Structure

Rawls and Pogge have coined and propagated the phrase **the basic structure** to refer to the social institutions that are the most important to the realization of human rights. These institutions have an effect on people which is, as Pogge says, "profound, pervasive, inescapable, and present from birth." The idea is this: the most important social institutions are the ones that shape the social conditions within which we live our lives. These institutions do not literally determine us, of course, but they do exert profound influence over the social context in which we freely make our choices and forge lives for ourselves.[17] Which specific institutions count as part of the basic structure of society? Something like the following list:

- *The mode of **economic** organization.* For example, in a given society, do free markets exist, or is the economy controlled by the government? How are goods produced and then distributed? Is money or barter the means of exchange? How are banks allowed to operate? What is the level of taxation—i.e. how much money do people get to keep for themselves—and how is the tax burden distributed? Are people allowed to hold private property?

- *The mode of **political** organization.* How is government established and operated? Is it a democracy or not? Who decides who rules, and what powers are given to the rulers? How are public choices made and executed? How is the civil service staffed—through patronage and family connections or, rather, by merit? Is there a division of power? Into which fields of human endeavour does government intervene?

- *The mode of **legal** organization.* Is there a written constitution or not? Is the judiciary separate and independent from other branches of government? Are judges appointed or elected? Are cases tried by judges or by juries? What legal rights do citizens have? Can people appeal legal decisions to a different level of court?

- *The mode of deploying **armed force**.* How are law and order secured? How are police officers recruited and trained? In what circumstances are they allowed to use force? When are people thrown, and kept, in jail? Do civilian authorities have ultimate control over the police and the military, and is corruption under control? What is the level of national defence spending, and how does that affect other public spending choices? When does the society deploy its army, navy, and air force?

- *The mode of delivering **basic social services**, such as education and healthcare.* Are basic levels of education and healthcare guaranteed to everyone? What is the ratio of private to public education and healthcare? What gets taught at school? Who gets into college or university, or into the various professions? How are hospitals funded? How are drugs and medicines produced and distributed?

- *The mode of **family** association permitted and encouraged.* Is marriage encouraged? Is divorce allowed? What rights do parents have over their children? What claims do spouses have on each other? Are same-sex unions permitted? How are family groupings treated by the legal, education, and the tax systems?

How a society answers the questions under each of the above headings will, obviously, come to exert over time "a profound, pervasive, and inescapable influence" over its members, and indeed from the very moment they are born. And how a society shapes the six kinds of institution will come to have an enormous effect over who gets the objects of their human rights claims.[18]

Figure 9.2 summarizes the focus of our human rights claims. To a large extent, our human rights claims are claims *on the basic structure*, and *on everyone to do their part* in shaping the basic structure in a rights-respecting way.[19]

Rights Violation

Individuals *directly* violate human rights when they take away the object of another person's human rights (e.g. by stealing). They *indirectly* violate human rights when they fail to do their part to shape the basic structure appropriately (e.g. by evading taxes). Institutions violate human rights either when they take away the objects of people's human rights or permit this to happen, or when they fail to provide the needed objects or the secure context in question.

It is important here to distinguish between *intentional* and *non-intentional* violations. An **intentional violation** occurs when an institution can, but chooses not to, respect human rights. Institutions guilty of intentional human rights violations are wicked and morally decrepit, like the government of Nazi Germany. From a human rights point of view, these governments are *not* legitimate and are in no position to complain when their

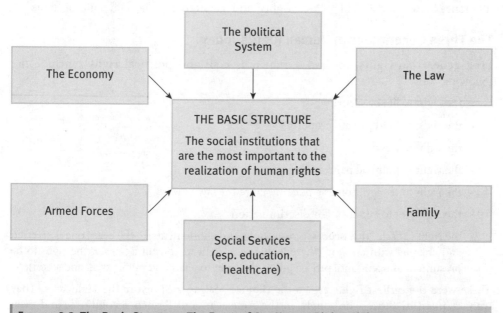

FIGURE 9.2 The Basic Structure: The Focus of Our Human Rights Claims

people rise to resist them in an effort to reform the government structure in a way that supports human rights.

An **unintentional violation** occurs when an institution wants to, but cannot, respect the human rights of its citizens, such as when it lacks the resources to satisfy the people's rights. Unintentional human rights violations have occurred in a number of countries in sub-Saharan Africa. These countries need help to fix their institutions in order to create and put in place rights-respecting resources. They need *assistance* rather than *resistance*.[20] We will return to this subject in Chapter 11, on international development, when we look at efforts to help the poorest countries gain the resources they need to meet the human rights claims of their people.

INTERNATIONAL HUMAN RIGHTS LAW

As mentioned above, the UDHR is viewed as the most inspiring and influential human rights document, but it has no legal weight. What *does* have weight are two global, multilateral human rights treaties that were inspired by, and which attempt to capture and realize, those rights enshrined in the UDHR. These are the International Covenant on Civil and Political Rights (ICCPR) and the International Covenant on Economic, Social and Cultural Rights (ICESCR). Both treaties were originally drafted and ratified in 1966, and came into force after a grace period in 1976. There are two treaties, as opposed to one, owing to the Cold War politics of the day: the capitalist West endorsed the ICCPR, while the communist East endorsed the ICESCR. Since the Cold War's end in the early 1990s, however, most countries in the world have signed and ratified *both treaties*, meaning they have committed to realizing the rights listed in the UDHR for all their people. What exactly, though, is the difference between "civil and political rights" and "economic, social, and cultural rights"?[21]

The Three Generations of Human Rights Today

First-generation rights, otherwise known as **civil and political rights**, include the following:

- the right to life or security
- the right to hold private property
- the right to freedom
- the right to political participation
- the right to recognition as a person before the law
- the right not to suffer unfair discrimination
- the right to basic **"due process"** protections and entitlements, in the event one is arrested and charged with a crime (these include the right to consult a lawyer, the right to be presumed innocent until proven guilty, the right to a fair and public trial, and so on).

These were the earliest rights ever to be claimed, dating well before the Holocaust. They were claimed by those who fought in the American and French revolutions, and even before then, in England in 1215, they were written into the **Magna Carta** (literally, "Great Charter"), commonly agreed to be the world's first rights document.[22]

Second-generation rights are also known as **socio-economic and cultural rights**. They began to be claimed during the Industrial Revolution, starting around 1750. They include:

- the right to material subsistence (or at least the guarantee of a welfare income sufficient to purchase material subsistence)
- the right to basic education (i.e. primary and secondary school education)
- the right to basic healthcare and public health measures (like inoculations)
- the right to form a union
- the right to basic safety standards on the job
- the right to more robust forms of equality beyond non-discrimination.

The last point includes, especially, greater income equality as well as the provision of additional socio-economic opportunities for the worst-off.

These second-generation rights are completely in line with the development of the modern welfare state, as described in Chapter 3, wherein the wealthy pay additional taxes to provide governments with extra resources, which are then (in theory) used for schools, hospitals, and income support for the poor.[23]

Third-generation rights are not generally known by any other term and are harder to define. As a group, they lack the internal coherence of the first- and second-generation rights. They are not included in either the UDHR or its two "ICs," but they are included in many other international human rights treaties. They are the most recent generation of rights claims—dating approximately from 1960 to the present—and they tend to feature especially cultural and environmental claims. These would include:

- the right to clean air and drinkable water
- the right to environmental protections more broadly (like the creation of conservation areas)
- the right to even "thicker" forms of socio-economic equality, like affirmative action hiring programs, with particular stresses on gender equality
- the right of minority groups to cultural and linguistic funding and protection, to save and enhance their culture for future generations.

One of the most interesting and important third-generation rights is the so-called **right to democracy**, claimed especially by those in the Global South who are sick of corrupt, incompetent, and authoritarian regimes. Claimants argue that only an accountable, elected, democratic government can serve their vital needs for poverty relief, economic growth, modernization, and improved quality of life.[24]

The move from first- to third-generation rights (summarized in Table 9.2) is *not only* a chronological move *but also* a move in terms of cost, controversy, and contestedness. First-generation rights are the most widely accepted, the least controversial, and, most believe, the least costly; the costs and controversy escalate when we move to second-generation rights and on to third-generation rights. Most societies now accept second-generation rights, but this acceptance has come only after a period of rejection, during the Cold War, when they were associated with communism. Third-generation claims are still very much

Table 9.2 The Three Generations of Human Rights

Generation	Examples
First-generation rights (a.k.a. civil & political rights, CPRs)	• life/security • liberty • private property • non-discrimination • political participation • due process protections
Second-generation rights (a.k.a. socio-economic & cultural rights, ESCRs)	• material subsistence • basic education • basic healthcare & public sanitation • greater economic equality • to form unions and organize for better working conditions
Third-generation rights (TGRs)	• greater equality (esp. gender equality) • environmental protections • cultural protections (esp. for minority groups) • democracy (esp. for the developing world)

up in the air. For example, only in 2010 did the UN General Assembly pass a resolution declaring drinkable water to be a human right. Sometimes third-generation claims can seem exaggerated and unclear in their implication, as when a distinguished panel of climate change scientists in 2010 declared it to be a human right "not to be subjected to global warming." That said, who can deny developing countries their need for democratization, or women the goal of true and fair equality with men?[25]

Studies in Technology

A Human Right to the Internet?

In May 2011, a UN panel appeared to assert a new human right, namely, to access the Internet and all its information. Do you agree that the Internet should be a human right?

Two things seemed to prompt the report of the UN's Special Rapporteur on Freedom of Expression and Opinion:

1. The passing of a law, in both Britain and France, allowing the governments there to "kick off the Internet" anyone found guilty of severe and repeated copyright infringement.
2. The shutting down of Internet access to roughly two-thirds of the population of Syria, presumably by the government there, in an attempt to block anti-government messaging and information-sharing.

It's interesting, and politically instructive, that the UN criticized both developed/democratic countries and developing/**authoritarian** (i.e. undemocratic and military-ruled) countries—reminding us that no nation has a perfect human rights record. Yet the underlying issue remains provocative: is it really true that we do, or should, have a human right to access the Internet?

Those in favour would stress how much daily life has changed since **the Information Revolution** began: can you imagine your life without your cellphone/smartphone, your Facebook, your YouTube, your Twitter, and your multiple e-mail accounts? Many would say to be deprived of Internet access would harm their interests, exclude them from social reality, make their work and life harder and more costly, and deny them access to a limitless range of useful—even vital—information (about health, finances, education opportunities, etc.). There have also been recent cases where the use of this technology—especially in the Arab world and in Southeast Asia—has substantially helped organize political resistance against rights-violating regimes.

But critics of this proposal may wonder about the cost and feasibility of this. After all, Internet access requires computer and/or smartphone access: how exactly are we going to ensure universal access to those not inexpensive pieces of technology? More basically, Internet access requires electricity, and experts estimate that close to one billion people worldwide lack reliable daily access to electricity. Using the Internet also requires fundamental

Should Internet access be a priority in this underdeveloped Nigerian village? How much would it help the people there? Would the infrastructure costs of setting up Internet access be better spent on other improvements? (© Claudia Dewald/iStockphoto)

literacy and typing skills—skills that are not evenly found across the globe, especially among some of poorer nations of the Global South. (See The Global Digital Divide in Chapter 3.) Just think about that: what you take for granted in your "wired-in world" is something that billions of people—*billions*—have *never* experienced. Is that lack of Internet access a shameful disgrace and a violation of rights? Or is it simply a harsh consequence of relative poverty and underdevelopment? (And are those without Internet access better off anyway, as Facebook and Twitter, not to mention all the gaming and pornography sites, can be such a colossal waste of time?)[26]

Global Human Rights Treaties

We've seen that the most influential pieces of international human rights law are the UDHR and the two covenants, the ICCPR and the ICESCR. Since then, there have been many human rights treaties, both global and regional—too many to list in full. Some of the more high-profile global ones include:

- the Convention on the Rights of the Child (CRC)—this is actually the most widely ratified human rights document in the world
- the Convention on the Elimination of all Forms of Discrimination Against Women (CEDAW)
- the Convention on the Prevention and Punishment of the Crime of Genocide (CPPCG)
- the Convention on the Elimination of all Forms of Racial Discrimination (CEFORD)
- various treaties relating to the rights of indigenous or native peoples, refugees, the physically and mentally challenged, and prisoners.[27]

Global Human Rights Institutions

What global institutions exist to help ensure that these treaties are respected and that human rights become realized? We saw in Chapter 5 that there is a world court—the International Court of Justice, or ICJ—that has ruled on some human rights issues (relating almost exclusively to the ICCPR and *not* to the ICESCR). However, we saw that *only* governments can take each other to the world court, and that they must *both* volunteer. Governments that violate human rights probably aren't going to be eager to do that. Moreover, the ICJ cannot *enforce* any decision: the losing country must voluntarily comply. That's *not* real enforcement.

Partly to overcome this, the UN's General Assembly created a **High Commission on Human Rights**. Based in Geneva, the commission receives annual reports from UN member nations regarding how they are fulfilling their commitments under the ICCPR and the ICESCR. The commission also fields complaints from countries about other countries' human rights records. The commission then calls in officials representing the various members for fact-finding and questioning before issuing a public summary, reporting on every country's strengths and, especially, weaknesses on the human rights front. While the Commission can do nothing beyond this, it is seen as having had some influence, since governments—even the very worst ones—can be quite sensitive to criticism about their human rights record. The commission's activity thus serves as a kind of *public shaming*, designed to spur change in a pro–human rights direction.[28]

Evidence of the commission's influence comes from a recent battle over control regarding the commission itself. A group of countries with poor human rights records grew tired of, and angry with, all the criticisms they were receiving. So they hatched a plan to vote for each other as a group, when new vacancies arose on the commission (where countries serve terms for a few years but then must give up their seats to make way for "fresh blood"). The result was that the commission was essentially hijacked by some of the world's worst human rights violators—Cuba, Iran, Sudan—and they made special efforts to drag in for questioning countries with strong (but admittedly not spotless) human rights records, like the United States (over the living conditions of its homeless population) and Canada (over its treatment of Aboriginal people). But recently, other countries have caught on to this cynical strategy and have fought back to put countries with generally good human rights records on the commission, which has since been rebranded the Human Rights Council (to signal a shift in perspective).[29]

At the head of the council sits the **high commissioner**. This is an individual office, sort of like a secretary-general for human rights. The high commissioner operates the council on a daily basis but can also—much like the secretary-general—travel to human rights "hot spots" to call the world's attention to problems in need of immediate assistance. The current high commissioner is South African Navi Pillay, who succeeded former Canadian Supreme Court justice Louise Arbour in 2008.[30]

In the end, this might not seem like much in the way of global enforcement of international human rights law: a high commission (or council), led by a high commissioner, that can give bad publicity and public criticism, and the ICJ, which can rule but not enforce. And so it *does* remain true that the political forms of international law are the most poorly structured and weakly enforced, as they are the most controversial and demanding. It remains true that it is *national*, and *not international*, structures that, by and large, determine whether any of us have our human rights respected. That may change in the future—and better, surely, to have what is there than nothing at all—but this currently remains a fact.

Regional Human Rights Treaties and Institutions

Among the most important *regional* human rights treaties are the following:

- the African (or Banjul) Charter on Human and People's Rights
- the Inter-American Convention on Human Rights
- the European Social Charter
- the Cairo Declaration on Human Rights in Islam
- the Charter of Paris for a New Europe
- the Helsinki Final Act (for improving relations between former Eastern bloc communist countries and the West)
- the Asian Human Rights Charter, which is the most recent of this set.

Note how each of the world's major regions has its own regional human rights document.[31]

For each regional human rights document there exists an international human rights tribunal or court, which hears cases involving alleged human rights violations. These international "remedies," as lawyers call them, can be accessed only once one has *completely exhausted all the national or domestic remedies* in one's own country. So, if you believe your human rights have been violated, you must first launch lawsuits within your own country's court system, and lose them all (both trials and appeals), before an international court will hear your case. Even then, a favourable decision from the international court might not mean much beyond a moral victory for you and bad publicity for your government: most of the regional international courts are powerless to enforce their decisions (much like the world court). The one important exception here is Europe, which easily has the world's most advanced and effective regional human rights system, with dozens of treaties and an effective, active court that has shown itself willing to make bold decisions and enforce them as well. Consider the following example.[32]

Case Study: The European Human Rights System

Say you're a citizen of France, but of Arab ethnic descent and of Muslim religious belief. Imagine that you were taking part in a public protest. The French police felt that the protest was getting too rowdy, and they moved in aggressively to break it up, using tear gas, shields, and batons. You get hit, placed under arrest, and spend two days in jail—whereupon you are released without charge. You come to believe that the French police violated your human rights. You believe they violated your security of the person, your freedom, your due process protections, and your right not to be discriminated against (you feel you were singled out because of your different skin colour and dress).

Let's say you decide you want to sue for **restitution**: perhaps an official apology, plus some money to compensate you for your pain and time. Your first step would be to file a lawsuit in French domestic court. If you lost, you could then file an appeal to a higher-level French appeals court. You could even have your case heard by the French Supreme Court. If you lost all the way up, you would then have the right to file a lawsuit with the EU human rights court. If it found in your favour, the court could order the French government to pay you your award by a certain date and, moreover, fine the French government for every day beyond that date, if it was late in giving you restitution. That's real enforcement—"cash justice," as some say.[33]

OTHER TOOLS FOR HUMAN RIGHTS

Does the powerlessness of most international human rights courts mean that we're out of options when it comes to trying to help citizens of a foreign country who are suffering violations of their human rights? Not at all—it just means that international human rights law is a limited tool that may not be very effective. But there are other tools, and essentially these are the tools mentioned in Chapter 4, on foreign policy: diplomacy, incentives (economic "carrots" and "sticks"), sanctions, and armed force. Each of these has been tried

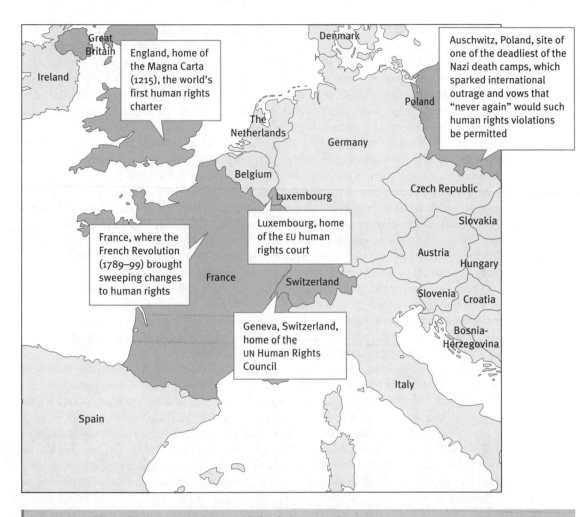

Great Britain

Ireland

Denmark

Poland

England, home of the Magna Carta (1215), the world's first human rights charter

Auschwitz, Poland, site of one of the deadliest of the Nazi death camps, which sparked international outrage and vows that "never again" would such human rights violations be permitted

The Netherlands

Germany

Belgium

Luxembourg

Czech Republic

Slovakia

Luxembourg, home of the EU human rights court

Austria

Hungary

France, where the French Revolution (1789–99) brought sweeping changes to human rights

France

Switzerland

Slovenia

Croatia

Bosnia-Herzegovina

Geneva, Switzerland, home of the UN Human Rights Council

Italy

Spain

FIGURE 9.3 Sites of Relevance to Human Rights in Western Europe

in the cause of protecting human rights, to varying degrees of success, depending on the nature of the case.

For example, we saw in Chapter 5 that the European Union lists respect for human rights as one of its criteria for membership in the EU. The enormous benefits of becoming an EU member served as a powerful economic carrot—a positive incentive—in persuading former communist societies in central and eastern Europe to improve their human rights records so as to be worthy of admission. During the Cold War, the United States tried to do something similar by bestowing "**most favoured nation**" (MFN) trading status on certain countries—offering them economic advantages in exchange for improving their own human rights records. Still in place, MFN status has now become so widespread that it has lost some of its effectiveness in this regard.[34]

The US also carries out a low-key, pro–human rights diplomacy with China. The EU and countries like Australia and Canada do the same. No one is willing to employ harsher measures with China, as it is a great power and everyone wants a profitable trading relationship with the world's most populous emerging economy. Yet many have substantial human rights concerns with China, which is still a communist (or, at least, authoritarian) state. Chinese citizens enjoy no rights to political participation, nor such basic personal freedoms as freedom of speech and the press or even the freedom to choose how many children to have (as we saw in Chapter 2). There are even substantial restrictions on where one can live and the profession one can enter, as China struggles to manage its massive population. Finally, there is the issue of Tibet, mentioned in Chapter 3. China considers Tibet part of its traditional territory, and rules it with an iron fist, whereas opponents— such as the Buddhist monks, as led by the Dalai Lama—view Chinese measures as violating their rights to sovereignty and self-rule, as well as to freedom and political participation. Taking this all in, countries around the world—but especially in North America and Europe—have *sometimes* publicly criticized China for its human rights record. China, in reply, returns the favour by publicly criticizing some human rights weaknesses in the US (the homeless, say, or the poorest visible minorities) and in Europe (say, its bloody history, or the conditions of such groups as the Gypsies/Roma). In reply to that, the US, say, will invite the Dalai Lama to meet the American president at the White House, and then China will devise a diplomatic payback scheme, and the low-stakes, back-and-forth diplomacy over China's human rights record continues in that fashion.[35]

With other countries—less rich and powerful—a more forceful approach, involving sanctions and force, is often used to pressure them to improve their human rights records. For instance, the US has applied sweeping sanctions on Cuba for decades to express its strong opposition to the communism imposed on the island nation by its regime. And in the very late 1990s, the international community was willing to go to war with the leaders of Bosnian Serbia and Serbia proper, all in the name of human rights. The Serb leaders of the day were authoritarian and militaristic, and they engaged in a process of **ethnic cleansing** in an effort to drive all non-Serbs out of territory the Serbians defined as belonging to a "Greater Serbia." Bosnian Croats, Bosnian Muslims, and Serbian Kosovars paid the price, which included mass rapes, killings, and forcible displacements. NATO stepped in with force to stop the Serbs and punish them for their mass rights violations, first in Bosnia and then in Kosovo. The second war resulted in the overthrow of the Serbian government, and the beginning of reconstruction there.[36]

Apart from diplomacy, sanctions, and force, human rights activists have some new tools to use to heighten human rights awareness and pressure countries into respecting human rights. These new tools include **civil society engagement**, NGO activity, and both traditional media and new media strategies. Consider the 2010 case of an Iranian woman, Sakineh Mohammadi Ashtiani, who was sentenced by an Iranian court to be stoned to death for adultery. Viewing such a sentence as a violation of her right to life, plus her right not to be punished in a cruel and unusual way, her supporters—especially women's groups—waged a campaign of Internet petitioning, information sharing, and lobbying, which brought international attention to the case and, apparently, caused the court to back down, at least in terms of its death sentence (although Ashtiani remains in jail). Human rights activists have learned the effectiveness of shooting videos of governments behaving badly, and then releasing the results globally on YouTube, publicizing atrocities and rights violations, earning the coverage of mainstream news media, and ultimately reaching those decision-makers who are empowered to do something further about it, in terms of the more traditional foreign policy tools. The new media strategies have proven especially effective at undermining government efforts to impose news blackouts and to control information about controversial measures, be it in Thailand, Burma/Myanmar, Sudan, Sri Lanka, or North Korea.[37]

Case Study: The Arab Spring

Perhaps the most sustained and sweeping pro–human rights changes occurring anywhere right now are happening in the Arab world. Collectively, these changes, and the protests that have led to them, are known as **the Arab Spring**.

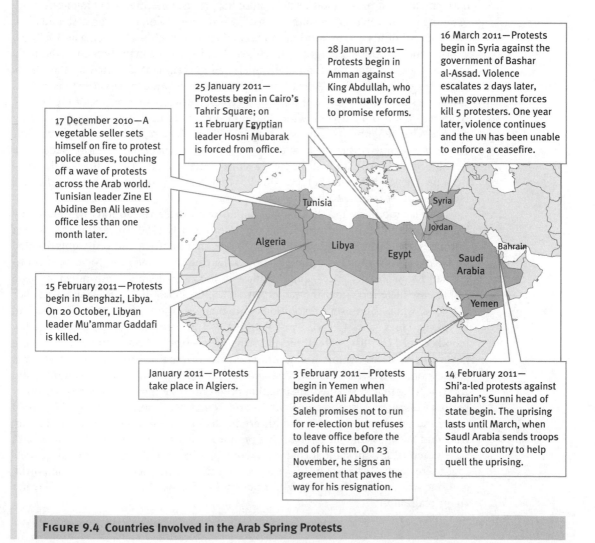

FIGURE 9.4 Countries Involved in the Arab Spring Protests

Arab is an ethno-cultural term, referring in the first instance to the shared ethnicity of peoples whose ancestors came from the Arabian peninsula. Also sharing the same language (Arabic), Arab peoples are also overwhelmingly (but not exclusively) Muslim, maintaining a shared belief in the Islamic religion (as defined in Chapter 3). Hence, "Arab" signifies a tight bundle of deeply important identity-makers, and the Arab people have formed the majority in the Middle East and North Africa for centuries.

For almost its entire history, and with only a few exceptions, the Arab world has been governed undemocratically. "Strongman" presidents, kept in power by the military and with next to no regard to the rights of the people, have been the norm. But in December 2010, something surprising happened in tiny Tunisia. A street vendor, Mohamed Bouazizi, became fed up after years of police abuses, including harassment, theft of his goods, extortion of his profits, and threats of violence. At the breaking point, Bouazizi—a young man of 28—set himself on fire in protest, and died. News spread of his act, by word of mouth and also via such social media as YouTube, Twitter, and Facebook. Enraged Tunisians took to the streets in protest, and eventually toppled their corrupt, unaccountable, unelected government. Inspired by the results of the protests in Tunisia, Arabs took to the streets to mount mass demonstrations and strikes in nearby Algeria and Egypt. Egypt, historically seen as one of the leading Arab nations, attracted worldwide attention during its uprising. Those demanding political change gathered en masse in Cairo's Tahrir Square, aided by new technologies and a regime unsure of how to respond to the unprecedented movement. "The Revolution will be Twittered!" became a slogan. However, it was another battle cry—"The people will bring down the regime!"—that proved prophetic, when the dictator Hosni Mubarek resigned after 30 years in power.

It is far too early to tell what the fallout from these revolutions will be. Many liken the present moment in the Arab world to the early 1990s in central and eastern Europe, when communist governments fell one after another, and pro-rights, elected democracies—eventually—came into power. During that time in Europe, each country had its own experience—quite painless in the case of some, with much struggle in the case of others—and the same pattern seems apparent in the Arab world. For instance, while there were revolutions and changes of government in Tunisia and Egypt, in Libya a nasty civil war—with NATO intervention—erupted. An equally bloody armed conflict, with ethnic and religious overtones, broke out in Syria, pitting government forces against a determined group of rebel insurgents. As of writing, it rages on, with Syrian allies China and Russia blocking any UNSC resolution, and NATO fearing that any armed intervention might provoke Iran and/or aggravate other regional disputes. Uprisings in Bahrain and Yemen were similarly met with armed force, and put down. Complex and uncertain pledges of reform were made in Jordan, Iraq, and Sudan, while the Arab Spring produced only token protests elsewhere, with little potential for substantial change, in countries like Saudi Arabia. Still, as of writing, there seems little doubt that this is a significant moment for the Arab world, and one with at least the potential for positive, enduring change in favour of greater rights realization.[38]

HUMAN RIGHTS NGOS

Human rights NGOs have been among the most vocal, active, and effective of all the international NGOs. **Amnesty International** is the oldest and best known. Formed originally in 1961 to help lobby for the freedom of those jailed purely for their political beliefs, Amnesty International has since grown across the world, engaging in nearly all fields of human rights activism, from letter-writing and political lobbying to helping to pay for defence lawyers and creating documentaries and other educational resources to highlight human rights for future generations. **Human Rights Watch** is also prominent. Founded in 1978, Human Rights Watch has focused more on the political and legal side of human rights issues, and on recording and disseminating detailed accounts of rights violation, such as torture at the hands of prison guards. Both Amnesty and Human Rights Watch have been resolutely neutral, concentrating not on supporting regimes or picking sides but, rather, on sticking carefully and expertly to the facts and to the law, and on standing up for those individuals who have suffered from human rights violations. As a result, these organizations are very credible and highly regarded—so much so, in fact, that they are often invited to the UN or into national courts, congresses, and parliaments to make presentations on particular cases or on human rights laws and emerging issues.[39]

Though the international scene is still, in so many ways, dominated by nation-states, NGOs have given a voice to individuals and non-state actors. Some NGOs even do such a good job that they attract government funding. Why would governments support non-governmental organizations? Because NGOs can—and often do—speak far more openly and with sharper criticism than state governments are typically comfortable using. Don't think that the US government always cringes and winces when Amnesty International has harsh things to say about political prisoners in China. Often, the government is grateful that the truth has been spoken in a way that will not bring Chinese retaliation upon the US.

Human rights NGOs—and international NGOs in general—perform the following vital functions:

- They call public, media, and government attention to important issues, widening the agenda and the scope of concern.

- They raise issues that often focus on protecting the world's least powerful, and most vulnerable, people.

A protester in Toronto makes a dramatic appeal for an end to the fighting in the Democratic Republic of the Congo. Westerners enjoy a right to protest without fear of being arrested or imprisoned for holding and expressing opinions that might not be popular with the government in power. Is that something we take for granted? Do you think that protest of this kind would be possible in the Congolese capital of Kinshasa? (© bilgehan yilmaz/iStockphoto)

- NGOs can sometimes help vulnerable people directly: by pressuring their governments to act, by providing funding and/or expertise, or by intervening with medical help to literally save their lives.

- NGOs typically concentrate on single issues, which allows them to be bolder, to develop more expertise in their areas of focus, and to be less subject than national governments or large corporations to "linkage." (**Linkage** is a government's joining one issue to another in order to manipulate a situation in its favour, as when China ties access to its huge and lucrative domestic market to silence on its appalling human rights record.)

- NGOs provide an educational function by conveying the sense, and sensibility, of their causes through articles, books, curricular content, documentaries, Internet content, and TV programming.

- NGOs provide a means for well-meaning, rights-respecting governments to further the human rights cause indirectly, should they be reluctant to tackle these issues head-on (as in the example, noted above, of the US and China). NGOs can thus end up being one more tool in the pro–human rights toolbox for influential national governments.

- NGOs both *apply pressure* to state governments and also *alleviate it*. They *apply* pressure when they push for positive change and action in connection with their agenda. They *alleviate* pressure when they perform social services that governments then don't have to do themselves, or (as just mentioned) when they voice opinions and criticisms of other governments in a way that spares the rights-respecting government from a direct international confrontation on the issue.[40]

WOMEN'S HUMAN RIGHTS

The human rights of women is a topic that merits special attention. This is so for at least two reasons:

1. a *before-the-fact* appeal to fairness; and

2. an *after-the-fact* appeal to good consequences.

We'll look at the second point first.

There is abundant evidence—especially from contemporary international development research—that greater emphasis on realizing the rights and well-being of women has two crucial payoffs. The first is a huge increase in infant survival and in the development and well-being of children. The second benefit is clear and measurable improvements in some of the most important indicators of development in a society overall, like lower crime, greater social stability, higher literacy, better access to and quality of healthcare, and even higher per capita income. In short, everyone benefits when the human rights of women are realized. If we want a better world, we must work harder to improve the well-being of girls and women around the world.[41]

In terms of the first reason, the before-the-fact appeal to fairness, there is plenty of evidence to support the view that women—everywhere, but emphatically in the developing world—are treated unfairly, and that their rights are *not* as fully realized as those of men. And this, we know, *violates the very spirit and core logic of human rights*, which insist on universality and equality. It's not for nothing that the biggest and most important global treaty addressing the human rights of women—the second-most ratified rights treaty in the world—is called **the Convention on the Elimination of All Forms of Discrimination Against Women** (CEDAW, 1981). An interesting note about CEDAW is that—shockingly— the US, alone among developed countries, has *never* ratified the treaty. In this, the United States joins such nations as Iran, Qatar, Somalia, and North and South Sudan. The reason seems to be the objection of con- servative Republican senators, who reject the perceived socialism of a number of strongly worded socio-economic rights in the treaty, plus a number of clauses that seem to support, or at least to allow for, abortion.[42]

> *Everyone benefits when the human rights of women are realized.*

An especially powerful picture of the unfair and unequal treatment of women worldwide comes from UNICEF, which provides compelling data on the difficulties and discriminations faced by women throughout their lifecourse, from birth to old age.[43]

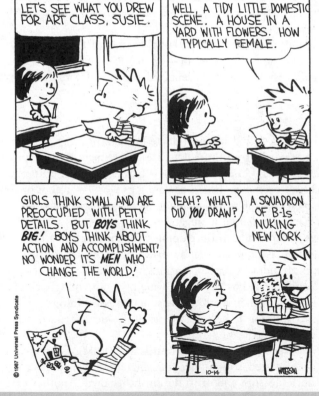

Why do you think it is that improving the human rights of women correlates with measurable improvements in development? (CALVIN AND HOBBES © 1987 Watterson. Dist. By UNIVERSAL UCLICK. Reprinted with permission. All rights reserved.)

Birth

Worldwide, every year, about 500,000 women die during childbirth or shortly thereafter from complications associated with childbirth. That's one every minute, and almost all these deaths happen in the developing world (which suggests that these are all *preventable* deaths, given sufficient investment in healthcare resources).

In terms of conception and the latest developments in reproductive technology, there is clear evidence that sex selection techniques are used to favour the selection of male children, and that in countries with population control measures (China, in particular), male children are most desired and selected for, resulting in the greater aborting of female fetuses and the abandoning of female infants.[44]

Childhood

Worldwide, boys get more nutrition and more education—and to a significant degree—than do girls. Girls are more involved helping their mothers perform domestic chores (like cooking, cleaning, and caring for siblings). This is to say that, in the developing world especially, girls *work more* on *less nutrition*, thereby hampering their healthy development. Boys are, in this way, better supported to learn skills and gain knowledge that will improve their earning power later in life.

Ironically, evidence from the developed world shows that when girls are afforded equal opportunities for education, they actually—on average—*outperform* boys scholastically. How sad, then, that an estimated 70 per cent of the world's illiterate people are females.[45]

Adolescence

Adolescent girls bear a clearly disproportionate burden of things like harassment, sexual assault or abuse, and sexually transmitted diseases. The effects of premature pregnancy and parenthood fall exceptionally on girls and their families, and in a number of developing countries, **girl brides**—even *child* brides as young as 8 or 9—are not uncommon. Pairing an adolescent, or even pre-pubescent, girl with a mature man, obviously, sets her up for a lifetime of inequality and potential subjugation.

Adolescent girls, especially in developing countries, are also especially likely to be drawn into prostitution, child pornography, drug addiction, sex tourism, and sex trafficking. (**Sex tourism** is an industry based on arranging for men from the developed world to travel to the developing world to pay for sex, mainly with young girls. **Sex trafficking** is the business of bringing women from the developing world into the developed world for sexual services or prostitution.) These are essentially modern forms of slavery, not to mention significant global public health hazards.

Some societies practise **female genital mutilation** (FGM), wherein an adolescent girl's genitalia are surgically altered, without her consent, either to ensure her virginity or else to enhance her partner's pleasure and/or to diminish her own. Another extreme practice—thankfully rare, it would seem—is **honour killing**, in which an adolescent girl or woman is killed (usually beaten to death) by a male member of her family for some perceived failure of behaviour, usually relating in some way to sexual mores.[46]

Motherhood and Mature Adulthood

The figure on childbirth-related deaths given above is relevant here, as is the issue (in the developing world anyway) of inadequate nutrition, supplements (e.g. folic acid), information, and medical care during pregnancy. We all know that, worldwide, women are (on average) much more likely to be the main caregivers for their children, which has serious impacts on the mother's income and career: first, her income is cut—temporarily or permanently—as she stops or cuts back on work to care for her children; second, all the added work of raising children and keeping house (cooking, cleaning, etc.) goes substantially unpaid. This combination, plus the education gap mentioned earlier, add up to a big **wage gap** between what men and women earn. The calculation and precise extent of the wage gap is disputed, but most agree that it is real, and big enough to be of concern. The UN has reported that two-thirds (67 per cent) of all poor adults are women. Experts have called this trend the **feminization of poverty**.[47]

Life for most women in the developed world is pretty good, when compared with what women in the Global South endure, and stands out as a standard to achieve for women struggling elsewhere. Over centuries of struggle, Western women have won the right to own property, have their own money, inherit from their parents, be considered legal persons, achieve any kind of education they can merit, become owners and directors of corporations, gain control over their reproductive futures, and vote in—and run as candidates for—public elections. Yet in some developing countries, especially those of the Arab Middle East, sub-Saharan Africa, some of the Pacific Islands, and Bangladesh—*none of this is true, even today*. At the same time, clear inequalities still exist in the West. The wage gap remains, and "career versus children" remains a complex and difficult choice for Western women, especially in the US, which is one of very few democratic nations with no federal law ensuring paid time off for new parents. One telling fact: as of 2008, only 3 out of 500 CEOs in the Fortune 500 list of America's richest companies were women, whereas 75 per cent of America's poorest 30 million citizens were female. Also interesting to note is that the US, again alone among developed societies, has never had a female head of state.[48]

Old Age

Women live longer, on average, than men. But this is cold comfort, as many of them live either in poverty or in situations (with adult children or, regrettably, some elder care facilities) where they are routinely subjected to **elder abuse**. It is often said, by feminist activists, that elderly women are doubly discriminated against: first in terms of gender, and then in terms of age. They may be taken advantage of either financially or in terms of their labour (e.g. if they are forced to provide unpaid care of their grandchildren or great-grandchildren).

Improving Human Rights for Women

The situations described above are all generalizations, holding water *only* on average and worldwide (wherein the statistics for the developing world pull everything down dramatically). But they nevertheless remain factual generalizations, together pointing to a huge worldwide problem facing women but affecting us all. How to make things better?

Obviously, the measures that are necessary and practicable will vary, depending on the country and region. But these areas of focus are most often cited:

- *Education.* In the developing world especially, governments must provide more schools and educational opportunities for girls and women, at every stage, from primary to post-secondary. Schools must feature a gender-inclusive and gender-aware curriculum for all students, and more female teachers are badly needed.

- *Sex and reproduction.* Governments must act to reduce assault and abuse of women, especially by legislating greater punishments for offenders. Women require more and better information about, and access to, hygienic sex and reproductive choices, and better healthcare overall. (Much more will be said on this in the next chapter.)

- *Domestic work.* Solutions are needed to reduce the unequal gender division in housework and child-rearing. Governments can help by offering greater rewards and/or pay for household work and encouraging fairer access to total household income.

- *Workplace.* Companies and workplaces must do their part to shrink the wage gap, and offer more promotions and advancement opportunities to women.

- *Legal and political structures.* Countries that do not yet guarantee women equal rights before the law must do so. Moreover, women must be given equal opportunity to have an effective say in the shaping of the basic political structure, which we've seen exerts such huge influence over the courses of all our lives.[49]

Canadian Insights

Canada's Human Rights Record

Canada is generally considered to be a fair-minded, rights-respecting democracy. It sports its own Charter of Rights and Freedoms (1982), which is vigorously enforced through the legal system. The Canadian Supreme Court has shown itself very willing to strike down legislation violating the Charter, and to uphold the human rights of individuals when they are threatened.

Canada also has a distinguished human rights record internationally. Four examples stand out in particular:

- Former McGill law professor John Humphrey is commonly credited as the major author of the final text version of the Universal Declaration of Human Rights.
- From 2004 until 2008, Canadian judge Louise Arbour served with distinction as the UN High Commissioner on Human Rights, using her high-profile post to travel several times to Sudan's Darfur region to highlight the widespread and alarming human rights violations occurring there.
- Canada has participated, with vigour, in recent military action on behalf of human rights: in Bosnia/Kosovo (during the 1990s); in Afghanistan (2002–present); and in Libya (2011).

- Canada, through its aid and development programs, has been a generous funder of human rights initiatives, especially those concerned with realizing the rights of women and children (see Chapter 11 for more).

This is not to say that Canada's record is perfect: every society has its share of human rights problems. Improving the quality of life and standard of living of the country's Aboriginal population has always been a challenge for Canada, and some would cite the country's historical failures in this regard as a significant blemish on its human rights record. And, of course, there are enduring issues regarding the achievement of equality and non-discrimination for all, especially women, the physically challenged, visible minorities, and sexual preference minorities. There are emerging human rights issues facing Canada, too—for example, some people believe that bullying (and, now, cyber-bullying) ought to count as a human rights violation, and treated much more seriously as a result.[50] Are there other areas you can think of where Canada has either distinguished itself or fallen short in terms of human rights?

CONCLUSION

This chapter inaugurates our final section, focusing on the well-being of individual persons, as opposed to the wealth and security interests of states. We saw how the modern human rights movement grew out of reaction to the Holocaust, and noted its basic values and commitments. We came to understand the point and function of human rights, how they are justified, and how they make claims on all of us, as well as on the basic structure. We witnessed the growth and nature of international human rights law and institutions, both globally and regionally. Given the limitations of the law in this regard, we also examined other tools for realizing human rights—diplomacy, positive incentives, sanctions, armed force, and NGO activity. Throughout, we explored vital, topical case studies dealing with the Arab Spring, women's human rights, the Internet, and Canada's human rights record.

REVIEW QUESTIONS

1. On the Web, locate and read, in full, the Universal Declaration of Human Rights. Are there any rights you disagree with? Anything you find surprising? What's your overall opinion of the quality of this influential rights document? (Perhaps, in answering, you might compare the UDHR with the rights document of your own country.)

2. Also on the Web, locate and read the highlights of a human rights treaty whose subject interests you (e.g. children, political prisoners, Aboriginal people). What rights are being claimed on behalf of these people, and why? (E.g. what do security and liberty mean *for children* as opposed to adults?)

3. Do you think human rights create international conflicts and problems? In cases where countries like China make silence on their human rights record a condition for trade and business deals, which side would you agree with—human rights, or trade—and why? What are the pros and cons of both sides?

4. Can we afford the genuinely *global* realization of human rights? Why, or why not? Can we afford *not* to realize them?

5. Referring to our Studies in Technology case study, do you agree that access to the Internet should be a human right? Why or why not?

6. In your view, are human rights merely Western, or are they truly universal? What implications does your view have for the place of human rights in international relations?

7. Research the Arab Spring and its latest developments. What have been its deeper causes? What does the movement imply about human rights, and what people want (and expect) from their societies? How, in your view, is the Arab Spring likely to turn out?

8. Reading this chapter's section on women's rights, what was your overall impression or concern? Do you agree that realizing women's rights will improve the world? Do you agree with the five fields most often mentioned for improvement? Would you suggest others, and why?

9. Do you think Canada should be proud of its human rights record, or not? Where do you think Canada can, and should, make the biggest improvements?

10. At chapter's start, we noted the famous cry that "Never Again!" should something like the Holocaust be allowed to happen. Has the international community kept that promise? Research and consider, for example, the near genocide in 1994 that happened in Rwanda. (I recommend you watch the searing documentary *Shake Hands With the Devil*.) What do more recent cases of mass rights violation say about human rights in the world community?

WEBSITES FOR FURTHER RESEARCH

Amnesty International www.amnesty.org
– leading NGO dedicated to ending human rights abuses worldwide

Bayefsky www.bayefsky.com
– for International Human Rights Law

Carnegie Council www.carnegiecouncil.org
– for information on ethics and social justice in international affairs

Human Rights Watch www.hrw.org
– NGO dedicated to promoting international human rights

UN High Commissioner for Human Rights www.ohchr.org
– for information on the UN's position on issues affecting human rights

NOTES

1. United Nations, *Universal Declaration of Human Rights* (1948). Full text: www.un.org/en/documents/udhr

2. B. Orend, *Human Rights: Concept and Context* (Peterborough, ON: Broadview Press, 2002). The contemporary human rights movement also drew heavily on a pre-existing "natural rights" tradition: see pp. 191–212.

3. M. Gilbert, *The Holocaust* (New York: Henry Holt, 1987).

4. Orend, *Human Rights* (op. cit., note 2); J. Caplan, *Nazi Germany* (Oxford: Oxford University Press, 2008).

5. M. Glendon, *A World Made New: Eleanor Roosevelt and The Universal Declaration of Human Rights* (New York: Random House, 2002).

6. J. Donnelly, *Universal Human Rights in Theory and Practice* (Ithaca, NY: Cornell University Press, 2nd edn, 2002).

7. J. Nickel, *Making Sense of Human Rights* (Berkeley, CA: University of California Press, 1987). See also A. Gewirth, *Human Rights* (Chicago: University of Chicago Press, 1982).

8. Orend, *Human Rights* (op. cit., note 2), pp. 155–88. But see, too, A. Pollis & P. Schwab, *Human Rights: Cultural and Ideological Perspectives* (New York: Praeger, 1979).

9. J. Narveson, *Respecting Persons in Theory and Practice* (New York: Rowman & Littlefield, 2002). See also D. Gauthier, *Morals by Agreement* (Oxford: Clarendon, 1986).

10. J. Rawls, *A Theory of Justice* (Cambridge, MA: Harvard University Press, 1971).

11. M. Walzer, *Thick and Thin* (Notre Dame, IN: Notre Dame University Press, 1994).

12. T. Pogge, *Realizing Rawls* (Ithaca, NY: Cornell University Press, 1989).

13. John Stuart Mill, *On Liberty* (Indianapolis, IN: Hackett, 1978 [1859]).

14. C. Graham, *Happiness Around the World* (Oxford: Oxford University Press, 2009); M. Seligman, *Authentic Happiness* (New York: The Free Press, 2002).

15. L. Sonneborn, *The End of Apartheid in South Africa* (New York: Chelsea House, 2008).

16. R. Dworkin, *Taking Rights Seriously* (Cambridge, MA: Harvard University Press, 1977).

17. Pogge, *Realizing Rawls* (op. cit., note 12).

18. T. Pogge, *World Poverty and Human Rights* (London: Polity, 2008).

19. Orend, *Human Rights* (op. cit., note 2), pp. 101–54.

20. Orend, *Human Rights* (op. cit., note 2), pp. 15–36.

21. *Twenty-Five Human Rights Documents* (New York: Columbia University Center for the Study of Human Rights, 1995); M. Ishay, *The Human Rights Reader* (New York: Routledge, 1997).

22. H.J. Steiner & P. Alston, *International Human Rights in Context: Law, Politics, Morals* (Oxford: Oxford University Press, 2000).

23. B. Orend, "Justifying Socio-Economic Rights," in R. Howard-Hassmann & C. Welch, Jr, eds, *Economic Rights in Canada and the United States* (Philadelphia, PA: University of Pennsylvania Press, 2006), pp. 25–40.

24. R.P. Calude & B.H. Weston, eds, *Human Rights in the World Community* (Philadelphia, PA: Penn State University Press, 3rd edn, 2006).

25. A. Vincent, *The Politics of Human Rights* (Oxford: Oxford University Press, 2010); M. Ishay, *The History of Human Rights* (Berkeley, CA: University of California Press, 2008).

26. S. Hick, *Human Rights and The Internet* (London: Palgrave Macmillan, 2010).

27. *Twenty-Five Human Rights Documents* (op. cit., note 21). See also the superb www.bayefsky.com

28. A. Iriye, et al., *The Human Rights Revolution* (Oxford: Oxford University Press, 2012).

29. A. McBeth, et al., *The International Law of Human Rights* (Oxford: Oxford University Press, 2012).

30. Office of the UN High Commissioner on Human Rights, www.ohchr.org

31. McBeth, et al., *International Law* (op. cit., note 29).

32. A. Hegarty & S. Leonard, *Human Rights: An Agenda for the 21st Century* (New York: Routledge, 1999).
33. M. Janis, et al., *European Human Rights Law* (Oxford: Oxford University Press, 2008).
34. H. Shue, *Basic Rights: Subsistence, Affluence and U.S. Foreign Policy* (Princeton: Princeton University Press, 2nd edn, 1996).
35. D. Hope, *China's Human Rights Record* (Victoria, NZ: University of Wellington Press, 2007).
36. B. Orend, "Crisis in Kosovo: A Just Use of Force?" *Politics* (1999), pp. 125–30; D. Rieff, *Slaughterhouse: Bosnia and The Failure of The West* (New York: Simon & Schuster, 1995); T. Judah, *Kosovo: War and Revenge* (New Haven, CT: Yale University Press, 2002).
37. A. Clapham, *Human Rights: A Very Short Introduction* (Oxford: Oxford University Press, 2007).
38. L. Noueihed & A. Warren, *The Battle for The Arab Spring* (New Haven, CT: Yale University Press, 2012). See also "The Interactive Timeline of the Arab Spring" by the UK's *Guardian* newspaper, at www.guardian.cok.uk
39. W. Korey, *NGOs and The Universal Declaration of Human Rights* (London: Palgrave Macmillan, 2001).
40. A. Hudock, *NGOs and Civil Society* (Cambridge: Polity, 2001); D. Forsythe, *Human Rights in International Relations* (Cambridge: Cambridge University Press, 2006).
41. M. Nussbaum, *Women and Human Development: The Capabilities Approach* (Cambridge: Cambridge University Press, 2001).
42. S. Ross, *Women's Human Rights: The International and Comparative Law Case Book* (Philadelphia, PA: University of Pennsylvania Press, 2008).
43. UNICEF, *2007 Report on the State of the World's Children* (New York: United Nations, 2007); www.globalissues.org ("Women's Rights"); N. Reilly, *Women's Human Rights: Seeking Gender Justice in a Globalising Age* (Cambridge: Policy, 2009).
44. R. Emerton, *Women's Human Rights: Leading International and National Cases* (New York: Routledge, 2005).
45. D. Bergoffer, et al., eds, *Confronting Global Gender Justice* (London: Routledge, 2010).
46. Human Rights Watch, *Global Women's Rights* (New Haven, CT: Yale University Press, 1995).
47. N. Thomsen & K. Culler-DuPont, *Women's Rights* (London: Facts-on-File, 2012).
48. M. Worden, ed., *The Unfinished Revolution: The Global Fight for Women's Rights* (London: Seven Stories, 2012).
49. R. Cook, *The Human Rights of Women* (Philadelphia, PA: University of Pennsylvania Press, 1994).
50. J. Miron, ed., *A History of Human Rights in Canada* (Toronto: Canadian Scholar's Press, 2009); A. Lui, *Why Canada Cares: Human Rights and Foreign Policy in Theory and Practice* (Montreal: McGill–Queen's University Press, 2012); Human Rights Watch, *World Report 2010* (New York: Human Rights Watch, 2010)—this is an annual report stretching back several years, on all the major countries and how well they do on rights realization.

Global Public Health*

"Many political borders serve as semi-permeable membranes, often open to disease and yet closed to the free movement of cures." —*Paul Farmer (b. 1959), professor of medical anthropology at Harvard University*[1]

LEARNING OBJECTIVES

After studying this chapter, you will be able to:

▸ define all the bolded key terms and concepts

▸ grasp how health interconnects with all other fields of international studies

▸ appreciate more fully what health and sickness mean, and the role of various health authorities in promoting well-being

▸ describe the largest and most important challenges confronting those who care about global public health, and explain and evaluate some of the proposed solutions

▸ have particular appreciation of "the social determinants of health," and the connection between socio-economic inequalities and the spread of disease and death (culminating in "the global inverse healthcare law")

▸ reflect, overall, on the significance of topical case studies examining maternal and baby health, tobacco, smallpox, North versus South, new health technologies, the distribution of food and water, differences in healthcare systems, and the health status of Canadian Aboriginal peoples.

INTRODUCTION

Global public health is one of the hottest, emerging topics in international studies. Only recently has its importance, and solid research about it, become understood. In this chapter, we shall define what health and sickness are, and canvass which health authorities are responsible for promoting the former, and fighting the latter. The quote above suggests that, while disease flows freely across borders, too often national governments have failed to co-operate effectively in solving common global health problems. We will come to understand what the major challenges are to global public health, giving equal time to creative proposals for their solution, or at least betterment. Though a clear picture will emerge of vastly different healthcare experiences around the world, it's clear that all of us are united in wanting health, and improved health status, for ourselves and for our societies.

---

*This chapter was co-authored by **Jennifer E. McWhirter**, PhD candidate at the School of Public Health and Health Systems, University of Waterloo.

HEALTH AND HISTORY

In spite of its newness as a field of study, global public health has been an issue throughout much of human history, impacting not only the lives of individuals but also the fate of nations. Consider just a few of the fascinating ways that health and history have come together:

- **The bubonic plague** (sometimes called the **Black Death**) travelled along the **Silk Road trading route** from China into Constantinople (present-day Istanbul), and from there into Europe, where it killed at least 25 per cent—and perhaps as much as 60 per cent—of the population in just 50 short years, between 1350 and 1400. This forever altered Europe's destiny. Research suggests that the plague spurred both **the Protestant Reformation** (beginning in 1517—see Chapter 1) and **the Scientific Revolution** (starting around 1550—see Chapter 2). In the first case, according to the theory, people interpreted the plague as God's punishment for their old religious failings, and so they sought to overcome them with a new religion. In the second, the plague prompted people to turn to science, instead of religion, to explain and deal with such devastating outbreaks of disease.[2]

- When Europeans set out to conquer the Americas and Australia—after their "discovery" of the New World in 1492—they found that the indigenous peoples living there lacked robust immunity to **smallpox** (discussed at length later in the chapter). There are those who believe that some Europeans made "gifts" of smallpox-infested blankets to the Aboriginal peoples, knowing that this would decimate these populations and ease the way for European settlers. Some historians, like E.A. Fox, have gone as far as likening this to the use of biological weapons in an armed invasion.[3]

- Outbreaks of disease and **famine** (i.e. crises of mass starvation) have often spurred large-scale emigration and diasporas. One of the more famous of these mass migrations occurred during Ireland's Great Potato Famine in the 1840s, when many Irish immigrated to North America.[4]

- For much of human history, health and medical knowledge have been appallingly bad, ill-informed and based as much (or more) on superstition as on fact. As a result, health-related behaviours have been, historically, deeply dubious and even dangerous. Before the 1900s, for instance, very few populations bathed or washed their hands regularly, had access to drinkable water and sufficient protein, or had ever seen a doctor or nurse in their whole lives. No wonder, then, that the average life expectancy of human beings worldwide was only about 30 years (!) before the Scientific Revolution began. The world average today is about 68 years. Improving hygiene and our understanding of health makes a profound difference on the length and quality of everyone's life.[5]

- Earth's human population used to grow at a slow and measured pace, often suffering setbacks during times of war, disease, starvation, and **drought** (unusually dry, rain-starved conditions that can kill crops and diminish the supply of water and food to crisis levels). But following improvements in healthcare (especially basic hygiene and **immunization**), as well as in agriculture and nutrition (crop yields, in particular), the human population hit a **tipping point** around 1750, and since then has not only *never fallen again* but, in fact, has *only exploded upward*, soaring, as we saw in Chapter 2, from about 1 billion in 1800 to almost 7 billion today. This incredible growth has had enormous implications for society, for pollution and the environment, and for the challenge of ensuring human wellness into the future.[6]

GLOBAL PUBLIC HEALTH AND OTHER FIELDS OF INTERNATIONAL STUDIES

One of the aims of this text has been to show how the different fields of international studies interrelate—for example, how population growth affects the environment, or how armed conflict affects the economy, and vice versa. These connections might not seem so obvious with global public health, and so it's worth our while to highlight them:

- There's an emerging field called **health and human rights**. It's concerned with arguing in favour of everyone's right to certain minimum standards of healthcare, but also with examining how violations of human rights (and not just rights like physical security but also more abstract claims, like equality) can lead to serious health problems and sickness. People active in this field work to uncover and publicize convincing evidence to link a country's poor human rights record to poor public health outcomes.[7]

- Another emerging discipline is **peace through health**. Scholars in this field argue that an often overlooked impact of war is its effect on public health. War affects the health and well-being of soldiers, of course, but also the health of their families and of civilian populations caught amid the fighting. The many physical and psychological traumas of armed conflict can affect millions of people and can last for decades following the end of battle.

- War also destroys infrastructure, including such public health infrastructure as hospitals, sewers, and water treatment and distribution facilities. As a result, war often leaves severe outbreaks of disease in its wake. A notorious example is the **Spanish flu pandemic** of 1919–20, which followed World War I and is estimated to have killed between 50 million and 100 million people worldwide—more than the war itself!

- War also, generally, consumes vast precious resources that could otherwise be spent on health. The peace through health movement advocates that prioritizing healthcare would, necessarily, leave fewer resources for war. Therefore, public health initiatives won't just improve the well-being of individuals: they will also contribute to a more peaceful world. There's another underlying conviction here: people who are truly healthy and happy won't involve themselves in something as dark and destructive as warfare.[8]

- There are significant connections between global public health and international law and organization, too. The UN's **World Health Organization** (WHO), based in Geneva, operates with the mandate to improve global public health.[9] The human right to minimally decent healthcare is enshrined in Article 12 of the International Covenant on Economic, Social, and Cultural Rights (ICESCR), which reads: "The States Parties to the present Covenant recognize the right of everyone to the enjoyment of *the highest attainable standard of physical and mental health* [emphasis

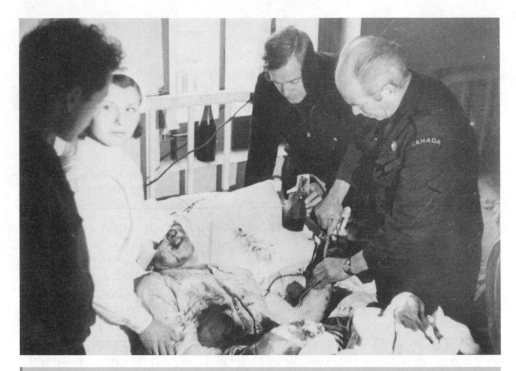

Dr Norman Bethune (right) performs a blood transfusion during the Spanish Civil War (1936–9). The Canadian thoracic surgeon made a vital contribution to the war when he established the first ever mobile blood transfusion service. How does this development fit within the history of global public health? (Geza Karpathi/Bibliothèque et Archives Canada/C-067451)

added]." There's also a recent treaty, in force as of 2007, establishing international health regulations and binding all UN member countries to co-operate in fighting the global spread of infectious disease.[10]

- Health has strong connections to the environment. Pollution causes many illnesses, and sick people are less likely to have the wherewithal to escape, or clean up, such dirty environments. There can thus develop a grim cycle of poverty and underdevelopment, and sickness and pollution, creating sad, persistent pockets of struggle and desperation.[11]

- In terms of aid, trade, and development, it's obvious that a sick population cannot work productively and contribute constructively to the growth potential of its society. To develop further, and to engage with the rest of the world economy, a country's people need to be healthy and capable.[12]

- Finally, health has robust connections even to the twin pillars of hard power: economic growth and military strength. After all, sick people cannot serve in the armed forces, nor can they participate in the economy as active producers, labourers, and entrepreneurs. And so, even the staunchest realist has strong reasons to want public health promoted in the general population at home. Indeed, the realist even has

A young girl walks through her backyard—a garbage dump—in Mexico City. What are some of the connections between health and living environment? (© Milan Klusacek/iStockphoto)

reason to be concerned about *global* public health, as pandemics, germs, and disease respect no national borders; and they can—and do—cross easily into even the most developed societies, sparking outbreaks of disease and even quite costly health crises. Consider, for example, how in the spring of 2003 SARS (severe acute respiratory syndrome) quickly spread from China and Vietnam into North American cities like New York and Toronto. (See Figure 10.1 below.)[13]

WHAT IS HEALTH?

Having looked at the historical context, and the connections to other aspects of international studies, we are now well positioned to launch our discussion of global public health. We need, then, to define three things: health, public health, and the global aspect of public health. In terms of the first, consider the WHO's oft-cited definition of **health** as "a state of complete physical, mental, and social well-being, and not merely the absence of disease or infirmity."[14] Or consider once more the language from the above-cited ICESCR, which resoundingly declares every person's right to "the highest attainable standard of physical and mental health." It is safe to say that these are **maximalist**, idealistic, and ambitious concepts of health, in that they seem to equate health with *perfect* health—i.e. optimal, fully developed, and even flawless human functioning.

Many critics have found this maximalist conception too idealistic, lacking in both restraint and realism. They propose, instead, a less ambitious standard of health— something more along the lines of Walter Glannon's useful definition of **health** as "the reasonably good functioning—both physical and mental—of a *normal* person within a

FIGURE 10.1 The Spread of SARS

Source: Based on www.scientific-computing.com/features/feature.php?feature_id=166

normal life span."[15] (**Sickness** or **illness** would thus be defined as bad or impaired functioning in the body or mind: an abnormal, obstructed, or damaged functioning that falls below the standard of what is reasonably good or normally achievable.) Simply put, when you're healthy, things work and you can function; when you're ill, you cannot function normally. Keeping this much more achievable standard of health—as normal functioning—in mind, consider what Figure 10.2 shows to be the major components of health.

WHAT IS PUBLIC HEALTH?

Public health differs from the practice of medicine. **Medicine** is focused *on individuals*—diagnosis, prognosis, treatment—whereas **public health** is focused on the health *of an entire nation*. Medicine, then, is *patient-focused*, whereas public health is *population-focused*. Medicine also tends to be more focused on treatment, such as when a patient visits a doctor because she's feeling sick. Public health, by contrast, is concerned more with prevention than with treatment. In many ways, the goal of public health is to prevent illness from happening, or from becoming widespread, rather than to treat it or cure it once it's already developed. This approach is desired not only to prevent suffering but also for reasons of cost and efficacy: as they (used to) say, "an ounce of prevention is worth a pound of cure."

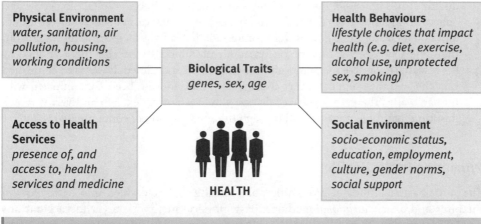

FIGURE 10.2 The Basic Elements of Health

Sources: Adapted from R. Skolnik, *Essentials of Global Health* (Sudbury, MA: Jones and Bartlett Publishers, 2008), p. 19; and based on determinants of health listed by the Public Health Agency of Canada, www.phac-aspc.gc.ca/ph-sp/determinants/index-eng.php.

A more comprehensive definition of **public health** is thus that it is concerned with

1. preventing disease and illness,
2. prolonging life, and
3. promoting health *during* life, through
4. the organized efforts of health professionals and health institutions.

Generally, public health is about trying to augment the overall health conditions of a population.[16]

Case Study: John Snow and the Tracing of a Cholera Outbreak

John Snow (1813–1858) was an English doctor, widely considered a pioneer in the field of epidemiology because of his role in sourcing a cholera outbreak in London in 1854. **Epidemiology** is the branch of medicine concerned with the spread and control of diseases and other conditions affecting public health. **Cholera** is an intestinal infection caused by bacteria in contaminated food and water; it causes diarrhea and vomiting and, if untreated, death from dehydration.

At the time of the London outbreak, it was common to believe that diseases like cholera were caused by breathing in "bad air" (this is known as **the miasma theory**). The correct theory—**the germ theory** (i.e. that microorganisms, like bacteria and viruses, cause disease)—would not become known until after Snow died. The good doctor visited houses in the area of the cholera outbreak in order to talk to people and collect information from them. He also mapped where the cases of cholera were found, and noted that all these homes were connected: they all got their drinking water from the same source, a water pump on Broad Street. Officials were convinced enough by his research to disable the pump, and the cholera cases declined. It was later confirmed that the well that supplied water to the pump had, indeed, been contaminated with human waste. The germ theory of disease would later help explain and verify Snow's intuition that cholera was spread through the consumption of contaminated water.[17]

Promoting Public Health

The most basic methods of promoting public health can be divided into basic *physical* methods and basic *educational* methods. Basic physical methods start with **vaccinations** and **immunizations** to prevent disease. At the community level, physical methods include:

- having functioning sewers and garbage dumps to separate garbage and waste from the population

- ensuring that people have access to clean, drinkable water (through water treatment and chlorination), along with access to sufficient food, clothing, and shelter

- draining stagnant water, to prevent mosquitoes, which spread many diseases

- gathering as much information about disease and death as possible (following the principles of epidemiology)

- having some health and safety measures in force in workplaces (to prevent work-related accidents and injuries) and in homes (to prevent, e.g., overcrowding and slum conditions).[18]

In terms of basic education methods, public health professionals work to promote "health literacy," which is, loosely, knowledge about the basic components of health:

- **hydration** (i.e. drinking enough water)

- **nutrition** (i.e. healthy eating)

- regular exercise

- good sleep

- **hygiene** (i.e. regular bathing and frequent hand-washing)

- avoiding such destructive addictions as smoking and drinking.

But, as we all realize, sometimes knowledge is *not* enough: it's the actual behaviour that makes the difference. And so public health officials try *not merely* to educate but also *to motivate*, for instance by promoting hand-washing and distributing hand sanitizer; distributing condoms; and lobbying for, and supporting, aggressive anti-tobacco measures. Summing it up, the WHO has defined **health literacy** more comprehensively as "the cognitive and social skills which determine the motivation and ability of individuals to gain access to, understand, and use, information in ways which promote and maintain good health."[19]

Public health is also very much concerned with (1) the extent of healthcare measures and coverage across a population; (2) the competence, quality, and efficiency of healthcare systems; and (3) the existence of effective plans to respond to sudden, sharp health crises, such as the recent SARS outbreak. We might conclude, then, that public health is concerned with threats to the overall health of a community, and with implementing the most basic and widespread measures for ensuring good general, or background, conditions for healthy living.[20]

Public Health Authorities

Most countries have public health units, departments, or ministries that are mandated to advance public health measures (as defined above). These range from local/regional public health offices to provincial/state-level ministries or departments of health. At the highest level, there are national departments/ministries of public health. Canada has both a federal Ministry of Health and Long-Term Care and individual health ministries or departments for every province and territory. The United States has its Public Health Service, which is headed by the surgeon general; there are also the National Institutes of Health (NIH) and the Centre for Disease Control (CDC), prestigious research institutes that gather public health data and perform advanced research on public health methods.[21]

Globally, as we've already seen, the major body overseeing public health is the World Health Organization, with a growing annual budget of between US$3 billion and US$5 billion. In addition to this international governmental organization there are various NGOs. Arguably, the most important is the Bill and Melinda Gates Foundation (funded by the Microsoft founder), which provides the most direct global public health funding of *any* organization, including the WHO and the US federal government. The foundation has an endowment of over US$36 billion (which is scheduled to grow to $60 billion with a donation from legendary investor Warren Buffet) and has annual payouts of over $3 billion in direct grants.[22] Another vitally important public health NGO is Médecins Sans Frontières (Doctors Without Borders), whose doctors volunteer their services throughout the developing world. A similarly important organization, Engineers Without Borders, focuses on building wells for providing drinking water. (There are a number of development agencies actively at work in this field, and they will be discussed in the forthcoming chapter on aid and development.)[23]

The Social Determinants of Health

Of special concern to all these public health authorities is a set of factors known collectively as **the social determinants of health**. These are aspects of social life and social organization (as opposed to individual biology or lifestyle choice) that have been proven to have substantial impact on a person's **health status** (i.e. the degree to which a person is either healthy or sick). The social determinants of health are, so to speak, "the causes of the causes" of illness: they create the context in which genes become disordered, or in which bad lifestyle choices become much more likely, producing sickness and disease (see Table 10.1).[24]

TABLE 10.1 The Social Determinants of Health

Social Determinant of Health	Description and Rationale
Income	Perhaps the most important social determinant of health: low income causes material and social deprivation, leading to ill health.
The social gradient	Health conditions are worse the farther down "the social ladder" one is.
Stress	Stressful circumstances adversely affect health because stress affects the hormones and nervous system, causing damage to the body over time.
Early life	Foundations of adult health are laid in early childhood and even before birth (i.e. during pregnancy, when the mother's health and nutrition are important to the unborn child).
Social exclusion	Social exclusion creates barriers to *education and access to health services*, and is psychologically damaging, thus increasing poverty and illness.
Social support	Social supports (friendships) improve health because they offer both emotional and practical resources and often influence positive health behaviours.
Employment and working conditions	Health risks associated with work can include *stress*, feelings of lack of control, exposure to harmful substances, repetitive strain, long hours, and dangerous physical labour.
Unemployment	Both job insecurity and the actual loss of employment can cause *stress* and depression and other medical problems, and can affect *income* (discussed above).
Food	A healthy diet is essential for good health, but may be influenced by how affordable or accessible nutritious food is.
Addiction	Alcohol, drug, and tobacco use are both a cause of and a response to social and economic disadvantage. They lead directly (e.g. cancer) and indirectly (e.g. job loss) to health problems.
Transportation	Healthy transportation means fewer road traffic accidents and more exercise. A lengthy commute can adversely affect health.
Education	People with higher education tend to be healthier than those with lower education, and this is closely tied to other social determinants (e.g. *income, unemployment*).
Access to health services	The sick need to be treated, but access may be influenced by the ability to pay for care, or the ability to take time off work to seek it.
Housing	Low-quality housing and homelessness negatively impact health (e.g. overcrowding increases transmission of disease).
Discrimination by social group (e.g. gender, ethnic group, disability)	Discrimination results in barriers to employment (reducing *income*), adequate *housing, health services,* and *education*, and causes *social exclusion* (see above).

Source: See especially M. Marmot & R. Wilkinson, eds. *The Social Determinants of Health* (Oxford: Oxford University Press, 2nd edn, 2005).

A TALE OF TWO CITIES: NORTH VERSUS SOUTH

Putting all of the above together, we can conclude that **global public health** is concerned with trying to augment the general health of the whole world's human population. But there are many—and massive—obstacles to meeting this objective. Not least of these is the fact that, as with so many areas of concern in international studies, there is a huge gap between the developed and developing worlds, in terms both of objective reality and of subjective experience. Consider three facts especially:

1. The average **life expectancy** is around 80 years in the developed world and just over 60 years in the developing world. That leaves a shocking 20-year gap in terms of the length of life itself. Indeed, as of 2010, the country with the longest average life expectancy is Monaco, at 89 years—a whopping 50 years more than the 39-year life expectancy of residents of Angola, at the very bottom of the chart. Life expectancy is the length of life one can, on average, expect to enjoy at birth looking forward. It is one of the most frequently cited and authoritative measures of public health, as it is seen to encapsulate within it so many of the other factors—social and individual—of health status.[25]

2. **Infant mortality** (i.e. the rate at which newborns die) it is on average roughly 6 per 1,000 live births in the developed world and about 70 per 1,000 in the developing world. The best rate is found, again, in Monaco, where just 1.79 out of every 1,000 infants die. The worst rate is, again, in Angola, where the infant mortality rate is 176 per 1,000, meaning that a whopping 17.6 per cent of all births in that country result in death shortly thereafter.[26]

3. The **global burden of disease** has to do with the difference between the **diseases of affluence** and the **diseases of poverty**—in other words, the main diseases (and causes of injury and death) in high-income, developed societies versus those in low-income, developing societies.

    It is important here to distinguish between infectious diseases and chronic diseases. **Infectious diseases** are those spread by infectious agents (e.g. bacteria, viruses, and parasites). Some are spread from person to person, but others (called **zoonotic diseases**) are spread from animals to people (e.g. swine flu) or from insects to people (e.g. malaria, as spread by mosquitoes). Examples of infectious diseases range from the common cold and influenza (i.e. the flu) to cholera, smallpox, malaria, measles, tuberculosis, and HIV/AIDS. **Chronic diseases**, by contrast, are *not* caused by infectious agents: in other words, they cannot be "caught." They are long-lasting diseases that progress slowly. They are frequently exacerbated by lifestyle choices and tend to have an onset later in life. Examples of chronic diseases include heart disease, stroke, cancer, diabetes, and chronic respiratory diseases (like emphysema).[27]

    In the developing world, infectious diseases remain major sources of both morbidity and mortality. (**Morbidity** is the cause or rate of sickness and disease; **mortality** is the cause or rate of death.) Table 10.2 charts, in descending order, the top 10 causes of death in the developed and developing worlds, according to the WHO. As you can see, the list of causes in the developing world includes such diseases as lower lung infection, HIV/AIDS, malaria, tuberculosis, neonatal infection, and complications from diarrhea, itself usually caused by water-borne agents. In other words, of the top 10

TABLE 10.2 Top 10 Causes of Death, Developing and Developed Worlds, 2008–10

	Developing World	Developed World
1	lower lung infection (pneumonia, influenza, etc.)	heart disease
2	complications from diarrhea	stroke
3	HIV/AIDS	lung cancer
4	heart disease	Alzheimer's
5	malaria	lower lung infection
6	stroke	colon/rectal cancer
7	tuberculosis	complications from diabetes
8	complications from premature birth	breast cancer
9	neonatal infection	stomach cancer
10	complications from birth trauma	road traffic accidents

Source: Adapted from World Health Organization, www.who.int/mediacentre/factsheets/fs310/en/index.html; B. Scaglia, *The Big Book of Death* (New York: Webster's, 2011).

causes of death in the developing world, the only ones that are *not* infectious diseases are heart disease, stroke, and complications either from premature birth or birth itself. In the developed world, by contrast, the *only* item in the top 10 causes of death that *is* infectious is lower lung infection (e.g. the flu, pneumonia). But this is in the middle of the list. Overwhelmingly, the top two causes of death are heart disease/stroke and cancer (in all its forms, with lung cancer being the leading one).[28]

The two cause-of-death lists in Table 10.2 are thus strikingly different. Consider some further facts that highlight the contrast between developed and developing worlds:

- HIV/AIDS is the leading killer of adults in Africa, whereas in the US, the top killer is heart disease.

- About 400 million people worldwide are infected with malaria every year; the disease kills roughly 1 million of those infected, almost all of them (90 per cent) in Africa.

- A total of 165,000 children die every year from measles, even though the immunization agent has been available in the Global North for over 40 years, and the total cost to make and distribute the agent would be US$1 per child.

- Tuberculosis (TB) still kills 2 million people every year, despite the fact that a cure has been available in the developed world for decades.

- It is estimated that 2.2 million children (under 12) in the Global South die every year from failure to receive the same immunizations and vaccinations that children in the North receive.

Interesting to note is the fact that cancer did not make the top 10 causes of death for the developing world at all. Is cancer, then, a "disease of affluence?" The research may suggest so, for now, but it is predicted that cancer will soon break into the developing world's "top 10" as the effects of the widespread growth of smoking in China and India take hold. Deaths from automobile accidents are also predicted to rise as the motor-owning middle-class grows rapidly in China and India in the decades to come.[29]

Worldmapper is an organization that illustrates certain statistics graphically using maps that have been altered to reflect certain numerical data. Figure 10.3, showing deaths from

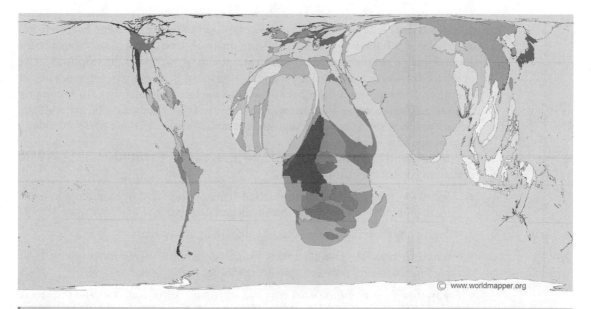

© www.worldmapper.org

FIGURE 10.3 Worldmapper's Representation of Easily Preventable Deaths Worldwide

Territories are sized in proportion to the absolute number of people who died from most preventable conditions in one year [2002]. In rich territories, deaths from most of these conditions are much lower except for infections in the elderly. For this reason they can be considered easily preventable conditions.

These conditions are divided into the following categories (with their contribution to the total deaths):

A. Infections/Infectious and parasitic diseases (59% of deaths). These are diseases spread directly or indirectly from person to person.
B. Respiratory infections (22% of deaths). These are infections of the ears and respiratory tract.
C. Maternal conditions (3% of deaths). These are conditions affecting women before, during, and after childbirth.
D. Perinatal conditions (13% of deaths). These are conditions arising in babies before or within one week of birth.
E. Nutritional deficiencies (3% of deaths). These are conditions due to food, vitamin, and mineral shortages.

These conditions caused 32% of all deaths worldwide in 2002, an average of 2,968 deaths per million people.

Source: Worldmapper, www.worldmapper.org/display_extra.php?selected=371. © Copyright SASI Group (University of Sheffield) and Mark Newman (University of Michigan).

preventable causes, is a fascinating example. Before examining it, consult an ordinary map of the world from your favourite source. Then, contrast it with the Worldmapper map in Figure 10.3. The latter shows a visual "bloating" of countries, based on the number of easily preventable deaths from disease and illness. Take note of how grossly distended the regions of the Global South become, and how shrivelled become those of the developed world.

Case Study: The Global Tobacco Epidemic

Tobacco use (via both cigarettes and chewing tobacco) is the *leading cause of preventable illness and death in the world*. Tobacco kills up to half of its users, and there are an estimated 1 billion smokers worldwide. In total, tobacco use is responsible for about 5 million deaths per year, or the death of almost 1 in 10 adults worldwide. Use of tobacco products is increasing on a global scale but decreasing in some developed countries. Smoking rates have been shown to decline significantly with increasing income and educational attainment. Tobacco use is a major cause of many of the world's deadliest diseases, including cardiovascular disease, chronic obstructive lung disease, and lung cancer.

In an effort to control the global tobacco epidemic, global health officials have concentrated on three main strategies:

1. increasing taxes on tobacco products, driving up their cost in an attempt to make them prohibitively expensive, thereby decreasing their use

2. controlling how and where tobacco companies can advertise

3. requiring cigarette manufacturers to include graphic image warnings on their packages, showing gruesome pictures of things like lung and oral cancer.

Globally, though, such efforts exist only in a small number of countries and thus serve only a small percentage of the world's population.

An important effort in the fight to control tobacco use is the creation of the WHO Framework Convention on Tobacco Control, which aims to protect people from the negative consequences of tobacco use by reducing consumption and exposure to tobacco smoke. It's a binding treaty (see Chapter 5) that has been signed by over 170 countries. It aims to accomplish its goals through pricing and taxation strategies, and through such non-taxation strategies as banning pro-tobacco advertising, increasing public awareness of tobacco's harmful effects, and protecting people from second-hand smoke in public places. Since its adoption by the World Health Assembly in May 2003, it has become one of the mostly widely embraced treaties in UN history.[30]

Improving Global Public Health

Global public health officials have a number of tactics for improving health worldwide. These include:

- vaccinations and inoculations
- distributing vitamins

- eradicating mosquitoes (through insecticide use and by draining standing water)
- sex education and condom distribution
- promoting exercise and nutrition
- augmenting health literacy.

But in addition to tackling tobacco, public health officials focus on four main areas in the fight to improve global public health:

1. reliable daily access to clean, drinkable water

2. access to nutritious food with sufficient calories

3. access to basic sanitation

4. access to a healthcare system that can be responsive, should preventative measures fail and individual treatment be needed.

We'll take a closer look at each of these in turn.

1. *Water*

Potable water—i.e. clean, drinkable water—is the most immediate vital human need, next to breathable air and sufficient oxygen. Nearly everyone in the developed world has secure access to potable water; in the developing world, by contrast, it is estimated that some-where between 1.1 and 1.2 billion people do *not* have secure access to drinkable water. For this reason, the construction and maintenance of water wells and proper water treatment and distribution systems are very high priorities in addressing this situation.

Another priority is making oral rehydration therapy, or ORT, available when emergencies arise from lack of potable water. ORT is a salt/sugar remedy that aids fluid retention, preventing children especially from dying of dehydration via diarrhea. An ORT packet costs only 2 cents (US) to produce.[31]

2. *Food*

Experts from organizations like the WHO and UNICEF estimate that about 1 billion people globally—with women and children in the developing world making up the vast majority—lack the minimal calorie intake needed for their stage of growth and life. Hunger and poor nutrition are thought to account for about 36 million deaths a year, and 20 million children are thought to be "severely malnourished" at any given time—nearly all of them in the Global South. Indeed, one of the sharpest contrasts between South and North is that being *hungry* and *underweight* is a major problem in the former, whereas *overeating* and being *overweight* are major problems in the latter. UNICEF, for example, reports that 28 per cent of children (under age 12) in the Global South are underweight; by contrast, in the United States, close to the same percentage of children (22 per cent) are either overweight or fully obese. Each condition gives rise to its own future health problems. With being underweight come stunted or challenged development, nutrient deficiency and bone loss, and a weak-ened immune system (which can result in further kinds of infections and illnesses). The negative health consequences of being overweight include a greater likelihood of diabetes, arthritis, heart disease, and some cancers, especially of the gall bladder and the colon.[32]

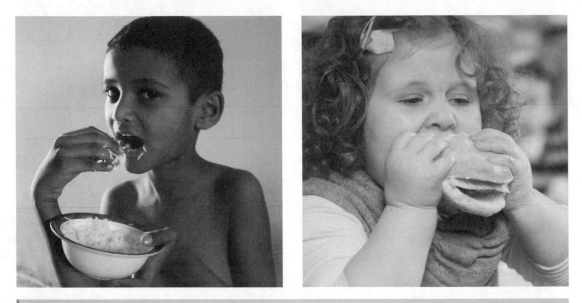

How would you tackle the disparity in the amount of *nutritious* food available in the North and the South?
(© Aman Khan/iStockphoto; © fatihhoca/iStockphoto)

Food problems in the South and in the North are very different. The amount of food wasted in the North is enormous, and the growth of obesity shows widespread problems relating to portion control, psychological issues with food, and—in spite of education and good access to information—a surprisingly high level of illiteracy about correct and healthful nutrition. Poor food choices are a real problem, whereas, in the Global South, the main problem is getting access to sufficient food at all. Experts agree that this is a *distribution* problem and *not a resource problem*: clearly (just look in any Western grocery store) there is enough food to go around, at least on a minimal calorie basis. The problem is ensuring fair and sustainable distribution of food in order to minimize the problems of obesity, food wastage, and unhealthy calories in the North, while ensuring that sufficient food resources are delivered to meet the minimum calorie requirements for everyone in the Global South. Aid agencies have come up with emergency food ration packs, which are very cheap to produce per unit. They stay edible for a long time, they require no refrigeration, and they have enough daily calories for a full-grown adult man. They are like toothpaste tubes filled with a form of peanut butter, heavily fortified with protein powder, sugar, sodium, and vitamins and minerals.[33]

3. *Sanitation*

The WHO estimates that about 2.6 billion people worldwide (but primarily in the developing world) lack secure daily access to basic sanitation services.[34] **Basic sanitation services** imply:

- access to water clean enough to bathe and wash one's hands in
- the separation of waste and garbage from living spaces

- some basic infrastructure for taking waste and garbage away and for bringing fresh water in. (It may also refer to access to electricity. Did you know that, in the developing world at this very moment, 1.6 billion people live with *no electricity whatsoever*?)

The reason sanitation is so vital is that sanitation problems have been shown to be the causes of dozens of some of the worst, most severe—yet also most preventable—diseases and illnesses. Two million children a year, for example, die from dehydration caused by diarrhea, itself almost always caused by drinking dirty water. Consider another fact: the Ganges River in India has 1.1 million litres of raw human sewage—urine and feces—dumped into it *every single minute* of *every single day*—a startling figure, considering that just one gram of feces in untreated water may contain up to 10 million viruses, 1 million bacteria, 1,000 parasite cysts, and 100 worm eggs.[35]

4. Healthcare

The WHO surmises that 1 billion people around the world—again, the clear majority being in the Global South, most of them women who live in the South's rural areas—lack access to *any* healthcare system at all.[36] In the developed world, by contrast, there are advanced and very sophisticated healthcare systems. These are **multi-tier healthcare systems**, featuring doctors, nurses, clinics, hospitals, research institutes, university departments, insurance companies, pharmaceutical companies, and various levels of government—themselves providing funding, insurance, regulation, and education—and these systems are *massive*, devouring large shares of the economic pie. For instance, in Canada's largest province, Ontario (with a population of 10 million), fully half of the entire budget of the provincial government goes to healthcare. In all of Canada, health as a sector of the economy is thought to represent about 9–11 per cent of the GDP; in the US, the number is thought to be 15–16 per cent of GDP. How do these numbers translate on a per capita basis? In 2009 in the US, total healthcare spending per capita was US$7,300; in Canada, it was US$3,800. (The OECD average—a reasonable proxy for the whole developed world—is about US$3,000 per person per year.) And how much do developing countries spend annually per capita on healthcare? Throughout Africa—which suffers the worst—experts estimate that the average is less than US$10 a year! Countries like Ethiopia spend only about $4 per person per year on healthcare. The WHO recently advocated that a minimally satisfactory number would be closer to US$60 per person per year.[37]

Two men drink from the Ganges River in India. Given what you've just read, what's your reaction to this photo? Would you bathe or wash your clothes in this water, much less drink it? (© Pep Roig/Alamy)

The reality is that the Global South suffers from extremely weak healthcare systems. The problems begin with severe human resources shortages: the **brain drain** of trained medical professionals leaving the South for the North is so serious that the WHO recently determined there are more Ethiopian-born doctors in Chicago than in *all of Ethiopia*. Those medical practitioners who *do* stay in the South face the colossal challenge of trying to treat massive populations with the most meagre of shoestring budgets. Consider the situation in Ethiopia: realistically, what medicines could be bought, stored, and effectively distributed to individuals (assuming they've been correctly diagnosed) on a per capita budget of $4 a year?[38]

> *There are more Ethiopian-born doctors in Chicago than in all of Ethiopia.*

In general, there's a consensus that the Global South, with about 75 per cent of the world's population, has only 30 per cent of the world's doctors and nurses. *Terrible infrastructure* makes the delivery of scarce healthcare resources difficult in the Global South, especially in rural areas, where roads are typically poor and refrigeration is non-existent, and yet where the people often display the greatest medical needs. *Political instability* and armed conflict can also block healthcare access. Finally, the developing world simply lacks access to some of the most needed medicines and treatments, as some of the world's largest producers/suppliers of drugs and medical equipment simply refuse to do business there, as they know the various governments don't have the ability to pay for their wares. This is the situation in parts of Africa, where HIV/AIDS is widespread and yet the drugs now used to best treat the virus are unavailable.[39]

A TALE OF TWO NEIGHBOURHOODS: NORTH VERSUS NORTH

The gap in healthcare resources doesn't exist only between North and South. One of the more interesting facts to emerge from the past few decades of health research is that a parallel gap exists *within* developed societies as well. It is consensus belief now, among public health experts like Michael Marmot, that the single greatest determinant of one's health status is socio-economic status, which, technically, includes not just one's annual income but also one's net worth, the prestige and influence of one's job and/or position in society, and one's level of education.[40] Greater than genetic endowment, greater than natural environment, greater even than personal choices about diet, exercise, and risky behaviours, one's income and socio-economic status correlate most strongly with one's health status. And it will come as no surprise to learn that, other things being equal, the *higher* one's socio-economic status, the *better* one's health; and, conversely, the *lower* one's status, the *poorer* one's health. Some illustrative facts:

> *It is consensus belief now that the single greatest determinant of one's health status is socio-economic status.*

- In breakthrough studies, known as Whitehall I and II, research teams led by noted epidemiologist and public health researcher Michael Marmot found that British civil servants at the bottom-most rungs of the corporate ladder were three times more likely to die an early death than those at the top.[41]

- In a surprising study, Canadian researchers found that movie actors who had won Academy Awards lived, on average, four years longer than their peers who had been nominated but had never won. Moreover, actors who had won more than one Oscar lived, on average, two years longer than those who had won only once.[42]

- Men who live in the wealthiest 20 per cent of Canada's neighbourhoods live, on average, more than four years longer than Canadian men living in the poorest 20 per cent; for women, the difference was two years.[43]

Marmot concludes, based on these and other data, that society is like the *Titanic*, the ill-fated luxury liner that sank on its maiden voyage across the icy Atlantic in 1912. After the ship hit the iceberg, first-class passengers survived on a disproportionate basis—in fact, almost all of them did. They had ready access to the lifeboats, they were assisted to the greatest degree by the crew, they were the first off the sinking vessel, and so on. Second-class passengers survived at a reduced rate, whereas almost all third-class passengers lost their lives in the dark, frigid ocean.[44]

Why do such strong associations—between wealth and health—exist? What have experts determined in this regard? Several things:

- Most clearly, *having more money provides one with more resources to deal with health challenges*. One can simply afford *more*, and *better*, healthcare.

- People with more money tend to have higher education and also ensure better education for their children. This means that *wealthier families usually have much higher health literacy than poorer people*. For example, in the US in 1995, 40 per cent of adult men whose peak educational attainment was high school or lower were confirmed habitual smokers; by contrast, only 14 per cent of adult male college graduates smoked.[45]

- *People with higher incomes tend to live in environments better for their health*. A Columbia University study showed that in the four biggest American cities, people living in the poorest neighbourhoods had a 70–90 per cent greater risk of heart disease than those living in the wealthiest neighbourhoods. Poorer neighbourhoods typically feature much greater pollution levels, population density, crime rates, and noise levels, as well as older infrastructure than exist in wealthy neighbourhoods. Rates of chronic stress, violence, illness, injury, and disease follow accordingly. There is also rock-solid evidence that poorer neighbourhoods have many more liquor stores, cigarette signs and sales, fast food restaurants, unemployed loiterers, drug dealers, prostitutes, and grocery stores with nowhere near the same quantity and quality of fresh produce and healthy eating options as suburban supermarkets.[46]

- *Our peer groups exert considerable pressure on our health and lifestyle choices*. We tend to socialize most with members of our own social class—in other words, our friends, our family, and our co-workers tend to share our socio-economic status. Since we are social creatures, we tend to share many of the same habits and lifestyle patterns of our peers. For example, the renowned Framingham Heart Study discovered that if your friend is obese, your odds of becoming obese increase by 57 per cent. If the friend is your *best* friend or significant other, odds of your own obesity go up by 171 per cent. As a result, some go far as to say that *health status is actually socially "contagious"*: you tend to get the same health problems as those around you. You get "infected" by either the health-positive or health-negative behaviours of those in your social network.[47]

Canadian Insights

The Health and Well-Being of Canada's Aboriginal Peoples

As we have seen, there are alarming differences in health, disease, and mortality between developed and developing countries. Even within countries, there can be great differences in the health outcomes of different populations. In Canada, a prime example of these differences is the disparity in health between the country's Aboriginal people and the rest of the Canadian population: the former simply do not enjoy the same quality of life as other Canadians and, as a result, have much poorer health outcomes.

Canadian Aboriginal people live shorter lives and suffer greater physical and mental health issues than their fellow Canadians do. The infant mortality rate among Aboriginal people is two to four times higher than it is for the rest of the Canadian population, and Aboriginal life expectancy overall is 10 years shorter for women and 13 years shorter for men. Aboriginal people also report lower levels of self-rated health compared to the rest of the Canadian population.

Aboriginal people are more likely than other Canadians to live in overcrowded housing (five to six times more likely for those living in the Far North or on reserve) and poor housing conditions (i.e. houses that are in great need of repair). These conditions lead to increased spread of illness, especially respiratory diseases like tuberculosis (TB). The incidence of TB in the general population is less than 1 per 100,000 people, but it is a shocking 158 per 100,000 people in the Aboriginal population.

Chronic diseases, as well as infectious diseases, are an issue for Canada's Aboriginal people. For example, the rate of type-2 diabetes is 11 per cent for Canadian Aboriginal people living on reserve but just 3 per cent for the general population. Poor diet and obesity are considered key contributors to diabetes, and poor dietary choices are very much connected to income and the cost and availability of healthy food. Because of the cost of shipping fresh produce, particularly during the winter months, it is much cheaper, in some places in the Far North, to purchase junk food like pop and chips than it is to buy fresh fruits and vegetables.

Many of these differences in health outcomes stem arguably from the poverty that Aboriginal people, including Aboriginal children, live in— whether on remote reserves or in the urban areas to which Aboriginal people are increasingly relocating. Consider that 80 per cent of urban Aboriginal children (under 6 years of age) live in poverty as it is defined by the UN. Aboriginal people have higher rates of unemployment than the rest of the Canadian population, and even those who are employed earn an average annual income that is one-third lower than it is for the rest of employed population ($22,000 vs $33,000).[48]

The important conclusion to draw is that not everyone in the developed world enjoys good health or decent healthcare. In fact, some studies show that certain especially vulnerable populations in the developed world—homeless drug addicts, some Aboriginal people living on remote reserves in Canada, some African and Latino Americans living in the toughest, poorest urban slums in the US, for example—carry health statuses *identical* to those of many people living in the developing world. There are deep pockets of poverty and health depravity in even the world's wealthiest societies. In terms of health, the *Titanic* is *everywhere*. Health inequality, linked to socio-economic status, is the universal rule and not the exception.

Some experts such as Marmot have gone further to make the following argument: it's not just that differences in income and socio-economic status *create* the health inequalities listed above; it's that inequality itself creates illness. Large studies have found that, in societies where there is *more* equality—in terms of race, ethnicity, gender, and income—there are *better* health outcomes (i.e. lower rates of injury and disease, faster recovery times, fewer instances of risky behaviours, and more healthy lifestyles). The United States is often singled out in this regard. For all the resources devoted to healthcare in America—which spends more on healthcare than any other country—the US lags behind most other developed nations in terms of key public health indicators. It especially lags behind western European and Scandinavian countries—like France and Sweden—which have public, universal healthcare systems and where there is much more equality, especially in terms of race, gender, and income.[49] Can such differences be merely coincidence? These researchers think not: specifically, they conclude that *the greater the social equality, the better the overall health outcomes*. Another telling statistic: according to the GINI index of income inequality, the world's 10 most *unequal* societies are all in the developing world: 7 are in Africa, 3 in the Caribbean and Latin America. By contrast, the 10 most *equal* societies are in all in western Europe and Scandinavia. And think of the differences in healthcare between these two regional groupings: from slim to non-existent in the first group to some of the highest-quality, most highly praised healthcare systems in the world in the second.[50]

GLOBAL POVERTY AND HEALTH INEQUALITY

These issues make us mindful of global poverty and its damaging consequences, especially on health. What is poverty? Experts distinguish between absolute and relative poverty. **Relative poverty**, which exists everywhere, is experienced by anyone whose assets and income are smaller than those of the people living in his or her immediate social context, whether it's a neighbourhood, city, or even country. **Absolute poverty** is much more serious, and is defined as a chronic inability to afford the basic necessities of life, such as water and food, and some clothing and access to shelter. The most commonly agreed-upon absolute poverty line is an income of US$2 per day per person (which translates into an annual income of US$730). By this common standard, *2.6 billion people worldwide suffer from absolute poverty*, the vast majority of them in the Global South. This number has remained largely unchanged since reliable data on this kind of poverty was first collected in 1981. It is estimated that one-third of the world's absolute poor live in India, and one-quarter in sub-Saharan Africa. As a result, a lot of the work in global public health goes on in these areas. However, owing to infrastructure issues, much of this work occurs in towns and cities, even though rural poverty is thought to be double that of urban poverty.[51]

Not only is there a shocking amount of global poverty, but there is stunning socio-economic inequality worldwide, and compelling evidence that the situation is becoming worse. For example, Europe and North America have, combined, roughly 23 per cent of the world's population, yet together they earn about 68 per cent of the world's income. By comparison, Africa and Asia together comprise 70 per cent of the world's population but earn just 27 per cent of the world's income (and most of that goes just to China, Japan, and South Korea). In tiny yet luxurious Liechtenstein, nestled between Austria and Switzerland, the average income per capita in 2009 was US$118,000; in Zimbabwe, it was just $200 (well below the absolute poverty line). In the US, probably still the world's richest and biggest economy overall, the average per capita income was $47,000; in the Congo, it was $300. It's commonly stated that the world's richest 25 per cent own 75 per cent of the world's economy, whereas the poorest 75 per cent own only 25 per cent. More graphically, the UN Development Programme reports that the richest *500 individuals* in the world together earn more than the *poorest 460 million*. Think about that for a moment: the combined income of just 500 individuals is greater than that of nearly half a billion people.[52]

As for evidence that income inequality is getting worse, both globally and even *within* most national societies, the University of California reports that in 1998, in terms of combined income, the world's richest 5 per cent out-earned the poorest 5 per cent by a ratio of 78 to 1. Today, by contrast, it's at least 115 to 1—the gap is growing. Looking just at the US, even the CIA, in its useful *World Factbook*, admits that *almost all* gains in income and assets since 1975 have occurred in *the richest 20 per cent* of the American population, creating a two-tier labour market in the country. This wealth split is reflected in healthcare coverage, with high-income Americans enjoying access to excellent, efficient care, but with low-income Americans often lacking access to any healthcare at all. (There is Medicare/Medicaid for the poorest of the poor, but no public medicine for the **working poor**—those earning enough to make them ineligible for state health insurance yet not enough to afford private health insurance.) It is estimated that about 40 million Americans lack healthcare insurance, and plans to ensure that all Americans have access to health coverage, under the Patient Protection and Affordable Care Act (2010) have been challenged in the courts. This is a gripping illustration, on a national level, of a fact about the international distribution of healthcare: that those who need healthcare *the most* have access to *the least*, whereas those who need it the *least* have access to the *most*. This is known as the **global inverse care law**.[53]

Case Study: Maternal Health

A graphic condensation of our North versus South narrative can be found by considering, in greater detail, how two women on opposite sides of the world commonly experience having a child. This fictionalized narrative summary of salient general facts will supplement our extended examination last chapter of women's human rights, while drawing attention to the importance of maternal and child health in global public healthcare.

Abeba is a 15-year-old school girl living in Ethiopia. Common features of her experience of childbirth and motherhood could include walking alone to a secluded area at the edge of her village, squatting on the ground, and delivering her baby on her own, without emotional or medical support or pain control. Because her body is still young and not fully developed, the baby becomes stuck as it moves down the birth canal, and because there is no doctor standing by to assist, this causes an **obstetric fistula** (i.e. a tear in the tissue between her vagina and rectum, or vagina and bladder) and a temporary stop in the flow of oxygen to the baby. Eventually Abeba delivers the baby, walks to the river to rinse off herself and her baby, and then returns to her village. Abeba survives delivering her baby but must care for it completely alone, and has very little knowledge about the best way to go about this. She goes on to have four more children but is eventually ostracized by her village and left by her husband owing to the constant leaking of urine and feces as a result of her unrepaired fistula (the hospital is very far away, and she could not afford to pay for the surgery in any event). She is never able to return to school, let alone work. She eventually dies of HIV/AIDS at the age of 29, leaving her eldest child, just 14, responsible for raising the younger children.

Susan is a 29-year-old woman with good health insurance, living in the United States. Common features of her experience of childbirth and motherhood might include arriving at the hospital with her husband, then being pushed in a wheelchair to a sterilized and sanitary hospital room specifically equipped to facilitate the delivery of a baby. She delivers the baby with the assistance of a doctor—one with specific training in delivering babies—and a team of nurses; her husband is by her side, and her parents are outside the delivery room. She is given an **epidural** (which numbs her body from the waist down to eliminate much of the pain of giving birth), and the baby is successfully delivered, its health checked by a nurse who then hands the infant to Susan. There are no complications, but if there were, a doctor is present to intervene. A lactation consultant visits Susan to instruct her on the method and importance of breastfeeding. After a one-night stay in hospital, Susan and her family return home to begin their well-informed journey of raising the baby. Susan takes one year of paid, job-protected maternity leave from her job, and when she returns to work, puts her baby in a high-quality local daycare. In two years' time, Susan and her husband have a second child, and they are able to enjoy seeing them both grow into adulthood and have healthy children of their own.[54]

THE OTHER SIDE OF DARKNESS

Much of this chapter is grim and staggering, both the general picture and the particular facts. Global public health is a tale of two very different "cities" indeed, and it's hard to be heartened in this regard. While that is all true, let's—before leaving this chapter—make ourselves mindful of the many positive stories and trends in global public health.

Case Study: Smallpox

Smallpox is a contagious disease caused by a virus that is usually passed from person to person. Symptoms include fever, headache, weakness, severe back pain, and sometimes stomach pain and vomiting. One of the most notable symptoms is the appearance of a rash, especially on the face, hands, forearms, and torso, consisting of raised, opaque, fluid-filled blisters with a dimple in the centre. The rash leaves deep, pitted scars on the faces of survivors, many of whom can suffer permanent blindness. In fact, in the eighteenth century in Europe, one-third of all cases of blindness were caused by smallpox. During the same period, smallpox was the cause of death of one in ten children in Sweden and France, and one in seven children in Russia. In fact, it was a major killer throughout the world for centuries, killing about 30 per cent of people who became infected with it. Even as recently as the 1950s, smallpox infected around 50 million people in the world *each year*. And yet today, smallpox represents perhaps one of the most well-known global public health success stories ever.

In 1798, Edward Jenner, an English scientist, discovered and developed a vaccine against smallpox. It was not until the 1950s, however, that the vaccine became widely available, thanks to advances that allowed it to be mass-produced and stored without refrigeration, as well as to a technological breakthrough in the type of needle that could be used to administer the vaccine to people. With these capabilities, the WHO in 1959 proposed a plan to eradicate smallpox entirely through mandatory vaccinations, and in 1965, the United States government offered technical and financial support towards the effort, helping to spur it forward. As a result of vaccination efforts, by 1966, smallpox infected around 10–15 million people—far fewer than the 50 million people infected with the virus during the 1950s. By 1980, the WHO was able to declare smallpox to be the first disease in history to have ever been eradicated. Since then, there have been no naturally occurring cases of smallpox in the entire world.[55]

Other Successes

Smallpox is only the most spectacular global public health success story. Consider, too, the following:

- Since 1900, enormous strides have been made in medical knowledge, with huge impacts on global public health. Average life expectancy has gone *way up*, and infant and child mortality *way down*. The human population has experienced enormous growth as a result. Simply put, far more people are now living much longer, and much more healthily (and presumably happily).

- The economic resources being devoted to healthcare—or to health, broadly defined— are growing every year, worldwide. Health is one of the economy's fastest and most consistently growing sectors.

- The availability of health information, though imperfect, has never been higher, thanks to the Internet.

- The percentage of children worldwide who are fully immunized and vaccinated has gone from about 5 per cent to close to 50 per cent.[56]

For many of the biggest global public health problems, plausible solutions *are* known, and are being implemented. Water supply problems are being addressed with water well construction and ORT in emergency cases. Emergency food shortages are being met with protein packs (though the only viable long-term solution is to have food resources redistributed to reduce waste and obesity in the North and increase subsistence consumption in the South). Hand sanitizer is being made available to tackle immediate problems in sanitation, and there is agreement on the need to construct sewers and garbage dumps, as well as other crucial infrastructure (like electricity). Mosquito nets and spraying are being used to stop the spread of insect-borne viruses.

> *Growing the developing economies is arguably the best way to improving public health around the world.*

Improving global healthcare systems will take money and resources. It goes hand in hand with reducing the global poverty that creates the conditions for poor health and shoddy healthcare. Progress on these fronts will be discussed in the forthcoming chapter on aid and development. For now, we can say that growing the developing economies is arguably the best way to improving public health around the world. We shall see that there are many tools in the trade and development toolbox to help achieve this goal. Figure 10.4, below, summarizes this point and, in essence, the whole chapter.

CONCLUSION

In this chapter we have seen how health interrelates with all other fields of international studies. We defined health, public health, and global public health. We witnessed the staggering nature of global public health challenges, but then also canvassed a number of promising proposed solutions. Throughout, we have seen evocative case studies that bring the issues to life. We concluded by noting how crucial alleviating poverty is to overcoming many global public health challenges, and it is to that subject that we will turn in the next chapter.

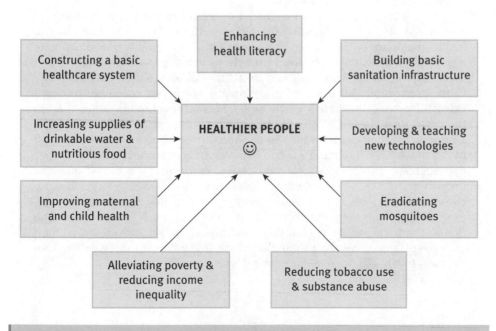

FIGURE 10.4 Main Strategies for Improving Global Public Health

Studies in Technology

The Phone Oximeter

We close out this chapter with a happy tale of high-tech hope. Suppose you're a doctor who needs to test the blood oxygen level of a patient in a remote location in the Global South, far from a medical clinic or hospital. There's an app for that. The Phone Oximeter is a small, low-cost mobile device that tests oxygen levels in the blood, developed by researchers at the University of British Columbia. It's essentially a finger sensor that can be connected to a mobile device, such as a smartphone or laptop computer equipped with the appropriate software. With the appropriate app, also developed by the UBC research team, it will display physiological information such as heart rate, respiratory rate, and oxygen level in the blood on the screen in a simple, user-friendly way. In fact, the screen display uses symbols instead of words to convey information, aiding medical professionals to make medical diagnoses and decisions, regardless of language. It also enables the information to be transferred wirelessly in real time—say, to the closest hospital—possibly saving patients a visit and maybe even costs. Although this technology is still in the testing stage (currently in Uganda), one of its strengths is that the device works with an existing technology: cellular phones are surprisingly common in many developing countries, much more so than landline telephones.

How, exactly, could such a device improve global public health? As mentioned, while health crises are quite common in the developing world, health clinics are much less so. Because the device is mobile, it could enable a medical professional working remotely to test a patient's blood oxygen level without extensive equipment or a hospital visit. The researchers say it has applications for monitoring patients when under anaesthesia (death rates from anaesthesia are much higher in the developing world than in the developed world). It can also be used as a diagnostic tool to check for a condition called **preeclampsia** (a dangerous complication related to high blood pressure) in pregnant women in developing countries. Without proper management, preeclampsia can be dangerous for both the mother and the unborn baby, and can even be fatal. Death from preeclampsia is much more common in developing countries, owing to a lack of diagnosis and management and low **prenatal care** (care for mother and baby before birth). The Phone Oximeter would enable this condition to be diagnosed, so women who have it and know they should be monitored will be more likely to make the long trek to the hospital for medical attention.[57]

REVIEW QUESTIONS

1. Research a public health crisis that had a significant impact on the history of your country. (Consider, e.g., recent outbreaks of SARS or H1N1, or historical cases of smallpox or tuberculosis.) What were the effects on your country? How was the crisis addressed by public health officials? How successful were they?

2. Offer your own definitions of health and sickness. Referring to Figure 10.2, consider what you believe to be the main ingredients of both individual and public health.

3. Did it surprise you to learn the Gates Foundation donates more to global public health than any other organization? Who ought to be responsible for healthcare and health promotion—and why?

4. Research the big "macro-stats" on health and illness in your own country: life expectancy, infant mortality, and the burden of disease/rate of morbidity. Compare these to the appropriate demographic data of other countries (pick one neighbouring country and one further away). What accounts for your country's performance? Where are the biggest needs for improvement?

5. A lot of recent research stresses how much of our own health is affected by its social determinants, as opposed to the potent (yet indirect) effects of our genes and the direct (yet often gradual) effects of our individual lifestyle choices. Explain how the social determinants of health have impacted your own personal health status.

6. What is your reaction to Figure 10.3, the Worldmapper representation of healthcare needs around the globe? How do such representations help or hinder our understanding of international realties?

7. If you were a public health official in Canada, how would you go about improving the health of Canada's Aboriginal population? Using three specific examples, with evidence to back them up, describe how you would go about this challenge and why your three areas of focus would be the key ones to concentrate on.

8. There's an impressive body of research linking inequality and poverty with low health status and high rates of disease and death. Reflect on this and what it means for the continued split of the world into developed versus developing societies. Do we owe the global poor more resources, if only to improve their health and well-being?

9. Describe your reaction to reading the two experiences in the case studies on giving birth and rearing children. What is the significance of these contrasting stories to international studies?

10. In terms of public health, our "tale of two cities"—the Global South and Global North—seems grim and tragic. Do you think we will be able to turn it around, say by using the strategies diagrammed in Figure 10.4? Why or why not? Will noble heroes emerge, or is the situation too far gone?

WEBSITES FOR FURTHER RESEARCH

The World Health Organization www.who.org

Kaiser Family Foundation on Global Health http://globalhealth.kff.org
– offering data and information on the US's role in advancing global public
  health

Public Health Agency of Canada www.phac-aspc.gc.ca
– Canadian government agency responsible for promoting public health
  in Canada

Health Canada www.hc-sc.gc.ca
– Canadian federal health agency responsible for overseeing public health
  research and initiatives

US Centers for Disease Control and Prevention www.cdc.gov
– American federal agency collaborating with state health departments to
  promote public health in the US

Médecins Sans Frontières/Doctors Without Borders www.msf.ca
– Canadian branch's website offers "field blogs" that detail some of the
  organization's work

NOTES

1. T. Kidder, *Mountains Beyond Mountains: The Quest of Paul Farmer, A Man Who Would Cure the World* (New York: Random House, 2011). Paul Farmer is also the editor-in-chief of the academic journal *Health and Human Rights*.
2. J. Nohl & C. Clarke, *The Black Death* (London: Westholme, 2006)
3. S. Watts, *Epidemics and History: Disease, Power and Imperialism* (New Haven, CT: Yale University Press, 1999).
4. J.S. Donnelly, *The Great Irish Potato Famine* (London: The History Press, 2008).
5. J. Riley, *Rising Life Expectancy: A Global History* (Cambridge: Cambridge University Press, 2001).
6. M. Gladwell, *The Tipping Point* (New York: Little, Brown, 2000); J. Weeks, *Population: An Introduction to Concepts and Issues* (Belmont, CA: Wadsworth, 11th edn, 2011).
7. R. Cook, *Health and Human Rights* (London: Ashgate, 2007); S.P. Marks, *Health and Human Rights: Basic International Documents* (Cambridge, MA: Harvard University Press, 2006).
8. N. Arya, et al., *Peace Through Health* (London: Kumarian Press, 2006); G. Kolata, *Flu* (New York: Simon and Schuster, 2001).
9. K. Lee, *The World Health Organization (WHO)* (London: Routledge, 2008).
10. World Health Organization, *International Health Regulations, 2005* (Geneva: WHO, 2008); full text: www.who.int/ihr/9789241596664/en/index.html
11. B. Cartledge, *Health and The Environment* (Oxford: Oxford University Press, 1994).
12. D. Phillips, *Health and Development* (London: Routledge, 1994); J. Clift, ed., *Health and Development* (Washington, DC: IMF, 2004).

13. A. Price-Smith, *The Health of Nations* (Cambridge, MA: The MIT Press, 2002); S. Elbe, *Security and Global Health* (Cambridge: Polity Press, 2010).
14. Preamble to the Constitution of the World Health Organization as adopted by the International Health Conference, New York, 19–22 June 1946, and signed 22 July 1946 by the representatives of 61 States (Official Records of the World Health Organization, no. 2, p. 100) and entered into force on 7 April 1948.
15. W. Glannon, *Biomedical Ethics* (Oxford: Oxford University Press, 2004).
16. R. Browson, et al., *Evidence-Based Public Health* (Oxford: Oxford University Press, 2nd edn, 2010).
17. S. Hempel, *The Medical Detective: John Snow and The Mystery of Cholera* (London: Granta, 2006).
18. Browson, *Public Health* (op. cit., note 16).
19. WHO, "Health Promotion. Track 2: Health Literacy and Health Behaviour," www.who.int/healthpromotion/conferences/7gchp/track2/en/
20. C. Shah, *Public Health and Preventive Medicine in Canada* (Toronto: Saunders, 5th edn, 2003).
21. Shah, *Public Health* (op. cit., note 21); R. Hamowy, *Government and Public Health in America* (New York: Edward Elgar, 2008).
22. Bill & Melinda Gates Foundation, "Foundation Fact Sheet," www.gatesfoundation.org/about/Pages/foundation-fact-sheet.aspx
23. R. Parker & M. Sommer, *Routledge Handbook of Global Public Health* (London: Routledge, 2011).
24. J. Mikkonen and D. Raphael, *Social Determinants of Health: The Canadian Facts* (Toronto: York University School of Health Policy and Management, 2010): www.thecanadianfacts.org; R. Wilkinson & M. Marmot, eds, *Social Determinants of Health: The Solid Facts* (WHO: Europe, 2003): www.euro.who.int/__data/assets/pdf_file/0005/98438/e81384.pdf; this discussion and parts of Table 10.1 also draw on M. Marmot & R. Wilkinson, eds, *The Social Determinants of Health* (Oxford: Oxford University Press, 2nd edn, 2005).
25. Riley, *Rising Life Expectancy* (op. cit., note 5); *The CIA Annual World Factbook*, 2010.
26. Riley, *Rising Life Expectancy* (op. cit., note 5); *The CIA Annual World Factbook*, 2010.
27. WHO, "Topics: Chronic Diseases," www.who.int/topics/chronic_diseases/en/
28. WHO, "Top 10 Causes of Death," www.who.int/mediacentre/factsheets/fs310/en/index.html
29. R. Beaglehole, ed., *Global Public Health: A New Era* (Oxford: Oxford University Press, 2009).
30. WHO, "Framework Convention on Tobacco Control," www.who.int/fctc/en/index.html; WHO, "Fact Sheet: Tobacco," www.who.int/mediacentre/factsheets/fs339/en/index.html
31. WHO and UNICEF, *Meeting the MDG Drinking Water and Sanitation Target: The Urban and Rural Challenge of the Decade*, (Geneva: WHO, 2006); full text: www.who.int/water_sanitation_health/monitoring/jmpfinal.pdf
32. UNICEF, *State of the World's Children 2011* (New York: United Nations, 2011).
33. A. Sen, *Poverty and Famines* (Oxford: Clarendon, 1981).
34. WHO and UNICEF, *Meeting* (op. cit., note 31).
35. WHO, "Fact File: 10 Facts on Sanitation," www.who.int/features/factfiles/sanitation/facts/en/index1.html
36. WHO, *The World Health Report. Health System Financing: The Path to Universal Coverage* (Geneva: WHO, 2010); full text: www.who.int/whr/2010/en/index.html
37. J. Johnson & C. Stoskopk, *Comparative Health Systems* (London: Jones and Bartlett, 2010).
38. Ibid.
39. J. Law, *Big Pharma: Exposing the Global Healthcare Agenda* (New York: Basic, 2006).
40. Marmot & Wilkinson, *Social Determinants* (op. cit., note 24).

41. M.G. Marmot, M.J. Shipley, & G. Rose, "Inequalities in Death: Specific Explanations of a General Pattern," *Lancet* (1984): pp. 1003–6; M.G. Marmot, G. Davey Smith, S.A. Stansfeld, et al., "Health Inequalities among British Civil Servants: The Whitehall II Study," *Lancet*, 337 (1991): pp. 1387–93.

42. D.A. Redelmeier & S.M. Singh, "Survival in Academy Award–Winning Actors and Actresses," *Annals of Internal Medicine*, 134 (2001): pp. 955–62.

43. Mikkonen & Raphael, *Social Determinants* (op. cit., note 24).

44. R. Wilkinson & M. Marmot, *Social Determinants of Health: The Solid Facts* (Paris: WHO, 2003).

45. Ibid.

46. Ibid.

47. Ibid.

48. D.A. Herring, et al., *Aboriginal Health in Canada* (Toronto: University of Toronto Press, 2nd edn, 2006); E. Young, *Third World in The First* (London: Routledge, 1995).

49. Marmot & Wilkinson, *Social Determinants* (op. cit., note 24).

50. Ibid.

51. D. Hulme, *Global Poverty* (London: Routledge, 2010); S. Wisor, *Measuring Global Poverty* (London: Palgrave Macmillan, 2011).

52. S. Smith, *Ending Global Poverty* (London: Palgrave Macmillan, 2008); UNDP, *Human Development Report 2010* (New York: United Nations, 2011).

53. J.T. Hart, "The Inverse Care Law," *Lancet*, 297 (1971): pp. 405–12.

54. For more on maternal health, see the WHO feature on the subject: www.who.int/features/maternal_child/en/index.html; see also Liya Kebede's and Christy Turlington's respective initiatives on maternal and child health: www.theliyakebedefoundation.org and www.every mothercounts.org

55. WHO, "Fact Sheet: Smallpox," www.who.int/mediacentre/factsheets/smallpox/en/index.html; R. Levine. *Case Studies in Global Health: Millions Saved* (Sudbury, MA: Jones & Bartlett, 2007); Centers for Disease Control and Prevention, "Smallpox Disease Overview," www.bt.cdc.gov/agent/smallpox/overview/disease-facts.asp

56. Beaglehole, *Global Public Health*, (op. cit., note 29).

57. UBC Faculty of Applied Science, "Electrical & Computer Engineering in Medicine: The PhoneOximeter", http://phoneoximeter.org

International Aid and Development

"All that is valuable in human society depends upon the opportunity for development accorded the individual." —*Albert Einstein (1879–1955), Nobel Prize winner in physics*[1]

LEARNING OBJECTIVES

After studying this chapter, you will be able to:

▸ define all the bolded key terms and concepts

▸ distinguish between *aid* and *development*, and debate the merits of the purely quantitative, GDP-based concept of development and the more inclusive, qualitative Human Development Index

▸ analyze aid tables and charts to understand where development aid comes from, who the major players are, and what their objectives might be

▸ appreciate the history of aid and development policy: how each of the "three waves" had strengths and flaws and have fed into the contemporary model of "bottom-up pluralism"

▸ describe the major, and massive, challenges confronting those who care about underdevelopment and poverty, and explain and evaluate the various proposed solutions (such as the UN's Millennium Development Goals)

▸ gain particular appreciation of the role of NGOs and non-state actors in the development process.

INTRODUCTION

We ended last chapter discussing how alleviated poverty would go a long way to remedying many public health ills in the developing world. A major way in which countries try to help make the Global South wealthier is through programs of aid and development, and so this is the topic of the present, and final, chapter. We shall distinguish between *aid* and *development*, and then examine rival concepts of the latter. Then, we shall tour the history of aid and development programs, from their start after the Second World War right up to the present day. We shall see how much of the current wisdom behind development thinking accords with Einstein's quote above: that most of the resources ought to be aimed at developing the right kind of capabilities and skills within individuals, so that they will know better how, and be better situated, to grow their societies and help them become more mature, wealthy, and advanced.

WHY SHOULD THE DEVELOPED WORLD CARE?

We know from previous chapters that an enormous division exists between the developed Global North (a.k.a. the West) and the Global South, with the former being much richer, healthier, more stable and peaceful, better educated, and more technologically advanced than the latter. The Global South, it follows, is much more poor, sick, unstable, violent, unschooled, and "technologically behind" than the North. More disturbingly, the clear and vast majority of the world's population (75 per cent) lives in the Global South. Furthermore, many countries in the Global South used to be colonies of a handful of countries in the North—Belgium, Britain, France, Germany, Holland, Italy, Portugal, Russia, Spain, and the US have all had direct colonial holdings throughout the Global South. Many of these colonies were run for the benefit of the colonizer, with the latter setting up the colony in such a way that resources (both human and natural) were disproportionately sucked out of the colony to feed the economy and society of the colonizer. Put all these facts together, and you have a good case that the North owes it to try to help the South develop—in other words, the North should do what it reasonably can to make the South richer, more healthy, better educated, more stable and peaceful, more technologically advanced, and more integrated into the global economy. This is true not merely for reasons of morality, or of guilt and trying to atone for the sins of colonialism. There are also strong reasons of realist self-interest here for the North, including the following:

> *The North owes it to try to help the South develop.*

- If the South becomes richer, it will become a huge new market for goods produced in the North, augmenting international trade (see Chapter 6).

- Also, if the South becomes wealthier, fewer people will want to leave, further helping those societies to develop and reducing pressures on Northern societies struggling with immigration and refugee flows from the South (see Chapter 2).

- If the South becomes healthier, it will become less of a source of cross-border disease and infection, cutting down on the number of global pandemics originating in the South (HIV/AIDS and SARS are recent examples—see Chapter 10).

- If the South becomes more stable and peaceful, it will see fewer wars, necessitating fewer Northern interventions and making it less of a breeding and training ground for international terrorists (see Chapter 7).

- If the South becomes more developed, there will probably be fewer gaps and inequalities, and thus fewer tensions in global politics, leading presumably to greater co-operation and progress on such important international issues as human rights and the global environment (see Chapters 2 and 9).

AID VERSUS DEVELOPMENT

It's helpful here to make some initial distinctions. The first is between aid and development. Though the two terms are often used interchangeably, there's a growing consensus that it makes sense to recognize the following difference: **aid** is *short-term relief*, largely *humanitarian* in nature and taking the form of *donations and gifts*—whether cash or "in

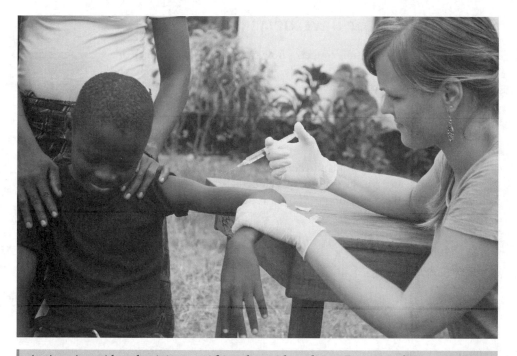

An American aid worker injects an African boy with medicine. Does providing vaccinations to children in the developing world count as aid or development? (© MShep2/iStockphoto)

kind" (i.e. goods). It is typically designed to help alleviate some sharp, sudden crisis within a society. Consider, for example, the response of the international community in 1983–5 to the crisis of mass starvation in Ethiopia, which sparked the famous "Live Aid" fundraising rock concerts that took place around the world. Or consider the 2010 response to the devastating earthquake in Haiti, or to the flooding catastrophe in Pakistan, both of which killed thousands, and left tens of thousands homeless. Ditto for the terrible tsunamis in Thailand (2004) and Japan (2011). There is an emergency, and aid is the response of the international community: short-term, humanitarian, gift-based, crisis-focused, and with the narrow goal of helping to alleviate the burdens of the society struggling with the event.

Development, by contrast, refers to a *slower and longer-term* effort, one intended not merely to help a country through a crisis but to truly grow a nation into a richer, smarter, healthier, more stable and sophisticated society—one with fewer problems and more successful and sustained social growth. To that extent, the timeframe for development is much longer, and the goal is broader and more ambitious than the goal of aid. And while development assistance might include gifts, it can also include *loans* (which have to be paid back), *direct investments* (which assume some return on the risk), or *advice and expertise* (i.e. services—as opposed to mere goods, such as blankets and medicines). So, the tools of development are *more*: they are *more complicated*, and they are aimed at *a bigger* and *longer-term goal*: the true transformation of the society in question into one which is substantially and sustainably better.[2]

Rival Concepts of Development

The second crucial distinction concerns how the extent of a country's development is measured. Traditionally, and more narrowly, this has been done by referring to the country's **gross domestic product per person** (or **per capita GDP**). This is a purely *quantitative* index of how much money (or income, or value) a society produces in a year, divided by that country's population. The result is something like a measurement of how wealthy that society is on a per-person basis. Table 11.1 shows the 10 most and least developed societies in 2009, according to this measure.[3]

But development experts, and economists, have long noted the drawbacks to relying on the GDP index as a measure of how developed a society is. First, it measures standard of living, as opposed to quality of life. **Standard of living** is this quantitative measurement of

TABLE 11.1 The 10 Most and Least Developed Countries by Per Capita GDP (2009)

Most Developed	Annual GDP Per Capita (in US dollars)
Lichtenstein	$118,000
Qatar	$104,000
Luxembourg	$81,000
Bermuda	$70,000
Kuwait	$57,000
Jersey	$56,000
Norway	$55,000
Brunei	$53,000
Singapore	$52,000
United States	$47,000
Least Developed	
Zimbabwe	$200
Congo	$300
Burundi	$400
Liberia	$500
Somalia	$600
Guinea-Bissau	$650
Sierra Leone	$700
Central African Republic	$750
Niger	$750
Afghanistan	$800

Source: Data from United Nations, *United Nations Human Development Report, 2009* (New York: UNDP, 2010); available at http://hdr.undp.org/en.

income per person, whereas **quality of life** takes into account other aspects of an enjoyable life, such as subjective happiness and the attainment of certain objective goods and goals, like an education and a healthy body. We all know that money, while important, is not the only thing in life. As a measure of development, per capita GDP is also flawed because it aggregates the total income in a society and simply divides it by the total number of people to arrive at an average number per person. But this glosses over clear differences in the **distribution of income** (i.e. how that overall wealth is shared within a society) and how that might affect our perception of how developed a society is. The distribution of income can affect our view of a country's development in at least two ways:

1. In an unequal society, where there is a large gap between rich and poor, it is possible that only the wealthy people living in posh neighbourhoods actually enjoy a truly developed life, whereas the poor people in downtrodden neighbourhoods might actually share more in common with the developing world than with the developed. Given this sharp split, should we judge the society, overall, to be developed or developing?

2. There is much evidence that societies characterized by a more equal distribution of income are happier, on average, than those that feature less equality. If happiness is part of the quality of life—and how could it not be?—then factoring in income distribution is vital to determining quality of life and, thus, the degree of development in a society.[4]

As a result, the **United Nations Development Programme** (UNDP) has constructed something it calls the **Human Development Index** (HDI). This is designed to move beyond aggregate income to include other measures of quality of life in a given society, such as:

- life expectancy
- infant mortality
- rates of literacy and disease
- rates of educational attainment
- distribution of income
- gender and minority equality
- self-reported satisfaction in life.

These are all in addition to per capita GDP. Table 11.2 shows the 10 most and least developed countries in 2009 according to this quite different measure.[5]

The drawback to using the Human Development Index is that it is *more complex* than using GDP, and it includes standards of development (for instance, income equality and educational attainment) that some believe to be *more controversial and subjective* than the straightforward monetary measure of wealth. That said, development experts currently tend to view HDI as the dominant method for evaluating the comparative development of countries.[6]

When comparing tables 11.1 and 11.2, note how *different* are the lists of the *top* 10, yet how *similar* are the lists for the *bottom* 10. The two lists of most developed nations have only Norway in common, whereas 7 of the 10 least developed countries appear on both lists. What does this suggest? It may suggest that *low income guarantees low development* (in other words, development costs money), but *high income does not guarantee high*

TABLE 11.2 The Ten Most and Least Developed Countries by HDI (2009)

Most Developed	Least Developed
Norway	Niger
Australia	Afghanistan
Iceland	Sierra Leone
Canada	Central African Republic
Ireland	Mali
the Netherlands	Burkina Faso
Sweden	Congo
France	Chad
Switzerland	Burundi
Japan	Guinea-Bissau

Source: Based on P. Haslam, et al., eds, *Introduction to International Development* (Oxford: Oxford University Press, 2008).

development (i.e. some people, and some nations, spend their money unwisely in ways that don't improve their lives over the long term). The most developed countries based on GDP include a number of tiny nations with either (a) huge natural resource endowments (especially oil and gas) or else (b) notoriously favourable tax breaks for the global ultra-rich. By contrast, the list of most developed countries according to HDI seems to adhere more closely to what most people think of when they think of highly developed and sophisticated national societies. Sadly, though, the least developed countries are mostly from one continent: Africa (see Figure 11.1).

SOURCES OF DEVELOPMENT ASSISTANCE

A third important distinction worth making is between *private* and *public* sources of aid and development. **Private sources** include all *non-governmental* sources, and the big subdistinction here is between *for-profit, corporate* development sources, on the one hand, and *not-for-profit, charitable* sources, on the other. The most relevant form of for-profit, corporate aid is what is called **foreign direct investment** (or FDI), made by a multinational corporation (a for-profit, private company that carries out business activities in more than one country—see Chapter 6). An example of an FDI by a multinational corporation would be the decision of a huge Northern company, like IKEA or General Motors, to build a factory in a Southern country to manufacture goods for the global market. This kind of decision boosts the development of that society by creating jobs and incomes for locals, by increasing the tax revenue available to the local government, and by tying that country's economy more closely to the international or global economy. Although FDI is one of the forms of economic aid most sought after by developing societies, it is also the most fickle: it represents the form of economic investment most likely to dry up in a recession, the most demanding of something in exchange, and the most prone to suddenly disappearing

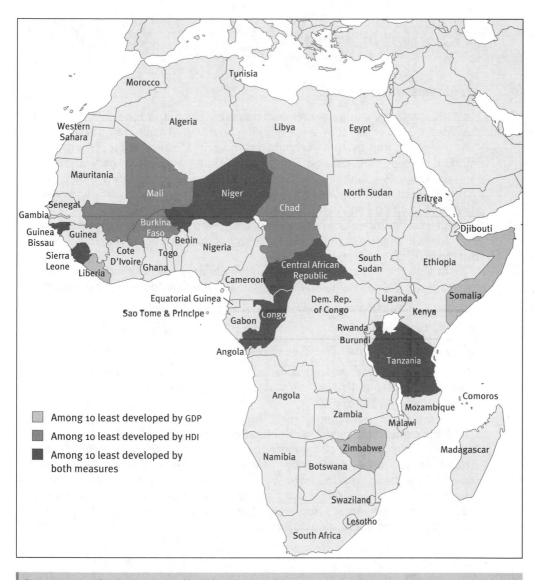

FIGURE 11.1 The Poorest, Neediest Continent: Africa

if the company decides there's a better deal to be had somewhere else. After all, the motives of the multinational corporation are *not* charitable: an MNC will engage in an FDI *only* when it is viewed to be in the company's economic interest. That said, FDI happens all the time—totalling hundreds of billions of US dollars every year—and developing societies capitalize on their cheap labour, land, insurance, and regulation costs to attract it.[7]

Why is FDI so prized by developing countries? There is a school of development thought that stresses the need to grow a robust manufacturing base in a society that wants to develop. After all, historically, this has been the case in every Northern society that went

Canadian Insights

Engineers Without Borders

In 2000, two young engineering students who wanted to make a difference decided that the skills they were learning could be of benefit to developing societies. Inspired by the work and example of Doctors Without Borders, Parker Mitchell and George Roter, both of the University of Waterloo, founded their own international development NGO, headquartered in Canada. They realized that the developing world could make enormous use of the practical building and design skills of engineers. They were also convinced that there were many like-minded engineers who were interested in helping to make a difference to the global poor, rather than just deploying their skills on behalf of large corporations.

At first, the organization was entirely voluntary, and worked on a shoe-string budget, sending volunteers over to rural Africa to focus on three things:

1. the construction and maintenance of clean-water wells

2. the building of effective irrigation (i.e. watering) systems on small farms

3. promoting the use of new, more resilient and productive seeds for crops.

The overall aim was, and remains, to improve both the life and health of communities in rural Africa, as well as to augment the incomes of poor, independent rural farmers.

From its modest beginnings, "EWB" now—just 12 years later—has 25 full-time employees, over 2,500 volunteer engineers and engineering students (who go overseas on temporary, project placements), and over 35,000 members, supporters, and donors. There are now 34 chapters of EWB across Canada. For their amazing hard work on behalf of international development, the two co-founders have received a number of awards, and been recognized with honorary doctorates from Queen's University in Kingston. And all of this before turning 30 years old![8]

on to become developed. Thus, attracting factories becomes a vital piece of the development puzzle, according to this theory. The government of China, for example, is clearly committed to this understanding, and has been aggressively luring factories by the thousands to its shores, to create goods for export sale back out into the global economy. For more on this, refer back to the discussion of export-led development and the role of international trade as a spur to development in Chapter 6.[9]

In terms of not-for-profit, private sources of aid and development, there are three big ones: churches, NGOs, and remittances. Churches have, historically, played a surprisingly large role in the interaction between Northern and Southern societies. This has not always been for the good, but then the same can be said of both businesses and governments. Churches have done especially well at providing some social and educational services to

Southern nations (though the latter has often, and obviously, been mixed with a mission-ary agenda). The Catholic Church has played, and continues to play, a huge role, especially in Africa and Latin America, though also in select Asian countries like Vietnam. The Mennonite Central Committee has been heavily involved in the Caribbean and Central America; ditto for the big US-based Protestant churches.[10]

There are many aid and development NGOs, and they range from well-known chari-ties like Care and Oxfam to learning societies like the World University Service of Canada and **technology transfer foundations** like Engineers Without Borders (discussed above). These NGOs are becoming increasingly important to international development as govern-ments look more and more to supporting and partnering up with charitable organizations to help them achieve overall development objectives.[11]

The third source of not-for-profit aid and development, remittances, should not be overlooked, especially as a source of additional income for people in developing societ-ies. When someone leaves or emigrates from a developing society to find work in a more developed one, the individual will often send a portion of his or her income privately to family members and friends back home in the developing society. These funds are known as **remittances**. It is hard, obviously, to measure accurately the contribution of remit-tances to a country's economy, but economists estimate that, for some countries anyway, remittances can be a huge source of hard cash revenue for people and, when they spend it domestically, for the whole developing society in which they live. Indeed, when it comes to the biggest sources of development assistance (by volume of dollars), most economists place private remittances third behind only government or public aid and foreign direct investment by multinational corporations.[12]

Public forms of aid and development are delivered by government-based agencies, either national or international. National governments, like the US federal government or the government of Canada, run development agencies and programs (called USAID in the US and CIDA—the Canadian International Development Agency—in Canada). When one nation provides aid, or **official development assistance** (ODA), to another, it's called **bilateral aid**. In addition to these national programs, governments also commit money to **multilateral aid**, primarily through UN-based global development programs, of which there are many, since the development of the Global South is a major aim of the United Nations, as we saw in Chapter 5. Some of the major UN agencies involved include the World Bank, the International Monetary Fund (IMF), the World Health Organization (WHO), the UN Conference on Trade and Development (UNCTAD), and the aforementioned UNDP. Most international development assistance, though, comes from an international body known as the Development Assistance Committee (DAC). The DAC is run by the Organization for Economic Co-operation and Development (OECD), a high-profile organization that carries out valuable economic research and provides advice to its member governments about how best to spend their development dollars.[13]

A perhaps surprising fact about aid and development is that only about 30 countries in the whole world—out of nearly 200—are givers, or **donor countries**. The rest are receivers, or **recipient countries**. This means that just 15 per cent of the world's nations are wealthy, "surplus" countries with the money, interest, and expertise to give development dollars and to craft aid programs, while a whopping 85 per cent of the world's countries need various degrees of aid and development assistance. The donor countries are essentially the members of the DAC—the United States, Australia, Canada, Japan, and the countries of western Europe and Scandinavia. Non-DAC donors include the oil-rich Arab states, notably Saudi Arabia. And that's it. Every other nation is lined up to receive aid and development assistance.[14]

Table 11.3 shows the top donors and recipients in 2006, the most recent year for which there is reliable, agreed-upon data. In terms of absolute dollar totals, the US is the leading donor country, and *always has been*, since development programs began after the Second World War. (Although, if you combine the figures from all the countries of the European Union—and the EU member states *are* beginning to blend their development programs into one—then the EU is the biggest donor.) However, when contributions are expressed *not* as an aggregate, absolute number but rather as a percentage of its GDP, the US actually gives *the least* of all the donor countries. The country that gives the most, as a percentage of its total national wealth, is actually either Norway or Sweden (they have flipped

TABLE 11.3 The Top 10 Donors and Recipients of ODA (2006)

Top Donors	Amount Given (in $US billions)
United States	22.7
Britain	12.6
Japan	11.6
France	10.5
Germany	10.4
Netherlands	5.6
Sweden	4.0
Spain	3.8
Canada	3.7
Italy	3.7

Top Recipients	Amount Received (in $US billions)
Iraq	4.6
Afghanistan	2.2
Vietnam	1.9
Ethiopia	1.8
Democratic Republic of the Congo	1.7
Tanzania	1.7
China	1.6
Poland	1.5
Egypt	1.4
Pakistan	1.4

Source: Data from United Nations, *United Nations Human Development Report, 2009* (New York: UNDP, 2010); retrieved from http://hdr.undp.org/en

back and forth recently). In fact, the Scandinavian countries—Denmark, Norway, Sweden, and Finland—are, alongside the Netherlands and Luxembourg, the only countries in the world who give 0.7 per cent of their GDP annually to international aid and development programs. This 0.7 per cent figure was unanimously agreed upon, as far back as 1970, as the ideal amount that ought to be given by all DAC members. The US gives about 0.1 per cent of its GDP, and Canada just 0.3 per cent. Only very recently have the Scandinavian countries hit the target—but at least, and finally, someone has done so.[15]

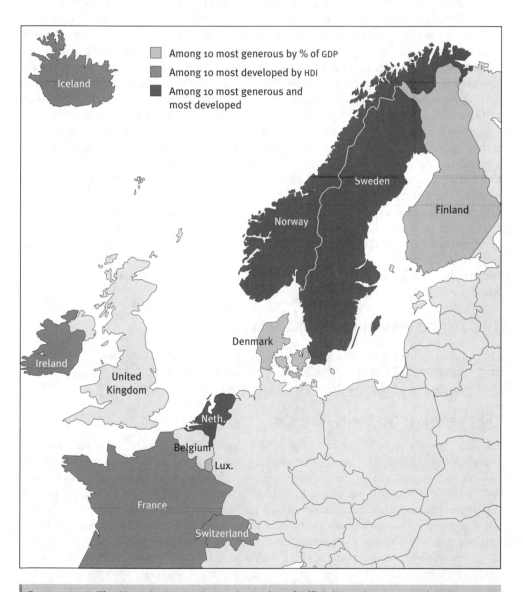

FIGURE 11.2 The Most Generous Donor Countries of Official Development Assistance

Table 11.3 shows that Iraq and Afghanistan are at the top of aid recipient countries, owing to the efforts of the international community (led by the US) to engage in expensive and difficult post-war reconstruction there (see Chapter 8). Also present are a number of countries from sub-Saharan Africa—some of the world's truly neediest nations—but also present are countries considered strategic allies by nations of the Global North. These include Egypt and Pakistan, whose people, no doubt, need the aid but which receive a disproportionate share that reflects more their support for the US-led war on terror than the genuine poverty of their people. China's appearance on the list will no doubt surprise, as will Poland's. But recall that both America and Europe want to cultivate China as an ally and ongoing trade partner—and it must be said that China still has a very poor, rural, interior population, in contrast to its booming urban coastline. Poland is enjoying investment from the EU, as well as rewards from the US for foreign policy support. Poland is also considered a historically important "buffer state" against the sway of Russia, and so both Europe and the US give the Poles aid and development for that reason, too. Vietnam's appearance on the list is owing to American efforts—all these years later—to help build up a country it once devastated with weapons of war. What the list in Table 11.3 shows, then, is that recipient countries are often *not* chosen on the basis of strict objective neediness but are selected for more subjective reasons having to do with either historical connections or forward-looking, realist strategies of foreign policy (see Chapter 4). And this is true of *all* donor countries, not just the mega-powers the US and the EU. Britain and France, for example, place most of their development dollars into those countries that they used to run as colonies—as, arguably, they should. And Canada tends to invest in member countries of the Commonwealth and La Francophonie, for reasons having to do with its own bilingual, bicultural history. The federal government also, increasingly, focuses on helping countries that have provided Canada with lots of recent immigrants (now Canadian voters), such as Bangladesh, China, Haiti, India, and Jamaica.[16]

THE THREE WAVES OF DEVELOPMENT

Official development assistance has undergone *three fundamental shifts* since it first began at the end of World War II. In the sections that follow we'll examine the features of each, their pros and cons, and how they have contributed to where we are today.

The First Wave: Top-Down, State-Centric Mega-Projects

The first wave of ODA lasted from about 1945 until 1975. Two factors dominated this period: the Cold War and a top-down paradigm of thought. In terms of the first, it was the US that began modern development programs at the end of the Second World War. As we saw in Chapter 8, on post-war reconstruction, the first determined effort to help poor, war-torn societies become developed nations was the Marshall Plan, which provided reconstruction aid to western and central Europe; Japan also received reconstruction assistance, under a separate program. But the end of World War II also marked the start of America's Cold War with Russia, and the US feared that poverty and underdevelopment could drive many countries to experiment with communism, causing them to leave the American sphere of influence and enter the Soviet Union's zone of control. To prevent this from happening, American foreign policy-makers decided to offer cash and aid, donations and expertise to those poor countries willing to stay on as America's allies during the long struggle against Soviet Russia. For the next 30 years, the amount and direction of US ODA was determined largely by American strategy during the Cold War. This is to say, crucially, that the motives behind aid and development were, overridingly, those of realist self-interest and *not* of idealistic altruism and giving for the sake of meeting the needs of the global poor.[17]

The nature of aid and development during this time was **top-down** and government-to-government (as shown in Figure 11.3). Almost all aid and development during this era consisted of direct cash-and-goods transfers from wealthy governments to governments in poor nations that were willing to sign on as allies during the Cold War. The thinking, or hope, was that local governments were in the best position to determine their own citizens' needs, and thus would use the cash and goods to do, and purchase, those things most required by the people. The result, in theory, would be a development-and-growth dynamic that moved aid from the top (i.e. the state or government) downwards and outwards throughout the rest of the country, eventually trickling down to reach even the poorest of the poor. Donor countries were confident that this model of top-down aid, generously given (some would say force-fed), would successfully trigger modern industrial development. (The confidence may have come from the then-recent wartime experience, when the American government took control over whole sectors of the US economy, helping to steer the nation to total victory. If it worked in war, policy-makers reasoned, why not in peace?)[18]

There *were* some high-profile successes of aid and development during this first wave. The reconstruction of Germany and Japan—especially their infrastructure and high-tech manufacturing capability—went over brilliantly, as we saw in Chapter 8. Other societies saw success with large-scale development projects, such as roads, bridges, irrigation systems, and dams and other hydroelectric power generation and infrastructure. These are examples of the sort of basic large-scale engineering enterprise that the top-down, state-to-state paradigm was best suited to achieve. Another success in this class was the Green Revolution, a good illustration of **knowledge transfer** and **technology transfer**. The Green Revolution saw the transfer of agricultural and irrigation technology from the developed to the developing world, resulting in greatly improved food yields, crop quality, and farm productivity.

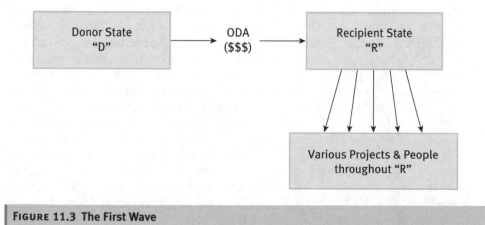

FIGURE 11.3 The First Wave

But in addition to these improvements, there were many problems with the first wave model of aid and development—problems that prompted big changes in policy by the mid-1970s.[19] Among these problems were the following four:

1. The cash or goods involved in aid and development during this time included huge **military transfers** designed to cement Cold War alliances. So for example, a donor country like the US might give rifles and jeeps to the government of an allied Third World nation, and then claim that the cash value of these goods was actually "aid" to that society. And while such military assets may have helped recipient governments patrol their borders and enforce the law, they did very little to help the poorest of the poor. As we saw in Chapter 7, most experts believe that over the long term, military spending is an uneven, unproductive way to grow an economy. As an expert once said, "This is true because, once you've shot your bullet, or fired your rocket—boom!—there goes your investment. And what kind of return do you get on that investment? Dead bodies and ruined infrastructure—and that's if it hits anything at all!"[20]

2. When cash was given from donor to recipient during this time, it was often in the form of so-called "tied aid." **Tied aid** is basically cash given with strings attached. Here's a common scenario: Donor "D" gives cash to Recipient "R" but insists that "R" use the money to buy goods and services from companies headquartered back in "D." You can probably imagine the grounds on which this plan was criticized. First, by having to buy from the donor country, needy countries couldn't shop around, meaning that they couldn't necessarily purchase what they needed at the world's best price. Second, this scheme appeared too much as though it was actually a clever, indirect way for a donor government to support and subsidize its own companies back home (without voters in the donor country knowing the full details). American companies belonging to the US military–industrial complex (Chapter 7) were notable beneficiaries of this arrangement. Either way, tied aid seemed *selfish* on the part of the donor and *sub-optimal* for the people living in the recipient nation.[21]

3. Not that the recipients were all angels, either. A major discovery (over the years) with the top-down, state-to-state paradigm was that it encouraged and fed enormous amounts of **corruption** in recipient governments. In particular, and most scandalously, government officials in recipient nations would simply skim off money from the ODA given them, and pocket it for their personal use. Not all of it, of course, but a surprisingly large portion, leaving little for the people it was actually intended to help. Consider the following, disturbing fact: following his death in 1997, it was discovered that Mobutu Sese Seko, the former long-time dictator of Zaire (now Democratic Republic of the Congo), had squirrelled away enough money in private bank accounts in Switzerland to pay—on his own—the entire national debt of his country. Of course, that was not how he was choosing to spend the money. How could this happen? A common pattern was this: a large amount of cash was offered, as aid, to a government sworn to side with America in the Cold War. The leaders of the recipient government thanked the Americans publicly, and profusely. They then stole a big chunk of the aid for themselves. With the leftovers, they devised a high-profile development project, like constructing a new building in their capital city. They generated huge publicity for the opening of the building, inviting US officials to see for themselves what their aid money

had accomplished. (Often, these development projects were **white elephants**—massive, impressive-looking [i.e. photogenic] projects that did little to develop the recipient society.) And then, insidiously, the leaders used the continued underdevelopment of their people as an excuse to ask for yet more money, from which they skimmed yet more, and so on. Some political leaders became cynical, ruthless experts at milking the aid system in this way, with very little net benefit to the poorest of the poor.[22]

4. Finally, even when the aid actually reached the poor, and even when it was decent and well-designed in terms of its content, aid experts worried that this kind of top-down approach only created **dependency**. Developing societies would become dependent on charity, they feared, as opposed to becoming independent self-starters. More cynical experts thought that the old aid system was actually *deliberately designed* to create dependency in this way. They argued that this system of aid was constructed as a kind of indirect **neo-colonialism**, to replace the older model of direct colonialism that was then falling apart (particularly with the dissolution of the British and French empires, as we saw in Chapter 1). Critics believed that the donated cash and goods were designed to make recipients dependent on donors and, thus, beholden to them—even to the point of becoming like little colonies, "Cold War Colonies" as it were—receiving cash and military goods in exchange for loyalty and for buying the merchandise of the mother country.[23]

The Second Wave: Structural Adjustment Programs

By the mid-1970s, the problems with the first wave model were all too apparent: donor governments knew that corruption was going on, and they could see that widespread development wasn't taking place. The recipients, for their part, resented the tied aid, and some of them actually played "hard to get" in the game of Cold War politics, so that they could receive benefits both from the US and from the Soviet Union. There were bad feelings all around, and things needed to change.

From the donor's point of view, two big reforms were required: (1) less, or no, corruption on the part of recipient governments, and (2) actual, concrete improvements in life and economic development for average, non-elite persons in the recipient state. Thus was born the **structural adjustment program** (or SAP) paradigm. The inspiration behind the SAP came from a shift in development thinking during this time. The notion that governments should simply be given limitless funds to spend on pet projects that might stoke economic development had become discredited. The new thinking was that recipient nations ought to "adjust the structures" of their societies, so that sustainable, broad-based development could take place. Once they did so, they would then be rewarded with cash and loans that they could use to fuel the process further. If they failed to do so, the aid and development assistance would dry up. But two questions remained: *which structures* should be adjusted, and *in what direction?*

There came to be an understanding that the top-down, state-centric model was flawed, and that social institutions *other than* government bodies needed to be provided with resources and power if development were truly to occur in a given society. The private sector—for-profit business, notably, but also the basic skill and enabling-sectors, such as education and healthcare—needed attention. There are parallels here to what we saw in our examination of human rights in Chapter 9. Essentially, policy-makers came to understand that it would take *all* the institutions in the basic structure—government, law, the economy, schools, and hospitals—*empowered together*, to make development work. So, the direction of reform was very much on the side of creating the social foundations that were shown to have worked in the developed world: decent education, functioning infrastructure, some healthcare, but above all, a free-market economy with a robust private business sector and an established, efficient, fair and public legal system to enforce "the rules of the game."[24]

In practice, then, donor countries and such multilateral aid-and-development providers as the World Bank and the IMF got together with needy nations at this time to change aid-and-development packages. The donors analyzed each recipient country's development situation and prescribed the institutional changes required. Once made, the taps of development funding were turned on again. But—crucially—the bulk of this funding was now awarded as *loans* rather than cash or goods, in order to combat corruption: after all, there's no point trying to steal what you eventually have to pay back anyway, right? The nature of the institutional changes prescribed over time during this period—about 1975 to 1995—came to look very similar from country to country, almost like a "universal recipe" for further development. These changes usually included the following five items:

1. Cutting back the state's presence in the recipient society's economy, in order to allow for the growth of private business and free-market enterprise. Several steps were stressed here: slashing subsidies to various industries, and on such consumer staples as bread and gasoline; slashing the size of the public civil service; and reducing government regulation to reduce the cost of doing business there.

2. Opening up the country to allow foreign companies (i.e. multinational corporations) to come in, own property, and invest in the growth of that society.

3. Improving the basic legal foundations of the society, in particular by eliminating incompetence and corruption in the legal system and by building confidence that a resort to the legal system could, and would, produce peaceful, productive solutions to disagreements. Areas of particular interest included business law and private property rights: it was seen as important to ensure that governments wouldn't interfere in an arbitrary way with business practices or property. This would allow the private sector to grow and to be able to count on its private property rights, under a government that would promote business interests.

4. Establishing strong and systematic anti-corruption measures society-wide, including in the government itself. These would include anti-bribery laws, complete with effective enforcement measures.

5. Bringing inflation under control. Inflation, we saw in Chapter 6, is the rise in the cost of goods and services—i.e. the cost of living—over time. Small, stable rates of inflation are generally considered acceptable—people can handle small increases, and can make necessary business and purchasing plans they can stick to—but big, rapid, and dramatic price hikes have proven to be very bad for an economy, causing shortages, black-market trading, and the erosion of peoples' savings and investment plans.[25]

It all sounds sensible, and in theory it was. Certainly, it was a vast improvement in the conceptual understanding of what should be targeted for reform, in order to enable development: not big gifts for government officials but, rather, institutional changes throughout society. Moreover, the SAP era did provide some clearly needed improvements among recipient nations—legal changes, anti-corruption measures, less dependence on government. But in practice, there were drawbacks with this second-wave paradigm as well, both in the short term and over the long term.

In the short term, many of these mandated measures were *enormously unpopular*, and caused dislocation and adjustment. The civil servants who got fired didn't like it. The officials used to taking bribes didn't like it. Protected local corporations didn't like losing their subsidies or having now to compete for local business with foreign MNCs. Consumers didn't like having to pay more for bread and gasoline. And, in practice, "bringing inflation under control" means a government has to raise interest rates—i.e. the price of money— making it more expensive to get a loan, pay a mortgage, make car payments, and so on. So dramatic were some of these changes, and some of their consequences, that widespread riots broke out—especially over bread and gas—and some governments were forced to back down, or else they lost power altogether. SAPs came to be known as "shock therapy," and rebranding the mandated measures "**IMF conditionality**" did nothing to increase their popularity.[26]

In the long term, the SAP era *substantially increased the indebtedness of developing societies*, especially in Africa and Latin America. Many societies made these institutional changes—or tried to, or (more commonly) tried to but then kept only some and had to back down on others—and thus got access to loans from the IMF, the World Bank, private Northern banks, and individual national donor governments. Loans, of course, have to be repaid, and it was thought that this approach would cut down on corruption, at least compared with the extent of corruption that went on when aid took the form of flat-out cash donations. But once they had been cleared for loans, many societies took out far more loans than they could afford, to the point where a great many developing societies today have enormous debt problems. Collectively, the Global South owes the Global North more than US$2 trillion.

Debt holds countries back for the several reasons. To start, loans have to be re-paid, with interest and service fees. Every dollar spent on servicing the debt (i.e. paying the interest) is a dollar that *cannot* be spent on development. Moreover, debt servicing turns the flow of money in the wrong direction, from South to North—a situation that is far from ideal in an aid-and-development program. (You can predict what the neo-colonialists have to say about this!) Even worse, the loan provisions didn't really prevent corruption very much, as developing world leaders in the 1970s and 1980s *still* skimmed money, knowing that the obligation of repaying and servicing the debt would fall to their successors. Finally, these debts, and the service fees, *must* be repaid; otherwise, the defaulting countries will be punished severely, essentially getting cut off from any future loans. And these repayments must be made in the hard currency they were originally negotiated in—usually US dollars—and some countries have very few industries that can bring in the hard foreign currency revenues to make these repayments. Try, for instance, repaying a huge debt in US dollars when your only sources of American currency are fickle, highly competitive, low-margin industries like coffee, chocolate, and clothing. Today, some countries are being squeezed very badly,

> *Collectively, the Global South owes the Global North more than US$2 trillion.*

struggling to repay loans from 30 years ago while still trying to find the money to invest in new and current projects (like building schools) that are desperately needed to improve the lives of their people.[27]

The Third Wave: Bottom-Up Pluralism

The end of the Cold War, in the early 1990s, and the awareness of the difficulties with the second-wave SAP paradigm spurred the generation of the newest wave of thinking and policy regarding aid and development. Not that things are completely different today: depending on the country and situation, structural adjustment programs are still used, tied aid is still given, and even state-to-state transfers of weapons-as-aid are still conducted. But there has been a very substantial shift in development thinking, which has brought about a new consensus among experts that an approach we might call "bottom-up pluralism" is the way to go (see Figure 11.4).

The first thing to note about **bottom-up pluralism** is the pluralism part. Development aid is no longer exclusively state-centric, a transaction carried out between donor and recipient governments. This shift to a paradigm emphasizing pluralism *decreases* both corruption in the recipient government and the temptation to engage in political manipulation in the donor government. There are now *many key players* in the development game, each with a different role to play and contribution to make:

- There are individuals in developed countries making private remittance payments to family members in developing societies.

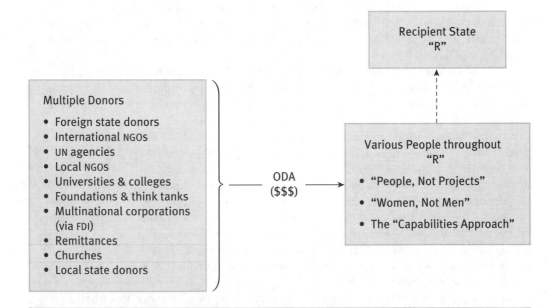

FIGURE 11.4 The Third Wave: Bottom-Up Pluralism

- There are multinational corporations building branch plant operations throughout the developing world, creating jobs, incomes, tax revenues, and international trade activity in societies that need all of the above.

- There are development charities and NGOs, in both donor countries and recipient countries, focusing on specific development tasks.

- There are foundations, think tanks, and whole university departments with a similar focus.

- There are international, multilateral institutions—notably the UNDP, the IMF, the World Bank, the OECD and the DAC—making heavy investments in the developing world.

- Last, but not least, there are still national governments—both donors and recipients—who remain major players. But, crucially, they are no longer the only players, and this explosion in number of participants is very beneficial.

In sum, no one agency can do it all, and too much power in the hands of any one kind of entity has always proved corrupting. The task is now really one of forming a co-ordinated partnership among all these players so that everyone is, so to speak, paddling in the same direction. State-centrism is dead; pluralistic partnership is the taste of the times.[28]

Hand in hand with pluralism goes the bottom-up reorientation. Gone is the notion of state governments being at the cutting edge of developmental changes, and heroically leading their societies onwards and upwards in wealth, power, and sophistication. They may have strategic roles still to play, and goodness knows governments can mess up the process, but confidence has been shaken in the belief that governments are the best leaders of the development process. It is now seen as *a many-factored causal process*, in which government has a role to play but alongside equally important players, notably the business sector, civil society institutions (like NGOs and the media), and basic enablement institutions (like education and health-care). In particular, the post–World War II notion that savvy governments could force-feed advanced development down the throats of their people with the right kind of agricultural and industrial projects has been completely discredited.[29]

> *State-centrism is dead; pluralistic partnership is the taste of the times.*

The development catchphrase of our time, indeed, is probably something like this: it's all about people, not projects. Experts and governments at the top know only so much (in spite of what they like to think they know). The true engines of growth and development in society are *not* carefully selected projects (like dam-building or constitutional reform) but, *rather*, the people on the ground. They know best the conditions in which they live . . . because they live in them. They know what the biggest problems are, and what might improve their lives, because they think about that every day. They know what would be a good business idea in their village, town, or city. And so on. The key development question then becomes: *how can we empower these people, so that they can turn these thoughts and experiences into reality, creating widespread growth in their societies?* This is a bottom-up orientation because the focus is on empowering and bettering everyone at the bottom—at the local level and throughout the nation—so that a broad-based momentum in favour of lasting, progressive growth can be started, with positive rippling effects upwards and outwards.[30]

Case Study: Micro-Finance

One of the best examples of this reorientation in development focus comes from the burgeoning field of what is called **micro-finance**. Some clever people got together and shared this thought: the flow of aid and development has been all wrong all along. The flows have been way too big—leading either to stealing or to debt—and they've been put into the wrong hands (i.e. the corrupt hands of officials, or the arrogant, mistaken hands of remote, self-styled "development experts"). Yes, let's give out a lot of money, *but only in tiny amounts*, across thousands of people, either as grants or as loans. We'll make people give us a small-scale business plan—say, buying 10 chickens, so they can sell eggs every day at the market—and, in exchange, we'll give them the $25 to make it happen.

My favourite story is of women in a village in rural Bangladesh—one of the least developed places on Earth—using their micro-finance money to buy, of all things, a cellphone (!), renting out its use to others. Their business boomed. People wanted to call their friends and relatives in the city, and poor farmers with no other means of checking the weather forecast—no TV, no radio, no newspaper—used it daily to call an information station to give them precisely that, allowing them to plan their daily agricultural activities much better.[31]

Micro-finance programs such as the one described above have sprouted up all over the developing world in the last 15 years, with huge success. One micro-finance bank, the Grameen Bank, even won the 2006 Nobel Peace Prize for its efforts, specializing in micro-finance loans to women in Bangladesh and India. Some of the important findings from the experiences of these micro-finance banks: the best customers are women; almost all the loans get repaid; the loans provide excellent seed money for small businesses; and they especially help women become financially independent of their husbands, which has led to more and better resources being made available to their children (e.g., food, clothing, and school supplies). It seems an outstanding way to stimulate real, widespread economic growth and development at the local level, amongst the poorest of the poor—the people with the greatest objective need for development assistance.[32]

The Capabilities Approach

Speaking of Nobel prizes, the one in economics was won in 1998 by the Oxford economist Amartya Sen. Originally from India, Sen has devoted his professional life to **development economics**. He is a leading thinker behind a current wave of development thought known as **the capabilities approach** because it focuses on building up a set of capabilities (or traits, or skills) within people, who thereby become empowered—or freed—to become productive members of society; this promotes economic growth and enhances the quality of life in their countries. Development is thus the freedom of the individual, leading to the freedom of the whole developing nation. But which personal capabilities, exactly, are we talking about?[33]

If we want people to be capable of being economically self-supporting, and capable of contributing to their society's advancement, what do they need? Don't think of massive

Studies in Technology

The mChip

To aid in the fight to improve public health in the developing world, there's a new device called the mChip. Invented by Samuel Sia, a professor of bio-medical engineering at Columbia University in New York City, it's a portable diagnostic tool the size and shape of a credit card. All it requires is one drop of blood from a finger prick, and the mChip can reveal a diagnosis within 15 minutes. It can diagnose a whole range of infections—including tetanus and hepatitis—and is currently being adapted to also detect HIV, syphilis, herpes, gonorrhoea, and more.

The mChip is easily portable, and eliminates the need to draw blood from a patient with a needle. It thus eliminates the need to refrigerate such blood samples, transport them to a clinic, analyze them there, and then return the information to the patient, along with treatment. All such things are very difficult, time-consuming, and expensive in the rural Global South. Moreover, the mChip is as easy to read as a home pregnancy test here in the developed world: the colour silver in the mChip's window reveals a positive diagnosis, which can be acted upon immediately by a healthcare practitioner.[34]

mega-projects like highways and hydroelectric dams; instead think of what an individual person needs in order to grow up into a self-supporting adult whose life both is enjoyable and improves the world. Well, the individual needs her life, obviously; and she needs, if not to be healthy, then at least to avoid the worst kinds of disease and sickness that would prevent her from being self-supportive. So, all kinds of basic, preventative healthcare measures are implicated by this new line of thinking about development—items such as those charted in Figure 10.4 last chapter: childhood inoculations; basic education about disease prevention, nutrition, diet, exercise, hydration, and hygiene; programs designed to control, or eliminate, disease-carrying pests, especially mosquitoes; and the most serious, sustained efforts at providing adequate supplies of clean drinking and bathing water, basic sanitation, and at least sufficient calorie intake for one's stage of life. These things are quite easy to list, yet note how much effort they imply, and how utterly different is the focus from before: instead of highways, healthcare; instead of office buildings, clean water and sufficient food; instead of massive loans, mosquito nets and childhood immunizations.

Today's big enemies of underdevelopment are no longer manipulative First World governments and corrupt local officials; they are the more basic and universal human struggles with things like hunger, thirst, and sickness. Poverty is also an enemy, as the worst kind of poverty is radically disempowering, dramatically limiting a person's options in life. Poverty also, obviously, is tied to issues like hunger and the inability to access medicines in the event of illness. Perhaps this is why the UN listed, as the very first item among its highly publicized **Millennium Development Goals** (or MDG, formulated in 2000 for achievement by 2015), the cutting in half of the world's worst rates of poverty and hunger.[35]

The UN's Millennium Development Goals

Ignorance, **illiteracy** (the inability to read), **innumeracy** (the inability to do basic math), and lack of knowledge and skills can prevent a person from earning a self-supporting living and contributing positively to the growth of society. And so education, especially for girls and women, gets huge emphasis in the capabilities approach. The UN has, as the second of its Millennium Development Goals, the achievement of universal—compulsory and free—primary education for all the world's children.

The middle goals in the UN's MDG all have to do with the health, well-being, and liberation of women and their children. As noted earlier, it's a firm article of development faith nowadays—but a faith backed by decades of cumulative fact—that *investment in women and children has the best overall payoff per development dollar.* (To best capture the current mood in development thought, add to the catchphrase cited above—"people, not projects"—the following: *"and women, not men."*) So the UN's development goals highlight the need to increase gender equality where possible and, by 2015, to cut by three-quarters the number of women who die every year while giving birth. The latter is considered a readily achievable goal, as childbirth is a procedure from which almost no one dies in the developed world. Two related MDGs are, first, to decrease by two-thirds the mortality rate of children under 5, and second, to reverse, or at least halt, the worldwide spread of HIV/AIDS, which hits women on a disproportionately high basis. Aid and development workers are now increasingly involved in doing things like distributing condoms and challenging cultural beliefs and practices that can lead to the transmission of HIV/AIDS (such as the notion that "real men" don't use condoms or that it's all right for a married man to have sex with prostitutes, even if

A billboard in Malawi carries the president's appeal to stop the spread of HIV. How would you design a campaign to change beliefs about AIDS in a developing country? (© Mark Boulton/Alamy)

it means returning home to infect one's wife). Efforts to challenge such beliefs and customs occur via **public health information and education campaigns** throughout the developing world, using the media (radio, billboards, posters, and brochures) and free medical clinics to spread the message and the tools (e.g. condoms) needed to realize it.[36]

The two final UN Millennium Development Goals are more abstract and systematic than the concrete and targeted goals mentioned above. One, which has already been discussed, deals with the critical need to forge—among the large plurality of players—a true and global partnership for development. Lastly, there is a desire to make sure that whatever projects are selected as being appropriate for a given society, they be environmentally sensitive and sustainable over time (see Chapter 2). In general, you can see how the projects imagined under the new capabilities approach seem so much more sustainable and environmentally friendly than the mammoth military and mega-industrial projects of old: schools and hospitals instead of weaponry and dams; injections and inoculations instead of new government buildings; micro-finance loans and classes on literacy and numeracy, not more military bases along the border.[37]

In convenient, bullet-point summary, the UN's MDGs are as follows:

- cut the worst poverty and hunger by 50 per cent

- achieve universal primary education

- increase gender equality

- decrease by two-thirds the mortality rate for children under 5

- decrease by three-quarters the number of women who die during childbirth

- reverse, or at least halt, the spread of HIV/AIDS infection

- ensure that new development projects are environmentally sustainable

- develop a global development partnership.

What follows is a bullet-point summary of the most popular (i.e., the most frequently funded and undertaken) contemporary development projects, based on changes in development thinking and policy:

- local water well construction

- basic literacy and numeracy education

- purchase and distribution of school supplies

- immunization and vitamin distribution programs

- mosquito nets and spraying

- distribution of organic fertilizers (to boost food growth yet cut down on polluting chemical fertilizers)

- sustainable irrigation projects

- micro-finance loans

- public health information campaigns

- women's rights, and women's health, information campaigns.[38]

CONCLUSION

This chapter wraps up our look, in Part IV, at how people have been trying to improve the lives of individuals everywhere, taking the focus of foreign affairs and international studies beyond traditional concerns with the power of states and the wealth of nations. In this chapter, we have looked at aid and development and canvassed different concepts of development, coming to see—through our history of the "three waves" of development policy—how the current state of the art has come into being. The focus today is on enabling individuals everywhere with the most basic capabilities they need to both survive and thrive. It is based on the conviction that if we enable people, then *they* will be the ones who will trigger the further growth and development of their own societies, resulting in measureable gains in human well-being around the world.

REVIEW QUESTIONS

1. Given the various problems, should there be aid and development programs at all? Why not just let everyone do the best they can for themselves?

2. Which do you find the best method for defining and measuring the development of a society? Why? Anything you'd change, or improve, even in your most preferred method?

3. Research an instance of an FDI by an MNC. Investigate the pros and cons of the impact of the financial investment upon the recipient country.

4. Consider the two maps in Figure 11.1 and Figure 11.2: Africa and Scandinavia. Pick a country in each region, and research what life is like there, and comment more broadly on how fair that is, or the broader lessons to be drawn for international studies from the fact of such enormous differences.

5. Why did the top-down, state-centric model of aid and development fail? What handful of things did it still achieve in spite of its drawbacks?

6. Why did the SAP model fail? What handful of things did it achieve regardless?

7. This chapter presented a positive view of the current wave of development thought and policy, "the capabilities approach." But other scholars have cautioned that it is too soon to pronounce this new policy a success, and that this third-wave model may be too local, not broad-based enough to actually generate clear and marked development *throughout* society. Thus far, which position would you most agree with, and why?

8. Imagine you are the head of state of a poor, developing country. Your nation has a huge debt, a huge population, a small economy focused on agricultural goods, and innumerable development needs. Given what we've learned in this chapter, what would be your development priorities, and why? What would you most request from the international community? What kinds of trade-offs or choices might you have to make?

9. Imagine you are the head of state of a wealthy, developed nation. You personally believe that your country can, and should, do more in terms of international aid and development. However, you know your people like to have low taxes and would prefer government energies to be devoted to helping the local poor and homeless. What could you say, or do, to talk your people out of their "aid fatigue" and into giving more to the global poor?

10. Research how well the international community has done meeting the UN's Millennium Development Goals thus far. Only a few years remain in the target timeframe: what is likely to be achieved? What will still remain to be done? Anything you'd add to, or change in, the MDG, should they be renegotiated for another set of goals and timelines?

WEBSITES FOR FURTHER RESEARCH

Canadian International Development Agency (CIDA) www.acdi-cida.gc.ca

Doctors Without Borders www.doctorswithoutborders.org

Engineers Without Borders www.ewb.ca

United Nations Development Programme www.undp.org

USAID www.usaid.gov

NOTES

1. A. Einstein, *World As I See It* (London: Citadel, 2006); W. Isaacson, *Einstein: His Life and Universe* (New York: Simon and Schuster, 2008).
2. G. Mavrotas, ed., *Foreign Aid for Development* (Oxford: Oxford University Press, 2010).
3. United Nations, *United Nations Human Development Report, 2009* (New York: UNDP, 2010); available at http://hdr.undp.org/en. See also R. Peet & E. Hartwick, *Theories of Development* (London: Guilford, 2009).
4. C. Graham, *Happiness Around the World* (Oxford: Oxford University Press, 2009).
5. United Nations, *Human Development Report, 2009* (op. cit., note 3).
6. P. Haslam, et al., eds, *Introduction to International Development* (Oxford: Oxford University Press, 2008).
7. S. Cohen, *Multinational Corporations and Foreign Direct Investment* (Oxford: Oxford University Press, 2007); T. Moran, *Harnessing Foreign Direct Investment for Development* (Washington, DC: Center for Global Development, 2006).
8. Engineers Without Borders Canada, www.ewb.ca
9. T. Moran, *Foreign Direct Investment and Development* (London: Institute for International Economics, 1998).
10. J. Lawlor, *The Church and International Development* (London: Universal, 1999).
11. A. Bebbington, et al., eds, *Can NGOs Make a Difference?* (London: Zed, 2008); M. Lindenburg, *Going Global: Transforming Relief and Development NGOs* (London: Kumarion, 2001);

A. Florini, ed., *The Third Force: The Rise of Transnational Civil Society* (New York: Carnegie Endowment for International Peace, 2000).

12. Haslam, *Introduction* (op. cit., note 6); S. Maimbo & D. Ratha, eds, *Remittances: Development Impact and Future Prospects* (Washington, DC: World Bank Reports, 2005).

13. G. Carbonnier, ed., *International Development Policy* (London: Palgrave Macmillan, 2012).

14. Ibid. See also UNDP, Human Development Reports, at http://hdr.undp.org/en

15. C. Lancaster, *Foreign Aid* (Chicago: University of Chicago Press, 2006); D. Mjinkeu & H. Cameron, eds, *Aid for Trade and Development* (Cambridge: Cambridge University Press, 2007).

16. C.D. Wright, *The Ethics of Trade and Aid: Development, Charity, or Waste?* (London: Continuum, 2011).

17. L. Picard & T. Buss, *A Fragile Balance: Re-Examining the History of Foreign Aid* (London: Kumarion, 2009).

18. J. Goldstein & S. Whitworth, *International Relations: Canadian Edition* (Toronto: Pearson, 2005); J. Stiglitz & G. Meier, *Frontiers in Development* (Oxford: Oxford University Press, 2000).

19. J. Perkins, *Geopolitics and The Green Revolution* (Oxford: Oxford University Press, 1997).

20. B. MacDonald, *Military Spending in Developing Economies* (Montreal: McGill–Queen's University Press, 1997).

21. R. Riddell, *Does Foreign Aid Really Work?* (Oxford: Oxford University Press, 2008).

22. D. Moyo, *Dead Aid* (New York: FSG, 2009).

23. W. Easterly, *The White Man's Burden* (New York: Penguin, 2007).

24. M.R. Abouharb & D. Cingaranelli, *Human Rights and Structural Adjustment* (Cambridge: Cambridge University Press, 2008).

25. P.-R. Agenor, *The Economics of Adjustment and Growth* (Cambridge, MA: Harvard University Press, 2004); J. Sachs, *The End of Poverty* (New York: Penguin, 2006).

26. J. Sachs, *Understanding Shock Therapy* (Boston: Social Market Foundation, 1994); J.M. Boughton & D. Lombardi, eds, *Finance, Development and The IMF* (Oxford: Oxford University Press, 2009); C. Weaver, *Hypocrisy Trap: The World Bank and The Poverty of Reform* (Princeton: Princeton University Press, 2008).

27. J.R. Vreeland, *The IMF and Economic Development* (Cambridge: Cambridge University Press, 2003); F. Tarp, *Foreign Aid and Development: Lessons Learnt and Directions for the Future* (London: Routledge, 2000).

28. G. Mavrotes & M. McGillivray, *Development Aid: A Fresh Look* (London: Palgrave Macmillan, 2009).

29. R. Rottenburg, et al., eds, *Far-Fetched Fads: A Parable of Development Aid* (Cambridge, MA: MIT Press, 2009); S. Ahmed & D. Potter, *NGOs in International Politics* (London: Kumarion, 2006).

30. P. Collier, *The Bottom Billion* (Oxford: Oxford University Press, 2008).

31. M.S. Robinson, *The Microfinance Revolution* (Washington, DC: World Bank, 2001); M. Harper, *Profit for the Poor: Cases in Micro-Finance* (London: Practical Action, 1998).

32. M. Yunus, *Banker to the Poor: Micro-Lending and The Battle Against World Poverty* (Washington, DC: Public Affairs, 2003); P. Smith & E. Thurman, *A Billion Bootstraps* (New York: McGraw Hill, 2007).

33. A. Sen, *Development as Freedom* (New York: Anchor, 2nd edn, 2000).

34. *Columbia Magazine* (Winter 2011–12), pp. 52–4.

35. S. Fukuda-Parr, *MDGs: For a People-Centred Development Agenda* (New York: Routledge, 2012). See also UNDP, Human Development Reports, at http://hdr.undp.org/en

36. M. Nussbaum, *Women and Human Development: The Capabilities Approach* (Chicago: University of Chicago Press, 2001).

37. M. Clarke & S. Feeny, *MDGs: Looking Beyond 2015* (New York: Routledge, 2011).

38. Ibid.

Conclusion

"Rich or poor, I shall be free. I shall not be free in this or that land, in this or that region. I shall be free everywhere on Earth." —*Jean-Jacques Rousseau (1712–1778),* *French philosopher*[1]

It seems like the biggest, most sweeping, practical question we can ask about international studies, having examined so many issues throughout this book is: will the world's future be better or worse than it is today? And in what ways? Can we look forward to **utopia** (a happy, peaceful, progressive future), or will we sink into **dystopia** (an unhappy, conflict-torn future, which marks regression from where we are today)?[2] No one knows for sure, and both optimists and pessimists can marshal various facts and theories to support their case. I leave it for your personal consideration. My own view is that while I *hope* the optimist is right, I *fear* the pessimist may be correct on some counts.

Indeed, throughout this book, we have seen strong clashes between competing concepts and visions, between rival realities and conflicting interpretations of our world. Even though the truth is often complex and nuanced, we have effectively examined many salient topics using, as our framework, **binary** (i.e. **two-sided**) **contrasts** that, in their own way, summarize quite helpfully so many subjects in today's world. Here are some of the more important contrasts that come to mind:

- realism versus idealism
- selfish interests versus impersonal obligations
- nation versus world
- the powerful versus the weak
- imperial core versus colonies
- developed versus developing
- North versus South
- the West versus "The Rest"
- urban versus rural
- man versus woman
- democratic versus non-democratic
- capitalist free-market versus alternatives
- industrial versus agricultural versus service economy
- spending versus saving
- free trade versus protectionism
- rights-respecting versus rights-violating

- technological versus not
- literate/educated versus not
- secular versus religious
- Abrahamic versus Dharmic
- moderate versus extremist
- conservative versus liberal
- liberal versus socialist
- nationalist versus internationalist/cosmopolitan
- rich versus poor
- insider versus outsider
- healthy versus sick
- well-fed versus hungry
- watered versus thirsty
- pollution versus population
- individual versus social
- global versus local
- war versus peace
- past versus present versus future
- and, once more, optimist versus pessimist.

COULD WORLD GOVERNMENT BE THE SOLUTION?

Perhaps one way to transcend all these sharp dualisms, and to make it more likely that the optimist can and will prevail, is to create an effective world government. Plenty of smart people through the ages—from Thomas Hobbes down to Bertrand Russell and beyond—have thought that this is the last, best bet for humanity's future.[3]

But don't we already have world government, you ask? The short, forceful answer is *no*; and I'm often surprised at how many people find this fact an eye-opener. We do *not* have a world government. The United Nations, you will recall from Chapter 5, remains a *voluntary association* of very different nations, and *not* a government above, and binding on, them. The longer answer is that while we do have *some aspects* of **global governance**—the UN, for example, does serve some useful global functions, especially in connection with technical, specialist, and operational issues like trade and health—these are patchy and do not add up to the kind of effective and far-reaching world government here in view.

Options for Global Governance

We might think of global governance options *on a continuum*, from the loosest, least governed model to the most tightly and highly governed (see Figure 12.1). We'll look at each model in turn.

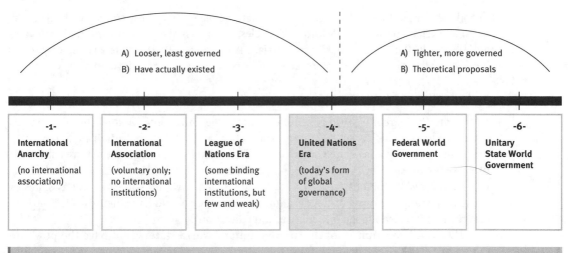

FIGURE 12.1 Options for Global Governance/World Government

1. *International Anarchy*

Featuring *no international association at all*, this model is characterized by international **anarchy** (literally "no-rules"—i.e. total non-governance, everyone for him- or herself) between nation-states. Arguably, this is the historical norm, dominating the landscape until the dawn of the so-called **international system**, better known as the birth of international law, beginning around 1650. (For more on international law, consult Chapter 5.)

2. *International Association*

This model marks the first attempt to create rule-bound and predictable foreign affairs, and is characterized by *some voluntary co-operation between states*, but no international institutions to bind them or to help them solve ongoing, common problems. This model, as old as the hills, was practised especially between like-minded countries and those sharing military alliances.

3. *League of Nations Era*

This period brought *some binding international institutions*, but only a few and with very narrow reference and power. As we saw in Chapter 5, the League of Nations was a precursor to the UN, from about 1919 to 1939. Some international institutions created around that time, like the Universal Postal Union and the International Labour Organization, still exist today.

4. *United Nations Era*

This model features *many binding international institutions*, quite a few of them effective, but very few truly global institutions, and no overall binding world government. The effective international institutions tend to have a narrower scope (e.g. bilateral or regional instead of global) and/or a narrower subject matter (e.g. functional or technical, instead of economic, or military, or political). This is the current state-of-play, where we are today with the international system: there's the UN and its agencies, but also massively powerful national states and blocs, like the US, the EU, China, Russia, OPEC, and NATO. There are also big disparities between nations rich and poor, powerful and weak, developed and developing.

5. *Federal World Government*

In this model, there is a *world government, but in the form of a federation.* In other words, there would be a single, non-voluntary world state, and it would be run like a federal government, say in Canada or the United States. The world government would have a finite list of powers over such matters as war and peace, and have sole responsibility for achieving the desired result. Nation-states like the US and Canada would still exist, but as states or provinces within the one world federation; as such, they would have their own list of powers (for instance, over language, culture, and education).

The world government of this **non-voluntary world state** would have the power to (1) gather its own tax revenue (and thus would *not* be reliant on voluntary contributions, like the UN is) and (2) enforce and bring to life its decisions, even on members who disagree (just as in domestic society—this would imply some robust police and military powers, and assets, for the world state). For it to be a true world government, it would need to have something like the traditional **three branches of government**

1.   a **legislature** (to debate, research, and craft laws)

2.   an **executive** (to enforce the laws, necessitating a supporting bureaucracy as well)

3.   a **judiciary** (to interpret laws and peacefully resolve conflicting interpretations of the law).

6. *Unitary State World Government*

This would be like the federal world government model described above *but in the form of a solitary (or unitary) central state.* There would be no autonomous nation-state provinces, although there may be something akin to municipal or regional administrations with very focused, practical functions like maintaining roads and sewers, fighting fires, handling garbage collection, and so on. (China and France are often described as close examples of unitary states: each has only a central government that dominates the political life of the country; and, while are some local authorities, they exist to carry out the wishes of the central government.) All the big, controversial, political issues would be handled at the level of the one, non-voluntary world government.

Thus, when we speak of world government, we mean the fifth and sixth models described above, which are well beyond today's current reality (model #4). With that, we return to the question: might world government be the solution we are looking for, for the future?[4]

The Case For World Government

Three strong arguments come up, again and again, in favour of the creation of world government.

1. *The Realist Argument*

Realists are often thought of as arch-nationalists. And they *can* come across that way. But their worldview actually indicates a strong, indirect argument in favour of world government, at least in theory. Recall, from Chapter 4, the "assurance problem," which realists view as the essence of international relations. According to realists, states cannot trust each other, which means that they are *fundamentally on their own* in this world. The only smart foreign policy is a selfish one. This situation fosters insecurity and a lack of trust and co-operation between countries, and this makes the international world such an imperfect and problem-filled place. A logical solution is the creation of a world government: create an effective world government—which, being over and above the level of states, can bring them all in line—and then states *won't have* this assurance problem, which seems to spark so many wars in particular. The "trust," or at least co-operation, will then be enforced, and thus could be counted on.

Those persuaded by this logic see world government as a viable solution to the assurance problem, one that could:

- mitigate or even eliminate war
- co-ordinate much more effectively economic growth and development in all countries
- deal effectively with the large number of cross-border issues, such as
  - pollution and global warming
  - drug and human trafficking
  - rogue regimes
  - weapons and drug smuggling
  - terrorism
  - weapons proliferation
  - refugee flows and migration trends
  - overpopulation
  - cross-border diseases, like bird flu
  - sudden crises of starvation, massacre, or natural disaster.[5]

2. *Previous Successes*

Not only do supporters of world government have a strong *theoretical* argument—regarding how the assurance problem points to the solution of a global state—but they also have strong *practical or empirical cases* to enumerate. (And this is true *even though* there has never actually been a world government.) They tend to cite two cases in particular: the United States historically, and the European Union (EU) today. Citing the US, they point out how weak, insecure, and unprosperous the early American states—Massachusetts, New York, Virginia, etc.—were until they formed an effective federal or central government to help them solve their common problems. Having done so, in the 1780s, they completed their quest for independence from Great Britain, and were able to spread their territory quickly across North America. When the central government of this young federation was later challenged by the secessionist South during the Civil War (1861–5), the victory by the North only consolidated the union further, leading to ever-higher standards of living and, eventually, to the worldwide projection of American force and culture—indeed, to the point where we now speak of the United States as the global hegemon. Imagine, then, the analogous gains to be made by the various countries of the world coming together to form a global government.[6]

The EU is an even better example, since it was formed freely by formerly bitter wartime enemies, and is composed of many different nation-states, speaking many different languages, and with quite uneven levels of development (as, say, between France and Germany on the one hand, and Slovakia and Slovenia on the other). Unlike the American case, it is a genuinely international or "supra-national" governance project, and shows how apparently huge differences—over culture, language, historical memory and scars, and levels of wealth—*can* be overcome. And it has been such an enormous success: continuous, relentless growth, both in membership and in economic development, to the point where it is, today, probably both the richest and most populous economic unit in the world. No country (as of writing) has ever left the Union, and there is a lineup of countries clamouring to get in.

Fans of world government conclude that if Europe can do it—Europe, with its sharp national divisions and savage history of armed conflict—then the world, for all its divisions, can do it, too. Europe, in fact, provides not only overall inspiration in this direction but also a detailed, recent, practical roadmap showing how to get there. As we saw in Chapter 5, following this roadmap would mean starting small, on practical and functional areas promising clear mutual gains (e.g. in international trade, or global public health), and then letting those consolidate and persuade people, before moving on to more ambitious political agendas (such as realizing human rights).[7]

3. *One World, One Government*

This final argument, articulated by Thomas Pogge, simply says: look at the facts. Back when the world was carved up into different families, tribes, cities, provinces, nations, or states, then it made sense to have levels of government appropriate for that level of development and interaction. But now things have changed, and our ideas about government and orga-

> Things have changed, and our ideas about government and organization need to keep up with the reality of our times.

nization need to keep up with the reality of our times. With globalization, the world's different peoples, cities, and economies are interconnected as never before. This interconnection is widening and deepening by the hour. With the emergence of one truly globalized world, we need one truly effective world government, to manage and regulate global activity. And we need this not just for the logical sense of (one-to-one) proportion here but, moreover, for the practical sense of dealing with all the cross-border problems and issues listed above and discussed throughout this book. Many of these problems, like the smuggling of drugs, weapons, and people, exist precisely because there isn't effective international co-operation and regulation between various national communities. *The problems arise because of the gaps between nations.* The very nature of these problems calls out for effective global governance to plug these gaps, if we are to have any shot at solving them, or at least bringing them under management and mitigating their worst effects.[8]

The Case Against World Government

Five arguments are most often trotted out in opposition to the idea of world government.

1. A Historical Observation

This isn't exactly an argument *against* world government, but it *does* need to be noted that Christian Protestants, in particular, are strongly opposed to the idea of world government. This is partly tied to religious reasons, relating specifically to what Protestants believe about how the world will come to an end: they believe that the rise of world government is foretold in the Bible's Book of Revelations to lead to "end-times." This form of world government will be an instrument of evil, and it will bring about the Battle of Armageddon—between Christ and Anti-Christ—leading ultimately to Judgment Day and God's final victory.

This point is also related to something more worldly and historical: the opposition between Catholics and Protestants. Even today, Catholics are much more comfortable talking about world government than Protestants are. I suggest this may have something to do with the fact that the Catholic Church, for over a thousand years, was the one and only church in Europe. That very fact alienates Protestants from the idea of world government: they indirectly associate it with the dominance of Rome, and their own persecution, and their own reasons for leaving the Church and setting up their own rival churches (often national in nature, and not universal in scope).[9]

2. The Anti-Socialist Argument

The notion here—a classical liberal one, as defined in Chapter 2—boils down to this: only a government-loving socialist would think that adding *yet another layer of government* to what we already have is going to improve anything. There are very good reasons to think that world government will *not* be able to solve the huge list and depth of international problems: risks of corruption, incompetence, favour-seeking by special-interest groups, gaps in knowledge, lags in time between policy idea and policy effect, and so on. Indeed, government—even *good* government—has failed to turn any one single national society into utopia, and so why should we think it could succeed on an international scale? These are the same kinds of argument that champions of free market economics give in advocating *minimal, not maximal,* government worldwide. The solution to the world's problems, they insist, is emphatically not *yet more* bureaucrats and *yet more* taxation and *yet more* forms to be filled and licenses applied for, *yet another* army, navy, and air force, *yet another* elected assembly, *yet more* scheming and self-serving politicians, and so on. There's a lot to be said for the forces of freedom, for the energy unleashed by *non-governance*, and for "letting a thousand flowers bloom."[10]

3. How Would We Get There, Actually? Obstacles and Enemies

This argument reasons that world government might sound great *in theory*, but *in practice* it's simply not possible to set one up. The closest we have, today, to a true world government would be the EU. There is no denying the incredible success that this institution has been, and the great improvement in peace and prosperity that it has brought to Europe. But that's just the point: its success is limited to the people of Europe. The big difference between the EU and a world government is that the latter would have to govern the entire planet. And the entire planet does *not* have the same cultural cohesion, shared worldview, same approximate living standards, same level of technology and development, that Europe does. For all their differences, the people of Europe do come out of a common civilization, Western civilization. Whereas, across the globe, there are *many different civilizations*, and they sharply differ in many vital ways, as we've seen throughout this book. The essence of this objection is this: the people of the world simply will not agree to the construction of an effective world government, because the differences between them run far too deep.

So then let's talk about the United States, also mentioned above. And let's talk about the US *not* as a good analogy for world government but rather, in practice, as *probably its biggest opponent*. Why? Beyond the reasons noted in the first point above (the US is historically Protestant, by majority), America is currently the global hegemon, as we saw in Chapter 1. Why, from a realist perspective, would it ever agree to help form a world government more powerful than itself? For all the competing demands put upon it, the US would surely prefer the status quo to a future in which it would have to obey a world government. Moreover, the US has already shown itself to be hostile, politically, to any international institution that it fears may hamper American interests (witness the International Criminal Court and, at times, even the UN itself, especially the General Assembly). Can anyone, then, really imagine the US surrendering its nuclear weapons and its massive military assets to a new world government? Or imagine American citizens agreeing to pay more of their tax dollars to a new world government—a government wherein they would *not* have majority democratic control over how such money got spent? In the absence of an imminent and ferocious catastrophe threatening the whole planet, it's—um—rather unthinkable to imagine such things happening.

And let's not single out the US. We saw in Chapter 5 how each of the "Big Five" permanent members of the UN's Security Council—the US, Britain, China, France, and Russia—has systematically blocked *any* attempt at real reform. We might ask, quite bitingly: *if we can't even fix the Security Council, how are we ever going to create a good global government?* In other words, we've got our hands full just with all the problems under global governance option 4 (see Figure 12.1); how are we supposed to leapfrog, magically, to options 5 or 6 and be ready for the problems there?

4. *Government Must Be Rooted in Community*

American political theorist Michael Walzer is the source of this argument. He says that all legitimate, permissible, and stable governments grow naturally out of the communities they govern. They come to *represent* those people, and in turn the people *consent* to being governed by them. A stable, effective relationship comes into being: the people consent, pay taxes, and support the system, and the government diligently tries to solve their problems and better their lives. But, Walzer insists, *there is no such thing as "the international community."* In reality there are many different communities in international life, and so any attempt to graft a global government on top of them all would be coercive, artificial, and doomed to fail. There need to be some commonalities of outlook, of experience, of general worldview, and a sense of trust, to create a true community; and only once you have such a community can you have a good government naturally and stably ruling over it. *We're just not there yet.* Globalization or no globalization, we're not even close, especially on values, as we saw in Chapter 3, on culture.[11]

(The supporter of world government would reply that there *are* common values globally, or pretty nearly so, such as human rights, which we discussed in Chapter 9. There may not be *many* of these global values, but they *are* real, and they are promising. Also, is it really true that successful government *must* be rooted in a sense of community? Why can't governments emerge out of *practical problem-solving*, and gain legitimacy by showing that they can solve problems well? That, and not the expression of common values, is what attracts consent and the willingness to pay tax. The example of Europe comes to mind once more.[12])

5. *Threat of Coercion and Global Imperialism*

Many people have suggested that the big problem with world government is that far from being a guarantor of world peace, it could itself become a massive threat to world security, and in fact might even become a global dictatorship. Now, the dictatorship reference might be extreme, but the better argument here concerns **risk management**: if we created a world government, and gave it government-like powers (including army, navy, air force, police powers, jails, control over taxation, interest rates, and budgets), then no other government on Earth could resist it. Indeed, in many ways, that would be the point of forming a world government: everyone would be forced to co-operate on these common problems, theoretically for the benefit of all. But what if, down the road, the world government was taken over, internally, by a group of extremists? This is not at all an uncommon occurrence in the history of governments around the world: indeed, has there ever been a country that hasn't had its government, at least temporarily, hijacked by damaging extremists? We would all be completely exposed to the threats and forces of such a rogue regime, with nothing but popular rebellion to fall back upon (when formerly we would have had armies, navies, and air forces of our own). It's just more prudent *not* to create such a creature, and to deal with the world's problems as best we can otherwise.[13]

KANT'S COSMOPOLITAN FEDERATION

All right, you might say, if world government is not the solution, then what is? Or are we just condemned to being where we are? Consider German philosopher Immanuel Kant's influential thoughts in this regard, offering us a middle-road alternative.

Kant, way back in 1795, wrote a famous essay called *Perpetual Peace*. There he argued in favour of what he called a **cosmopolitan federation**. He put forward a provocative thesis, namely, that "republican governments" (as Kant called them) *would not go to war against each other*. It followed that we should try to increase the number of these governments, as the way to increasing peace in the world.

Kant's **republican government** is one that would look quite familiar to us today. It respects and realizes the rights of its individual citizens, and governs with their consent. It's a limited government with no tyrannical designs, either against its own citizens' freedoms or against the territory or authority of any other foreign government. It has a free economy, urges its citizens to excel culturally and economically, and shows foreign visitors warm hospitality. Kant reasoned that a country like this would never start a war against another, similarly structured, country. It would not be domineering and tyrannical, and thus not a conquering force. And its people, since they would have control, would never authorize such wars in the first place. Kant thought that people are basically rational, and they don't want to start wars, which are so risky and destructive and do not seem to serve anyone's self-interest. Moreover, people living in a free society have all kinds of better ways to spend their time, to seek satisfaction, and to quench any competitive striving: arts, business, culture, education, the professions, personal romance, sports—you name it. These are the things that would occupy their time and thoughts instead of political conquest and territorial expansion.[14]

American political scientist Michael Doyle has, in our time, taken over Kant's early conjectures and put out a **democratic peace thesis**, suggesting that *democracies have never gone to war against each other, nor will they ever do so*, for reasons very similar to what Kant suggests. Note that Doyle's thesis, like Kant's, is only that republics/democracies won't go to war *against each other*—not that they won't go to war at all. In fact, Doyle notes that democracies can actually be quite belligerent when confronting non-democratic regime types, especially dictatorships, since they are convinced of their own moral superiority.

Looking at the facts, Doyle seems correct. Counting all major wars of the modern era (since 1750), the three countries most frequently involved in armed conflict have been the United States, Britain, and France. But, these countries, since becoming true democracies after World War I (once slavery had ended and women had won the vote), have, indeed, never gone to war against each other. And ditto for all the other democracies.

> If democracies really do never go to war against each other, then we need to increase the number of democracies worldwide so that we will have more peace.

Doyle's democratic peace thesis has received considerable scrutiny and scholarly support. Many have tried to prove him wrong, offering up possible counter-examples. But these have all been proven false, and there is now widespread consensus that the democratic peace thesis is valid. If so, it points one substantial way towards Kant's dream of "perpetual peace": if democracies never go to war against each other, then we need to increase the number of democracies worldwide so that we will have more peace. Theoretically, if every country were to become a democracy, we would then have a true and enduring solution to the problem of war. And, given the open and rights-respecting nature of democracies, we could also predict much greater co-operation and effectiveness on a whole range of other international problems, such as pollution, aid and development, and the growth of trade.[15]

Here's how Kant imagined this step-by-step dynamic, moving forward:

1. Several countries, themselves peaceful, prosperous, free, and rights-respecting, ought to form a club. This club is totally voluntary and has, as its main terms, the following: (a) each member must be committed to these values to join; (b) each agrees to defend anyone in the club if and when it is attacked by countries outside of the club; and (c) each member agrees to allow for free trade, science, and technology, and the free movement of peoples within the borders of the club.

2. Kant predicted that such a club would be a spectacular success (like the EU so far)—so much so that other countries would experience envy. The envy, or jealousy, would produce one of two responses: either irritation and attack or the desire to join. Kant said the club should freely allow other countries to join, so long as they keep to the terms of the deal. They might have to reform their own societies, so that they could

Can we ever solve war, as Kant's "Perpetual Peace" promises? Why, or why not? Might war, or at least military readiness, actually be essential *for* peace? Or is that just wishful thinking which props up the status quo? (© Bart Sadowski/1Stockphoto)

be "fit" enough to join the club. So be it; and only then would they get in. But if the envy provoked attack, the republican club would have the right to defend itself, and war would be on. Kant said that if and when the club beat back such an aggressor and defeated it in war, the club could, and should, forcibly transform the institutions in the aggressor state to republican, rights-respecting ones. The club could essentially create, by force, a new member for the club—*but only if first attacked*. We discussed some of these post-war reconstruction issues in Chapter 8.

3.   Over time (as in centuries, not merely decades), Kant predicted that the club would grow and grow, until a truly *global* cosmopolitan federation developed. Not a binding, institutionalized world government, but a voluntary club of decent, rights-respecting countries that could and would offer their people security and justice, peace and prosperity, and the freedom to pursue their own skills, interests, and happiness.[16]

Conclusion: Bottom-Up Pluralism, Revisited

The above is a rather hopeful scenario, and rather top-down, focused as it is on issues of governance and the structuring of the inter-state system. But throughout this book, we've seen lots of evidence that (a) a top-down focus can lead to, well, imperfections, and (b) hopeful optimism might strain against some salient facts. (See especially the clash between optimist and pessimist over the environment, in Chapter 2, in this regard.) Plus, if the last few chapters have taught us anything, it's that rewarding solutions to serious problems can come from unexpected places—in particular, from the ground up, and in "double particular," from a variety of actors, be they talented individuals, committed volunteer groups, passionate non-state organizations, or even (every now and then) decent governments and well-designed international institutions.[17] This perspective would thus recommend we place less hope in top-down solutions based on sweeping governance changes—such as a cosmopolitan federation—and more on the kinds of things we've seen in the "soft power" chapters, 9 through 11:

- enabling the basic capabilities of individuals
- respecting their human rights
- allowing them to be free
- welcoming the rise of non-state actors and new technology
- working hard on things like global public health, the development of the South, wealth creation, and improving environmental sustainability.

Baby steps, in other words, instead of grandiose visions.

But, as we've seen with some of the more successful recent international ventures—notably the EU—these two things *don't have to be exclusive*: we can have grand visions of a better world, and a better organized international system, while we acknowledge, at the same time, that the most effective way to get there is probably through targeted measures and small, functional improvements, adding up over time to a better, happier, and more liveable world.

NOTES

1. Jean-Jacques Rousseau, *Emile*, trans. A. Bloom (New York: Basic Books, 1979).
2. Classical depictions of utopias include Plato's *Republic* and Thomas More's *Utopia*. See also W. Morris, *News from Nowhere* (Peterborough, ON: Broadview Press, 2002). Classic accounts of dystopia include George Orwell's *1984* and Aldous Huxley's *Brave New World*. See also Margaret Atwood's *The Handmaid's Tale* (Toronto: McClelland & Stewart, 1985).
3. T. Hobbes, *Leviathan* (Peterborough, ON: Broadview, 2010); B. Russell, *Freedom and Organization* (New York: Routledge Classics, 2009).
4. R.J. Glossop, *World Federation?* (Jefferson, NC: MacFarland and Company, 1993).
5. L. Pojman, *Terrorism, Human Rights, and The Case for World Government* (New York: Rowman & Littlefield, 2006).
6. E. Foner, *Give Me Liberty! An American History* (New York: W.W. Norton, 2008).
7. J. Pinder, *The European Union* (Oxford: Oxford University Press, 2nd edn, 2008).
8. T. Pogge, *Realizing Rawls* (Ithaca, NY: Cornell University Press, 1989); T. Pogge, *World Poverty and Human Rights* (Cambridge: Polity, 2nd edn, 2008).
9. M. Noll, *Protestantism: A Very Short Introduction* (Oxford: Oxford University Press, 2011).
10. R. Nozick, *Anarchy, State and Utopia* (Cambridge, MA: Harvard University Press, 1974); J. Narveson, *The Libertarian Idea* (Philadelphia: Temple University Press, 1988).
11. M. Walzer, *Thick and Thin* (Notre Dame, IN: University of Notre Dame, 1994); M. Walzer, *Just and Unjust Wars* (New York: Basic Books, 1977).
12. B. Orend, *Human Rights: Concept and Context* (Peterborough, ON: Broadview Press, 2002).
13. Glossop, *World Federation?* (op. cit., note 4).
14. I. Kant, *Perpetual Peace and Other Essays*, trans. T. Humphrey (Indianapolis, IN: Hackett, 1983); B. Orend, *War and International Justice: A Kantian Perspective* (Waterloo, ON: Wilfrid Laurier University Press, 2000).
15. M. Doyle, "Kant, Liberal Legacies and Foreign Affairs," *Philosophy and Public Affairs* (1984), pp. 204–35 & 323–53; M. Doyle, *Liberal Peace* (New York: Routledge, 2011); M. Brown, et al., eds, *Debating the Democratic Peace* (Cambridge, MA: MIT Press, 1996).
16. Kant, *Perpetual Peace*, and Orend, *War and International Justice* (op. cit., note 14).
17. I'm grateful to one of the anonymous reviewers for stressing this.

Glossary

Throughout this textbook, key terms are bolded and defined where they are first introduced. This glossary cannot, and does not, repeat and define all bolded key terms here; instead, it collects and defines those that are referred to multiple times throughout the book, and that are thus of special importance. For discussion of important words and events not found here, please consult the index to find the chapter in which the subject matter appears.

absolute poverty *see* **poverty**

aggression the unjustified first use of **armed force** against another **country**. Any unprovoked armed attack that crosses an international border constitutes aggression and is a *casus belli* (lit. "cause for war"). Stated otherwise, aggression is the use of armed force to violate the two core rights that any legitimate, recognized country enjoys under **international law**: (a) **political sovereignty** and (b) **territorial integrity**.

aid help given to another country (hence *foreign aid*). It is short-term assistance, largely humanitarian in nature, mainly in the form of donations and gifts (whether cash or goods), and designed to alleviate some sharp, sudden crisis within that society. **Development** may include aid but usually goes beyond it.

ambassador a public official—a diplomat—designated to be the official representative of his or her country to another country. An ambassador works out of an **embassy**.

anarchy the absence of government (lit. "no rules," an ungoverned condition). Many realists (*see* **realism**) believe that the international system is an anarchy in which trust and co-operation between **countries** are very risky; this is called the "assurance problem," and it leads realists to their various **foreign policy** recommendations.

armed conflict the use of weapons and physical violence by each of two or more groups, each with the intention of inflicting damage and harm upon the other(s) in an effort to force compliance to their will.

armed force deliberate, organized violence, deployed as a tool of **foreign policy** to achieve a political objective. It can range from a show of force, like a military drill or exercise, or small-scale, "pin-point" force aimed at a strategic target, to all out classical, fully mobilized, "hot" shooting war.

autarchy a policy of determined self-sufficiency in economic matters. Based on the principle of being "beholden to none," autarchy is the drive for a nation to provide as much as it can for itself while minimizing any dependency on foreign relations or **international trade**. As economic policy, autarchy (and **protectionism**, with which it often goes hand in hand) is viewed today as a dated doctrine that is generally *not* good for the wealth of the people; **free trade** and **globalization**, though imperfect, tend to be viewed more favourably.

bilateral treaty *see* **treaty**

bucks and bullets *see* **hard power**

business cycle the recurrent flow of economic activity between periods of expansion and contraction (or "boom" and "bust"). When a country's **GDP** goes up, the economy is in an *expansion phase*, i.e. a growing phase; when GDP goes down, the economy is in a *contraction phase*, a period of recession or shrinking economic growth. Almost all economies experience this business cycle.

capitalism a kind of economic system that:

  (a) allows for the private (i.e. non-governmental) property ownership of the means of economic production, such as natural resources and one's own labour power;

  (b) allows businesspeople the freedom to set up their own businesses and to keep some of the profits they earn for themselves for their own private enjoyment;

  (c) encourages trading between buyer and seller as the means of distributing goods and services in the economy;

  (d) uses money as the means of exchange, to facilitate this trading (i.e. the buyer and seller in a transaction agree upon a price that is mutually acceptable); and

  (e) features a court system of public laws for the peaceful handling and non-violent resolution of economic disputes.

Capitalism is the dominant economic system of our age.

cartel a small group of suppliers that controls the majority of the supply of a particular good (e.g. oil). When they co-operate, the members of a cartel can heavily influence the price of the good in question. By cutting back supply, for instance, they can dramatically increase its price.) **OPEC** is a notable example.

civilization a pervasive culture (or way of life) shared by many countries and impacting a large region of the world over time. The countries of a civilization tend to have the same (or at least similar) systems of governance, law, and economics, patterns of living and settlement, types of food and subsistence, and kinds of **culture** (especially in terms of worldview, religion, and values). **Western civilization** is an example.

Cold War the global, multi-generational showdown lasting from the end of **World War II** until 1991, and pitting the United States and its allies against the Soviet Union (or USSR, which included Russia and several now independent republics) and its allies. The US and USSR were the two biggest winners of World War II (in which they were allies), but they did not trust each other, and each championed completely different social systems: the US, that of **capitalism** and **democracy**; the USSR, that of police-state, planned-economy (or command-economy) communism. The Cold War *was* a war in that it was very much a struggle between these nations as to whose social system would triumph and survive, whose would fail and collapse. But the war was "cold" in the sense that there never was a "hot war" exchange of live-fire hostilities directly between the two adversaries (largely because of fear that such might escalate into an un-survivable nuclear war). The US eventually won the Cold War when the Soviet Union collapsed in the early 1990s.

collective security *see* NATO

colonialism (*or* **colonization**) the process of founding and maintaining colonies, as part of a system of **empire**.

contraction phase *see* **business cycle**

country the most basic unit of international studies. There are over 200 countries in the world today. Generally speaking, countries are defined by four vital components: (a) a territory (and its resources), (b) a human population, (c) **culture**, and (d) a **state** or government.

culture how people live, think, and behave; a way of life.

declining power a country whose impact and stature are decreasing upon the world stage.

decolonization the process whereby an imperial core ends its control over its colonies, leaving them to become independent countries. The term is used especially to refer to the process in which European imperial powers gave up their colonies after World War II, from roughly 1945 until 1995.

deflation a decrease in the price of goods and services within a country. A high rate of deflation is associated with *recession*, i.e. negative economic growth. Deflation is the opposite of **inflation**.

democracy a style of governance that features, at minimum, regular, free, fair, and public elections. Democratic government is determined by the free consent of the people. It's historically associated with **capitalism**, **human rights**, and **Western civilization**, but, more recently, it has become a global phenomenon and aspiration.

democratic peace thesis the theory, started by the philosopher Immanuel Kant and recently extended and developed by political scientist Michael Doyle, suggesting that democracies have never gone to war against each other, nor will they ever do so. Kant argued that increasing peace in the world thus depends on increasing the number of democratic countries in the world.

developed world *see* **Global North**

developing world *see* **Global South**

development an effort (slower and more long-term than **aid**) aimed at helping a country not merely to get through a crisis but to grow into a richer, smarter, healthier, more stable, and more sophisticated society, with fewer problems and more successful and sustained social growth. To that extent, the timeframe for development projects is much longer, and the goals are broader and more ambitious than with aid. Development assistance can include gifts, loans (which have to be paid back), direct investments (which expect some return on their risk), or advice and expertise (i.e. services, as opposed to mere goods, such as blankets and medicines). Thus, the tools of development are more numerous and complicated, and are aimed at bigger and longer-term objectives for the recipient country (above all, the transformation of the society into one that is substantially and sustainably better). *See also* **sustainable development**.

diaspora the spread or dispersion of a specific group of people from its home territory into other countries, sometimes around the globe. The term was first used to refer to the dispersion of Jews beyond Israel beginning in the eighth to sixth centuries BCE. Recent examples include the Chinese diaspora and the Indian diaspora.

dictatorship a form of governance in which an unelected leader or "strongman" commands the government. His power rests on his control of the military, and its power, in turn, rests on the coercive (i.e. based on the threat or use of violence) force it exerts over society in general.

diplomacy a tool of **foreign policy** in which one attempts to persuade another country to adopt one's point of view and act accordingly. Diplomacy may involve talking, negotiating, lobbying, dealing, rational argument, or the offer of positive political incentives.

economic incentives the use of money, as a tool of **foreign policy**, to gain **leverage** on another country in order to influence it to act or behave in a particular way. Economic incentives may be either positive or negative (the proverbial "carrot" and "stick," respectively).

embassy the residence of an **ambassador** and headquarters for the diplomatic efforts and staff of one country inside another. The Canadian embassy in the US is located in Washington, DC. An embassy is considered an extension of the actual territory of the home country it represents.

emerging power a country whose economic and/or military stature is increasing on the world stage. China is often mentioned as a current example.

emigration the departure of people from a country to go and live somewhere else. It's the opposite of **immigration**.

empire a system of governance forged by military conquest (as opposed to the freely given consent of people) as part of a policy of **colonialism**. In an empire, there is an imperial core—sometimes called the "hub of empire" or *metropole* (lit. "mother city," the pole around which the rest of the empire revolves)—and then there are the colonies, which are the conquered and subjected lands that have become "dependencies" on the periphery of the empire.

environment Earth's various and most vital natural cycles and systems, upon which we depend for life and well-being: the atmosphere, the land, resources under the land, fresh water, sea life, the plant world, and the animal kingdom.

ethnic cleansing the process of trying to drive an entire, distinct people from a certain territory where they are settled and have been living as a community over time, usually so that one's own people can then move into and occupy the territory, in order to take it over.

European Union (EU) a regional, multilateral organization centred in Europe and held together with an extensive array of treaties, organizations, and, increasingly, shared beliefs and practices. It is often said that even though the EU was created as an intergovernmental organization, it should now be thought of as an entirely new kind of entity. Because of the breadth and depth of the integration it has successfully brought about between the nations of Europe, the EU is sometimes described as a "trans-national" or even "supra-national" institution. Recent financial difficulties have highlighted some weaknesses in its structure.

expansion phase *see* **business cycle**

export a good produced in one country, then shipped out and sold into another country. It is the opposite of an **import**.

export-led development a large-scale strategy for growing the national economy, using the tools of **autarchy** and **protectionism** to subsidize and grow select local industries until they are strong enough to compete on the world stage; at that point, **tariffs** are dropped and the country aggressively engages in **free trade** to maximize revenues from **export** sales. These revenues are used to develop society further, making it richer and more sophisticated. The most successful model of this in modern history is Japan following **World War II**; more recently, many other nations throughout Asia (notably China and South Korea) have begun trying to copy that success.

failed state a country whose government exists but can no longer effectively govern its people or provide for their vital needs. The government fails to do the most basic things people expect of their **state**: to keep the peace; to protect them from foreign invasion; to enforce law and order; and to ensure that the most important social services are provided. Somalia is often seen as a failed state, and many of the countries in sub-Saharan Africa appear on the verge of joining it.

fair trade a movement designed to help independent farmers, especially in the **Global South**, earn a *living wage* (an income one can actually pay one's bills with) by charging fair prices for products such as coffee, cocoa, sugar, tea, cotton, honey, bananas, chocolate, wine, and flowers. The movement appeals to consumers *not* on the basis of price (typically higher than the **free trade**, mass-market price) but, rather, on the basis of how good the products are, and how important it is for everyone to support independent farmers.

First World *see* **Global North**

First World War *see* **World War I**

fiscal policy a national government's policies, collectively, on how it spends money, covering issues such as the official budget, the rate of taxation, new spending measures, and so on. Fiscal policy is directly in the daily control of the (elected) government; **monetary policy** is *not*.

foreign aid *see* **aid**

foreign policy a national government's policies, collectively, on how it should relate to other countries and their national governments. Of special concern in foreign policy is how one should best relate to one's immediately neighbouring countries, as well as, more generally, to one's friends (allies) and enemies (opponents) around the world.

free trade the trade of goods and services between countries wherein the countries in question do *not* use any **protectionist** measures against each other. Free trade is trade that is **tariff**-free, quota-free, ban-free, and subsidy-free: what gets traded, and at which price and quantity, is determined solely by the market forces of supply and demand and *not* by any government regulation or intervention. Free trade is an extension of **capitalism**. A *free trade area* is a group of countries, often sharing a common geographical region, that have agreed to engage in free trade with one another; examples of free trade areas include the **EU** and the North American signatories to **NAFTA** (Canada, the US, and Mexico).

GDP *see* **gross domestic product**

genocide lit. "the killing of a whole people": genocide occurs when an entire cultural, ethnic, national, etc., group is targeted for murder at the hands of another. The preeminent example is *the Holocaust* (*c.* 1933–45), when European Jews especially (but also homosexuals and physically and mentally disabled people) were killed by German Nazis; shocked reaction to the Holocaust helped spark the contemporary **human rights** movement.

global digital divide a key aspect of the dramatic split between **Global North** and **Global South**, referring to the tremendous advantage enjoyed by people in the North based on how much more "plugged in" and technology advanced they are, especially with regard to the latest information technologies like the Internet.

global governance a term of art referring to institutional attempts at global problem-solving, ranging from loose initial efforts via the **League of Nations** to today's international institutions, notably in the **United Nations** system. It can also, however, refer more ambitiously to issues of needed reform, up to and including potential kinds of world government (as discussed in Chapter 12).

globalization the recent and increasing strengthening of ties between countries, mainly in the economic sense of **international trade** and the spread of free-market **capitalism** (accelerated by America's victory in the **Cold War**) but also in some social and cultural senses (especially regarding information technology, social media, and pop culture).

Global North a term of art referring generally to the more developed countries of the world, loosely equivalent to "Western societies" or **Western civilization**; *the West* and the *developed world* are other synonyms (somewhat more commonly used) that have superseded the now outdated term *First World*. All of these terms, generally, are used to denote countries that tend to be wealthier, better educated, healthier, less populated, more technologically advanced, more urbanized, more influential internationally, and more attractive to immigrants.

global public health a field of study and policy concerned with augmenting the general health of the whole world's human population. Tactics commonly used by global public health officials include vaccinations and inoculations, vitamin distribution, mosquito eradication, sex education and condom distribution, exercise and nutrition promotion, and augmenting *health literacy* (i.e. knowledge about health). But—in addition to tackling tobacco—four things stand out in terms of improving global public health:

(a) reliable daily access to clean, drinkable water

(b) access to nutritious food with sufficient calories

(c) access to a basic sanitation system

(d) access to a healthcare system that can be responsive, should preventative measures fail and individual treatment be needed.

Global South a commonly used term of art referring to the world's developing countries, a.k.a. the *developing world*. ("Global South" is much preferred to the outdated term *Third World*.) When compared with countries of the **Global North**, countries of the Global South tend to be more populated, yet less wealthy, less healthy, less educated, less technologically advanced, more rural, and less powerful, with higher rates of emigration than immigration.

global warming the recent, systematic warming up of Earth, as evidenced by the temperature record, thought to be responsible for producing climate change, among other potentially serious consequences (see Chapter 2). There is controversy around whether global warming is caused by human-made industrialization (especially the burning of such non-renewable fossil fuels as oil and gas) or, rather, by changes in solar activity and the consequent warming up of Earth's oceans.

Great Depression an enormous slowdown and shrinkage in the economy, worldwide, lasting for 10 years from about 1929 until 1939, creating vast unemployment and poverty. It ended because of the adoption of the **welfare state**, and because of increased government spending following the outbreak of **World War II**.

great powers those countries with the richest economies *and* the largest armed forces, which have true global impact in their decision-making. They include (among others) Britain, China, France, Russia, and the United States.

Green Revolution a movement, between 1940 and 1980, to export the latest know-how and expertise in agricultural production from the **Global North** to the **Global South**. Specifically, the Green Revolution involved introducing new methods of planting and irrigation, better fertilizers and harvesting techniques, and the use of genetically modified crops and foods (i.e. ones whose genes have been artificially manipulated so that they are more resistant to disease, and with superior durability and freshness). As notable result of the Green Revolution is that world grain production has tripled over the last 50 years. The movement is thus an important example of the kind of *knowledge transfer* and *technology transfer* that many experts believe is important for the South's further **development**.

gross domestic product (GDP) a measure of national wealth, summarizing the condition of, and level of activity in, a country's economy; it is the total value of goods produced and services provided in a country in one year.

hard power the use of economic resources and/or **armed force** to get what one wants in international relations. Summarized as the *bucks and bullets* approach to **foreign policy**, it means either buying or forcing the compliance of others to one's will.

health literacy *see* **global public health**

hegemon a dominant power in a given field, region, or area. A hegemon exerts "hegemony" (i.e. strong influence) over others. Brazil, for example, is said to be a regional hegemon in South America, while the US is said to be a truly global hegemon.

Holocaust *see* **genocide**

Human Development Index (HDI) a measure of a society's level of development that goes beyond **GDP** to consider life expectancy, infant mortality, rates of literacy and disease, rates of educational attainment, distribution of income, gender and minority equality, and self-reported satisfaction in life. The measure was recently crafted and introduced by the **United Nations**.

human rights universal moral entitlements that are sometimes legally recognized and realized, but sometimes not. They are claims to those objects considered vital to living a minimally good life, notably security, subsistence, liberty, non-discrimination, and recognition as a person. The most influential contemporary human rights document is the UN's Universal Declaration of Human Rights (1948).

idealism the **foreign policy** doctrine that says that the most important thing for countries to do is *not* to tend to their own self-interest but, rather, to contribute what they can towards the creation of a better world for all. Idealists believe in an ethos of universal improvements; they emphasize economic growth, **international law**, and **human rights** in foreign policy. An influential doctrine—especially among **NGOs**—idealism is opposed by **realism**.

ideology *see* **political ideology**

immigration the arrival in a country of people from another country, seeking to settle and create new lives for themselves. It's the opposite of **emigration**.

imperialism the process or policy of trying to form and maintain an **empire**.

import a good brought into a country for sale, having been produced in another country. It is the opposite of an **export**.

Industrial Revolution a set of dramatic changes in the production of goods, beginning in the early 1700s. With the invention of manufacturing technology such as the steam engine and the cotton gin, the machine-driven production of goods became possible, replacing the older approach of piece-by-piece, handcrafted production of goods. The first factories were built, especially in the middle of England, to take advantage of this, and to mass-produce as many goods as possible, eventually leading to such innovations as the assembly line. The Industrial Revolution had an enormous, utterly transformative, impact on society, making people much wealthier, creating goods much more quickly and cheaply, accelerating **urbanization**, and transforming the nature of work and the economy.

Information Revolution a term of art (styled after **Industrial Revolution**, **Green Revolution**, etc.) to suggest the dramatic and widespread transformative impact of advances in computer technology on everything from economic activity and communication to education and popular culture, especially in the **Global North**. Some situate the start of this period in the 1950s, when computing technology first made its appearance; for others, the Information Revolution did not begin in earnest until the early 1990s and the end of the **Cold War**, when the use and availability of the Internet became widespread. The Information Revolution is closely tied to **globalization**.

inflation an increase in the price of goods and services within a country. A high rate of inflation is associated with economic growth, but if it becomes too accelerated, it can cause serious problems (as described in Chapter 6). Most countries aim for small, controlled amounts of inflation (e.g. of 1–3 per cent per year). Inflation is the opposite of **deflation**.

insurgent forces revolutionary armed groups committed to the violent overthrow of the government of their society.

interdisciplinary lit. "among the disciplines." International studies is said to be "interdisciplinary" by using the tools and insights of *various* disciplines, both (a) to eliminate narrow-mindedness and (b) to arrive at a more thorough appreciation of the subject matter.

international law all the agreements and undertakings that different nations or countries make among themselves, presumably for mutual benefit. International law embodies a set of rules that serve as a code of conduct for countries. Though there are other sources, **treaties** are considered the gold standard of international law.

international public spaces places "un-owned" by any country. There are three such places currently recognized:
(a) Antarctica
(b) the "high seas" (in the middle of the great oceans)
(c) "near space" (i.e. the very high atmosphere, just before outer space).

international trade the movement of goods and services across national borders in exchange for money.

interstate system the prevailing order of international affairs, specifically regarding how countries relate to each other.

knowledge transfer *see* **Green Revolution**

laws of war a term of art referring to treaties that together attempt to regulate warfare. For the outbreak of war, the main piece of international law is the UN Charter (1945) and, to a lesser extent, the Hague Conventions (1899–1909). For conduct during war, the Geneva Conventions (1949) are the most authoritative.

League of Nations an international intergovernmental organization whose creation marks one of the first attempts at **global governance**. It existed from 1919 to 1939, created after **World War I**; having failed, it fell apart at the outbreak of **World War II**.

leverage the ability to gain an advantage and exert favourable pressure on another country. The tools of **foreign policy** are all designed to help one's country get leverage over other countries.

linkage a strategy for exerting **leverage**, in which a country makes progress on one issue contingent upon progress in another that is more favourable to it. For example, China frequently uses linkage when it makes international business deals dependent upon silence regarding its flawed **human rights** record.

literacy the ability to read. Literacy is vital to the development of a country and the growth of its economy. In terms of this textbook, it is an overall objective: to achieve a basic literacy regarding international, or global, studies.

living wage *see* **fair trade**

metropole *see* **empire**

middle powers countries with a level of influence/capability in between that of the **great powers** and the **small powers**. Typically, they are Northern, Western, developed, and quite wealthy societies, but they lack the population size, military force, cultural impact, and ambition to become great powers. Examples include Australia, Canada, and Sweden. The middle powers typically try to be active and good "international citizens," picking and choosing projects and missions in which they can play a globally constructive role. They tend to be like-minded and mutually supportive—unlike the great powers, which are often rivals and tend to butt heads on a range of issues—and middle powers are among the strongest and most enthusiastic supporters of global co-operation and such international institutions as the **United Nations**.

migrant workers people who have citizenship and a permanent home in one country but live temporarily, for work purposes, in another. They tend to work in industries that pay very little, and that are very labour-intensive. Agriculture is perhaps the largest example.

military capability the resources a country has to deploy **armed force**. Most countries have an army, navy, and air force, each using its own kind of weaponry.

military–industrial complex collectively, those people and companies—both inside and outside of the military—with a vested (sometimes greedy) interest in the business of war, including the national army, **private military companies**, mercenaries, arms manufacturers, etc.

monetary policy policies designed to control a country's supply of money, set out and overseen by a semi-autonomous central bank, aloof from party politics.

multilateralism lit. "many-sidedness": a preference for countries to co-operate internationally, for mutual benefit. Multilateralism is often associated with **idealism**, and opposed by **unilateralism**.

multilateral treaty *see* **treaty**

multinational corporation (MNC) a large business operating in several countries.

NAFTA the North American Free Trade Agreement, a regional multilateral **treaty** between Canada, the United States, and Mexico, on the flow of goods and services between these three countries, which came into effect in 1994. NAFTA is a **free trade area** that grew out of, and extended, the 1989 Free Trade Agreement between Canada and the US.

nation a group of people that sees itself as a people, in other words, as belonging together in some meaningful sense as a unit that has its own identity and that is separate and distinct from other, comparable groups.

nationalism generally, a recognition of, and attachment to, one's **nation**. More specifically, and historically, nationalism often implies the impulse of a nation to get and form its own separate country, governed by a **state** of its own choosing.

NATO the North Atlantic Treaty Organization, probably the most important military alliance of our time. Composed originally of America, Canada, and the nations of western Europe, and now of central and eastern Europe as well, NATO is an alliance dedicated to mutual defence, or *collective security*, in the event any one of its members is attacked. It was founded in 1949 with an eye, especially, to protecting western Europe from a ground invasion by the Soviet Union during the **Cold War**, but it survived the end of that conflict. NATO currently is in action in Afghanistan, where it has been operating since the September 11 terrorist attacks on the US.

non-governmental organizations (NGOs) all charitable **non-state actors** that have a humanitarian or social movement function, such as promoting respect for human rights or for environmental protection.

non-state actors all non-governmental associations or institutions. Some of the most important and influential types of non-state actors include businesses and corporations, churches and religious groups, charities, sports leagues, fan clubs, social movements, terrorist groups, and interest groups.

North American Free Trade Agreement *see* **NAFTA**

North Atlantic Treaty Organization *see* **NATO**

numeracy the ability to do basic math, especially in its practical applications (e.g. in business or in balancing personal household budgets).

OPEC the Organization of Petroleum-Exporting Countries, one of the most important **cartels** in the world. OPEC was founded in 1973, mainly by the Arab states of the Persian Gulf region, for two reasons: (1) to increase the price of oil, thus generating more money for themselves, and (2) to punish the West—especially the United States—for its ongoing support of Israel. The formation of OPEC generated an "oil crisis" in Western countries from roughly 1973 until 1985, characterized by *stagflation*—significant **inflation** and stagnant economic growth occurring at the same time.

peak oil theory a theory predicting negative economic consequences once oil production reaches its peak (or maximum output)—beyond this point, there will be less and less oil to extract, yet more and more demand for it (owing to population growth and industrialization). Most peak oil theorists speculating about when we will reach this point believe that we are, worldwide, at peak oil right now.

political ideology ideals and values surrounding how best to run a country, and how to organize its people and shape their way of life. Chapter 3 details the three most influential contemporary ideologies: conservatism, liberalism, and socialism.

political sovereignty the right of a group of people to rule themselves. "Political" refers to power or to *polis*, the ancient Greek word for a group of people living together as an ongoing community. *Sovereignty* means the entitlement to rule, literally to have the power of a king or sovereign; to be sovereign is to be self-ruling, acknowledging no higher authority over oneself. More fully, then, political sovereignty is the most basic right of a country, in modern **international law** and global affairs, to make its own laws and to govern itself, *provided*—crucially—that it respects the right of all other countries to do the same.

poverty Experts distinguish between absolute and relative poverty. *Relative poverty*, which is everywhere, is poverty experienced by anyone whose assets and income are small relative to his or her immediate social context, such as the neighbourhood, city, or even country. Much more serious is *absolute poverty*, the chronic inability to afford the basic necessities of life, such as water and food, clothing, and access to shelter. The most commonly agreed-upon standard of absolute poverty is an income of US$2/day/person (which translates into an annual personal income of US$730). By this common standard, 2.6 billion people worldwide are thought to suffer from absolute poverty, the vast majority of them in the **Global South**.

power the ability to get what one wants. *See also* **hard power**, **soft power**.

precautionary principle a maxim of environmentalism stipulating that if you're unsure of whether a practice is safe—or if you think it *might* be dangerous or polluting—then, as a matter of prudence, you ought *not* to proceed. For example: even if we are unsure about the role of humans in causing **global warming**, it would be better, and safer, to change our behaviours and minimize any possible damage we're causing than to wait until the human role has been proven, at which point any change in behaviours might be too late to reverse and repair the ill effects of our actions. (The environmental skeptic replies by urging us to consider the clearly negative consequences of, say, hastily cutting back our greenhouse gas emissions: namely, economic damage for the North and dashed development hopes for the South.)

private militias armed groups that are *not* part of any country's official military. They may be either political or mercenary in nature: in other words, they either have a private political agenda of some kind or they simply sell their military services to the highest bidder. The latter kind—the mercenary kind—are referred to as **private military companies (PMCs)**.

protectionism the use of government power in a manner inconsistent with **free trade**. Protectionist measures are hurdles or obstacles placed by the government on **imports** in order to protect certain domestic goods or industries. The most common protectionist measure is a *tariff*: a tax on foreign, imported goods, which increases their price, making them unattractive to consumers (relative to competing local or domestic goods). The United States, for example, levies tariffs on Canadian softwood lumber to protect American lumber companies. Other protectionist measures include quotas, product bans, and government subsidies.

Protestant Reformation a sixteenth-century movement demanding changes in the structure, teachings, and practices of the Catholic Church, which prompted, when the demands were denied, the establishment of Protestant and Reformed churches. The bad feelings that ensued led to violence (see **Thirty Years War**) and to the eventual split of Europe along religious lines, into a mainly Protestant north and a mainly Catholic south. The Reformation ended the religious monopoly of the Catholic Church in Western civilization.

proxy wars wars fought indirectly between major powers, wherein the powers use local pawns or "proxies" to do their fighting for them, so they don't have to engage each other directly. The Cold War was filled with proxy wars—such as in Vietnam and Afghanistan—as the US and USSR did not wish to confront each other directly, lest nuclear war result.

realism a **foreign policy** doctrine that says, first and foremost, that one's nation or country must look out for its own interests and advantages on the world stage. "Looking out for number one" is a way of life for realists, and it expresses an ethos of national egoism. Realists emphasize the pursuit of power, wealth, and national security in foreign policy. A very influential doctrine—especially among policy-makers—realism is opposed by **idealism**.

recession *see* **deflation**

refugees people who have been forced to leave their home countries involuntarily, usually because of war or persecution. Refugees seek "asylum," or a safe haven, in another country, and then often go on to settle there, as immigrants.

relative poverty *see* **poverty**

religion from the Latin *religio*, lit. "re-linking" or "linking back." This refers to a supposed link between humanity and the god (or gods) who created humankind, as well as the universe. Different religions are characterized by their different views about the nature of the divine, how the universe came to be, and how humans ought to relate to the divine and to one another. Chapter 3 details the similarities and differences between such "Abrahamic" religions as Judaism, Christianity, and Islam, and such "Dharmic" religions as Hinduism, Chinese folk religion, and Buddhism. Religiousness is opposed by **secularism**.

rogue regime a country that has established itself as a bad international citizen. It typically refuses to play well with its neighbours while actively creating trouble and instability on an international scale. It breaks the rules, goes its own way, makes the world worse, and is difficult to resist or discipline. A possible current example would be North Korea.

sanctions a tool of **foreign policy**, marking a shift away from *positive* incentives and mutually beneficial deal-making, towards *negative* incentives: threats, non-cooperation, punishment, and actions taken deliberately to thwart the interests of the other country. Sanctions can vary in level, intensity, and effect. "Targeted sanctions" are measures of punishment, un-cooperation, and interest-thwarting focused upon hurting *only* the elite decision-makers in the target country. Sweeping sanctions are those measures of punishment and uncooperation that either deliberately target or at least directly affect *the majority of citizens* in the target country.

Second World War *see* **World War II**

secularism a non-religious approach to life. Secularists tend to fall into one of three categories:
(a) atheists, who believe that there are no gods

(b) agnostics, who don't take a firm stand on whether any gods exist, and who are simply not motivated by, or interested in, religious concerns at all

(c) secular humanists, who prefer to substitute for a religious code their own systematic code of beliefs, one that refers *not* to the divine but only to humanity and to the need for human beings to treat each other decently, at minimum by respecting universal **human rights**.

Secularism is opposed by **religion**.

small powers countries that can be either developed or developing, located in the North or the South, and that have only a small degree of impact on international decision-making and global life. Typically, the population, economy, and military of a small power are simply too tiny for it to exert much influence globally. Examples range from the Czech Republic in Europe to Chile in South America, and from the Caribbean islands to the various island nations in the South Pacific.

soft power the use of one's language, ideas, values, and culture to bring about the compliance of others to one's will, especially in **foreign policy**. The spread of one's **culture** is thought to create a commonality of worldview, a mutuality of interest, and a reservoir of good will, which bolsters one's ability to get what one wants.

sovereignty *see* **political sovereignty**

stagflation *see* **OPEC**

state the government of a country: the group of people responsible for making, and enforcing, the rules that regulate the collective life of a people and that thereby make an orderly social life possible within a given territory. Every country has a government, and often it is the single most powerful association, or institution, in that society.

sustainable development economic progress that is based not on creating growth for its own sake—much less as much growth as fast as possible—but on stimulating growth that is measured, paced, reasonable, and consistent with the world's "carrying capacity" (i.e. the human population Earth can support with its resources). Sustainable development is about growing an economy—i.e. making people richer and better off—in a way that can continue over the long term. Some think sustainable development is at odds with **capitalism**, others not.

tariff *see* **protectionism**

technology transfer *see* **Green Revolution**

territorial integrity to be real, the abstract right of **political sovereignty** must imply some secure space on which a group of people may live and enjoy self-rule. A community or country has a right to some liveable territory and is considered to be the general "owner" of all the natural resources on, under, or above, its land. That's the "territorial" part; the "integrity" part refers to that group's right not to have other countries invade its territory and try to take its resources. A community needs not just *to have* territory and resources; it needs to be able to *count on having* such resources moving forward.

terrorism the deliberate use of **armed force** against civilian populations—as opposed to military targets—in hopes that the resulting spread of fear (or terror) among the people will further a narrow political agenda held by the terrorist group.

theocracy a regime in which the state uses its power to realize and enforce a religious vision. Any theocracy implies a blending of church and state.

Third World *see* **Global South**

Thirty Years War an intense and widespread war fought over religion, in Europe, from 1618 to 1648. It ended with the **Treaty of Westphalia**, which had a far-reaching impact on **international law**.

treaty a contract between countries, spelled out in a formal, legal document. It is a promise to *do* something, typically with the expectation of some benefit. A *bilateral treaty* is made between two countries; a *multilateral treaty* is made between many countries. There can also be regional treaties, operating within one region of the world, and global treaties, which most or all countries in the world have agreed to.

Treaty of Versailles the peace treaty of 1918–19, which ended **World War I**.

Treaty of Westphalia the peace treaty of 1648, which ended the **Thirty Years War**. It is considered highly significant as both the first modern legal expression of religious tolerance and, moreover, the birth of modern **international law**, enshrining the norms of **territorial integrity** and **political sovereignty** for every country.

unilateralism lit. "one-sidedness": the willingness (or even preference) of a country to do what it wants internationally, regardless of what other countries think. It is often associated with **realism**, and opposed by **multilateralism**.

United Nations (**UN**) an international intergovernmental organization, created after **World War II** in 1946. It marked a renewed attempt at advancing global governance, after the failure of the **League of Nations**. The UN Charter, which details the aims and structure of the UN, is one of the most successful global **multilateral treaties**, and almost every country in the world is a UN member. Headquartered in New York, the UN has important offices in Paris, Geneva, and The Hague. The various parts and functions of the UN, as well as its strengths and weaknesses, are outlined in detail in Chapter 5.

urbanization the growth of cities at the expense of the countryside. Urbanization has been a relentless trend, in both developed and developing countries, over the past 200 years. The majority of the world's people, overall, now live in cities (though the majority of those in the Global South are still rural).

war an intentional and widespread **armed conflict** between groups of people. This is true whether these groups are *within* one country, engaged in civil war, or in *different* countries, engaged in classic international warfare.

weapons of mass destruction (**WMDs**) weapons capable of large-scale life and property destruction, including nuclear, chemical, and biological (NBC) weapons.

welfare state a government with a positive, robust, and intervening role to play, especially with regard to constructing a "social safety net" for the worst-off of its citizens. This is done (at least ideally) through the taxation system, by using revenues generated by taxing the wealthy to provide welfare payments to the very poor and unemployed and to pay for publicly funded infrastructure, education, and healthcare systems. The welfare state constrains, and counteracts, some aspects of free-market **capitalism**, resulting in a so-called "mixed economy"—the norm for societies throughout the developed world.

West, the *see* **Global North**

Western civilization (**1**) with reference to geography, western Europe and the **colonies** it created, especially throughout the Americas and Australia/New Zealand. (**2**) with reference to shared values, a set of beliefs about how, ideally, to run a society. These shared values, detailed in Chapter 1, include individualism, **human rights**, **democracy**, and free-market **capitalism**.

World War I an enormous war, waged mainly in Europe but with serious worldwide implications (given the spread of European **imperialism** around the world), fought from 1914 to 1918 between mainly "the Allies" of Britain, Canada, France, and the United States on one side, and Germany, the Austro-Hungarian Empire, and the Ottoman Empire on the other. (Russia, which had been on the side of the Allies, left the war in 1917—just as America was joining—to attend to its own domestic political turmoil.) Though the Allies gained a short-term victory, cemented by the **Treaty of Versailles**, many historians argue this war was inconclusive, and merely paved the way for **World War II**.

World War II the biggest war in human history, fought all across the world, with more than 60 countries involved by war's end and resulting in at least 50 million people killed. Lasting from 1939 until 1945, the war pitted "the Allies" of America, Britain, Canada, France, and Russia (as the Soviet Union) against "the Axis powers" of Germany, Italy, and Japan. (The United States did not enter the ar until 1941.) The war ended with an Allied victory, resulting in the unconditional surrender, and near total destruction, of Germany and Japan in particular.

Index

Page numbers in **bold** refer to pages where key terms are defined.